Professional Wrestling Intellectual

A compilation of Writings by Joseph L. Babinsack, Jr.

Pro Wrestling Intellectual

Copyright 2008 Joseph Babinsack

All Rights Reserved.

Publisher: www.btpress.net

Printed in the United States

Joseph Babinsack can be reached at chaosonejoe@yahoo.com

Special Thanks!

In no particular order…

My wife Kimberly, Bruno Sammartino, Dave Meltzer, Christopher Cruise, Larry Matysik, Ron "Magnificent Flying Bat" Russitano, Brian Trammel, Georgiann Makropoulos, Irv Muchnick, Dr. Keith Lipinski, Leonard Chikara-son, Gabe Sapolsky, Dan Madigan, J.R. Benson, Bryan Alvarez, Scott Johnson, Dave "The Truth" Prazak, Patricia (Mom) Babinsack, Gilbert (2nd Dad and Father-in-Law) Chriest, Michael McIntyre, Jim Boyd, a few people named Corey, Jeff Yandora, Michael Friedlander, Bill Defazio, Josh "uhm, thanks for the reference" Hvizdos, Raf Gulas, Phil Spagnolli, all eight of my siblings, and my beloved dog Dee Dee…

And everyone else who gave me opportunities, encouragement and review copies!

Joe Babinsack

For My Father…

About the Author!

Joseph Babinsack is a graduate of the University of Pittsburgh, 2004, with a degree in English writing.

But it's not that simple, as he began study at Pitt in 1986 as a Chemical Engineering student, switching to English in 1990 or so, and departing the University in 1992. At that point, he became a full time comic book store worker, at the Phantom of the Attic in Pittsburgh, until he landed a dream job with Friedlander Publishing Group's newly formed Game Division. Shortly before that company filed bankruptcy, he departed for a decade long anguish at an employer he will only reference as "corporate hell." He began 2008 with another dream level job, with RAM Software Systems, as a Trainer/Tech Support/Document Writer.

He has worked in the "Pen and Paper" gaming industry, with game co-author and design credits, notable in work with the Collectible Card game genre, and he regrets the "one that got away."

He has written about professional wrestling in various media for more than 20 years, and has written in various Western Pennsylvania publications for half as long.

He has reviewed hundreds of DVDs and scores of books, mostly related to professional wrestling, but also in the worlds of literature, politics, comic books and other miscellany.

He has had his picture on the back of a comic book (Cerebus #169) and has written gaming articles in a national magazine (Knucklebones) and has received compliments on his writing from Wrestling's only Living Legend.

He currently writes multiple columns per week for the Wrestling Observer Newsletter's Online site: www.wrestlingobserver.com (now merged with www.F4online.com)

He also writes a weekly column on professional wrestling and MMA for the Allied News (Grove City, PA) and writes often for www.pop-damage.com

He currently lives in Butler, Pennsylvania with his wife, Kimberly.

Introduction

If my Dad knew, some thirty-five years later, that introducing me to the world of professional wrestling (by watching it on TV, by attending Civic Arena shows, and by letting the concept work itself out in his son's mind) would result in me being an internet wrestling reviewer, commentator and, well, journalist, I'm not so sure he'd believe it. If he could believe that, would he believe that I could write for one of the most prestigious web sites in the world, that I could gain review copies from the best of wrestling promotions and book publishers, and that I could put together a book of my writing, with the assistance of many major names and promotions in the business?

Of course, the biggest and most impressive thing to him would have to be talking to Bruno Sammartino, more so that I've gained the Champ's confidence, and his blessing on rewriting his 1990 book, and likely some other book writing projects.

For a steel worker living in Natrona, Pennsylvania (just outside of Pittsburgh) and a second generation pro wrestling fan himself, there would be nothing as spectacular as his son befriending Bruno, let alone being hopeful of telling Bruno's story to the world!

Now, I've been writing publically about professional wrestling for 20 years, even though most of that first ten years was Usenet posts, on rec.sports.misc and rec.sports.pro-wrestling. Eventually, I wrote for smaller, local publications, and then smaller web sites, and after I finally graduated from the University of Pittsburgh with a degree in English writing, I went for the big times – there's nothing bigger than the Wrestling Observer Site.

Dave Meltzer has been my biggest influence in the world of professional wrestling. It was the very early 1990's that I started following the Wrestling Observer Newsletter, and it has been a weekly ritual in my life ever since. Just ask my wife, who knows once that newsletter comes in the door, I'll be AWOL for a few hours, pouring over small font types, and ingesting the latest industry news.

Once upon a time, 6pm on Saturdays fulfilled that nigh religious observance, and then it was 9pm on Mondays -- plus that weekly reading of the Observer, until a few years back, when the religious watching of TV wrestling turned into semi-regular DVD viewings.

Dave and I don't always agree, but I respect his reporting immensely, and no one in the business has the handle on the industry – its faults, its entertainment, its realities and overall, the reason why so many millions watch it even when it's not so good. As I've said, I've religiously read Dave's insights, stories and wisdom for decades, and whether he knows it or not, I call him a mentor.

Five years ago, I was able to put a review up on his site, and I have been doing so on a weekly basis (and often twice a week) ever since, and I greatly appreciate the opportunity. Without that foot in the door, I would never have gained so much insight, would have never exchanged emails with Irv Muchnick or JR Benson, or made phone calls to Larry Matysik and Terry Funk, or contacted a dozen other names --- authors, promoters and talented wrestlers.

Today, www.wrestlingobserver.com is www.f4wonline.com, and I'm still churning out the reviews. It started off with books, moved into DVDs, and then I got comfortable with doing more and more commentary. The only things I haven't reviewed are video games…. that's to avoid the gamer mentality in me, wanting desperately to avoid another addicting game medium. (It's bad enough I'm a triple-threat geek: comics, games, rasslin.)

I've written for a number of Pittsburgh area publications, mostly entertainment magazines, but some serious stuff like The Front, where I interviewed Shane Douglas; and eResources, where I interviewed Terry Funk and Dixie Carter; and I now write for The Allied News out of Grove City, with a MMA/wrestling column.

But the single most important moment in my professional wrestling experiences has been a phone call I received two years ago, on a Sunday afternoon. Chris Cruise and Georgie – Georgiann Makropoulos – had both contacted me by email, demanding my phone number. I had already gone through the "Bruno wants to call you" scenario once, and I didn't think it would happen, just couldn't believe I would ever have that opportunity.

But it did happen.

No thrill matches the one that I got when I picked up the phone. "I've never met you" he said, "but I get the impression you know a lot about me. I'm not sure if you recognize my voice…." We both laughed at that one. Who could not recognize the distinguished voice of Bruno Sammartino?

And since that day, my understanding of the sport of professional wrestling has been raised to a new level. I've talked with Bruno, hoping to do so every week, and utterly thrilled when I do. Admittedly, I've dropped Bruno's name a few times too many, but put yourself in a weird situation or two, where you're only claim to fame is writing extensively about professional wrestling – wouldn't you claim to have spoken often to the Living Legend, who is a cultural icon in Pittsburgh, the Northeast, and all the world?

Joe Babinsack

I'm sure you would, if it were true. And it is.

I've felt that every step of my wrestling and writing career has lead to something, and now I'm realizing what that is, and it is tantalizingly close, and with the publishing of this book (thanks to Brian Tramel of rasslinriotonline.com) I'm one more step closer.

Right now, that thing is to bring Bruno Sammartino's life story to a bigger audience, and to reveal to the world (both wrestling and 'real' one) the realities that proclaim Bruno as the greatest professional wrestler of all time.

Sure, he won't say that, but I will.

But along the way, I need to express my own views on the professional wrestling industry, hone my craft in writing, and establish myself as someone to read on the subject.

To me, professional wrestling is an artform. It is a multi-dimensional entertainment concept that actively engages its audience, and demands a creative input on levels that are often lost on an ignorant mainstream.

To me, professional wrestling isn't a base and simplistic show, dominated by the WWE to the point that anything else is irrelevant.

To the contrary, I believe that the WWE offers a simplistic version and vision of the professional wrestling industry, debasing the once glorious platform for talent, ignoring traditions and altogether producing a vile, most often ignoble, at times far too raunchy, and most of all, a show completely disdainful of the fans.

For decades, I've considered it an honor to be a professional wrestling fan, and I still do. I consider it an industry that deserves the kind of attention that Dave Meltzer pays it, that boasts of exceptional human beings like Bruno Sammartino, and offers a world that can be debated, analyzed and intellectually pursued, as well as enjoyed as a fan.

Along the way, I've encountered many products, books and DVDs worthy of praise, but few that truly address what I feel about the sport we call professional wrestling, and the depth of what it is to be a fan of the entertainment form.

It is my hope to expand the understanding of the artform, and to prove that professional wrestling can certainly be an intellectual pursuit.

That's the purpose of doing this book, and I hope you enjoy what I have to say.

Pro Wrestling Intellectual

Table of Contents

Bios of Pro Wrestlers
Jay and Mark Brisco 10
Christopher Daniels 14
Claudio Castagnolli 18
Jack Evans 21
Nigel McGuinness 23
Shirley Doe 26
Ricky Reyes 29
Takishi Morishima 32
Roderick Strong 35
Vincent Nothing 40

Book Reviews
Bang Your Head 45
How Dr. Death/Dr. Life 49
King of the Ring 53
Wrestling at the Chase 57
Journal of a Journeyman 59
Ref. of an American Dream 62
The Mouth of the South 65
Death of WCW 68
Between the Ropes 73
Turning the Tables 76

Bruno Sammartino
Secrets of a Survivor 79
Great Debate 08 82
Gretest Wrestler 86
Great Moment 95
Response 101
1990 Autobiography 105
Rewriting the book 108
Synopsis 112
Adv's in Larryland! 117
Studio Wrestling 120

DVD Reviews
Set it Off 128
Ballpark Brawl III 134
Better than/Best 137
Clash/ Cancer 141
JCW vs PWU 146
Strong vs Evans 153
Overload 156
Best of Raven 158
Project Mayhem 161
Cibernetico&Robin 164

Controversies
Tangled Ropes 170
Eddie Guererro 171
Flair: End of an Era 175
Flair: Legacy 179
ChokeHold Pts 1 & 2 183
Extremely Strange 192
Should Vince Resign? 200
Pro Wrestling Kid Style 204
Vampiro 208
Listen, You Pencil Necked Geeks! 212

History
Bodyslams in Buffalo 216
Rassler from Renfrew 219
Lucha Libre 221
Hardcore History 224
One of the Boys 227
Pain and Passion 230
Mondo Lucha a Go Go 233
Misawa/Kobashi 238
Ring of Honor Title 242
Tributes II 247

Philosophy
This is a Shoot 251
Kowalski's Blueprint 254
Lack of Passion 260
War on the Fans 264
Sport and Spectacle:/Mazer 268
Formulas for Success 272
Steel Chair to the Head 275
What happened to Jobbers? 280
SuperChampionship 283
What Makes a Great Promotion 286

Women's Pro Wrestling
Women's Pro Wrestling Today 291
Cheerleader Melissa vs MsChif 294
SHIMMER Volume Six 300
ChickFight V 304
Glow 310
SHIMMER Volume Eighteen 313
Sara Del Rey 317
MsChif 320
WSU: Dawn/New Day 322
Cheerleader Melissa 325

Favorites
ROH 5th Year Fest/NYC 329
Last Call: Raven & Sandman 336
Best of Dragon Gate 339
Brody 343
Omega: Uncommon Passion 346
Walter Kowalski 351
Pure Dynamite 354
More Than Just Hardcore 358
Pile Driver 361
Cage of Pain II 366

Miscellaneous
Pro Wrestling Field Guide 371
Want to Be a Wrestler? 373
Out of Texas 377
Pro Wrestling Illustr.#100 379
Gaming Addiction 383
Synopsis: Greatest Moments 385
Eight Suggestions for TNA 388
Who'd Win: Goldberg/Austin 393
Ken Patera 398
St Louis Wrestling Vol 2 401

Shirley Doe

Ricky Reyes

Professional Wrestling Intellectual

Bios of Professional Wrestlers

Christopher Daniels   Takeshi Morishima/Bryan Danielson   Roderick Strrong/Jack Evans

Jay and Mark Briscoe

Been up and down since I turned seventeen
Well I've been on top, and then it seems I lost my dream
But I got it back, I'm feelin' better everyday
Tell all those pencil pushers, better get out of my way

"Gimme Back My Bullets, "Lynyrd Skynyrd

Tag Team Wrestling has been dying on the vine for the past decade, and when the signature teams of the WWE at the turn of the millennium – The Hardys, The Dudleyz, Edge and Christian – got stale from fighting themselves for too long, and subsequently broke up or moved on, it seemed like the final chapters were being written.

TNA may have had some of those great teams, and perhaps with expanded time, they may reappear as a focal point or even just as a well stocked division. But when the most prominent TNA tag team of the past several years – America's Most Wanted – has been mired in meaningless support positions and has teased a break-up far beyond general fandom even caring about them as a unit, the resounding lack of emphasis on a southern wrestling staple really strikes home.

Aside from flourishes in Japan, and variants of the concept in Mexico, there aren't very many places where tag teams seem to mean anything.

But as it has proved in a variety of pro wrestling traditions, the Ring of Honor promotion continues to tout the best examples of tag team wrestling known today.

At the top of ROH for much of the year had been the duo of Austin Aries and Roderick Strong. Now, those belts are held by Chris Hero and Claudio Castagnoli, who provide a interesting challenge, both in storyline and in talent, as they have taken up the emotion and extended the duration of the heated CZW/ROH war.

But over the summer, the return – and slow build – of what appears to be the tag team of the future has been playing out.

Mark and Jay Briscoe have shown that potential, and in ROH's more traditional booking sensibilities, guided by Gabe Sapolsky, they are obviously being slotted for things much bigger and better than even Aries/Strong.

In the past, great teams have usually been thrust upon the fans. I can vividly recall that Saturday evening when the Road Warriors appeared, destroying their opponents after a few weeks of whispers, a phantom title change and already an expectation that forced their reputations to soar.

Not to discredit the Warriors, but the sleight of hand was necessary. While they had the ground breaking image, the inherent power and enough of a pro wrestling background to make themselves over huge, their gimmick – so to speak – was based upon ignoring the offence of their opponents, or looking huge and monstrous beside lesser endowed individuals, and otherwise depending upon solid workers to make them look good.

Cut to the 1990's, and the Steiners, who had unquestionable amateur backgrounds, had paid their dues, but also rose to a great reputation not merely by innovation, ability and sense of wrestling, but also by cutting off their opponents and denying to give much offense to anyone they deemed inconsequential.

As products of All Japan, the famed "Miracle Violence Combination" of Terry Gordy and Steve Williams was the evolution of tag wrestling to its peak. They had the experience, as well as the inherent power, and because of their promotion and its stable of excellent pro wrestlers, their matches had the give-and-take, and their presence was all the more important because they were well-rounded performers.

The teams in the WWE were always a bit lower on the scale of greatness because of a general disinterest – which got worse as time went by – by the powers that be about technical matches, emotional outputs or building long term feuds. But the obvious greatness of the British Bulldogs, the Hart Foundation, perhaps Demolition, and the later the New Age Outlaws, all pretty much depended upon give-and-take, not just destroy your opponents and make yourself look good while defeating the nature of professional wrestling.

Once again, while the Road Warriors paved a path of destruction across the known world, across the NWA, the AWA and many parts in between, they mostly fizzled in the WWE atmosphere because they never really learned all the aspects of working a match.

Which brings me back to the Briscoes.

Pro Wrestling Intellectual

Two things came to mind when watching these guys for the first time: First, they have unlimited potential. Second, they are obviously students of the sport. Add to that their position in the ROH promotion, and the ultimate guidance of Sapolsky's booking.

With a lesser restraint, an no eye towards the future, the Briscoes would have waltzed in, beaten up the competition, and held the belts until they got a call-up. We would all call them great, but would they be?

Just watch these young pro's in action. They not only sell for their opponents, but they work the match. They not only innovate, but they work with their opponents to make the company look good. They don't just run roughshod over smaller guys, they take dives to get out of the ring, give great expression, and get worked over in double teams.

That first match I sat down to watch was against the Irish Airborne. Jake and Dave Crist don't exactly match up physically with the Briscoes, but they present a high-flying, innovative style that matches up quite perfectly with the Briscoes. And the match is quite excellent. Not because of the winners of the match, but because of the talent displayed.

And that, to me, is the essence of professional wrestling. The Briscoes aren't about going through the motions, they are about telling a story and giving the fans an excellent show. While I cringe at every leap they take over the top rope to the floor, and shudder (as well as marvel) when reading about their exploits in Detroit, because that level of dedication, insanity and self-destruction does not readily translate into a long career.

However, all it takes is a few minutes to see just how dedicated these guys are, and how much potential they have in this sport. To some (especially mainstream types) they may need some thickness, but they have a solid combination of power, speed, technical prowess and innovation in double team moves as well as general violence. But they work to a pin, they sell strong, and they don't do much

Joe Babinsack

that isn't smooth or at least realistic. That alone puts them above most talent featured on weekly or syndicated shows.

And the most impressive part is watching the Briscoes develop over time. They aren't just going through the motions. They aren't merely basking in well deserved accolades, or relying upon phantom pushes or burying their opponents as they rise to the top. One year down the road, they'll match up against the Crists and put on another excellent show. Down the road, they'll fight Colt Cabana and Ace Steel and sell for the smaller guy, and transition from comedy to violence just as smoothly. And for years to come, one can imagine them battling Austin Aries and Roderick Strong in a variety of ways, each time raising the bar, each time putting on a more spectacular show.

So, here are the Briscoes in ROH, in a slow build to becoming one of the all-time greats, learning with some of the best, gaining experience at all levels of competition, going over talent while raising the bar of excellence in tag team matchups, and not winning the big matches while maintaining the momentum of the team of the future.

"But I keep on workin' like the workin' man do
And I've got my act together, gonna walk all over you ..."

That theme song just gets better and better.

CHRISTOPHER DANIELS

Christopher Daniels is an enigma.

*T*here are few current wrestlers who have such an extensive track record of working for so many promotions. At the same time, there are few current wrestlers who have a reputation as being one of the best technical performers. And yet, here's Christopher Daniels, a journeyman who should be a feature player in TNA's X Division, getting a rather lackluster "repackaging" from the promotion.

With a beard and cyberpunk markings, maybe Daniels is poised to do great things in TNA. His past strongly suggests that he can. Whether as the leader of The Prophecy in ROH, or as the glue to the all-but-forgotten Triple X grouping in TNA just but a few years back, Daniels has the look, the experience and the ability to be a top notch heel.

Even after his WCW debacle/debut that got him signed to a contract, he was positioned to be a major player. But that was something like six years ago. And the aforementioned groups he lead were after that. And yet, there's still something missing. But its never been for a lack of effort.

Christopher Daniels broke into the business with Chicago's Windy City Pro Wrestling in the early 1990's. Since then, he's been everywhere in the United States that one can imagine going, and has joined a select few in appearing on air for WCW, WWE and TNA. Throw in the reputable and technical excellence of ROH, and that number dwindles to a select, elite few. That he has also been able to change up his look and gimmick and be respectable in Japan is also of note.

As the "Fallen Angel" Daniels has cultivated a gimmick and a somewhat unique look. Playing off the goth/underground/cyberpunk subcultures, and obviously influenced by the worlds of comic books and games, Daniels seems to have gotten it. Perhaps, unfortunately, he works in an industry where remaking images and creating new concepts always seems to be the way to a successful gimmick.

But it's not like Daniels is his gimmick. He's an accomplished wrestler, and his influence and positioning in promotions from UPW to Ring of Honor have proven his ability to work the major independents. His presence and working with several of wrestling's next generation of promising stars, from Samoa Joe to AJ Styles, has helped formed his reputation, but still, others move on and gather the accolades.

When Daniels made his debut on a Monday Nitro, January 23, 2001, he was in the midst of a much anticipated infusion of new blood into the sagging promotion. With Michael Modest, he was with a wrestling colleague from UPW, and they were set to make their mark on the industry. It was a great match, that would have springboarded the pair to the big time. But Daniels nearly broke his neck on a botched moonsault attempt. You can see the situation unfold on UPW's Bodyslam: the Making of a Pro Wrestler.

Fortunately for Daniels, he avoided major injury and was also offered a contract. But by the time he was ready to wrestle, getting involved in the Sting/Vampiro feud, WCW was out of luck. His contract was readily dismissed in the McMahon buyout. Far too many marketable and potential names and salaries were ignored, and it was likely a bad break for Daniels, who wasn't the recipient of a lucrative 'sit at home' situation.

But other things appeared, and Daniels even appeared on a few WWE broadcasts: once, as a masked Conquistador, and another in challenging TAKA Michinoku for the oft forgotten Light Heavyweight Championship on the equally forgotten Shotgun Saturday Night.

Daniels, less forgetably, was a featured wrestler in the opening of Ring of Honor.

His refusal to abide by the Code of Honor, a defining measure of respect in the promotion, set him apart as a heel. By refusing to shake hands after losses, the undercurrent of dissent was well suited to his "Fallen Angel" persona, and it was played up even further in the creation of The Prophecy as a heel group, which he lead.

Donovan Morgan, another UPW alum, battled Daniels, but a mutual respect ensued. They added Xavier to the group, and it dominated the early days of ROH by holding the Tag Team Titles and the ROH singles Championship. Daniels feuded primarily with Low Ki, even bringing in Samoa Joe as a hired hand.

But strange situations ensued when scandal rocked ROH, and in the midst of a heated feud with the Second City Saints, with a rotation of members that now included Dan Maff and BJ Whitmer, Daniels was put "out of commission." Now feuding with CM Punk, Daniels took a Pepsi Plunge through a table, and it would be 16 months before he reappeared.

Already working with TNA, he was in the midst of a heel grouping with, ironically, Low Ki, and also Elix Skipper. The team of XXX played off the old Freebirds 'any two of the three' concept, and captured the TNA Tag Team Championships, and feuded with America's Most Wanted. Subject to Russonian booking insanity, XXX would be dismantled. To be fair, the grouping was always in flux due to Low Ki's Japan commitments, as well as Daniels' own worldly and national bookings.

Daniels first real major push as a singles came with a series of matches with Jeff Jarrett in 2003. That lead him back into the X Division, where he competed at the top of that distinction for a while, and where he held the X Division title for 150 days – the longest reign of the belt in TNA history. Along the way, he defeated Skipper, Shocker and other X Division notables like Chris Sabin and Matt Bentley, as well as ROH player Austin Aries.

The Title was hotly contested by AJ Styles and Samoa Joe, with Daniels first holding it, and then losing it in a spectacular match at TNA's Unbreakable.

Meanwhile, Christopher Daniels returned to ROH, where he challenged ROH Champion CM Punk. Punk was headed to the WWE, and ROH talent was hell bent on keeping the Title with the promotion. Daniels would become a solid roster member of ROH from then on to the present. His abiding by the Code of Honor became an interesting backstory for ROH's 100th show, in which he met Claudio Castagnoli in a match, and praised him as the future of ROH (only to see Claudio turn his back on ROH in the awesome war with CZW. Daniels seemed conspicuous in his absence.)

In ROH, Samoa Joe became a rival, and Daniels would continue to be linked to Samoa Joe, as a victim of a concussion after a tag match in TNA. He further put Joe over as a monster, with Styles acting as concerned partner who threw in the towel to protect Daniels' career. This would lead to another three-way match, in which Christopher Daniels regained the X-Division Championship, only to lose it back to Samoa Joe.

It was another strange twist that brought Low Ki back to TNA. Daniels was scheduled to wrestle Jushin "Thunder" Liger, but that direction was scrapped behind the scenes. A mystery opponent turned out to be a re-named Low Ki, wrestling now as Senshi. They put on a great match.

Strangely enough, AJ Styles was in the picture as Daniels' partner, and they gained the Tag Titles, then feuded in a great series of matches with the newly formed LAX. The LAX squad of Homicide and Hernandez, guided by Konnan, traded the belts until finally vanquishing the high flying pair.

Daniels went back to the X-Division, and won the X-Division belt once again, but then lost it back to Chris Sabin. This lead to the "repackaging" deal which really doesn't seem like much of a change for the long time veteran.

In ROH during this repackaging, Daniels formed a team with ex-Generation Next member Matt Sydal, and captured the ROH Tag Team Titles on November 25, 2006. They would lose to the Briscoes on February 24, 2007 after some top-notch title defenses.

Christopher Daniels, linked to Marilyn Manson's "Disposable Teens" in both ROH and in a perverted mix in TNA, continues to live his reputation as a top-notch player in the industry.

While he has held far more belts than I would dare list, and has been a major impact figure in ROH, TNA and as a comedy wrestler (mostly in Japan as Curry Man,) he seems still positioned just under the main event level, and seems – more than most of TNA's roster – to be a victim of short-sighted booking and a lack of emphasis on its great roster smaller, but technically awesome and high flying talent.

Repackaging always comes with a promise and a push. I certainly hope that Christopher Daniels will be allowed to make the most of this opportunity, as he has done in the past, in virtually every promotion he'd been a part of, and in a variety of different methods.

CLAUDIO CASTAGNOLI

Yes, it's another installment of "wrestlers you should know" and the subject today is

Claudio Castagnoli, aka "Double C" and "the Most Money Making Man"

Ok, somehow that last moniker sounds like a bad translation from the Swiss (or French or German or Italian or whatever they speak in the Alps.)

Funny story: the first time I watched "Double C" in action, he was pitted against another oft-comedic grappler, who's Developmental Deal with the WWE actually stuck, that man being Colt Cabana.

I spent ten minutes screaming "Double C" stands for Colt Cabana too, you idiots!

But my respect for ROH grew from that day.

Back to "Quad M" and his bio:

The person we all love as Claudio Castagnoli began his career training in Switzerland by SigMasta Rappo, who in himself has an excellent name. Claudio billed himself as Tenshi Takami in his first experiences in the German promotion "westside Xtreme wrestling"

Shortly thereafter, he hooked up European grappler Ares, and formed a team called "Swiss Money Holding" His training continued in England under Dave Taylor, and SMH was invited by Chris Hero to wrestle in the U.S. -- for CHIKARA and IWA Mid South, and to receive further training by Hero.

Swiss Money Holding was no trivial note, and the team captured gold in several promotions, including German Stampede Wrestling, International Pro Wrestling: United Kingdom, Independent Wrestling Association: Switzerland, and the Swiss Wrestling Federation (where CC held the "Powerhouse Championship twice as well.) Castignoli also held the wXw World Heavyweight Championship on two occasions, plus the gold with Ares on three occasions.

SMH faced a break up, as Ares would stay in Europe (to reform SMH with Marc Roudin,) when Claudio secured paperwork to wrestle full time in the United States. Double C worked appearances for CHIKARA and Ring of Honor, and gravitated to Combat Zone Wrestling to link up with Chris Hero.

Joe Babinsack

It was 2005 that the "Kings of Wrestling" were born, being Castagnoli and Hero, and the pair grabbed the CZW Tag Team Championship in short order, then seized the CHIKARA Tag World Grand Prix in 2006 (a few days after losing the CZW tag straps) which billed them as the first "Campeonatos de Parejas"

Few teams have had the independent level success as the Kings of Wrestling, as they went to ROH and dethroned long time ROH Tag Champs and dominant (sorta former) Generation Next faction members Austin Aries and Roderick Strong on September 16th of 2006.

The Kings of Wrestling were associated with Queen's "We are the Champions" and they certainly deserved the opening music:

Less than one month later they won their second CZW Tag Team Championship at "CZW Last Team Standing" on October 14th.

They held three versions of Tag Team Championship gold for a month, before losing away those CZW belts to BLKOUT (Sabian and Robbie Mireno) then the CHIKARA belts to Team FIST (Gran Akuma and Icarus) then finally the ROH belts to Christopher Daniels and Matt Sydal.

Castagnoli was a star on the rise, and the WWE took notice.

The Kings of Wrestling were to be no more, and after a loss to the Briscoes at "ROH Final Battle 2006" the team split in storyline fashion, as Chris Hero turned on Double C and aligned with mouthpiece Larry Sweeney.

Castagnoli was reported to have signed a Developmental Deal with the WWE, after appearances on RAW backstage as a policeman, and in tryouts for Deep South Wrestling. However, the deal was quickly and mysteriously nixed, with claims of paperwork problems (strange, since he was already working full time in the US for a year) and perhaps the dreaded attitude problems.

Listed at 6'5" with extensive training, experience, a fascinating personality and comedic presence, plus being a modern update of the Million Dollar Man gimmick, with a distinct European style and accent, it seems baffling why the WWE would cut ties with Claudio Castagnoli so quickly.

Armed with the Ricola Bomb (a cross armed, sit-out power bomb) and other versions of Ricola (cross arming) plus the dreaded European Uppercuts and assorted, renamed versions of staple wrestling holds, plus the ever present Halliburton (a metal briefcase,) Claudio was an established star on the rise, with potential and at least a look that make you look.

Pro Wrestling Intellectual

Rejected by the WWE, he turned back to the indy circuit, and seemingly had to prove his loyalties. At the first King of Europe Cup, he represented CHIKARA in the 16 wrestler tournament in Liverpool, England, but lost in the opening round against long time partner and now rival Chris Hero.

He appeared on ROH's inaugural PPV "Respect is Earned" and teamed with Matt Sydal (who ironically now is reported to have his own WWE Developmental Deal -- did someone get the names mixed up or what?) to take on the Briscoes. It was a typically excellent match, and it earned a rematch with a partner of CC's choosing. He picked Chris Hero but they lost on June 9th of this year.

Firmly in ROH's fold, Claudio won the 16 man, two night tournament called the "Race to the Top" which earned him a title shot at ROH dominant champion Takeshi Morishima at "Death Before Dishonor V". It was a effort that gained him crowd recognition and with every near fall, a hope that he could unseat the Japanese powerhouse.

He earned a rematch of sorts, in a three way match with Brent Albright taking on the ROH Champ at "Caged Rage" and was a logical choice for the grand tournament for the restoration of the NWA World Heavyweight Championship, where he competed in the "Terry Funk" bracket.

He won opening rounds against Pepper Parks and oft CHIKARA roster mate Sicodelico Jr, before losing to one of the favorites (and three-way rival) Brent Albright in Charlotte.

In yet another tournament, Claudio participated in the second Pro Wrestling Guerrilla "Battle of Los Angeles" just a few days ago, matching up against Doug Williams and PAC.

There are few true "blue chippers" in the independent wrestling circuit, but Claudio Castagnoli continues to appear as one of the biggest and most experienced wrestlers not on one of the weekly national shows, as he typically towers over his opponents, but matches them with speed, skills and superior psychology.

JACK EVANS

*I*t is appropriate that Jack Evans has emerged from the self-destruction of Generation Next as one of the new ringleaders of a Ring of Honor faction. The association, once formed by Alex Shelley, and lead to greater glory by Austin Aries (and tag team mate Roderick Strong) was comprised of established stars and two stars of the future: Matt Sydal and Jack Evans.

With Aries turning into a Starr for TNA, and Strong seemingly more satisfied being a bedrock for ROH and its sister promotion, Full Impact Pro, the split of the more dominating force in ROH over the past two years seemed inevitable. Already, Sydal had mostly broken away, and captured the ROH tag titles with Christopher Daniels. Already, Aries and Strong had declared the dismantling of Generation Next.

But the Aries/Strong alliance persisted, and Evans seemed still closely aligned.

When Strong finally made the turn on Aries, Evans has turned his back on both, saying he'd get his own "crew" for future battles. With well established connections to Dragon's Gate, Calgary's Stampede and now Wrestle Society X, it seems as though Evans is poised to make an impact in ROH in the year to come.

Over the past few years, Evans has been building the foundation of a successful career.

Before reaching the age of twenty-five, he has wrestled extensively in Japan's Dragon Gate promotion, with its high speed, innovative and 'wrestling of the future' mentality. It's kind of hard to not apply those same notions to Evan's style, even before heading across the Pacific pond. Being trained by Bryan Alvarez, and the Harts, he holds a legacy in his style that few can boast of, and his peers, Harry Smith and TJ Wilson, are equally poised to make their names in the sport.

Linked early and often with the renegade known as Teddy Hart, Evans has been more his equal in the stunts and high flying, but not so much in the unpredictability aspect. Armed with a spectacular array of splashes, sentons, somersaults and moonsaults, cartwheels and suplex, often with a literal twist or two (and a half) thrown in for good measure, Evans is the epitome of a generation inspired and improving upon the backyard wrestling craze, combining some of the speed of the Japanese lighter junior heavyweights with the spectacular dives of the Luchadores.

Pro Wrestling Intellectual

Jack Evans started with ROH in late 2003, and stayed with the promotion even after his tag partner turned on him, and (once again) did his best to burn bridges instead of building foundations. Known as the "Aerial Emperor" and "Jack Evans from the Heavens" and having ties to Canada, Japan and the best of the cruiserweights, Evans has definitely paid his dues.

Another interesting connection of Evans is to the brief but sensational display of high flying that was Blitzkrieg. With his short-lived career already in retirement, Blitzkrieg gave the name, and mask, to Jack Evans. Evans has wrestled under the Blitzkrieg II name from time to time. One major nod to his mentor is what's called the "Ode to Blitzkrieg," which starts with a standing shooting star press, with a corkscrew thrown in, and is followed up by a standing senton (also with a corkscrew.)

Having worked in Calgary, and then ROH, Evans has done the opposite of Hart, and his career, while not as impacting (he's not been featured on the main stage,) his innovation and high flying exploits have lasted longer than his mentor. Combining the two strands of wrestling legacy, Evans has proved his worth to Generation Next in terms of innovation and tag teaming with Roderick Strong.

He signed on to a commitment with Dragon's Gate, and three months of 2006 in Japan, training and becoming part of Cima's group (the Blood Generation.) While Evans participated in Generation Next's big feud with ROH's Embassy faction, the seeds for splintering were sown when Cima came to fight for the prestigious ROH Tag Titles.

Evan's own list of accomplishments is growing. He was the AWA Pinnacle Heavyweight Champion , the Open the Triangle Gate Champion in Dragon's Gate (a six man championship, which he held with members of Blood Generation,) the Jersey All Pro Tag Team Titles (with Teddy Hart!) and the Pro Wrestling Unplugged Junior Heavyweight Championship.

Generation Next disbanded by name in June of 2005, with the four players removing their merchandise. But once again, the loose alliance seemed to be stable until recently. Before that, he became involved with the innovative and futuristic WSX program on MTV. While the future of WSX remains muddied, the experience and the exposure will only spur Evans on to bigger and better things.

Jack Evans can be found on the internet, and has an active forum on his site, which also provides contact information. http://www.myspace.com/kcajsnave
http://www.jackevanswrestling.com

Many DVD's featuring Jack Evans can be found at www.rohwrestling.com

Joe Babinsack

NIGEL MCGUINNESS

"I've realized here recently, that perhaps like life itself, wrestling isn't about winning or losing, it's about being who you want." Nigel McGuinness

The list of English born wrestlers who have made an impact on the world scene isn't terribly long, but certainly is significant. Whether Nigel McGuinness can live up to his potential, and the legacy of those preceding him, remains to be seen, but he has certainly begun to be noticed by the fans.

With a look that crosses Billy Idol and the British Bulldogs, punk rock and European style technicality, he certainly is readily recognized no matter what the promotion.

McGuinness carries with him the display of technical skills that seems to be a hallmark of his countrymen. Perhaps one aspect of it lies in the somewhat alien approach, in terms of movements, holds and wrestling, or maybe something even deeper, in that there seems to be a sort of thought process that is inherently different from the US mainstream mentality

There are two central quirks to the wrestling style of McGuinness. One is a sense of momentum generated by backing through the ropes, more specifically when he leans back over the middle rope before springing off into what will usually end up in a lariat on the opponent. McGuinness also incorporates this sort of springboard-similar addition to various other maneuvers.

The other odd creation of Nigel McGuinness is a handstand on the top turnbuckle. From this position, he basically invites the opponent into running at the corner, which creates opportunities for him to set up a variety of counters or offensive maneuvers.

His primary "finisher" is the Tower of London, which often gets set up with the unorthodox corner work. This is a 'cutter' type hold, which starts with the feet of the opponent on the top turnbuckle, McGuinness holding the head and dropping down. Once again, that weird sort of momentum comes into play.

Different seems to be an operative word for Nigel McGuinness.

While the Pure Title in Ring of Honor is most associated with him, strangely enough, he was not the first holder of the title. He was, however, the last, and held the belt for 350 days. The essence of the Pure Title revolved around rope breaks. Also, no punches to the head were allowed. Three rope breaks were given to each wrestler, who would spend them to escape a submission or a pinfall, or lose one (after being warned) if a punch was thrown. Once used, the wrestler could not escape a loss via the usual technicality of using the ropes to break up the situation. Coupled with the Title changing hands on a countout or disqualification, the rules were readily exploited by a heelish approach.

This is why it seemed so natural for McGuinness to maintain the belt for a year.

A world traveler, Nigel McGuinness has recently been doing regular tours of NOAH, typically teaming with Doug Williams and/or Bison Smith. He has been a regular on quite a few US indy promotions, especially the Heartland Wrestling Association, where he got his start in this country.

He has a site, www.nigelmcguinness.com, which has an extensive record of his matches since January 10, 2004. Among the highlights are his winning and losing the Pure Title, his defenses -- defeating Samoa Joe, Homicide, Austin Aries, Christopher Daniels, Bryan Danielson, among others, and the loss of the belt in a unification match with Bryan Danielson.

Another highlight was a loss to Naomichi Marufuji in a GHC World Championship match – the NOAH promotion's belt, in one of the first defenses of that title in the US.

Less significant appearances by McGuinness include a match with Shark Boy on the 2005 version of TNA's Genesis PPV. He also appeared on a WWE Sunday Night Heat show. The concept of a genuine punk rocker in either of those mainstream promotions seems impossible, and perhaps it is to the betterment of his career that he hasn't had his unique style destroyed by the WWE or his character relegated to a few moments of nonsense in TNA.

A quick search of www.rohwrestling.com will provide readers with a tremendous opportunity to see Nigel McGuinness at his best. His Pure Title reign is resplendent with unique approaches, creative booking and a style and pace of wrestling not often seen on the mainstream stages. Whether crafty heel or crowd-pleasing hooligan, McGuinness seldom fails to get the audience to respond, and he is poised to break out from his anonymity to full blown star, perhaps rising to the level of Danielson or Samoa Joe.

Armed with his Union Jacked iron (stories of which suggest either a defensive weapon or another approach to being different,) and sporting spiffy ROH merchandised T-Shirts, Nigel McGuinness is set to make his mark on the pro wrestling industry: Pro Wrestling NOAH in Japan seems to be establishing him as a regular, and the upcoming departure of

Joe Babinsack

Samoa Joe perhapsleaves a high card roster spot open for the likes of this English punker with the strange mannerisms and unique approach to the sport.

Shirley Doe

"If you hate me, I've done my job.

Too many heels want the fans to applaud them for their fancy moves. I'd rather get inside your head, fill you with jealousy and force you to try to take me down at every opportunity.

Because the more you try to destroy me, the stronger I get." -- Shirley Doe

www.shirleydoe.com

Questionnaire:

1. Are you comfortable with your real name out in public, or only your ring name?

    I'D PREFER MY RING NAME ONLY.

2. Who trained you?

    BENSON LEE STARTED ME, I HAD A LOT OF SEASONING FROM T RANTULA AND LORD ZOLTAN, AND FINISHED OFF WITH DORY FUNK, JR.

3. Why did you get into the industry?

    I WAS BORED AT HOUSE SHOWS AND JUST KNEW THAT IF I GOT THE CHANCE TO GET IN THE RING, I COULD DO SOMETHING EXCITING AND CONTRIBUTE.

4. How would you describe your style?

    I KNOW HOW TO WRESTLE, YET CHOOSE NOT TO.

5. Where do you see yourself in ten years?

    TEN YEARS IS A LONG TIME. MAYBE ALIVE?

6. What is your favorite match?

    OF MINE? I REALLY ENJOYED WORKING HENTAI AND BALLS MAHONEY, AS WELL AS TRACY SMOTHERS. NOT OF MINE, I PREFER ALL JAPAN OF THE EARLY 90S, TEXAS GLORY DAYS AND TURNER SATURDAY NIGHTS AT 6:05.

7. Either or:

    a) Heel or Face? **HEEL.**

    b) Hogan or Flair? **FLAIR.**

    c) Health or Wealth? **HEALTH.**

    d) Fame or Talent? **TALENT**

    e) Family or Fortune? **FAMILY**

    f) Story or Highspot? **STORY**

8. What is your hidden talent?

> **I WRITE COMIC BOOKS AND HOPE TO ENTER THAN FIELD SOMEDAY. I CAN ALSO PLAY BLACK SABBATH'S IRON MAN ON ANY INSTRUMENT, INCLUDING THE TELEPHONE AND THE PAN FLUTE.**

9. Your lasting impact on the industry will be what?

> **GEE, I DON'T EVEN KNOW. MAYBE SOME OF THE PEOPLE I'VE TRAINED WILL GO ON TO DO THAT.** [Note: Shirley Doe has helped train the a number of regulars on the IWC roster, including Jason Gorey, HENTAI, the Gambinos, and Shiima Xion.]

10. Who are your wrestling heroes?

> **THE FUNKS, JUMBO TSURUTA, MICK FOLEY, BRUISER BRODY, STAN HANSEN, BARRY WINDHAM.**

11. Is there anything else you'd like to say to your fans?

> **I APPRECIATE ANYONE WHO COMES OUT TO THE SHOW. I DOUBLY APPRECIATE ANYONE WHO BUYS ME A DRINK AFTER THE SHOW. NOTE: I LIKE DIET AND JACK, DIET AND RUM, YUENGLING AND WHEN WITH LARRY SWEENEY, WHITE RUSSIANS.**

There's an interesting picture of Shirley Doe with Dory Funk Jr; Doe with that sort of Charles Manson on goth steroids look, Dory looking all serious and stuff. I guess it proves the training connection, and impresses that, indeed, Shirley Doe "knows how to wrestle."

He's been wrestling for at least the past six or seven years, and while based mostly in the Pittsburgh area, he holds the longest reign as International Wrestling Cartel Heavyweight Champion (defeating Eric Xstasy, in a match refereed by Mick Foley and Chris Wood,) and was the first to defend that belt in Japan, making it a true world championship.

In defense of the championship, he defended against the likes of Chris Hero, Balls Mahoney (with whom he traded the belt,) Steve Corino, Sterling James Keenan, Tracy Smothers, until losing to Dennis Gregory in the summer of 2006.

The Unholy Alliance became a major IWC faction, until being recently thrown out of the promotion. That alignment centered on Shirley Doe, Sebastian Dark and HENTAI.

To call Shirley Doe a psychological heel would be an understatement.

He's a 'get them riled up' type of wrestler, more interested in telling the story that displaying flashes of athleticism, and vastly more interested in entertaining in his own perverse sense of style. He describes his own style as a combination of "old school brawler" but it's obviously updated with submission holds and power moves, retrofitted with headbutts! and far more reminiscent of Keijii Mutoh than The Great Muta.

Doe bristles at the notion of working high-spot style matches, greatly preferring ring psychology.

Armed with his big three weapons – the Shining Wizard, the roaring elbow (called the Magic Bullet) and the Superterrorizer – a sort of reverse suplex/stunner move. He's also used, as his finisher, the Sillyhead. That finisher started out as a DDT variant, then changed to Sillyhead 2, then Sillyhead 33, an inverted Death Valley Driver.

The collection of jewelry in Does closet is a strong showing of Western Pennsylvania's finest promotions, and a few nearby ones as well. The grand jewel being the IWC Heavyweight Title, which he held on two occasions.

He also held the "High Stakes" title of the IWC - a belt where the champion dictates the specialty match to decide the championship.

Along the way, he's held the VCW Title, the Pittsburgh Wrestling League "Triple Jeopardy" title, the UWL Junior Heavyweight title, the CWF Mon-Valley Title, and several Tag Team titles (USWA Ohio, PWX, PWL and UIPW) – notably with HENTAI, as well as with Devil Bhudakahn.

Shirley Doe has been a force to be reckoned with in the International Wrestling Cartel, and his exploits in the Unholy Alliance, and now moving beyond, should be interesting to those who hearken back to the sadistic villainy of Kevin Sullivan.

Joe Babinsack

RICKY REYES

One of the main purposes of my efforts is to shed some light on talented wrestlers who may be "under the radar" of the mainstream fans. Many of these individuals are well-established and known to fans of a particular independent level federation or even culture, but sometimes even the best of pro wrestlers don't get the appreciation they deserve until they hit the mainstream.

Since the industry is replete with talented individuals who never get that opportunity to shine, and a select few who catch a break and get to the big show, it makes sense to me to shine a spotlight on people who should get recognition, and to give props to the promotions that feature these individuals, but most of all, to let the more mainstream fans know who's out there, and why they should know about them.

That being said, I turn my attention to and individual who has been appearing on my TV screen from a variety of promotions.

Ricky Reyes is that man.

It would be cheap to simply call him a cross between Taz and Homicide, so I'll just lay that first analogy out there on the fly. Reyes is a strong style wrestler with a bad attitude and a heel demeanor that suits him well. Beyond that, he was a member of one of the most touted tag teams of a few years back – the Havana Pitbulls—and a strong member of ROH's Rottweilers.

With Reyes, it's not the Kotohajime or the Cop-Killa, it's the Dragon Sleeper as his finisher.

He has proven it to be unbreakable with his steamrolling through the ROH student wrestlers in 2005, which "angered" Austin Aries and lead to a series between the two. Aries could not break the hold, but took advantage of the situation to score a pinfall victory in the first encounter. In the second, Reyes refused to break the holds as Aries reached the ropes. After both occasions, Gen Next team member Roderick Strong was out for the save.

A tag match which pitted Reyes and Homicide against Aries/Strong culminated the short feud, but established the Dragon Sleeper as a powerful finisher.

Pro Wrestling Intellectual

But it was a few years earlier, notably in ROH, where Reyes hit the radar screen of most hardcore fans. Teaming up with Rocky Romero, they made up the tag team of the Havana Pitbulls, and made a huge splash in debuting against the Briscoes in a non-title match, and joining the Rottweilers faction, lead by Julius Smokes, and including Homicide (and later Low Ki.)

Shortly thereafter, the Havana Pitbulls defeated ROH Tag Team Champions (of the Second City Saints faction) Colt Cabana and CM Punk. Until Aries and Strong rose to the thrones, the HP had the longest reign, and plowed through opponents, including Evans/Strong, Maff/Whitmer, Special K, and others. Eventually, they succumbed to the Maff/Whitmer pairing

The partnership began to crumble, although the Rottweilers won 2005's Trio's Tournament. After that event, Romero and Reyes seemed headed in opposite directions, and definitely in ROH. They tagged in other indies, but with Romero headed to New Japan as the fourth incarnation of the Black Tiger, the legacy of the Havana Pitbulls (also known as Los Cubanitos, based on the nation of birth of both the members) seems to have lasted longer than their highest profile championship run. In fact, at the ROH "100th Show" it was Reyes and Homicide who challenged then-champs Aries and Strong for the title belts.

Reyes then began his "bully" streak at ROH, and has now been settled into a solid heel role throughout the independent circuits.

He has continued to wear tights with the "HP" insignia, which seems confusing if you don't recognize the wrestler.

"HP" of course stands for the Havana Pitbulls.

The pair were well known for their strong style work, stiff moves and ability to just beat up on their opponents. Romero turned out more of the high-flyer, with his CMLL experience, but Reyes has been known to throw himself into a mean plancha. Reyes is a suplex master, and throws the stiff kicks associated with his typical style. One of their favorite finishers was the Cuban Missile Crisis, where one hits a backbreaker, and the other does a knee drop.

Ricky Reyes was headed back up the ROH charts, disposing of various mid-carders with his dangerous Dragon Sleeper, when he ran head first into Delirious. It was a great set up and an impressive win by the masked insanity known as Delirious, but it seemed to derail any sort of push given to Reyes in ROH. Ironically, Reyes would debut in CZW and joined "The Blackout" faction to help Eddie Kingston win its version of the World Heavyweight Championship.

Since then, he's been appearing at various Northeastern indies, but also appeared across the country at Pro Wrestling Guerilla and UPW. At PWG, he forces newcomers to prove their mettle, not so unlike Taz in ECW. In ROH, recently, the inevitable last straw was done to end the Havana Pitbulls. Ricky Reyes turned his back on Rocky Romero in a tag team encounter, perhaps sending the legacy truly into history.

Ricky Reyes has certainly proved his mettle. He is currently the International Wrestling Cartel Heavyweight Champion, and has held the UPW Light Heavyweight Championship.

Of course, he is more known for his tag team work. With Rocky Romero as the Havana Pitbulls, they held the Empire Wrestling Federation belts on four occasions, the UPW Tag Team Championships, as well as the aforementioned ROH belts. With Joker, they held the Pro Wrestling Unplugged Tag Team Championship, and continue to struggle to reclaim that belt.

Listen for "Bulls on Parade" by the appropriately named Rage Against the Machine, as it heralds the appearance of one of the independent circuits stiffest and strongest competitors. As Reyes told the English language version site of New Japan Wresting a few years back, "we never liked the good guys, we always liked the bad guys"

That doesn't seem all that surprising….

DVD's of note:

ROH: Let the Gates of Hell Open: The Best of The Rottweilers
Reborn: Stage One
Testing the Limit
Trios Tournament
Hell Freezes Over
Best in the World, 100th Show

PWU: Vendetta

Takeshi Morishima

Morishima has a look that is hard to get around.

The baby-face look worked so well for Sid "not the singer" Vicious, even with that mostly chiseled physique, because he just towered over people. It didn't matter about his indifference to the sport, or his propensity to play softball instead of headline, Sid got a great response. Maybe because he just looked like a kid who turned into a monster, maybe because of that boyish charm.

Takeshi Morishima ain't no Sid. He shows passion and works a hell of a lot harder in the ring.

Before Adrian Adonis got way too bloated, he complimented Jesse Ventura as a wrestling machine. Adonis, too, had that soft look and had the workrate of a ring general. More so, Adonis had the ability, once he did get too big, to make everything look so easy. He was fat, well experienced and yet could get the crowd riled up, and perform his craft with seemingly a minimal effort.

While Takeshi Morishima isn't that bloated, he does have that sense of minimal effort, despite his powerful moves and dangerous, high risk maneuvers. Many times, it just seems like he briefly shakes off a miss, and moves back on the attack, barely making an effort.

With Terry Gordy, the bashful fat kid just wowed you with his determination and power. Gordy had the blessings of size, power and presence from an early age. He was also well protected, with Michael Hayes as the mouthpiece and Buddy Jack Roberts as the ring veteran.

Gordy is, in many ways, the template from which Takeshi Morishima springs to mind.

Like Gordy, Morishima is a big bulky kid, with a mop of long hair draped over his eyes (no mullet here) and big in the middle and with a strong foundation.

He looks soft, moves soft, but belies that softness with a powerful array of attacks. From the lariat and the "bowling over" -- where he hits the ropes and spins across, knocking over a sitting opponent, to the missile dropkick.

Joe Babinsack

Most impressively, the dangerous back drop driver, made famous by Steve Dr. Death Williams, in which a rather routine back suplex is made much more dangerous by gripping down, forcing an opponent to land on his upper shoulders, neck and head.

With Morishima, there are aspects of all of those people and more.

Already touted as the "future" of the heavyweight pro wrestling scene in Japan, he's been slowly groomed from his days in the All Japan Pro Wrestling Dojo, through the schism that created Pro Wrestling NOAH, and through some impressive tag team work, having held the NOAH Tag Team Titles, twice with Takeshi Rikio, and once with Mohammed Yone.

That Morishima could hold the weight of his destiny on his broad shoulders is hard to question.

Even the Cauliflower Alley Club has tagged him with the "Future Legend" award this year. Whether his knees can hold up is a more painful one.

Morishima has proven a dedication and a capability worthy of all the accolades. Few men as large as him have regularly attempted the missile dropkick, or the cartwheels or the top rope attempts. Then again, few have sold for lighter and talented wrestlers as he has, which undoubtedly has endeared him to his generation of workers, who are otherwise smaller, faster and more acrobatic.

Since his debut in Ring of Honor, he's disdained the "code of honor" which involves an opening handshake and a traditional ring announcement of the match. Instead, he simply attacks his opponent when in proximity, disdainful even of the opening bell.

While the match with Samoa Joe, before Morishima won the ROH title, seems somewhat odd, the use of Joe as a measuring stick is not. Joe is the prime time legend of ROH, and Takeshi Morishima had to face him before being able to stand up to the ROH Championship. While a rematch with Joe seems distant if not unlikely, such a title match would be immediately called a classic by fans.

Since winning the title from ROH's other living legend, Homicide, Morishima has gotten mixed reviews and reactions. But it's going to take some time to click. Already it's going on ten years of ring experience for Morishima, and will his tenure as ROH be the start of his prime?

Even with, and likely because, of that lauded ROH fan base, the acceptance of a much touted newcomer is easy to pull off. And when he wows the fans and does the big man

Pro Wrestling Intellectual

stuff (like hand springs, dives and missile drop kicks) like no other, you can get caught up in the excitement. But the other end is that it's difficult to create a heel, even a monster heel, out of someone everyone in ROH either appreciates or also considers as a talent destined for greatness.

One of the problems is that we no longer live in the era of the monster foreigner.

Worse, ROH is by far the promotion most removed from such heel/face delineations, having far more of a Japanese feel to the matches, the match-ups and the interactions between roster members. In other words, Takeshi Morishima is a monster Japanese invader in a promotion heavily geared towards the Japanese mentality and traditions and respect.

While his ROH history is growing, his achievements are notable in other groups. He has won the championship in 3CW, in Harley Race's WLW and Tag Team gold in NOAH.

Inevitably, Takeshi Morishima will return to the Land of the Rising Sun, and challenge the greats – maybe Mitsuhiro Misawa – for the GHC Championship.

But his time in ROH is now, and as the current World Champion of the most technically minded promotion in the United States, Morishima is being tasked to take on the giants of the independent wrestling universe, as well as the top two "mainstream" promotions.

All told, it's going to be fun to watch him succeed.

Joe Babinsack

RODERICK STRONG

No remorse, no repent
We don't care what it meant
Another day, another death
Another sorrow, another breath
Metallica, "No Remorse"

February 16th of this year saw a typically brilliant tag team match involving the renowned duo of Austin Aries and Roderick Strong against ROH Tag Team Champions Matt Sydal and Christopher Daniels. While much of the audience may have expected (or wanted) a title change, the champions laid another pinfall loss on the team that had been touted for much of the previous year as the world's greatest tag team. But the duo of Aries and Strong had been in a funk for months, having lost to the Briscoes in a brutal two out of three falls match, and once again, Sydal and Daniels -- the past and future of ROH -- were victorious.

A tease of sorts ensued. Matt Sydal acting the cocky winner, as Christopher Daniels attempted to bring him back down to reality. It was an ironic display, considering Daniels' eventual promo on the ROH fans.

But it was merely a tease for something else.

Generation Next had been dissolved months previously. Matt Sydal, once a prospective member of the group, had broken off before Aries declared Gen Next obsolete; Sydal challenging the team back then for the Tag Team gold with a few partners. They did not succeed, and the pairing of Strong and Aries endured.

It endured through a tumultuous stint in TNA, which tested the loyalties of both men, and saw Aries stay on as a roster member with TNA, while strong sought his fame and fortune in the indies. They remained the Tag Team Titlists in ROH even while Strong made a bigger name for himself in Pro Wrestling Guerilla, IWA and Full Impact Pro. Aries saw a name change to The Austin Starr.

With a shared tenacity, they complimented each other. Aries flashed high flying moves and high impact maneuvers, as Strong worked opponents methodically, chewing them up with chops, dozens of variations of the back-breaker, and ever working to a submission, or simply to soften up the opponent for Aries to finish them off with a 360 splash.

Pro Wrestling Intellectual

In an era where tag team competition had been reduced to nothingness, this duo embodied the greatness of the art form.

But this is not the history of that tag team. The bond remained, and the ROH Tag Team champs defeated all comers, from Dragon's Gate factions to ROH roster stars of the past, present and future, as well as the last vestige of the CZW war. But the ROH crowd, vociferous and appreciative, was more into their own former world champion, Austin Aries, than the eventual title holder of the FIP promtion.

They chanted "Austin Aries ... stomp stomp ... stomp stomp stomp" after each win. Sure, the comback chants for Roderick Strong grew as an afterthought, but he was always secondary. Even after the losses piled up, the fans chanted for Aries... then Strong.

Back to February 16th, and the chants rang out once more.

But before the crowd shifted into any sense of appreciation for good ole Roddy Strong, out comes Davey Richards, ROH newcomer, equally tenacious, and an oft met opponent of Strong's in FIP.

With a bit of distraction by Richards, Roderick Strong blindsided Aries with a sweet version of a backbreaker, and ended the association that was the best tag team in ROH history, and in many ways, also the world considering the past year and a half.

Unlike the nonsensical, "let's get a great pop" mentality of booking tag teams to turn on one another, this one had the drive, the motivation and the purpose behind it. Here's Roderick Strong sitting in the shadows no more. Here's Roderick Strong sick and tired of losing. Here's Roderick Strong showing his true loyalties. Here's Roderick Strong usurping the mantle from a faction that died months previous. Here's Roderick Strong finally taking a leadership role, much like Aries did when he took over Generation Next so long ago from Alex Shelley.

Richards laid a promo on Aries, and Strong declared himself the leader of the "No Remorse Corps" and established themselves as the lead heel faction of ROH, targeting Austin Aries and his associates, and potentially Jack Evans and his gang. The NRC has since added Rocky Romero to the group.

####

He is called the "Messiah of the Backbreaker" and with little argument. Sure, it's a bit of a daring moniker, but when was the last time a wrestler was so associated with, not a thousand holds, but seemingly hell bent on a creating a thousand variations on a particular maneuver? In an interview with Alan J. Wojcik in 2003, Strong counted seventeen version of the backbreaker in his arsenal. "There's the "F-Bomb" which is a blue thunder backbreaker. There's a flipping Canadian backbreaker, a belly to back backbreaker and a hip-toss backbreaker." he said.

There comes a point where it becomes pointless to count and describe them all.

Strong throws them out left and right once he gets the best of an opponent, beating them down and softening them up for the coup de grace -- the Stronghold. This is a version of the Boston Crab, where Strong firmly plants his knee in the back of the opponent, and raises the guy's body up a bit, creating excessive force on the small of the back.

Once again, a focus on the back, and his repertoire of holds includes variants starting from a crucifix, as well as power bombs and a powerbreaker (where he drops the guy not on the mat, but on his own knee.) Throw in the Falcon Arrow and some gut buster variants, and you've got the sense of Strong's methodical attacks.

Excepting for his vicious streak in dealing chops on his opponent's chest.

A match with Roderick Strong is a match were the opponent's chest is raw meat for the next night's festivities. You can see that in his classic battles with Bryan Danielson. With Strong, for the past few years, you might beat him, you might survive, but as the enforcer of the faction Generation Next, you paid the price and it showed for weeks after.

Roderick Strong has an appearance that reminds one of Davey Boy Smith, far before the unfortunate addition of muscle mass to shine on the big stage. His myspace page (http://www.myspace.com/3464450) touts Pure Dynamite as his favorite book, and we can only hope he's learned from that gem.

"People try to do too much instead of doing the right things," he told Corey David Lacroix of the Slam! Wrestling site. "It's not about how many things you can do, it's how many things you can do right and that's one thing that people tend to forget. You need to work on bettering yourself all around instead of just moves. Everybody wants to be the cool move guy. There's way more to wrestling than cool moves."

Thus Strong comes across, as a wrestling machine akin to Chris Benoit, without the high risk stuff, showing a sense of long term survival instincts that should do him well.

The story on Strong is that he grew up in Tampa, got a scholarship in football, and followed his father into training to be a pro wrestler. A few sessions and a meeting with Harry Smith helped him decide to make the leap into the industry. His trainers are listed as Jim Neidhart, with additional training by The Warlord, Prince Iaukea and Tim Mahoney, as well as his father.

He started with IPW, Independent Professional Wrestling, and shortly thereafter formed a tag team with "brother" Sederick Strong. That team capture Tag Team gold in 2002, and held the belts before losing them to Scoot Andrews and Mike Sullivan in a steel cage match. That began the slow turn on his brother, and one night, the Strong Brothers and Agent Steele came to the ring to save Mike and Todd Shane from a beat down by the Alliance of Defiance. Instead, Steele and Roderick turned on Sedrick and continued the beat down.

With a growing sense for the business, he moved on to bigger and better things.

Most of those moments came with Ring of Honor, and his face and wrestling can be found in numerous DVD titles. He has also began to forge a name with Pro Wrestling Guerrilla, and perhaps began his No Remorse Corps alliance with Davey Richards in that promotion, as they gained the PWG World Tag Team Championship on November 17 of 2006 by beating B-Boy and Super Dragon.

He has held numerous titles in numerous promotions: IPW Tag Titles and Cruiserweight title, the NWA Florida X Division title twice; the American Wrestling Federation Heavyweight Championship; the Florida Intertainment Wrestling Championship; and the Lethal Wrestling Federation Championship.

As well, there's his domination with Austin Aries as ROH Tag Team Champions.

Of the most notes, is his current streak as Full Impact Pro Champion, which again can be seen on numerous DVDs, on sale at fullimpactpro.com

He defeated Bryan Danielson for the FIP Championship on November 10 of last year -- putting his career at stake as a stipulation -- and has taken on a slew of challengers since, a mixture of independent level heavy hitters and rising stars.

Roderick Strong is a name to remember, and one to watch if you're into old school, Bruno Sammartino inspired wrestling. Strong is far from flashy and more methodical than even Chris Benoit, but has proven his ability to wrestle with the best of them, and if that's your favorite form of entertainment, go out and grab some DVDs from FIP, ROH or PWG and enjoy his work.

Pro Wrestling Intellectual

VINCENT NOTHING

Vincent Nothing is a mostly Ohio based pro wrestler, who's ring gear caught my attention. Well, his talent and ring presence and look were there as well. But by sporting a "Symbol of Chaos" tattoo on a shoulder and shorts festooned with half the eight-arrowed star on each leg, I became intrigued with the philosophy and outlook of the man.

That, plus the whole atmosphere and attitude of Awesome Intense Wrestling made me want to understand some of the leading players. As one of the first champions of that promotion, why not start there?

I decided to dust off the old questions, questions which I've tossed at a few notables, and have decided to get back into the bio and interview concepts that I dropped last year.

Considering the seeming explosion of new talent, and opportunities for that talent to shine on dozens of indy level promotions, I feel a duty to expose these overachieving but often overlooked wrestlers to a wider audience.

Vincent Nothing has held the Absolute Intense Wrestling Heavyweight Belt, and has traveled across Ohio, Michigan and Indiana. He has also teamed up with the awesome Christian Faith, in a tag team called Faith in Nothing -- an interesting power team that could give many an indy tag team a run for the money -- or the belts.

But Nothing is more than just a potential tag team superstar. A proponent of the "Strong Style" and with a take-no-prisoners attitude, Vincent Nothing is a presence in the indy world that should soon be making waves, and knocking down doors, and you should know the name.

Joe Babinsack

And so, without further ado, I present, Vincent Nothing

1. Are you comfortable using your real name, or only your ring name?
My ring name is Vincent Nothing – my real name is Vincent; there is no confusion.

2. Who trained you?
I was trained by Chris Cole at the MCW School in Ohio. Chris is an extremely knowledgeable and experienced wrestler who has had the opportunity to compete in some amazing places, including Japan.

I have also been fortunate enough to informally learn some in-ring, but mainly out of ring lessons (respect, etiquette, fine tuning, etc.) from JT Lightening – who, in my opinion, is one of the greatest veterans in my area.

3. Why did you get into the industry?
I've always been into physical competition. I'm a physical person and have always kept myself in shape through weight training and exercise – from there, it is a natural progression to become involved in sports.

I played football and amateur wresting in my teenage years and from there progressed further into what I focus on today: mixed martial arts (submission wrestling, kickboxing, etc.) and pro-wrestling.

4. How would you describe your style?
Suplexes, Strikes, and Submissions. I am into the technical aspect of grappling and submission holds, with a blend of Japan Strong Style striking and suplex maneuvers.

5. Where do you see yourself in ten years?
As far as wrestling goes, I'd like to establish myself at the "next level" by that time. We all have dreams of making it to a grander scale – what that scale is depends upon the person. Being fortunate enough to wrestle as a means of making a living is a goal. I'd also like the opportunity to tour Japan.

I don't see myself lingering in the business – I'd like to accomplish those goals in the next 5+ years or be out of the business completely.

6. What is your favorite match?
I can't point towards one particular match as my favorite, but I love working tag teams with my partner, Christian Faith. He is an amazingly agile wrestler for his size (or any size) and we have a great chemistry together.

Pro Wrestling Intellectual

7. Either or:
    a) Heel or Face? — **Heel**
    b) Hogan or Flair? — **Definite fan of both, but Hogan**
    c) Health or Wealth? — **Health, I don't know what I would do without it -- I've never had wealth, so it is easier to continue life without it.**
    d) Fame or Talent? — **Both very important in this business for separate reasons, but I think it is better to be underrated than overrated – Talent.**
    e) Family or Fortune? — **Family/Friends, again, having never tasted fortune it is easy to say that I can live without it.**
    f) Story or Highspot? — **Both – although admitting, I'd rather watch highspots.**

8. What is your hidden talent? **I can rip phone books in half.**

9. Your lasting impact on the industry will be what?
I'd like to be remembered for my ability as well as never getting tied up in politics. I am in this business to wrestle and put on the best show that I can for the fans. Egos are left outside of the ropes – all that matters when you are in the ring is giving the fans their money's worth.

10. Who are your wrestling heroes?
Old school wrestlers I really enjoy are Bruiser Brody and The Road Warriors. Today I would love a chance to wrestle Doug Williams or Masato Yoshino, they are two of my favorites.

11. Is there anything else you'd like to say to your fans (or to me)?
I'm constantly improving and am far from peaking at this point. Expect new things. Also, thanks to the ones who support me and thanks to you for this.

12. What's up with the Symbol of Chaos?
13. Is there a philosophy behind your name/symbolism?
I'll group these two questions together because they piggy back off of each other.

In a lot of cultures and religions especially there are creation stories – most talk about the earth or the heavens forming and coming forth from Nothing. Roman mythology specifically gave this Nothingness a name, Chaos. So Chaos is really the beginning of everything, it is where everything came from, but essentially it is Nothing – is that philosophical enough for you? Chaos is balance; it is absolute balance to the point of no one characteristic outweighing another – it is equal parts good/evil, love/hate, light/dark, etc.

Chaos is Nothing, and Nothing is Everything. That's where it all comes from.

14. What are your goals in the industry?
This goes a lot with question #5. I'd like to make an impression and get myself established on a bigger scale. Short term, I'd like to increase my bookings outside of the OH area and work some promotions on the West Coast and eventually overseas in Japan.

15. What's the deal with AIW?
AIW had a very unique element at its conception. Unfortunately a lot of internal problems ravaged the company and took it off its initial course until it split. The two products of the split both currently run good shows in Cleveland, OH and both have gone different directions. The group retaining the "AIW" name is distinguishing itself by using a lot of indy stars from across the country. Another local (Ohio) promotion doing a lot to set itself apart from the pack is Hybrid Wrestling. If you have not yet done so, you should definitely check them out.

Pro Wrestling Intellectual

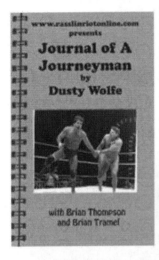

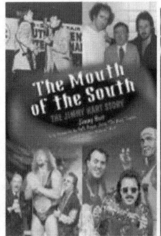

Book Reviews

Joe Babinsack

Bang Your Head: The Real Story of The Missing Link
Book Written by Dewey Robertson and Meredith Renwick

There are quite a few individuals who use the third person in describing themselves and their exploits. It often becomes annoying, arrogant and unbecoming. Sometimes it becomes endearing, but rarely is it appreciated.
After reading the efforts of Dewey Robertson to escape the demons he imbued in his strange alter-ego of The Missing Link, it is a very important and thankful thing that Mr. Robertson addresses his former persona in the third person.

At times, there seems to be a lack of clarity in the story, even despite the smoothness of the writing and the naturalness of the voice of Dewey Robertson. But once the reader understands the nature of The Missing Link – that here's a guy who readily states "I lived the gimmick 24 hours a day. I didn't speak to anyone for nearly eight years and sank into a fog of addiction" – one should recognize that, above living and breathing, the reality that Robertson can produce a coherent thought, let alone put forth a strong book about his life, demons and exploits, is something to approach with admiration and awe.

There are great similarities between this book and two others: Mick Foley's Have a Nice Day, and Bill Watts' The Cowboy and the Cross. While it lacks some of the details of Foley's book, Robertson has a far stronger, traditional pro wrestling base and enough insight and far-flung experiences to make the comparison. And while Bang Your Head lacks the preachiness (and religious slant) of Watts, it certainly tells the tale of a man who found a way to claw himself out of a real mess of a life.

At times the story seems to lack the details initially promised. The abusive relationship between Dewey and his wife seem lacking. Here's a guy who relied upon his wife (who sported the name Sheena as his public "handler" in many regions) to literally guide him around his profession and through his vices for many long years. "With her driving me everywhere I was free to drink as much alcohol and smoke as much pot as I wanted after a match." The nuts and bolts of it all seem to be glossed over, but then again, the deep and personal hurts inflicted upon his marriage is readily admitted to have destroyed it, and maybe Robertson is far more the gentleman to admit to even worse things, but not exploit his failings at the expense of his former wife.

Thus the real criticism comes into play in the rehashing of some of the WCCW years, and the whole Von Erich string of tragedies. But then again, in a story full of consequence, abuse and recovery, the juxtaposition between larger than life twenty-year olds who paid the ultimate price for fame, addiction and untenable lives and the continuing saga of the guy who was generations older and readily admits that "I was with a bunch of new guys who were 10 to 15 years younger and you'd think I would know better than to let them influence my behavior." That Robertson survived while far too many of that younger crowd was decimated seems to be a great example for another generation far removed, but frighteningly drawn to the perils of the pro wrestling world.

The Missing Link's tragedy is one of addiction: to alcohol, to marijuana, and the steroids.

Of the three, alcohol is traditionally the most destructive, but that was the least of Dewey Robertson's troubles. He shows that his abuse was a mask for a bipolar disorder, and that his addictions created in him an abusive personality, a long string of horrible decisions, and a vagabond lifestyle that deprived him of a lucrative career's earnings, as well as his family's happiness and his relationship with his wife.

The Link was basically "discovered" by a Sports Illustrated article on pro wrestling in the 1980's – he had toiled for years in various NWA stages, but had just created the gimmick which would bring him fame and fortune – but from that centerfold he was brought up to the big stage of the WWF's explosion on the national scene. It is hard to imagine the heights his career could have reached, since his issues affected him – making him asocial, hard to work with and hard to reason with – and drove him from the big stage in rapid order. His recollection and comparison to the careers of other McMahon shepherded superstars (from other promotions) suggest that his walking out of the WWF was a major mistake.

McMahon certainly has tested newly acquired talent – having them put over established names, testing their egos, repackaging them.

While the reality may have been that there was little comprehension of the Link's potential – by the WWF, its managers (Bobby Heenan, Jimmy Hart) and the creative forces, his impact and lasting impression, created mostly outside the WWF's formative years.

The Missing Link – the character that Dewey Robertson developed – was an archetypical wrestling staple, the beast-man who was abused by his evil manager and who was innocent underneath it all, and can produce a long term storyline, with a satisfying face turn and all the lucrative merchandising and lifelong appearance opportunities that would ensue.

As it happened, Robertson needed all of his brief fame to keep him able to move on to the next territory as he encountered the rapidly changing industry.

Joe Babinsack

With a high octane lifestyle, having picked up the drinking bug (rekindling genetic tendencies) in the Carolinas, partying through Kansas City, discovering weed along the way, and starting in 1978, taking full advantage of chemical enhancement, The Missing Link persona seemed to have hid the deteriorating social skills, not to mention the aging process.

I think some of the background of his travels became tedious, but then again, I'm rather well versed in World Class, Mid South and the like, so if you've read or seen those stories, it becomes another perspective on a well known subject. For those mainstream fans who don't know what happened, it does provide the rationale for the demise of pro wrestling and around Texas in the late 1980's

Green paint covers a lot of flaws, and the wild-eyed creature – who never spoke, who was guided by his wife through the backstage and the travel, and who relied upon a minimalistic wrestling display by evoking emotions with a primitive appearance, no-selling to display his strength, and gradually connecting with the younger fans.

Could the Link have gone far in the WWF -- as a bridge between George Steele and the wackiness of the early 1990's? It doesn't take much speculation to agree. While the disconnect between his portrayal and the WWF's understanding and use of him in that short span seemed a large gulf, there was nothing done to the Link to make him leave, he seemingly got upset over doing a job to Paul Orndorff (who at the time was a lot more untouchable than a newcomer to the promotion.) Robertson himself relays how at least one contact in the WWF begged him to come back.

One has to wonder if the structure and lifestyle of the WWF at that time might have threatened the very essence of the Link's core – the addiction and the partying – far more than anything else.

As Robertson explains earlier in the book, his dedication to working out helped to alleviate some part of his raging hormones, altered by the chemicals he freely imbibed, injected and inhaled into his middle age body. His mind was already masked from realities of being bipolar, the periods of depression and mania would haunt him worse once he got himself off of the stuff.

In the unconquered land of the WWF, he was removed from his co-dependency, put in situations where his reputation and appearance meant little to the establishment, and he would have had to rebuild a relationship to a new fan base. Add to that the work schedule which relied upon constant and excessive traveling -- instead of the many, many hours of driving in a car, which provided the privacy and layers of co-dependency that enabled him to live an out-of-control lifestyle.

Eventually, the Link hit the bottom, much like many of the regional promotions where he gained much of his fame and squandered much of his fortune. The dollars are added up in many ways, and the financial foundations of his lifestyle (while often not adding up, but hey, here's a drug addict living in his own world) come across as an interesting insight into the career choice of a pro wrestler.

The money was gone, and it prevented him from keeping up with the steroids, and ironically, that layer of rage and testosterone may have brought him down to more manageable mood swings. But alcohol and marijuana remained to taunt him. He eventually returned to his native Canada, got some real jobs, but lost them to his addictions.

He kicked the alcohol habit, but could not readily control the weed and could not remove himself from that temptation, despite his best intentions on helping troubled youths and important position in shaping and serving such institutions.

While the battles with cancer seem a bit rushed, they are also there to explore. Ravaged by some of the typical afflictions of the professional wrestling world: alcoholism, steroid abuse and painkillers (in the form of smoking dope) the Missing Link remains a strong symbol of the worst of this career choice. While there are books with more specifics, more exciting lifestyles and more emotional dramas, I can't help but place this book up among the top tier of wrestling books. And for anyone who dreams of such a life, here's your kick in the ass in terms of the worst case scenarios: broke, broken, fighting for your life, your family and your sanity. And waking up one day, finally getting your life together, looking back at the decades wasted and wondering where it all went.

Dewey Robertson, however, has seemingly kicked the Link back to the ring, and away from his real life. He has been known to play the part, but not live the life. And we can all hope he can keep it that way.

Joe Babinsack

Steve Williams: How Dr. Death Became Dr. Life
Book Written by Steve Williams with Tom Caiazzo
Sports Publishing LLC

There's much about the Steve Williams autobiography that has been done before, but in the end, it's not about novelty but presentation, and to that end, it's a very strong book.

Much like the Bill Watts to me, it's a story of a hard-nosed wrestler, with almost inherent family difficulties due to the industry, who went through hard times, found religion, and is back on track to being a productive and worthwhile human being.

Much like most pro wrestling veterans, there is an overfocus on "protecting" the sport, and a strangely warped reality in doing so. Much like many books on the subject before his, this Steve Williams book can no longer shock or titillate with the stories that went on behind the scenes.

Much like the many untold tales, and the already written ones, of the past decade, there are far too many names that are no longer with us, far too many who have died in the excesses of the industry, and far too many who were too young when it happened.

Steve Williams, like most others who have written their own stories, is a survivor of a business that continues to eat its young with its wealth and fame and dependencies and abuses.

Unlike most other books by professional wrestling veterans, Steve Williams fought a dual battle. His wasn't simply the story of overcoming an industry of death, but also the overcoming one of the prime movers of death in the world.

The one time "Dr. Death" Steve Williams fought and conquered cancer.

So it is that story that tends to dominate the several themes of the book. One thread is the wrestling industry and his own history in it. Another is his life story, coming from Colorado through the University of Oklahoma, playing football for Barry Switzer and wrestling (albeit part-time.)

A more heartening tale is his coming to terms with the Lord, and his overcoming the odds, to where he is now an agent of Life, not Death. The wages of sin, as the Bible says, is Death. Thus the renouncing of the old name and the claiming of the new.

But first, the old life is explored.

Pro Wrestling Intellectual

Williams was a stud athlete and destined to greatness. There were those, like his wrestling coach, Stan Abel, who felt he could have been an Olympic wrestling champion if he focused on the sport full-time. But still, he was highly recruited and championship material at the college level in football, and won two championships at the Big Eight conference in wrestling.

Professional football could have been his calling, but he was drafted by the USFL, to the New Jersey Generals team owned by Donald Trump, and a coaching staff better suited for the XFL. How else do you explain how they took a highly prized offensive lineman and slotted him as a nose tackle -- without sufficient hands-on training -- then dumped him from a guaranteed contract before the season ended?

Williams had already been in the partying scene in high school, and jumped in the wrestling world during his college years.

With the mentoring of Bill Watts, Steve Williams took the name "Dr. Death" from his amateur wrestling demeanor to the professional stage. Contemplating his future in football, he was already turned off by the decision making in that industry. He would once again run into the idiocy of corporate politics in the world of WCW, but his stay in Mid-South was one of better experiences, learning the ropes from the veterans and being involved with one of the better run promotions of the wrestling world.

It also provides fascinating and interesting tales, and a wealth of quotes from the industry's most storied names. From Jim Ross to the Rock-n-Roll Express, from Bill Watts to Buddy Landell, the road trips, the bar fights and the wrestling world comes alive in the words of Steve Williams.

About the only complaint I have with the book is the use of the term "shoot" and its derivatives. Not that I'm going to argue with Dr. Death, but in the year 2007, the exposure of the nature of pro wrestling just doesn't need that layer of veneer. But Steve Williams is as "Old School" as one can get, being well versed in the culture of Japan, and well aware of the history, honor and customs of the sport in that nation.

Williams, despite the several influential individuals in his pro wrestling career, admires Watts, yearns for McMahon's graces, but never strays from the world of pro wrestling created by the late, great Giant Baba.

The really interesting and juicy part of the book is the free association chapter at the end, where names are named, and thoughts are presented. If you want to know how Old School can sound like, take note of the thought processes of Steve Williams as it comes to who and why he can still slight certain individuals. Most of whom are well deserving and logical from his story.

Strangely enough, the career of Steve "Dr. Death" Williams was well established and heading for greatness in this country, until Bill Watts, and the UWF, and its most deserving champion slid into obscurity with the merger into WCW.

Williams avoids the details on the background of the UWF, which is somewhat odd, but once again, Williams is distinctly the type that isn't going to say bad things about people he respects. That doesn't account for a great book, but for an honest one. And the details of his life, which is the essence of the book, more than make up for that.

But within WCW, Williams ran into the kind of politics he had not encountered, and the sort of decision making that he already had. The clique that was the upper echelon of WCW in the late 1980's was something that Williams neither cared for, nor about. He speaks of his opportunities to "play nice" and be social, but he never cared.

Which meant that threats and contract negotiations became hostile, as well as his portrayal on TV eventually being downgraded. Obviously the interaction between kingpin Dusty Rhodes and Williams was a problem, and the potential of unification between UWF powerhouse Williams and WCW legendary headliner Flair was destined to fizzle out.

Steve "Dr. Death" Williams didn't exactly play nice when he wasn't wanted.

The connection between Japan and Williams began a few years earlier, as Williams and Antonio Inoki met at a WCCW big event, with the quite obvious result. But respect was created, and Williams did tours for New Japan for a few years, and went full time after the fiasco with WCW.

While the insight on the Japanese wrestling scene could have been more in depth, the book does provide a look at the differences, and through the great quotes from friends and acquaintances, and the ever present stories, there is a picture painted of the professionalism, the differences in cultural acceptance, and the magnitude of dealing with a career that suddenly is thousands of miles away from home.

That Williams excelled, and not merely survived in Japan, is a testament to his spirit.

The one fascinating "omission" is the transition from New Japan to All Japan. Once again, "old school" rules take precedence. Whatever happened with Inoki never gets a full explanation, and that Williams takes on Baba as a father figure and a most trusted and respected industry leader cannot be seen without its significance, knowing of the intense rivalry between Inoki and Baba.

The value of Steve Williams to Baba's promotion is vast, considering the efforts and lengths taken to smooth over some of the demons that plagued him, and the inevitable legal entanglements. Even with being barred from the country for a year, Williams was brought back into the fold.

As I mentioned earlier, the terminology most readers of this site would comprehend and use seem to blend a bit into Japanese industry mode from the pen of Steve Williams, but one can also respect the efforts he takes to protect the business. Also, with his status and celebrity in Japan, it doesn't take long to realize that a translation would ensue, and that culture undoubtedly is a bit less forgiving of exposing the business as the fans are in this country.

Even so, Williams maintains that "old school" mentality. He makes some strong statements about his work with the WWE and WCW in the late 1990's, and some of the nonsense with which he got sidetracked into. About the only painful aspect of the book is that it does come across as an appeal for work in the industry, especially as a trainer for future stars. As big as Dr. Death was, as schooled as he became, it's equally a shame that he's not in such a role as it is that he's asking to be considered for it.

There are many, many personal stories, insights and touching moments, many of which I could not justify to explain in a brief review.

The life journey of Steve Williams is a battle, and being a veteran of the professional wrestling industry for more than two decades, reaching the pinnacle of success on two continents, and claiming a legacy of being one of the toughest guys in the business, it really comes as no surprise about the outcome.

A transformation from "Dr. Death" to "Dr. Life" (of sorts) comes about in a voice that is consistent, tough and believable, much like the no-nonsense wrestler that Steve Williams always has been, and continues to be.

But like a great wrestler displaying his talent, Steve Williams makes the story all the more interesting, and all the more satisfying in taking part in it.

Joe Babinsack

King of the Ring: The Harley Race Story
Book Written by Harley Race with Gerry Tritz
Sports Publishing LLC

There seems to be two predominant personality types in pro wrestling. Those who create a flamboyant persona, living large and projecting themselves like superstars, whose exploits can always be taken with a grain of salt, and whose gift with the microphone usually exceed their wrestling prowess.

The other is the kind of guy that seldom goes over-the-top: the kind of guy that exudes toughness without talking about it; the kind of guy who can scare with a glare, a sentence or merely through mentioning of his name. That's the kind of guy who creates a legend, not who lives the legend.

That's Harley Race.

Fans nowadays don't always see those sorts of personalities. Homogenized and scripted, we see names without character, different faces with the same body type, wrestlers with little history or drama or quirks to support a reputation.

With Harley Race, all those modern conventions were turned upside down.

Here's a guy that exuded character – toughness, capability and the aura of a champion – without effort. Here's a guy that everyone knew could stand toe to toe with a Giant (and slam him!) Here's a guy who never looked like a physical powerhouse, but like the feared submission masters of old, he could withstand the worst and deliver in equal portions.

Harley Race is a guy who became his reputation, and who filled out the whispers of his legend as it preceded him, as he traveled the worlds of professional wrestling, interacting with the other legends, whether it be the Funks, the Harts, Johnny Valentine or Ray Stevens, the AWA or Japan, Shohei Baba or Vince Jr. But Race never had to trumpet his success. He wore that NWA Heavyweight Championship Eight times, and eight times he lifted the legacy of that belt to new heights.

Bret Hart gives two words in association with Race: Tough. Respect.

From the inception of his wrestling career, toughness was his way of paying dues. He started off by working on the Zbyszko farm, doing chores and learning how to escape submission holds, as applied by the legendary Stanislaus Zbyszko and the younger

Pro Wrestling Intellectual

brother Wladek. When he was at the level to be tested, he impressed Gus Karras and his boys, and was drawn into the carnival wrestling circuit in the Missouri area.

But it wasn't always in the ring where his torments assaulted him. Automobile accidents seem to have tortured the man's life, and one destroyed his early family. Out of action for a year, he never gave up on his career. And he was gifted by the great Eddie Farhat – The Shiek – with payments while he was out of commission. Farhat would never accept repayment of that loan.

It was in the AWA where he began to make his career, his legend as we know it. With Larry "the Axe" Hennig and learning from the greats, he was able to hold his own. Tag team championships came his way, and despite some setbacks with injuries, he took it to another level.

Always enamored with guns, Race gave his legend an even more dangerous twist.

Pranks were always the backstage fun of the industry, but few were ever spoiled as the one perpetrated by Johnny Valentine and Jay "the Alaskan" York. I think the details are better left for the reader, but Race proved that gunplay was not something he played around with.

And so, when he went to confront the WWF when it encroached on his territory – Kansas City – in its expansion mode, no one expected him to be without backup, and even Hogan knew of that reputation, and the tension backstage must have been overwhelming. But consider it, and consider the balls on both sides of that fence: Harley Race walking out in the arena, showing his unmistakable face to an audience that would wonder why he was there. The WWF crew, backstage, knowing how badly they were damaging the champion's business, knowing how little difference there was between legend and man.

Race claims to have lost $500,000 in the Heart of America promotion formed to stem the growing tide that was the WWF. Even so, he turned down one of the biggest offers to jump in the industry, simply because he was the NWA Champion, and he would have to live with such a decision.

In the 1970's to the mid 1980's, Harley Race was the epitome of a champion.

In many ways, the flamboyant wrestler's were made by the legendary ones. Not that, say, Dusty Rhodes needed Harley Race, but take away the victory, the belt winning victory against the undisputable NWA Champion in 1979, and what does Dusty have to talk about for the next decade? Ric Flair still had the skills and the look and the promise, but take away his feud with Harley Race in the early 1980's, and one must question how enduring, how reputable, how tough the fans would have considered the "Nature Boy."

And so it was with his career in its waning years, with his profits sucked away by a desperate ploy to throw up a firewall against the WWF, and with a huge event being staged to prove the NWA's viability, that Vince McMahon Jr made Mr. Race an offer he couldn't refuse.... And is it any wonder that he refused it?

Race claims a scuffle broke out after the refusal. I for one would not dispute Harley Race's account in his own book. Vince at the time was buying everything, even on credit, but he was plowing over the old school, and getting Harley Race, at that moment, at that point in the war, would have destroyed the NWA. Not just because of the timing and the disruption of Starrcade, and the denial of transition from Race to Flair, but because of whom Harley was, and what he meant to the industry.

Like I said, the flamboyant types always need the legendary types to put them over in the end, and how much more flamboyant was Hulk Hogan at the time? How much higher up the food chain would Hogan have gone if he was the one to soundly beat the legend of Harley Race instead of Ric Flair? Fans argued Flair over Hogan in terms of wrestling ability for a decade because of that reality. Not that it would have meant much in the long run, because Hogan and McMahon had the momentum and the outlets and the mainstream appeal, but it isn't difficult to read between the lines and listen to the words, and especially since Harley inevitably did go to the other side, it is logical to understand the inherent need for Hogan to beat Race.

But it didn't happen on Vincent K. McMahon's terms. It happened on Race's terms.

When the time came when the NWA could no longer support him, financially, and could no longer tolerate him, because the torch had to be passed, Race then brokered his deal with the WWF. Hence the King of the Ring and one of the weirdest characters for the WWF, even at the time of cartoonish figures and often outlandish, over-the-top portrayals.

That Harley Race jumped to the WWF was rather inevitable, that he got so much respect, and was given so much leeway shows how much his reputation meant.

According to Race, they wanted him to be an effeminate, royal character. More Gorgeous George than perennial champion. But Race wasn't going that way, and who would make him? Hogan, who saw his gun? McMahon, who scuffled after the initial refusal? Anyone on the roster, who all knew his reputation up close and personal?

Pro Wrestling Intellectual

Race's career faded away, but he was still prominent in the industry. Injury and accidents dogged him, and he moved to WCW as a managerial figure, to toughen up Lex Luger and to give some restraint and championship aura to Vader.

Later, he would do work as a process server, once again using reputation and toughness to stand up to criminals, as he once did in his early career. Between 1996 and 1999, he served some 500 warrants.

But Race's family life became much more kind to him, as he met BJ and eventually married. They have been known for their community service, and the best barbeque parties in Kansas City for the wrestlers who know and respect him. Of which there are many.

In participating with the World League Wrestling promotion, Race leant his name and legacy and has given many students an in to Japan, and a look from the WWE. "Shut up and Wrestle!" is the promotion's catch phrase that needs to be taken seriously by many.

In Japan, he was one of the living legends, having gone from "Handsome" to "Mr. Pro Wrestling" after winning his seventh NWA Championship. He remains respected in NOAH and with the fans who want wrestling, and wrestlers, to be tough and respected.

In the world of pro wrestling books, there are few that really stand out. In some instances, it is because of the riveting portrayal, in others, because of the behind-the-scenes details, and some, the brutality and the reality. King of the Ring has all of that, but more so, it has the aura of authenticity of one of the industry's most legendary figures. Because Harley Race is humble and has no need to brag, and the book captures his championship aura, it is simply a must read if you want a real insight into this crazy industry.

Joe Babinsack can be reached at chaosonejoe@yahoo.com. I look forward to suggestions and commentary.

 As an aside, if you can imagine Steve "Mongo" McMichael and his dog Chico, you can imagine me (a lot softer) and my little white chihuahua, Dee Dee. She passed away this weekend and my wife and I are devastated. If you have a dog, give him or her a hug….

Joe Babinsack

Wrestling at the Chase
Book Written by Larry Matysik
ECW Press

"Chandeliers, tuxedos, evening gowns -- and wrestling!"

When reading "Wrestling at the Chase" by ECW Press ($18.95,) I was impressed upon the drastic difference between the current scene and the seeming utopia that was St. Louis wrestling in the Sixties and Seventies.

During that era, the world of professional wrestling was fragmented, with several large regions, and an assortment of smaller organizations: many cooperating, many engaged in constant political and territorial conflicts, but all coexisting. They shared talent and an overall sense of what professional wrestling was, but the freedom existed for wrestlers to travel the country and the globe, learning new styles, experiencing differences in cultures, local rules and local expectations.

All this created a fan friendly atmosphere, because promoters had to cater to the interests of the local fans, not Television executives. Talent exchanges were ongoing, and fresh faces, styles and tactics appeared on a regular basis.

Now the WWE dominates the landscape, and all decisions are funneled to a billionaire so far removed from reality that constantly overrules the applause of his own fans, buries talented wrestlers who do not conform to his mysterious standards, and then pushes the same, overmuscled and underperforming types in a style that became bland before the current millennium.

In St. Louis, at the Chase hotel complex, things were different. The promoter was Sam Muchnick, a one time sports reporter, who forged a legacy as NWA President, a golden era that lasted from the Fifties to the Eighties, until the machinations of Vince McMahon, owner of the now dominant WWE, basically stole the city away.

Muchnick featured the best wrestling in the country, and used foreign talent, a mixture of traveling stars from various large promotions, and a style that focused on realism. As NWA Champion Lou Thesz is quoted in the book, "many promoters had come from the carnival era and never got out from under the tent… [Sam] brought credibility to the business." A legendary sports writer in St. Louis, Muchnick brought respect and honesty to the business

Pro Wrestling Intellectual

The organization of Muchnick is detailed: he wrote on note cards every event promoted: match results, attendance figures and the gate. Muchnick's sports background and honesty created a foundation for a successful promotion, and the admiration of his city (in an industry called "crazy, bizarre and dirty.") As Joe Garagiola, the initial TV announcer and former Pittsburgh Pirate said, "we had lawyers and politicians and doctors at ringside. I saw the mayor ... there one night... it was the place to be, it became a social event."

Larry Matysik, who wrote the book, lived a wrestling fan's dream, writing about the sport as a sixteen-year old, connecting to Muchnick in an exchange of letters, and basically interning until earning his college degree. Although warned often by Sam about "a nasty, horrible business, filled with double crosses," Larry Matysik stuck with the promotion, learning through "osmosis" about booking matches, dealing with talent and successfully running the operations

St Louis was the place to work: it provided payoffs higher than anywhere else, and featured only the best. It was promoted without foolish gimmicks, illogical angles or to keep its regulars happy. In fact, it had only a small roster of local talent, often imported from nearby Kansas City, and instead relied upon the top names from across the country to fill up monthly cards, usually at the Kiel Auditorium.

St. Louis' reputation was worldwide, as the NWA was often sustained by political actions directed by Sam Muchnick. After a period of potential discord in the early 1970's, St Louis gave Bruno Sammartino a winning streak, setting him up for main events and against the NWA World Heavyweight Champion, just to show that Muchnick retained other options than the NWA title holder.

It was Sam Muchnick's connections, political savvy and reputation that kept the NWA together; his vision of professional wrestling allowed the talent to shine. Muchnick only brought in the best. He let them perform their art, and work the crowd, with very few restrictions. Unlike other promoters, he never consistently paired factions of 'good guys' and 'bad guys' -- most of the well received matches were between faces, or between heels!

Working St. Louis, Sam Muchnick is quoted, "was tough, but we never lost money here."

Catering to the fans, and making money doing so? Someone get Vince McMahon on the phone!

Joe Babinsack

Journal of a Journeyman

Book Written by Dusty Wolfe with Brian Thompson and Brian Tramel

RasslinRiotOnline

"Guys like the Fargo's, Red Bastien, Terry Funk, Dick Murdoch, Johnny Valentine, and Roddy Piper wouldn't stand a snow balls chance in hell today. Simply due to the fact that they wouldn't be allowed to be themselves." Dusty Wolfe.

Dusty is a Texan, a world-traveler and a one-time Hollywood Blonde. He is, as the tile screams, a journeyman wrestler, with little presumption and no disdain for the moniker. He has been a booker, an organizer of world tours (Singapore, India, South Africa and other wild locales.)

Dusty comes to grips with the lifestyle of a true professional. Not just the pampered life of a superstar, who can now spill the beans for another big payday, but a man who made a living and worked, partied and paid for it while it happened.

His tale is an honest book.

One that reveals his regrets (missing most of the lives of his three children, and several failed marriages;) his 'success' in terms of actually living out a career as a professional wrestler, and learning an awful lot about the industry; as well as his accomplishments – overcoming a painful and debilitating disease, bouncing around the indy promotions and getting some good paydays from the WWF, from the WCW and from fans and promoters across the world.

Journeyman, in terms of Dusty's life, is a great phrase to call someone who has seen it all, knows a lot more than he's credited with, and has the track record of being a true veteran of the sport.

Considering the miles he's flown, traveled and experienced, Dusty Wolfe truly is a journeyman, who has taken each tour, each stint, each date worked as a step in his rugged life.

What is it about the life of Dusty Wolfe that deserves further scrutiny?

Well, telling that story is Dusty himself, in the book, and I just can't do that justice by rephrasing it. What I love about the book is the constant stream of stories, insights and gritty reality of road life.

Pro Wrestling Intellectual

What I love is how open and honest Dusty is about how his career destroyed his family life – especially his marriages – all the while he was able to lean on his mother ("Big Mama") to help rear his boys. The only sidestep is his daughter, Dana, who was with her mother more often than not.

While there are some flaws, much are understandable. This is a 200 page book packed with details and information. There's always a perception that it should be deeper, longer and more informative, but especially in terms of someone steeped in kayfabe, there's a reality that getting so much is well worth getting.

The places where I wished I saw more (and let me say that this isn't a Larry Z situation where too much was self-edited out) was when Dusty talked about Bruiser Brody, Dick Murdoch and Andre the Giant.

Then again, we didn't hear the obligatory Andre drunk two cases of beer story, only the "Andre did like me, and I was lucky" slant.

A deeper look at the Brody situation would have been much appreciated, though. Wolfe obviously knew the man, and had his friendship. But then again, and the same thing is true with Murdoch – this isn't the story of anyone but Dusty Wolfe, and I'd likely complain if he did talk too much about other guys. What is especially impressive is the strength of Dusty's connections in the business. He worked for Blanchard, for Jarrett, for Graham, for Jovica/Colon and for Vince. He worked for WCW, for various outlaw promotions and for shady promoters across the world.

And he sloughs off the notion that he booked and ran several tours for several guys, all the while dropping names like Tony Atlas, Bundy, Brody, Murdoch and assorted other journeyman, to fill out his cards and his several week tours of exotic locations.

Some locations are certainly scary enough. Whether tales of machine guns in Malaysia, troops in India or police pull-overs in Mexico, this is a man who faced far more than just his opponents, or con-artists or a wife gunning for a divorce!

But getting back to the contacts, it was amazing to read how some off-beat promoter in Texas was looking for the Ultimate Warrior for booking purposes in early to mid 1990's, and sure enough, Dusty makes a few calls and puts them together.

Then, as shady promoters are want to do, the deal fell apart, and Dusty provides insight into the reality of the urban myths of two (or is it more?) Ultimate Warriors.

Joe Babinsack

Pain is the purview of a professional wrestler, especially one who transitioned from the regional realities of the early 1980's up until the truly modern, WWE dominated era today.

Wolfe was there for the deaths of several close associates, including Brody, including Murdoch. He was impacted by Eddie Guerrero's untimely death – helping people contact Chavo Classic. (He ironically was also not so fond of Chavo for other reasons, early on in his career.)

Maybe you haven't heard of Dusty Wolfe, but you certainly saw him, or his influences, if you have followed the sport over the past twenty five years: He was there to help the American Starship break in. (That's Scott Hall and Dan Spivey if you need to know the trivia.) He was there to help babysit Zeus. (That's the movie made rival of Hulk Hogan after the No Holds Barred fiasco.) He was there as a Hollywood Blonde, learning from Jerry Jarrett and also from Eddie Graham.

And, like I said earlier, he gained the confidence of Bruiser Brody and Dick Murdoch, and from their reputations, that isn't an easy feat to accomplish.

But after reading the book, I can readily understand the appreciation. Dusty Wolfe is honest, a good story-teller and was crazy enough to hang with the party types, and solid enough to be trusted by the best of the business.

Now, going back to complaints, I wish Dusty et al would have spelled out Ken Johnson and Ken Timbs more than just naming Ken T. and Ken J., but the associations he had with his trainer, and long time tag team partner were moving and important.

The absolute important aspect of this book is that it is the story of a professional wrestler who has seen it all, and who has no particular axe to grind. This isn't the story of professional wrestling over the past 25 years, it's the story of the career of one of its unsung heroes.

And because of that, I'd highly recommend this book. It's another perspective of the business, and one that you must read if you really want to appreciate this business.

Dusty: Reflections of an American Dream
Book Written by Dusty Rhodes, with Howard Brody
Sports Publishing LLC

Dusty Rhodes remains an endearing figure in the sport of professional wrestling.

If not, there would be no way he could get away with selling all the B.S. he spews forth.

According to Big Dusty:

- He broke up the Texas Outlaws. Dick Murdoch was such a disgusting slob, and he just knew he'd be better off as a single. When he gave notice to get away, Murdoch all but begged to go with him.

- Vince Sr. begged him to stop VKM from going national. This was during a phone call while the elder McMahon was on his death bed.

- The role that Hulk Hogan held in the WWF expansion was originally supposed to be for Dusty Rhodes himself, but he blew off a movie deal with VKM and their relationship soured.

- The whole problem with Crockett's promotion in the 1980's was … Crockett. If he hadn't wanted to move the offices to Dallas, it might have all been fine.

- The Baby Doll envelope was a shoot. Oh, it was a work, but there really were photographs in there, and it was a rib on Dusty. But the only way anyone's going to know what's in there is if Nickla Roberts tells it.

- Dusty going to the WWF ended up being a series of ribs on WCW, and it was meant to make him a mediocre character, but that all backfired and it was the most financially rewarding period in Dusty's career (and he didn't have the stress of being the boss.)

- "there's only one and original "Dusty Finish" and you're just going to have to read the whole book to find out exactly what that is."

- Dusty can book a fabulous dream card, and book the bookers and promoters as well.

- "yellow finger" is the best nickname for Hulk Hogan ever.

- As much as you can imagine Dusty using all this profanity, it's really frightening how it flows naturally to his writing. Sometimes I'd sooner see phonetics, since Dusty's enunciations were part of the package (If you weeeeel!) but wow, there's no mistaking the "voice" of the American Dream.

One of the best parts about the book is the wealth of quotes and the insight provided by them. There were a few chapters early on where I'd sooner see some of the story go off on a tangent from the quotes, instead of just ignoring them, but in the end, its Dusty's book (co-authored excellently by Howard Brody.)

I just wish he'd come clean about some of the nonsense. The whole Dusty Finish stuff really needed to be explored, instead of using a chapter to skirt around the issue and pretend it's all a concoction of internet writers and unabashed critics. While its certainly true that Virgil Runnels didn't invent the concept of swerving the fans into thinking they've seen a title change, then pissing them off by basically screaming "fooled you!" when they watch TV the next week, no one ran it into the ground like Dusty did.

And while that probably wasn't the root cause, and certainly not the only cause, for tearing down Crockett's promotion, it has and always will be a strong example of what not to do to the fans.

The crazy thing about the book, again, is that Dusty can be so charming even while half the stuff he says can't possibly be accurate. The whole "Vince Sr. was a saint, Vince Jr. was the devil" storyline seems great to the oldtimers, but really, if you look back at the time frame, there was an overlap between VKM's expansion plans and Vince Sr.'s being alive. As much as Vince Sr. had respect and respected the "arrangement" I still can't see how VKM would go against his father's wishes about dominating the industry, while taking care of so many of his father's loyalists. There's a strange disconnect there somewhere.

Even stranger is how Dusty all but proves that VKM was running many of the shots before he officially took over: with this big movie deal (Dusty balked at merely getting a "Garden payoff" for his role, co-starring with Superstar Billy Graham), and with the setup of the Hulk Hogan role, and the way the second generation Vince slipped so naturally into the kingpin role.

But Dusty is the ever popular self-promoter. Just like his booking, he's the center of attention, with or without the belt. He's also always getting the shaft, and all the nasty stuff that gets dumped on him ends up backfiring.

But he's still so damn entertaining.

He's the common man, the man of the people, one of the first guys to seriously appeal to minorities on the national stage. Before the era of Hulk Hogan, or as he calls him, "yellow finger" because of all the merchandising millions made (and I can't for a second not see the green eyes of envy in that name calling,) Dusty was the guy who made the most of the least. Unlike Hogan, Dusty relied on his gift of gab first, and a unique appearance second, to fully utilize a simple set of moves and often a rather pat sequence of finishing moves to charm large audiences everywhere. While Hogan played the role of cartoon superhero who was entertaining to watch and vicariously live through, Dusty embodied a sense of 'if he can do it, I can to' which was captured perfectly by the "American Dream" concept and also, arguably, by the VKM "Common Man" persona, which as Dusty said, really was him in just another package, and really wouldn't have worked with anyone else's charisma but his own.

And despite the over-the-top presentation, most of that ends up being true. At least it has truth at the core of it. Even when he's getting emotional and personal, like with the Dustin estrangement and reconciliation, Dusty proves true to his patter. He says so much, but

Pro Wrestling Intellectual

reveals so little, and at the same time he's motivating, captivating and compelling all at the same time.

I have two distinct Dusty remembrances. The first is that famous match with Superstar Billy Graham. HBO ran that often in the mid to late 1970's, and while I can't recall the promo's (which I can't imagine them not airing with those two guys) I'm always recalling that sequence of Irish Whips into the corner and the eventual double count-out. There were two guys who told a story in the ring, two guys giving and taking and making a spectacle out of a match where they didn't fly all over the ring or perform awesome or technical moves. They just got down to the basics and boy, was it ever riveting.

Which is why, when Dusty rails against the acrobats and the high flyers, I'm not exactly approving, but at the same time, I understand what he's talking about. Dusty is nothing without the psychology of telling a match, and that he can't comprehend the high spot fests of too much of the modern product, isn't something I'd hold against him.

The other vivid memory of Dusty is the Road Warriors turn. A friend of mine in college wrote down the speech he gave afterwards, and I need to dredge that up from my notebooks, because once again, Dusty turned on the charm, and with his cadence, his speech patterns and his emotional ties to the audience, he spilled his guts and made you want to see that match.

Unlike so many of today's talents. I mean, who could say something like "If Sting has to drag me to the ring in a wagon, I'm going to …." And not only do you get it, not only do you believe, but you simply want to see it happen.

So when Dusty speaks of putting 20,000 or 21,000 asses in the seats, I believe him. If I stop and think about it, I can pick apart the logic and the facts and the emotional draw, but the next time he opens his mouth (or writes words on the paper) I can't help but being drawn into the story, no matter how much b.s. he spews, how many facts he butchers or how utterly preposterous it is -- because of the way it sounds and the way he speaks.

I mean, really, if you're going to watch two guys fight, do you root for the fat polka-dot clad guy who grabs his crotch and spins his fingers and bleeds a lot, or do you root for the overmuscled clod who puts his hands to his ear, and points his fingers and sweats a lot?

One guy gets the yellow finger, and one guy gives it.

Dusty Rhodes proves in his book that his legend is unshakable and his charm transcends generations. While some of the statements and facts are arguable, the quotes about him are reflective of his appeal and the fan testimonials are endearing. It is impossible to comprehend how Virgil Runnels has created such a character as Dusty Rhodes, has lived the life and has created such a legend, but here he is, decades later, in his own (unmistakable) words and he's still got it, he never lost it, and he never will.

Joe Babinsack

The Mouth of the South: The Jimmy Hart Story
ECW Press
Book Written by Jimmy Hart

To say that Jimmy Hart was at the center of pro wrestling for the past forty years is … hard to argue.

In Memphis, he participated in the stock angles and was heavily involved in one of pro wrestling's most famous celebrity involvement. He then jumped to the WWF at its point of national domination, and migrated to an affiliation with the great Hulk Hogan, whom he followed into WCW, and has been linked to the icon ever since, popping up as a sort of herald, promoter and details manager from time to time, whether it be XWF, TNA or even back with the WWE.

Hart's book is so different from others. He has proven to be a rather selfless individual, always shilling, but always for the promotion, the talent or a purpose beyond him. Hart is also probably the most apolitical politician in the business. There is little doubt where his allegiances lie, but he rarely speaks ill, participating in promotional wars by simply making his side stronger.

Stranger still, Jimmy Hart has got to be the most successful promoter, in the strictest form of the word, of all time, not in terms of profit, but simply by marketing and advertising locally.

If there's one thing to take away from the book, it's the attention to detail and the incessant need of wrestling promotions to work the local towns and cities, to work radio and other forms of communications, and to constantly work to advertise the next show.

Of course, his experience in the music business, with the Gentrys, and one hit wonder success with "Keep on Dancing" and subsequent attempts to keep the band and name alive on the national, then local scenes, well qualified him to take his fundamental knowledge of earning a living and translate it into the pro wrestling industry.

Hart's stories are interesting, even if already known, and his takes are a bit too careful for colorful retelling. Nonetheless, the perspective and the insights are there. Just not always glaring.

I would have loved to read more about Andy Kaufman's fascinating comedic mind, but Hart does a tremendous job of detailing that period, with the great angles, and the involvement of the inquisitive Kaufman. "Jimmy, why is it done that way?" is how Hart recalls Kaufman's curiosity. Perhaps the only regret is that Jimmy doesn't always reveal the whys and wherefores. But when he does – by using the interactions of that strange mix of Kaufman's comedy and curiosity and Lawler's wrestling fundamentals, often smoothed over by Hart himself, one gets a glimpse of the big picture of pro wrestling like few have every described.

Hart's music talents cannot be overlooked. From writing and producing songs for the WWF, for the Thunder in Paradise show, to WCW, and undoubtedly others, Jimmy Hart's contributions to how we have watched and listened to pro wrestling over the past few decades cannot be adequately measured. He also needs to be lauded for Curt Hennig's "I Hate Rap" song!

That one interesting slam that Jimmy Hart takes is in defense of his long time employer. Hart speaks of Jerry Lawler's assessment of Hulk Hogan's career outlook at his Memphis debut.

The build up to Lawler's revelation that the pre-Hulk Hogan version of Terry Boulder wanted him to manage his career, Hart's insight and follow up are best left to reading the book, but the money quote is this: "Are you crazy?" Lawler said, "That guy will never draw you a dime in professional wrestling. He doesn't have what it takes."

Hart's shortly thereafter states "He denies the conversation ever took place. But I know the truth."

When the book is almost a studious avoidance of controversy and personal affronts, so one can only take this detail as utterly factual. Or utterly representative of Hart's personal loyalty having shifted from Lawler to Hogan decades ago. Regardless, what's the point of making such a statement up? Hogan's career needs no embellishment. Perhaps it is a receipt on Lawler breaking Hart's jaw thirty years ago, and Hart's unique approach to negativity – it's just about the only place in the book that the typical ebullient Hart goes off on anyone in any real manner.

Hart opens the book with a look at his itinerary before a big event. While the top brass is working over the details of the show, Hart has already attended to the promotional aspects, and to a degree which many seem to overlook. He's going to be in the ring with a radio personality, gaining lots of air time and a connection with (or against, for that matter) thousands of fans of that show.

Translating promotional efforts into attendance figures is something with which Hart is obviously well experienced, and much comfortable with despite his tenure with WCW.

Have there been any managers on the same level as a Jimmy Hart, around the ring? Sure. But the irony is that Hart approaches detailed work before and after the events, and is far more valuable on the microphone of a radio show than when using his megaphone on the periphery of the ring. His music talents were always there, and his ability transcended his on-screen persona.

What's strange to me is how different Hart is as a manager. Growing up on the triumvirate of Blassie, Albano and the Grand Wizard, Hart simply doesn't add up: His promos were buffoonish, he had no physical presence, nor did he ever exude any sort of danger. And yet, despite or because of his presence, his managerial role endured. Hart clearly shows his understanding of building to the big bump, his reverence for the sport's history, and a clear knowledge of fundamentals of promotion, marketing and connecting to fans.

History has proved the longevity of Hart, and his association with Memphis had to have contributed – where else would he have learned the fundamentals of producing an ongoing, popular and enduring version of pro wrestling. While the likes of WCCW exploded and imploded, while the AWA suffered from delusions of grandeur, while ECW captured the hearts of hardcore wrestling until it broke, and while WCW rose to soaring heights and plummeted into oblivion, Memphis stuck around, capture the last breaths of that Texas promotion and that Minneapolis one, and managed to be more extreme than Philly, more creative than the WWE and simply endured.

Hart, likewise, seems to have had an inner sense, managing to move on at the right time. He hung on to the name of the Gentrys longer than most of that band cared to be called a band, and then hooked up with Lawler and Jarrett. Once that run went too long, he leapt at the chance at the big time, and obviously maintained a long term business connection to Hulk Hogan. Despite not being on air for years, I'm sure he'd still pop a crowd with his immediately recognizable look.

Pro Wrestling Intellectual

The Death of WCW
Book Written by R.D. Reynolds and Bryan Alvarez

The WCW Nitro era was, by any perspective, a great story, and the team of Reynolds and Alverez do an excellent job of retelling it.

Reynolds is famous for his WrestleCrap.com site and his book, WrestleCrap: The Very Worst of Pro Wrestling. Of course, much of the downward spiral of WCW can only be described in that phrase -- "The Very Worst of Pro Wrestling."

Alverez continues to produce the Figure Four Weekly newsletter, and cohosts the Wrestling Observer Live radio show, and does much for this web site.

The combination has the background, insight and ability to analyze the realities of WCW and the avenues by which it self-destructed from heights of success and money making. If you've forgotten the legacy of WCW and the craziness that propelled it from WWE beater to doormat, this is a great way to understand its demise.

Or you can start watching TNA.

The running theme of WCW's demise is one that is well known to modern fans, and hasn't seemed to disappear despite the obvious and documented results. Simply put, and anyway you want to look at the history of professional wrestling, when the promotion fails to connect with the fans, and fails to please the ticket paying, PPV ordering and merchandise buying fan base, then that promotion is doomed.

With WCW, the backing of major TV and Cable networks (and the rich history and favoritism of Ted Turner on TBS/TNT) prolonged the life span of the promotion. With enough business acumen, the cyclical nature of pro wrestling would have been expected to kick in, allowing for a down period before picking up again.

But with WCW, that very promise of permanency seemed to be a curse more than a blessing. Far too many of the major players simply expected and assumed that wrestling would never die. Those sorts of assumptions were proven fatal for a major portion of the industry.

At its height, WCW employed some 260 people. At its height, the sale price of WCW was expected to be $500 million. Some time shortly before that, it was regularly beating the then WWF in a ratings war. WCW had under contract virtually every important name in the business in the 1990's (not named McMahon) and it featured on a weekly basis the biggest matches possible.

Of course, with all the records set on the way up, it only positioned itself to set new records on the way down. And this book clearly describes that fall.

Overkill seems to be the most basic term to use. That, plus the egos of four notable names: Eric Bischoff, Vince Russo, Hulk Hogan and Kevin Nash. The overwhelming evidence of the mismanagement, the under production of the booking schemes, the stubborn indifference of its top star, and the impossible to understand politicking of another influential star are interwoven in the tragedy that was WCW.

Underlying the facts and figures of WCW are some contradictions. The realitiy of WCW's winning the ratings battles wasn't quite meteoric, nor was it all that dominant. Nor was the WWF's reclamation of top status.

Nor is it completely fair to say that WCW stayed too pat on the top. WCW actually did allow Goldberg to rise to the top, and then cut his legs off. WCW actually created an atmosphere where the likes of Chris Jericho were able to attract impressive attention -- and then they cut his legs off. WCW actually kept trying to kill Ric Flair, but could never put the stake in his heart -- they just kept cutting his legs off. WCW did present a stage where Luchadores and Japanese talents and the "extreme" and groundbreaking concepts ECW got their first true national stage to shine on.

But then they cut their legs off as well.

ECW seems to get a short stick in the story, as overlooked in the rise and fall of WCW is the acquisitions of several "major" pieces of talent, including Benoit and Malenko and Eddie Guererro, including Raven and Public Enemy, including Rey Mysterio Jr and Juventud Guererra, including some lesser names and some really painful losses to the hardcore promotion's rabid fan base (Perry Saturn, Shane Douglas, Big Al (formerly 911) and others.)

The funny thing to me is that WCW's inability to capture the essence of ECW's promotion and talent, but simply steal some of its storylines, seems an apropos indication of why they couldn't reinvent themselves.

The WWF, on the other hand, got it. They stole the "attitude" and the hardcore wrestling, and incorporated it enough to build momentum and then created the atmosphere where Steve Austin caught the attention of the fans, and Vince McMahon joined the mix.

But that's another story.

While the facts and figures are sprayed across every page of this book, another weakness is the avoidance of charting, graphing or comparing numbers. Also, a timeline would have been a great addition. Just like the stories behind WCW were compelling, the numbers also told the story. Again, the numbers are there, but not readily digested.

Then too, the stories of the "big four" of WCW's demise are there, but not there.

The book is an analysis piece, and as that, it's great and a great read. I spent four days on it, and the story is so compelling and the writing so smooth that I can't say enough about the book, its content and its storytelling.

What the book isn't is an in-depth look at the behind the scenes happenings and anything more than a superficial analysis of the company and its product. Good or bad, fair or not, that's the reality of "The Death of WCW."

That being said, the chapters are great for what it is, but not for what could be told. There really needs to be chapters for Bischoff, Russo, Hogan and Nash. Few others had "real" power, influence or detrimental effect upon the promotion. Eric Bischoff deserves the credit for building WCW to stellar heights. Unfortunately, and the reality of this seems to fall through the cracks of the book, he created a foundation -- or lack thereof -- of disdain for management, talent and long term direction.

Sure, Bischoff brought in the invasion concept and did it right, and did it spectacularly.

But he lost control of his troops, and permitted Hogan and others to write their own rules and influence hiring and establish the precedence of saying no. Bischoff was the "ATM" because he was money, but he was obviously unable to manage his success, and if you cannot manage your success (and your people) at the peak of making money, there's no way you can regain control, instill discipline or hope for the best when it is on the downslide.

Vince Russo came in as a golden boy, but he also came in with a gloating disdain for the fundamentals of pro wrestling. In a company already reeling because of a disconnect with its fans, the hiring of Russo completely severed the ties.

WCW was built upon the southern tier of fundamental professional wrestling. It sought realism, wrestling skill and good fights. The upswing of WCW provided that. It was all about big name matches and match ups, it featured some really great feuds, and in the early build up of the nWo, there was a great and acceptable heel faction seemingly balanced by WCW home talent.

All was good, but before Russo, it was already downhill.

The nWo was, with little doubt, the greatest faction in pro wrestling. It was cooler than the Four Horsemen, and it was also vastly more powerful. But heels who are cool and powerful seem to rapidly play out their hand.

Sting became the counterbalance, and that was still reasonable, but once the nWo seized up every viable opponent -- much like the bully kids on the playground pick the best so they will always win and never lose -- once that happened WCW was no more.

Nothing more to back, nothing more to follow.

WCW killed itself and killed off its mainstream fan base. Once you've lost them, who do you have?

I continue to wonder if the ratings success of the cable wars was simply a trick of numbers, or more likely, the draw of real competition. But all competition demands a winner and a loser, and once the battle was becoming obvious and the momentum shifted, what worse decision could be made than to declare a loss.

Taking Vince Russo away from the WWF was that declaration.

Once again, the fundamental fan base of TBS and TNT wrestling was its southern roots. By bringing in one more Northerner to the fold, and giving him absolute power, what did that signal other than "we don't care about or fans."

And the story of Russo is long told and overly problematic.

Russo doesn't believe in a century of professional wrestling, of matchmaking and building up names, of building up big matches and of connecting with the fans.

No, Vince attempted to remake the industry, and simply used the staples of the sport and its history, those events, scenarios and situations that drew heat, without regard to the inherent need of emotional investment, let alone time and sequential aspects of the sports/entertainment form.

It's like watching basketball and seeing a last second three point shot tearing down the house, and expecting to recreate a last second three point shot every other segment on TV, and then acting incredulous when the fans don't care.

Pro Wrestling Intellectual

A three point shot is a three point shot, but when it gets set up properly -- when it is at the last minute, when it can win the game, and when the home field fans are hoping for the best possible outcome -- that's when it becomes magical!

Vince Russo has proven by booking, words and his own history that he has utterly no concept of the fundamentals of professional wrestling. Hogan proved that he had creative control, would use it, and would only serve himself in the end.

Nothing else can be interpreted from his actions. Whether or not Hogan actively played politics backstage or not is immaterial. Hogan only acted for Hogan's sake. He turned heel to earn enormous dollars. He resigned only to earn enormous dollars, and when time came - at any point, with any person, and to any extent, he chose to sit instead of build for the future.

He wanted to prove he was the draw, and he manipulated his appearances to that effect, until the reality played out that no one cared for him as a performer.

Kevin Nash was Hogan, without the icon status, and with twice the effort to manipulate.

At first, he was the good guy backstage, the funny one, the guy everyone liked.

By the time he presented himself as the incarnation of Dusty Rhodes, as a booker who was only concerned with himself (and friends, of course) he was well on his way to becoming locker room poison. And he spent the rest of his WCW tenure playing games to improve his stock instead of improving the viability of the company.

That must have been fun, but what good it did for anyone is beyond my understanding.

But to get back to the book and not the story, the book does a great job in distilling those facts, figures and intertwining storylines into a coherent presentation. There are some tangents and some points which are out of order (Jim Hellwig as Warrior directly impacts the health of Davey Boy Smith; Smith's story is injected long after that storyline is explained) and then they go into some things, including the resurrection of WCW, that don't seem all that important in the end. But this is another great book which stands alone as a testament to bad pro wrestling, as well as a great nostalgia piece for those too squeamish to follow the implosion as it happened.

It would serve as a nice gift to a few current owners of professional wrestling companies, and would be much more insightful than losing another few tens of millions of dollars.

Joe Babinsack

Between the Ropes: Wrestling's Greatest Triumphs and Failures
Book Written by Brian Fritz and Christopher Murray
ECW Press

One tangential realization from reading this book is that so much of pro wrestling's history has been exposed on local radio shows like Between the Ropes on WQTM 740 AM, in Orlando. Of course, the newsletters like the Wrestling Observer are the main sources of much of the news and history of the sport, but sometimes it takes hearing the stories from various voices that makes it click.

While certain dominating forces can write their own history, the talent that actually lived that history has already told many of those tales and have continued to voice their opinions on a much smaller scale. By presenting a history of the last fifteen or so years of professional wrestling, much based on the interviews conducted on their radio show, Brian Fritz and Christopher Murry provide a great deal of depth, authority and perspective that just isn't found anywhere in the mainstream.

What really makes the book special is the connections between the WWE, WCW, ECW and TNA that would never be presented in the mainstream, otherwise. For the millions of fans who walked away from the business over the past half-decade, this is a great way to catch up on the sport, not just in terms of history, not just in terms of what actually happened, but as a way to read about what happened to your favorites (and not-so-favorites) as well as a way to learn about the existence of TNA.

While the book can come across as a rehash to in-depth readers of the Observer, and I am one of those for certain, I quickly realized that for once, a wrestling book is targeting a mainstream audience that probably doesn't already know all of this stuff. And in that regard, it rises to the top of the lists of wrestling books.

The first section focuses on WCW. And because of familiarity, proximity and access to a vast array of WCW's talent, the guys at "Between the Ropes" are able to provide an excellent history of the downfall of that promotion. These guys spoke to Eric Bischoff, to Hulk Hogan, to Randy Savage, to Sting, to Vince Russo and Ed Ferrara, as well as to Chris Jericho and Shane Douglas and Terry Taylor and JJ Dillon. In other words, they hit the full gamut of perspectives, and by doing so, they weave a history that isn't overfocused on management's side, or the big guns, or even the lesser known talents.

When these guys can quote Bret Hart about coming in, or Bobby Heenan about why he wanted out, when they talk shop with Jerry Lynn or Larry Zbyszko, when they note the

Pro Wrestling Intellectual

views of Scott Hudson or Ric Flair, it just takes the book up to another level. Not that any of the other books -- the ECW histories, or the WCW recaps or the WWE books are inherently untrustworthy, or their authors voices not authentic, but in reading "Between the Ropes: Wrestling's Greatest Triumphs and Failures" you cannot help but realize that the history presented is shaped by the interactions with powerful, insightful and influential people, and it is all laid bare without an agenda.

Well, in terms of a corporate mentality. I think the agenda is clearly to present the history as best as possible, and in that sense, Fritz and Murray hit a home run.

There are some places where having interacted with the likes of Eric Bischoff or Vince Russo, the perspective shows favoritism. However, having interviewed and being photographed with Vince McMahon, Stephanie McMahon and Jim Ross, that pendulum swings a lot of ways. But it is tied together with a consistent voice, and an ongoing theme of presenting the facts and shaping an overall history which moves in and out of the major promotions of the past decade and a half.

There is some shifting of perspective from WCW to ECW. While the Between the Ropes guys are complete fans of pro wrestling in all its facets, because of proximity they had greater access to the WCW product. With ECW, there's no sense that anything isn't accurate or wrong, but as I've harped before, it is difficult to view ECW from a historical perspective without having experienced it firsthand. It is easy to focus on who left when, and all the backdoor politics, but the true star of ECW was its fans. I don't think that came across. (But then again, Fritz and Murray aren't spitting on them like Vince McMahon is.)

But to get back to the theme, it's hard to doubt or fault the book when they've interviewed Heyman, Douglas, Van Dam, Taz, Simon Diamond, Cyrus and the like. They've got the perspective of the workers at hand, from the top of the company to some of the more obscure (to the mainstream) talent.

The WWE years are a bit more superficial. Unfortunately, the WWE has some policies which make access to talent difficult. (and access to review material equally as difficult, in case anyone ever wondered why I don't review WWE books!) That being said, the guys used their contacts, and the information provided by wrestlers before and after their WWE contractual relationships are very much more pertinent to the shaping of pro wrestling history than those muzzled (or unavailable) by management fiat.

While I question some of the inclusions (the XFL impacted pro wrestling and WWE, but was it a "Failure" that needed inclusion in this history? And the slavish devotion to Mick Foley?) the overall picture painted was fascinating considering the voices heard. Steve

Joe Babinsack

Austin and Jim Ross come to mind, and what's more interesting is reading some of these quotes, and realizing who's in working mode and who's spilling his (or her) guts.

Once again, the draw of the book is that if you think you know everything about WCW, WWE, ECW or TNA, this book will prove you a little wrong. If you missed out on any of those promotions by walking away in the past few years, it will fill you in beyond expectations. And if you want to learn about TNA, well, there aren't many choices.

That the guys had Vince Russo and Jeff Jarrett on the show at various points in time does shape the fondness they have for the first few years of TNA. While I tend to disagree on that matter, it is interesting to see the happenings and the initial involvement of Dixie Carter in the promotion.

In light of Russo's return to the fold, it does shed a lot more questions having read this book. All the power plays and backbiting done seem to make it strange that anyone would ever let him back into a decision making role!

Once again, the individuals interviewed tell the stories. Mike Tenay and D'Lo Brown, Christopher Daniels and Ron Killings, Dixie Carter and Jerry Lynn.

The cool thing that surfaces is the interconnections between the promotions, in terms of talent, that those who didn't follow them all would miss. Jerry Lynn gets interviewed while in WCW, while in ECW, while in the WWE and then in TNA. Shane Douglas has a similar path. Mike Tenay intertwines through WCW and TNA. Jarrett skips ECW but was in the other three.

Which is again the main point. Frits and Murray obviously have a passion for the industry, and got some great interviews with highly informative talent throughout the era of the Cable TV wars and through the downfalls of WCW and ECW, and through the rise of TNA. They got to deal with talent on all sides of every fence, from disgruntled to satisfied, from being stiffed on paychecks to getting outrageous contracts.

And in doing so, and in talking intelligently to the sport, its players and then, to its fans, they have provided an enormously successful and enjoyable book. If you know someone who needs to know this stuff to be better informed on pro wrestling (not just what the WWE wants you to know,) it is probably the most important single book on the market today.

Turning the Tables:
The Story of Extreme Championship Wrestling
Book Written by John Lister

Lister is an English journalist who previously published Slamthology, which detailed his interests in the American version of professional wrestling. In Turning the Tables, he provides another strong perspective on the subculture of professional wrestling, through the renegade ECW product and its most hardcore fans. Unlike the previous DVD release on ECW and the upcoming book by that overbearing corporation that bought the rights to the ECW name (but apparently not the secrets of crowd interaction, let alone respect for the fans, talent and tradition) Turning the Tables is an unauthorized and uncensored account of ECW's history.

By combing through insider newsletter accounts, fan websites and other news outlets, as well as watching the tapes of the shows, Lister provides an in-depth picture of what made ECW work. With nut-and-bolts details of various important events, including "The Night the Line was Crossed," the NWA tournament backstab by Shane Douglas, the New Jack/Mass Transit incident in Revere, and a detailed listing of the bankruptcy, this book has far more depth on the history than those that will rely upon sound bites, carefully orchestrated memories and an eye to the wrestling politics of the McMahon family.

What I find great about the book are the details of the storylines and how Paul Heyman (ECW's prominent creative head honcho) interweaved various plotlines, characters and motivations into a seamless product. Turning the Tables features the background of not only the big matches, but also the streams of run-ins, plot twists and dates of major feuds and matches. In a DVD format, a match and a voiceover provide visual and commentary. But with this book, the reader gains insight into the overall picture of how the fans interacted, were lead and almost always participated in the show.

One fascinating tale is the story of the first "Three Way Dance", which is not the Douglas/Funk/Sabu match, but the much anticipated battle between the tag teams of Sabu/Taz, Benoit/Malenko and Public Enemy. Having participated in Tom Misnik's first Internet conventions, I witnessed the festivities and the awesome spot where, at the culmination of a Public Enemy versus Sabu/Taz "Double Tables" match, the newly christened "Crippler" Chris Benoit interfered to power bomb Sabu onto the prone Rocco Rock, with them all going through a table.

Joe Babinsack

Sabu would abruptly leave ECW for bookings in New Japan, creating animosity and an eventual return to battle Taz at the first ECW PPV. The back story on all the behind the scenes machinations of that story are provided; as are the details on the Raven/Dreamer feud, Mick Foley's various contributions as heel and face; the various jumps to WCW and WWE, which destroyed the company; and lots of promo material, from Terry Funk, Mick Foley and the off-color introductions of the oft-forgotten Joel Gertner.

Because of all the licensing deals involving the music, the previous DVD's featuring ECW have always seemed to be missing something: the manic drumbeat of "Thunder Kiss '65" by White Zombie to open the show, the bumper music between commercials, which often featured Killing Jokes "Millenium"; or the various intro music, including Deep Purple's "Perfect Strangers", the Offspring's "Keep 'em Separated", and Alice in Chain's "Man in the Box" (bonus points if you can name who had what song!)

Obviously, a book doesn't sound better than a DVD with strange music, but the acknowledgement more than makes up for it. The transformation of The Sandman from beach bum to goth-inspired metal head anti-hero is well chronicled. I'm somewhat annoyed that Lister overlooks the influence of fellow Brit writer Neil Gaiman's Sandman comic book character in the mix, but the "Sandman is Blind" storyline, which elevated Jim Fullington to major heel status and cemented Tommy Dreamer as a face acceptable to the hardcore fans.

Within that storyline is the essence of what was ECW, including how and why it continues to this day as a spontaneous chant when fans see awesome work in the ring. Whether castigating wrestler's who "screw up" in the ring, giving homage to those who do death-defying stunts, or simply showing exuberant appreciation for wrestlers and bookers who return the favor, the insane atmosphere that was in ECW still haunts the WWE and cannot be duplicated, no matter how the audience is manipulated. "Attitude, effort and talent" are what Lister calls the focal points of the fan's appreciation of being there, being involved and creating more than just a performance in the ring, but also being players in the big picture, through audience participation, communications that went in both directions and through respect that was maintained.

"Indeed, formulaic chants are now little more than a cliché for the fans who truly believe they are part of the show. In ECW, they were."

Turning the Tables: The Story of Extreme Championship Wrestling, by John Lister, retails at $15.99 US, and can be found at various web sites, including www.highspots.com

Pro Wrestling Intellectual

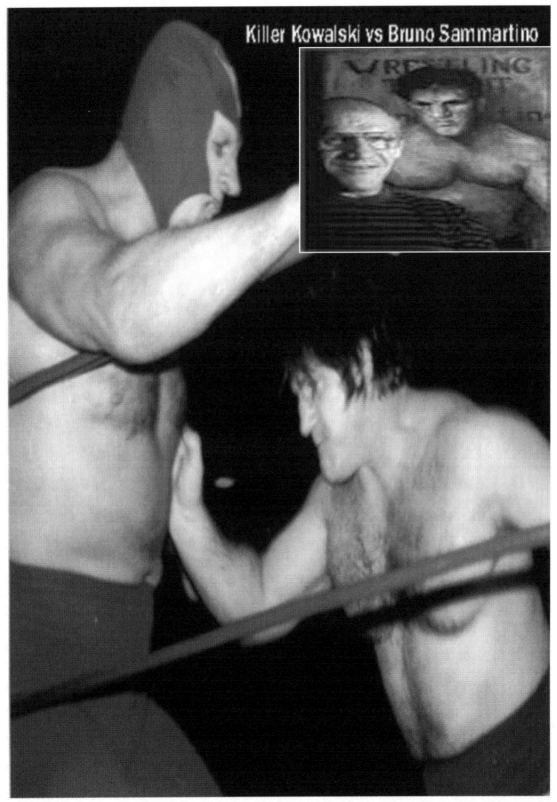

Killer Kowalski vs Bruno Sammartino

Joe Babinsack

BRUNO SAMMARTINO

"Secrets of a Survivor"
WPXI TV, Pittsburgh
June 25, 2006

This show was a nostalgic look back at Bruno Sammartino's life, from his ordeals in Italy during WWII, touching upon his early obstacles in the realm of professional wrestling, noting a few near-misses with plane crashes, and zooming through his dominance of the pro wrestling world in the 1960's and 1970's.

It was definitely a mainstream piece, with not much in terms of wrestling facts, figures, numbers, dates or the like, nor did it dwell on many names or specific matches. The show was hosted by WPXI's regular anchor David Johnson, with support from main sportscaster John Fedko. It was greatly respectful of professional wrestling, which may seem surprising, but knowing of Bruno's reputation and legendary status in Pittsburgh, as well as his own personality and presentation of the sport, its hard to imagine it being anything else.

The first 1/2 hour was Bruno's story of a child, dealing with the devastation of a war-torn Italy, his situation where his dad went to America for a better life, but was unable to bring his family over for almost a decade. The story's central theme was Bruno's ability to survive, but it was moreso a tribute to his mother, Emilia. The show is deeply personal, spliced with a current interview of Bruno, photos taken from the autobiography, stock photos and an ongoing pitch for a DVD, poster and other materials (which can be found at www.brunobrunobruno.com)

Several of his stories of survival stand out from that period. He breaks down while describing the time when two Nazi's actually set out to search the mountains where many hid, and how they lined up dozens to be executed, only to be saved by the chance arrival of some Italian men of the village coming back to check on things. He describes the efforts of his mother to gather food by sneaking back to the town, while he and his siblings fearfully waited on the top of the path, watching for a sign of her.

Pro Wrestling Intellectual

The young Sammartino was afflicted by disease and recounts how he may not have survived if not for his mother taking care of him.

When he was finally health enough to make the voyage across the Atlantic, it was another trial, a trip on a violent ocean during the worst season for such a journey. When he finally met his father (he was far too young to remember him when he set forth for the US) he was suprised at the sight of this older guy.

At first the promises of streets paved in gold proved disappointing, as Sammartino was bullied and out of place in Pittsburgh's Oakland neighborhood. But a friend got him involved in weightlifting, and Sammartino would take his interest in lifting and bodybuilding to local heights, and went to York, PA to get noticed by national figures in the sport.

He met Carol, soon to be his wife, while she was still in high school. It was only after being married that she learned of his career interests in professional wrestling.

While the details of his breaking into pro wrestling is glossed over, the program does touch upon his being blacklisted. The names (and clips) put forth from the 1960's are Killer Kowalski, Gorilla Monsoon and Ivan Koloff. They mention Koloff as a rival, but don't dwell upon the historic title change.

Strangely enough, but highly favorable to the piece, there is no mention of the McMahon name, despite dancing around the blacklisting, despite dancing around the issues of his rush to return to the ring after breaking his neck, and suitably as the program ends after his second reign as champion ends at the hands of Superstar Billy Graham.

That the McMahon feud was ignored serves to avoid a lot of unpleasantness and bitterness.

Bruno's position on pro wrestling, as someone who continues to live protecting the sport, was nicely played. There was no cynicism or questioning of the living legend. Two things did come to mind as a bit revealing, especially considering Bruno's adherence to kayfabe.

When they discuss his winning the match against Buddy Rogers, he did mention the locker room talk between various wrestlers, and some sort of arrangement to get Rogers into the match, an arrangement that promised the victory to Rogers. Of course, less than a minute into that match, Sammartino won to begin his first and longest reign as WWWF champion, and proceeded a long run of headlining Madison Square Guardian There is mention of Sport's Illustrated's article showing Bruno, along with Mickey Mantle and Willie Mays, as the highest paid athletes one year.

Another part where Bruno gets really close to exposing things is when he discusses his return to the ring, as part of the "undercard" of the Ali/Inoki card. The show completely ignores the reasons why "they" desperately wanted Bruno wrestling at the event, and notes that the air date was the 30th anniversary of that match. Bruno acknowledges that his match with Stan Hansen only went two minutes, and all he did was "punch and kick" until Hansen got a bloody nose and the referee DQ'd him. He describes the fans as being happy with the result.

As with most TV, there was lots of rehashing but strangely a lot of stock photographs. To me, what they called MSG was actually the Civic Arena. One clip that aired over and over was a marquee with Bruno Sammartino/Superstar Graham on it, but they never delved into that title change, either.

They aired a clip of David when he was 8-9-10 or so, hoping that his Dad would retire to spend more time at home, but never delved into the feud between father and son.

By avoiding a lot of the negativity, it came across like a puff piece, and far more bent on nostalgia and a mainstream audience than aiming at the wrestling crowd, or real reporting on Bruno's history, but considering that the airing did a 6.0 in the ratings

(According to Dave Meltzer's latest issue of the Wrestling Observer Newsletter) that was obviously the goal and it most likely exceeded its expectations.

The Great Debate '08: Race/Sammartino NWA/WWWF Kayfabe Commentaries

So I open up two packages in the mail on Friday, one has Raven/Sandman from Big Vision, and the other … this gem featuring eight time NWA Champion Harley Race, and two time, twelve year WWWF Champion Bruno Sammartino.

Where's the head's up from Chris Cruise and Georgianne Makropolous, I say!

Let me say this, if you haven't seen Bruno recently at one of his many appearances, signings or guest attendances, this is a great way to see how he looks, how he's feeling and how spot-on he is about the business. Harley Race, too!

Bruno's presence is just awesome and on display here. No matter what question is thrown at him, he's answering with the wisdom of fifty some years in the sport, and a perception that isn't clouded by billionaire owners, sycophantic fan boys or other people too close to the business to see the forest for the trees.

His answers are insightful. His thought process is well on display. And he's not pulling any punches. I can definitely feel for Harley and his "Bruno said it all" responses. It really wasn't much of a debate, and not because Harley Race is dwarfed by Bruno's knowledge of what works and what doesn't.

It's because Bruno just doesn't hold back.

I mean, I'm still working on a publishing deal for rewriting Bruno's autobiography, and I'm thinking, man! Bruno, save some for the book!

But it doesn't matter. Bruno is a font of information, and despite his negativity towards the business he helped put on the map in many ways, he exudes more understanding of what it should be, could be and was, than almost anyone else in existence.

I dare anyone to watch this DVD and not come away with the notion that Bruno didn't just live his career as a professional wrestler, he MADE his career as a professional wrestler.

You want insight on Ali/Inoki? Bruno could have had that match, if the national promoters didn't back out of supporting Vince McMahon Sr and didn't want to pony up big money for the benefit of the New York promotion.

Joe Babinsack

You want to know what Bruno really feels about Vince Jr?

Buy the DVD. You won't be disappointed.

Kayfabe Commentaries really digs deep in research, and they throw an assortment of questions at the two legends. Some questions are slow pitches, others curves, but these guys are hitting them out of the park at every chance.

And the insight is incredible. Here', we've got two stellar talents in the business, and two of the toughest guys around, and they just KNOW what they're talking about:

Steel Cages? What's the better city, St. Louis or New York? Villains and Heroes.

Squashes. Ribs. And are newsletters good or bad for the sport?

All these are answered and much, much more in an 85 minute DVD. I'm growing to love Kayfabe Commentaries, as they provide in-depth insight into the business, without the foolishness, condescension or antipathy that too many announcers hold for the sport.

This DVD also explodes the notion that Bruno is just this bitter old guy, who just rails on the sport that made him, who just doesn't "get it" and who just has an axe to grind with Vince McMahon.

Not only that, but it shows how far Bruno has gone with the modern understanding of the industry. He's well informed and well in tune with what far too many fans are feeling with the business. No respect for the history, no respect for the audience – just vulgarity, just profanity, just over-the-top sex and everything that wrestling wasn't back in the day.

But even at his most vociferous, Bruno's thoughts aren't for himself or his legacy, they are for the workers. When Rick McGraw died at the onset of the steroids/drug abuse era, it obviously hit Bruno hard.

Four years after retirement, he came back to the sport, and the whole backstage scene had changed. This is all on the DVD, so I'll avoid spilling the beans. But the point is, Bruno's disgust was never about just the product, it was about the health of the boys.

If you want Bruno and Harley on booking, on what makes professional wrestling great, on who would win between a boxer and a wrestler, it's all in here.

Pro Wrestling Intellectual

A couple of interesting and controversial topics come up, especially in regard to perspectives provided by Harley and Bruno, where you might expect there to be a heated debate.

Ric Flair is one.

Believe me; Bruno is passionate about his opinion of the Nature Boy. Well, not just THAT Nature Boy, but the more modern one. One of Bruno's pet peeves is wrestlers who don't mix up their styles, who don't seem to care that their talents are on display for the same audience, and sometimes the same exact people.

Predictability?

Say what you want about Bruno, but if you didn't experience him in his day, if all you know about him is watching some blow-off match on YouTube, then it is easy to say that you DON'T KNOW BRUNO.

Bruno learned about wrestling by watches greats like Rocca and Carpentier. But he also learned for himself that when he made it big, he wouldn't just rely on the same spots to get himself over.

What's interesting to hear is what Race thinks about the whole issue. Race is hesitant to name who he thinks the greatest wrestlers are, but he's more in agreement with Bruno than you may think.

Race also annihilates any notion that the WWWF was simply a regional promotion, talking about how Bruno main evented in St Louis, in Japan and Australia.

Moreso, the debate offers insight into the realities that working the largest arenas, working them often and working a large circuit of populous cities defied any notion of a region, especially considering that Bruno was responsible for keeping the fans coming.

The debate explains that Race, as NWA Champion, would come in to meet the regional champion, or regional top star, and that match wasn't worked all over the circuit. It was an aspect of the NWA and its formula, for sure, but then again, the success or failure of a promotion wasn't wholly based on the NWA Champion's drawing power – it was on the region itself. Call the WWWF a region all you want, but it lived and thrived on Bruno's drawing ability, and his presence, and his ability to connect with fans, and in every major city in the Northeast.

Joe Babinsack

No other professional wrestler, in the history of the sport, could hold up to the rigors, demands and drawing power that Bruno displayed in his eight year 1960's run, let alone the fact that he proved his power when the formula didn't hold with Morales or Backlund.

Anyway, I could go on, but let's get back to the DVD.

Kayfabe Commentaries, with its dedication to the industry, it's amazingly interesting questions and the forum for greats to provide details, stories and true histories of the sport, is proving to be a valuable player in the DVD market.

And the Great Debate '08 is certainly one of its best offerings to date.

Joe Babinsack can be reached at chaosonejoe@yahoo.com. Look for Rey Misterio in Tijuana 2 DVD (by Bob Barnett!) to be reviewed soon, plus the Warrior's comic book, and many more wrestlingbooks and DVDs…Life goes on.

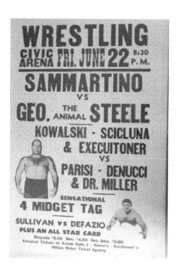

Pro Wrestling Intellectual

The Case for Bruno Sammartino

<u>Who is the greatest professional wrestler of all time?</u>

We've heard all the accolades about Ric Flair over the past few months. We know the names of legend, like Lou Thesz, like Ed "Strangler" Lewis, and the big names of yesteryear, the ones the old school claim were real wrestlers, and of whom I won't argue against.

So, how do you measure greatness?

Can it be based on the "it" factor, or the drawing power (compared as apples and oranges, decades apart) or the number of championships won (and lost?) And, in building the case for greatness, can it be done without tearing down the contenders?

For Bruno Sammartino, the case must be made, and in respect to the man, I must do it with the passion, power and Integrity that is not just the legacy of Bruno, but the essence of his professional career and public face.

For the record, I'm not a nuts and bolts historian. This isn't about getting into the details, but building a case, logically, emphatically and with the analysis and historical perspective than is necessary.

In ten points I can argue why Bruno Sammartino is the greatest professional wrestler of all. Ten points of establishing why he surpasses others, why he embodies the sport, why he, above all, can challenge for the title of champion of champions.

Arguments are the hallmark of fandom…. Here are mine:

By the way, let me put some perspective on the WWWF territory. It is easy to relegate the "Northeast" as a smaller region than, say, the entire United States of America. But let's not overlook the vast populations of the Northeast. From Boston to Pittsburgh, and as far south as Washington DC and Baltimore, every major city was of the top 20 in population up until the 1960's.

To dismiss New York, Philadelphia, Boston, Pittsburgh, Baltimore, Washington DC, the various smaller cities of New York, the state of New Jersey, and the New England area, plus Pennsylvania, is to dismiss up to 50% of the population of this country.

It is equally arguable that the NWA, in not promoting heavily in the Northeast, hardly covered the United States, as it would be to say that the Northeast is a minor region.

1 Bruno Sammartino was the longest reigning Heavyweight Champion in the United States.

Lou Thesz was the NWA Champion for over ten years. Ten years and three months, to nail it to that detail. He held the belt on three occasions.

Bruno surpassed that mark by nearly a year. He had two reigns, the first being seven years and eight months long. That first, historically dominant reign speaks of a longevity that will likely never be challenged.

We can talk numbers of titles, but the duration of the reign seems far more important to me. And in that regard, Bruno surpasses the measuring stick of the great Lou Thesz himself.

2 Bruno Sammartino dominated the professional wrestling industry in the 1960's,

and for much of the 1970's. Well, dominated maybe is not a good enough description...

It is a documented fact that Sammartino was all but offered the NWA championship, even while he held the WWWF version of the World Heavyweight Championship.

Sure, the rivalry was nowhere near the level of WCW/WWF in the 1990's, but the reality was there: Sammartino was considered such a draw, such a dominant force, that the NWA was willing to take ½ a month of his schedule instead of controlling a full month of their own championship.

I'm not so sure how that can be dismissed.

Bruno had the offer, but turned it down, with the obvious reality that he had enough income, work and a tough schedule working for the WWWF alone, and knew he'd be destroyed by a non-stop schedule.

How do you argue the depth of this? This was an era when arena attendance was where the profits were made.

Pro Wrestling Intellectual

This was an era where the NWA bespoke of its own gallery of truly deserving champions. And yet… the biggest and most prestigious of professional wrestling organizations all but begged to have a part time champion?

How much of a draw was Sammartino? One can get lost in the numbers, but consider the logic: One half of Bruno Sammartino's presence was worth more than a completely controlled NWA Heavyweight Champion.

3 Bruno Sammartino's salary level in the 1960's compares strongly to the highest paid athletes in sports.

Whether we look at Major League Baseball – the dominant sport of the culture at the time – or the NFL and AFL, or even Professional Golf (notably Arnold Palmer,) the numbers floated around for Mr. Sammartino, that of $100,000 per year, cannot be duplicated in the modern era.

Steve Austin danced at income ranges approaches that of Baseball and Football stars, but briefly and not quite at the same level. And to raise Bruno's impact further, keep in mind that merchandising was not even a blip on the radar compared to the T-shirt sales, branded products and other lucrative items (that yellow styrofoam finger comes to mind as well) that propelled wrestlers to high salaries.

Bruno, however, rubbed shoulders with the likes of Willie Mays and Sandy Koufax and other baseball superstars, not because of merchandising, but because of base salary.

The range of salaries for professional football was around $60,000 average in the 1970's, which is why some football greats like Wahoo McDaniels moonlighted in wrestling. $100,000 was the upper stratosphere of most sports, and even pro golfers like Arnold Palmer were doing $125,000 per year at the peak of income in that era.

It's hard to comprehend a wrestler today making tens of millions of dollars per year.

I'll admit that changing entertainment and sports values makes this another apples to oranges comparison. But once again, who today, and who over the past thirty years had consistently pulled in a salary comparable to the superstars of other professional sports?

Joe Babinsack

4 Who has the legacy of Bruno Sammartino?

Bruno commands the stage at every even he attends. People in Pittsburgh stop and respond, often in an orderly fashion, to his presence: at baseball games, at boxing events and of course at charity events.

Sure, it's Pittsburgh and it's Bruno's adopted hometown, but Pittsburgh wasn't the heart of the old WWWF. That was Madison Square Garden. New York. But talk to the old-timers in Philadelphia. In Baltimore, Boston or parts in between. Bruno was the champ in Washington DC and in other Pennsylvania cities, from Allentown to Altoona.

We can talk about how The Sheik burned out Toronto, and how Jack Tunney turned to Ric Flair to re-establish it, but can we overlook how Bruno Sammartino sparked his career in Toronto, after being blackballed in the business by McMahon, by speaking his native Italian and drawing as an ethnic hero?

But Bruno Sammartino being Italian was only a portion of his legacy.

Pittsburgh has its many hues and many places of origin for its strong immigrant history, but Italian neighborhoods aren't dominant by far, in the 96 odd ethnic magnets that comprise the Steel City.

Bruno wasn't just the hero of the Italians, but of the working men of many national origins. Slovaks and Poles are more prominent in the City of Champions, but no one, no matter where they called their ancestral home, hesitated one bit about their champion's fluency, his accent or his real home town.
Neither, it seems, did the citizens of cities across the Northeast, and across most of the continent as well.

And, by Bruno's passionate loyalty to Baba, one has to add other lands to that mix.

5 Bruno Sammartino wasn't just the face at the foundation of what is now the WWE,

he was the man who came back time and time again to restore the promotion to prominence, to bail it out from potential disaster, and he was a part of the national establishment of the WWF.

Pro Wrestling Intellectual

Yankee Stadium is the House that Ruth Built. While to argue that Madison Square Garden was made the wrestling capital of the world by Sammartino's efforts would ignore many years of history, one cannot avoid the fact that Bruno Sammartino headlined MSG for reportedly 200 events.

Furthermore, one can argue that the WWWF was built on the massive shoulders of the Italian Superman. Take away Bruno from the mix, and Vince McMahon Sr isn't the mover and shaker in the industry in the 1960's, with no regard to the happenings of the NWA, no interest in booking that champion, and no concerns about raking in the profits.

Bruno's ability to call his shots is another point, but his endurance built the WWWF. Having the dominant champion meant a revolving door of challengers, who could be made just by standing up to the man. Having that pecking order, that brilliant formula, that awesome combination of promotion and wrestling mind, that all built the organization up.

But was it Vince Senior as promoter, or Bruno Sammartino, as champion, that propelled the success? The period between Bruno's first loss and second reign cements the argument.

His return after Pedro Morales' title reign re-established the WWWF as a major player. His return brought the numbers back: his magic, his presence and his wrestling mind and talent. Re-establishing the formula worked its wonders.

So what happened with Morales? What happened with Bob Backlund a few years later? If it was just the draw of an ethnic champion, why didn't Morales draw? And if it was the sheer talent, why didn't Backlund, a superior wrestler, with the All-American pedigree, raise the bar of success?

To dig deeper, was it not Bruno Sammartino, coming back way too fast from a serious neck injury, who brought the crowd in to watch the debacle of Antonio Inoki and Muhammed Ali on closed circuit?

The McMahons all but begged Bruno to put in an appearance, and there were apparently promises of a return on the receipts for his efforts. He did wrestle a match. It was a four minute match which once more highlights Bruno's awesome understanding of the sport and its fans.

Four minutes seems like nothing. But consider:
A)   Bruno wrestled enough to show he could

B)   Bruno wrestled enough to protect his health
C)   Bruno wrestled so that the fans would want more
D)   Bruno wrestled to save his boss from a financial loss

And, history will show, that he succeeded like he always did.

Jump ahead nearly a decade later. Bruno Sammartino is still a name to be reckoned with. His ability and presence was more than just helpful to the expansion of Vince McMahon Jr's business brilliant business game plan.

Whether it was setup or pure coincidence, Bruno's talent and aura persisted: to work a tag team match, to take the place of a headliner who missed a show, to step right in an carry an arm of a three-pronged canvassing of the nation.

6 What can be said about Bruno's schedule? Was it any less than the NWA Champions of the era? Did it pale to the TV face time of the Ric Flair era?

Bruno worked styles like few others. He could do power. He could wrestle with the best of them. And he had the unique presence, charm and credibility to work however he wanted come the mid-seventies.
It's funny to read complaints about his style.

Sure, he didn't work the highspots or the crazy acrobatics that are almost expected today, but he worked like few others. But Bruno's forte was credibility. He simply was the champ. He had the power.

He worked at his profession and protected it by his actions, his aura and his attitude.

Far too many people seem to take too much stock in technical presentations and all the flash and glitz and glamour. But professional wrestling isn't just show, it's the fashioning of illusion. Maintaining credibility is an awesome undertaking.

In establishing credibility; working at psychological, booking and emotional levels; and simply by presenting himself as a true champion, Bruno Sammartino proved his greatness.

But even so, his schedule as champion was not one to overlook. He ran his own promotion, worked dates as WWWF champion, and still found time to do spots and tours across the nation, in Canada, in Japan, and still the NWA wanted him on board.

And still, he worked long and hard, and with a completely physical style.

7 Bruno was able to call his spots like no other.

Who turns down the NWA? Who leaves a title reign, twice, not because of being pushed out the door, but because of his own volition?

Consider this: Bruno Sammartino had title reigns lasting over eleven years. He likely could have had reigns over fifteen, if not twenty years.

He was just that good, he was just that loved.

Bruno built up a reputation that he was in demand across the world, and he could simply lose the WWWF belt, and tour sporadically, and not lose income or drawing power or any sense of loss.

And when he wanted to come back, there was no hesitation.

With no diminishment of his connection with the fans.

8 Moments

A) Lifting Haystacks Calhoun
B) Defeating Buddy Rogers in less than a moment
C) The Face versus Face battle against Pedro Morales
D) Ivan Koloff (more below)
E) Winning back the belt from Stan Stasiak
F) Breaking his neck with Stan Hansen
G) Rematch with Hansen
H) Losing to Superstar Billy Graham
I) The Larry Zbyszko angle
J) Cage match with Zbyszko at Shea Stadium

And the list goes on. Every formulaic but well crafted title challenger from the 1960's through the 1970's was a compilation of moments, angles and building perfect challenges.

Bruno had a way with the sport like few others. There are some who could completely out-wrestle him, but very few who could out-think him. And one of the vastly important aspects of Bruno's career was his ability to be a professional wrestler in terms of talent and presentation, in terms of crafting the illusions and maintaining his reigns.

The very fact that so many of Bruno's challengers could come back to make more money with him bespeaks a depth of knowledge and appreciation and understanding of the workings of professional wrestling that very, very few have ever displayed.

9 I keep coming back to the moment where Ivan Koloff beats Bruno for the belt.

The numbers are unimportant for the argument, but should not be overlooked.

But consider these points:

A)   After some eight years of a title reign, there is no "We've seen history" pop. Imagine that today, or over the past twenty years. Even the biggest stars got a "Thanks, goodbye" ovation and reaction. Even the most minor changes have gotten pops for a title change. Not here.

B)   There is no violent reaction, either. Bruno had too much respect from the fans for that.

C)   The depth of the emotion was simply awesome. Better wrestling minds than mind have commented upon the connection Bruno had with the fans. This was it, on display, and without any sense of restraint.

D)   Just try to wrap your brain around this: more than ten thousand people, and no heckling, no heel fans, no boos and no cheers. That's a display of greatness that cannot ever be reproduced.

Ever.

E)   That moment was the end result of crafting of nearly eight years of interactions with the crowd, the establishment of credibility and the sheer emotional investment of the fans.

10 Integrity is the essence of Bruno Sammartino.

From his championship aura and his unparalleled passion for the sport, in all its forms, to the very core of being called a professional, Bruno is simply the greatest.

Pro Wrestling Intellectual

Can you question Bruno's motivations? His reputation? His earnestness?

Bruno Sammartino went through a period after his last stint with the WWF where he seemed utterly bitter and had an axe to grind with the industry. And yet, what did he do? How did he take his anger out on the profession that he loved?

At the time, he crusaded.

He spoke of the ills of the drug use he saw backstage. He screamed concerns of the use of steroids and enhancements that were creeping into the industry. He took his campaign to the media, and spoke with passion and veracity and from his heart.

And now, fifteen and more years later, how prophetic have his words been?

Furthermore, his testament to his own integrity is his turning his back on a profession he no longer saw as upholding the legacy he built. For years, he could have simply answered an affirmative to the requests of the most powerful man in the industry. He could have profited by his image, in merchandising, videos and DVDs sold to new generations.

Any other man would crumble at the temptation.Not Bruno Sammartino.

His greatness needs no statistics, it needs no petty arguments nor foolish tear-downs of competitors, nor a trashing of the industry or a bemoaning of why he has been so forgotten or overlooked, so underappreciated and often blatantly ignored.

All I truly know about Mr. Sammartino, and his legacy, is that I am a third generation professional wrestling fan, and watchedhim as a young boy, and knew him by the words of my father and grandfather, both now long gone.

That, my friends, is more than good enough for me.

But the further studying, reading, listening to my betters and to the voice of Bruno himself, all prove it to an exponential degree. My arguments are my testament to his greatness, and I hope to honor him with my proofs.

Joe Babinsack

One of Professional Wrestling's Greatest Moments
Ivan Koloff defeats Bruno Sammartino for the WWWF Championship

Date: January 18, 1971
Place: Madison Square Garden
Federation: WWWF

"I pulled myself up off the mat and for a second it wasn't clear to me what had happened. I thought at first that something was wrong with my ears. I couldn't hear a sound! ... The whole Garden was as quiet as a tomb.

Then I started hearing little cries, whimpers. Talk about emotional moments, this was one that really got to me. I heard sobbing. I heard cries. Someone called out, "Bruno, you're still thebest. We love you, Bruno.

--Bruno Sammartino: An Autobiography of Wrestling's Living Legend

The History
Bruno Sammartino won the WWWF Championship on May 17, 1963. His reign of almost eight years, his no-nonsense style – rooted in his powerful strength and raw wrestling ability, and his interview style of appealing to the fans for support, all contributed to make him one of the most popular professional wrestlers of the era, and definitely the most popular in the WWWF's Northeastern United States base.

Bruno arrived in the United States after WWII following his immigrant father, accompanying his mother and siblings to the Pittsburgh area. His ability to speak Italian became integral to his appeal and drawing power, and coupled with his raw power and wrestling skills honed by practicing with University of Pittsburgh grapplers, he would ultimate rise to the WWWF championship. According to his own biography, Sammartino had grown weary of the rough travel schedule imposed upon him as champion, and actually refused to consider a merging of the WWWF and NWA titles because of the potential of being away from home even more.

With a growing family, a business interest in the Pittsburgh area promotions,and an eye towards slowing down his schedule, the prospect of losing the prestigious belt should not have been a surprise.

Ivan Koloff had emerged in the WWWF as a force to be reckoned with. The typical cycle of matches in the federation focused on new challengers to the popular champion. Koloff

began a run at the top of the WWWF in 1970, beating everyone in his path. The "Russian Bear" was a powerhouse, relying upon a bearhug and feats of strength, not terribly unlike the champion's repertoire. Unlike Sammartino, however, Koloff showed greater agility and a tendency towards using the ropes to jump on an opponent. That would lead to the pivotal moment
in the match.

Sammartino had held the belt for nearly eight years: seven years and eight months to be exact. He had not lost in the WWWF in ten years, and was in the prime of his career, a career which saw him headline Madison Square Garden over 200 times. The match with Ivan Koloff was his one hundred and eleventh title defense.

The Moment

The match had proceeded well past the fourteen minute mark, when Ivan Koloff gained the upper hand. "The end came with startling suddenness as Koloff hurdled off the top rope and hit Sammartino full force in the neck area." [Scranton Times] From the blow, the prone Sammartino was unable to stop the three count. Referee Dick Kroll counted the champion's shoulders to the mat in a stunning decision. It came without interference or cheating, a clean win by the powerful challenger. A new Champion for the WWWF was to be crowned.

For security reasons, it had already been determined not to hand over the belt to the Russian in front of a reported sellout, with probably more than 20,225 fans filling Madison Square Garden, breaking the record gate at $85,554 in receipts. That fear of the fans' response to a title change had haunted the WWWF for decades, and would remain a concern throughout the next two title changes.

Impact

The match between Bruno Sammartino and Ivan Koloff ended Bruno's first reign as WWWF Champion, which was a very long run by modern standards. That it happened at Madison Square garden, ending a streak of one hundred and eleven defenses of the title, made it more memorable. The unique reaction of the heavily partisan crowd – a complete silence – heightened the historic nature of the moment and left a lasting legacy.

That a Russian defeated the American superstar in the midst of the cold war created great heat on Ivan Koloff, establishing him as a main eventer for the next decade, and gave him the basis for a solid and notable career that
stretched into the 1990s and beyond.

The booking aspect of the victory was the transition in the WWWF between two hugely popular ethnic wrestlers without ruining the popularity of either man. Pedro Morales was given the opportunity to run with the heavyweight championship, and immediately and successfully filled the seats at Madison Square Garden and other WWWF strongholds.

Tangent (I)
Ivan Koloff's short reign

The "formula of success" for Vince McMahon, Sr. was to have a popular wrestler hold the belt, and have challengers try to dethrone the popular title holder, usually after draws, disputed or otherwise controversial finishes. Thus it was only days until McMahon engineered the title match between Koloff and rising ethnic star being groomed for a long title reign, 28 year old Pedro Morales.

Pedro Morales had been wrestling since the 1950's, and mostly in California. In the mold of Antonino Rocca and Miguel Perez, who were the popular and Dominant tag team of the past two decades, Morales was able to capture the attention of another major ethnic group in the New York area. As Sammartino was to the Italian community, Morales -- hailing from Culebra, Puerto Rico -- was expected to be for the Latino community. Pedro Morales was introduced to the WWWF fans as the United States Heavyweight Championship, which further bolstered the draw for his WWWF title match.

Ivan Koloff only held the WWWF belt until February 8, 1971 – at the "Battle of the Champions" where he lost to Pedro Morales in a match that was just short of eleven minutes long. The card drew a reported 21,118 fans, and $86,885. The main event ended on another one of the WWWF's staples – a disputed finish. While Koloff held Morales in a full nelson, the challenger climbed the turnbuckle and pushed off, with both wrestlers ending on the map, both in seemingly a pinning predicament. Morales was declared the winner, which elicited a huge response from the crowd.

And so the primary result of Sammartino's loss was the transitioning to a new baby face title holder.

Tangent (II)
Ivan Koloff: Star Creation

Ivan Koloff was made as a headliner from the victory against Bruno Sammartino, and may very well have been a major force in the WWWF during the 1970's. His career was launched by the victory and he headlined in various promotions across the world: the

AWA, the IWA in Japan, the NWA and remained a prominent heel and tag team champion through the next three decades.

Until 1971, Koloff was a relative unknown in the WWWF and his career was still learning the craft, but was perceived as talented. Koloff had a brief run, holding the International championship in Montreal, in the late 1960's, but had only known at the bottom of the card in the WWWF. A match alone for the belt would have solidified him as a star, especially after doing well in the first match, setting up the typical series for a strong challenger. But by beating the seemingly undefeatable Sammartino, Ivan Koloff was now a name to be reckoned with.

The industry in that era was known for brief runs in the various regions across the United States, and once Koloff lost the WWWF belt, Koloff went on to make use of his reputation as the man who dethroned Sammartino in many regions and across the world. He sustained a solid career, in singles and in tag teams, for over twenty years, retiring in 1994 (but still wrestled sporadically into the 2000's.) He would go on to be a Florida and Georgia Tag Team Champion, an NWA Tag Team Champion, and an NWA Six-Man Tag Team Champion.

Koloff's first run as a headliner came against perennial titleholder Verne Gagne in the AWA. In a stint in Japan's IWA, he teamed with Mad Dog Vachon to grab the IWA World Tag Team champion belts in 1973. He bounced around a bit, but returned to the WWWF with Sammartino again Champion, for a short series, in which he was ultimately pinned in a much heralded steel cage match.

After Sammartino got his revenge, Koloff bounced around various US Regions. In 1977, he became the WWA World Champion. Later that year he started his more familiar role as a tag team specialist, and held a portion of the belts four times in the NWA's Florida promotion. He would then hold the Georgia version of the NWA belts with Ole Anderson, and later with Alexi Smirnoff twice in 1980. As Georgia went national, he held those belts on several occasions, and was also a fixture in the Mid-Atlantic region, where he held tag belts, the TV championship, and eventually introduced his "nephew" Nikita Koloff, who was slated to be a major headlining force for the NWA, and linking him to the Koloff name certainly helped in laying the foundation.

With Nikita, and with Krusher Krushev, Ivan was the leader of the Russian contingent that held the NWA 6-Man tag team championship belt, and later the NWA's United States tag team championships in the mid 1980's, and the waning of the Cold War. While he was becoming a foil for the now baby face Nikita Koloff, who turned away from the Russians to join Dusty Rhodes as the Superpowers, Koloff's career was waning as well.

Ivan Koloff maintained an international presence as a headliner. He had held the NWA Canadian championship out of Toronto and had a bloody feud with Angelo Mosca. In 1989, the WWC's championship in Puerto Rico, which became the last significant belt in his collection that spanned the world, and four decades of a solid career.

Tangent (III)
Bruno's post-Championship era

Bruno Sammartino, in much need of a rest from the hectic schedule as WWWF Champion, went into a brief inactive period. He followed that with a softer schedule, headlining across the country and the world based on his reputation and charismatic presence. According to his autobiography:

"For about a month, I didn't do anything. I decided to be good to myself and I quit training so as not to put any kind of stress on any part of my body. After a while, I started feeling much better. After those four weeks, I went back to training. Guess I couldn't live without it."

The eight years of his championship reign took a toll on his body. As the champion, and with the blue collar work ethic of his adopted home town, as well as the wrestler's reality of only being paid when working, Sammartino had not taken time off. He was an established headliner across the globe, and his schedule in the WWWF alone kept him on the road. The champion was expected to headline the main events in his territory, and his drawing power made him attractive to other promotions, even for one-shot events.

Once he lost the belt, Sammartino was able to schedule a less hectic pace, and using his reputation gained in the Northeast, continued to headline across the United States, and do tours in Japan. In St. Louis, he teamed with Dick the Bruiser in a memorable team called Annihilation Inc. and won the WWA Tag Team belts.

But this time, he was able to soften the schedule and take time off between more lucrative tours, instead of being expected to headline the never ending WWWF's programs in Boston, New York, Philadelphia, Washington DC and work in his own co–promotion (the WWA) in Pittsburgh.

Bruno slowly returned to the WWF, first doing spot appearances in Pittsburgh and Philadelphia, but eventually started making waves. At a tag team match with champion Pedro Morales against the Japanese duo of Toru Tanaka and Mr. Fuji, both were blinded

Pro Wrestling Intellectual

by the heel duo's throwing of salt. After a flurry of punches they realized the mistake of attacking each other. But to the surprise (and delight) of the crowd, the restarted the brawl, and were separated by the locker room and referees.

This set up a unique situation, and the first-ever WWWF "face vs. face" World Title match on September 30, 1972. The match-up featured the WWWF's two most popular wrestlers, who had never fought each other, and the natural grudge of a former champion wanting a shot at the title for which he had yet to have a rematch. This historic match went to a grueling 65:05 draw, full of mat wrestling and exchanging holds, and left undecided who was the better man among the current and former champions.

That issue went unresolved, as Stan Stasiak defeated the Latino star for the WWWF belt, and lost it promptly to Bruno Sammartino, who returned to a full schedule with the promotion after healing up and spending some much desired time with his family.

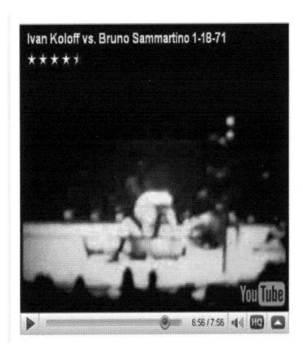

Joe Babinsack

A Not So Subtle Response to a Local Talk Show Host's Drivel

Great spirits have always encountered violent opposition from mediocre minds.
--Albert Einstein

The issue of greatness will always be a measure of great argument, just as much as it is the application of subjectivity and personal bias, let alone belief and perception.

In terms of professional wrestling, there are a few interesting opportunities in the region to acknowledge greatness, and to otherwise make some comparisons.

In the next month and a half, two appearances will be made in Western Pennsylvania, notably in Elizabeth, PA, a town 15 miles south of Pittsburgh.

One is an appearance by Ric Flair, sponsored by highspots.com and the International Wrestling Cartel. The IWC isn't exactly international, although it has defended its main belt (the Super Indy Title) in Japan, and the New Japan promotion once committed to a defense of the IWGP Junior belt (by now WWE contracted talent, and former IWGP Junior Heavyweight Champion Low Ki.)

Flair, by most accounts, is the most glorious wrestler in the past twenty five years. The internet pundits, nitterati or glitterati, depending upon your own personal point of view, rave and rave about Mr. Flair.

Ric is no longer with the WWE, the promotion that dominates the professional wrestling scene, even though he had the highest profile match (arguably, I must add, to avoid the nitpickers) at last year's WrestleMania XXIV. After a dispute over the summer, the WWE and Flair parted ways, and ever since, he's been charging upwards of $75 for fans to sit ringside, watch him in action and/or have autographs and/or interact with "The Man."

Another appearance, on March 20, is by the Ring of Honor promotion, which has strong links to the movie, "The Wrestler" – which, tangentially, should be rolling out locally within a week or so….

ROH is, in my own humble opinion, the greatest wrestling promotion around.

(Well, if we're not talking about exclusively women's professional wrestling, in which I'd call SHIMMER the best!)

Pro Wrestling Intellectual

We can debate up and down about whether the WWE is better than ROH. On most every substantial, financial or attendance result, ROH loses by ten miles. In terms of perceptions of passion, talent and matchmaking, I'll go with ROH, but die-hard WWE fans aren't going to bother debating me.

So, let's turn back to Flair… and the question of greatness, and the simmering battle between blow-hards and die-hards.

Recent events in Pittsburgh, namely an article in the Post-Gazette by Dean Fleischman, have suggested that Bruno Sammartino be honored at the new Hockey Arena being built, with a plaque, a street or statue, dedicated to the greatness of the man, his importance to Pittsburgh, and the drawing power he exuded.

A recent show by the Pittsburgh NBC TV affiliate listed Bruno as the 36th most important Pittsburgher.

The debate was taken up, in typical smarmy nitpicking, by a certain local (and once national) radio DJ/sports talk host, who questioned Bruno's greatness, due to his local drawing power.

Somehow, when Frank Sinatra sang, of New York City, "If I can make it there, I'll make it anywhere" the concept gets lost in parochialism.

If you want to read Bruno's life story, his 1990 autobiography is being reprinted, and is available at www.rasslinriotonline.com, at a cost of $24.95 plus assorted niceties.

Many people question the book, because of Bruno's steadfast adherence to keeping professional wrestling true to the fans and the nature of its entertainment form. While I can understand that sentiment, I reject any sense that it takes away from the book's honesty, integrity or worthyness.

Bruno's greatness is only exemplified by the book!

The question of how to measure greatness hasn't been made easier in modern times. We live in the world of YouTube, where seeing is supposed to be believing, even if seeing isn't the whole picture, or is taken out of context. We live in the world of Wikipedia, where fictions can be massaged into facts, and opinions often masquerade as truth. We live in a world of the Internet, where thoughts travel at speeds unheard of, and yet picking and choosing what to read, understand and digest are even easier than reality… or research for that matter.

On top of it all, we live in an industry not just dominated by a single entity, but one increasingly dominated by a fanbase that only knows that singular entity. Which isn't so much a condemnation of the WWE, but an acknowledgment that professional wrestling is the WWE, and seldom strays from that position… even if the WWE isn't merely the WWE, but an evolution of the WWF before it, and the WWWF before that.

That sentence, to many of today's fans, is likely undecipherable.

Can we compare apples to apples, or apples to oranges, or even time frames to time frames? Sure, the times they are a-changing, to quote Dylan. (And I mean Bob Dylan, not Dylan Thomas or Dylan from 90210, or the Dylan we call Hornswoggle.) The way professional wrestling works these days, a week is like a month is like a year in old school terms.

Old School? Heck, for all the debate about greatness, Old School, in professional terms, is something potential of a great tangent. But for our purposes, let's not call Hulk Hogan of the Old School, and let's agree that Lou Thesz is way Old School.

And let's not start to quibble about the greatness of either of those two pillars of the sport.

Because neither stands up to the man I speak of. But there I go again.

We can speak of greatness, but what is the measure, and by what logic do we speak?

In the "conventional wisdom" it has become not the number of years of being a Champion, but the number of times that Championship was lost.

In the "conventional wisdom" we speak of Regional Titles with aplomb, but conveniently overlook that the largest part of a certain great's title reigns occurred in the East…

In the "conventional wisdom" celebrity status trumps all. Being plastered on TMZ is far more important than an ethnic social club celebration. Being arrested, divorced or hiring high profile lawyers trumps the quiet respect of a legend secure in his own history.

Being Infamous trumps being famous any day.

As most political pundits observe, "conventional" wisdom is often something to ignore. The accumulation of opinions, cherry-picked facts and fast moving talking heads who merely blather their own carefully constructed arguments. The worst of these fans tear down greatness, inserting their own opinions as the basis for measurement.

But how does one measure a man?

Greatness, in the sports world, has been turned on its ear in recent times. Is Mark McGwire great despite his "supplemental" issues? The slugger is likely to find it hard to get into the Hall of Fame in his sport. Likewise, Barry Bonds is vilified in many circles. The NFL has former superstars that had greatness written all over them, and have tarnished, if not destroyed, their reputations through varying degrees of criminality.

Should we measure greatness by acts, actions and reputation?

Should we measure greatness by records, financial considerations, and achievements?

The strange thing is, either way, one simply cannot compare the likes of Ric Flair against the likes of Bruno Sammartino.

For Bruno, it comes down to integrity and the facts: Dominance, duration and dedication on one man's part; his real life merits; his legacy in-ring and out; his campaigns to clean up the industry at a time when it made him a pariah; his steadfast determination to avoid hypocrisy and selling out.

We can all be, according to Bobby "the Brain" Heenan, "Fair to Flair" but to be fair, we must point out the warts and the spotlights. And, to be fair, there are far too many blemishes, far too many questions and far too many issues to be raised in making the case of greatness.

For me, I'll take the Living Legend over The Man any day of the week.

Joe Babinsack

Bruno Sammartino: An Autobiography of Wrestling's Living Legend

I've not been too shy about writing about Bruno Sammartino over the years, and having been fortunate enough to have kept in contact with the Living Legend for much of the year, I have tended to avoid overdoing it.

Several things over the past month have popped up, which makes ignoring such news really stupid for someone who would call himself a professional wrestling journalist, so allow me to present a few items of interest for Bruno fans, and likely, fans of the professional wrestling industry (in one way or another!)

####

I was alerted to the reprinting of Bruno Sammartino's 1990 autobiography a few weeks back, and my apologies for not getting this news out more quickly. The guys at www.rasslinriotonline.com – the same people who did a great job with Dusty Wolfe's "Journal of a Journeyman" have worked out a deal with Sal Corrente and Bruno Sammartino himself, to reproduce the original autobiography.

They've included some new photos, and completed some much needed editing of the book. The price is $24.95, and it's available at www.rasslinriotonline.com

Now, some interesting bits and some background on the 1990 book:

- For one, the book was available only in the Pittsburgh area, with a print run of 10,000 copies. From what I understand, some promises were made for a national run, but that never occurred. Bruno has told me that he never got a dime for that book.
- Part of the deal with www.rasslinriotonline.com, which I've heard from both sides, is that all proceeds will go to Bruno. Since the guys at rasslinriotonline have many projects in line for next year, they are looking to get their name out as a significant publisher of professional wrestling books.
- I've heard from Bruno, and anecdotally over the years, that the original book sells for $80 and $100 a shot on ebay. The book is relatively rare, and again, not having been marketed or available outside of Pittsburgh, if you want one, you have had to pay a steep price to get one. (Do you think any Pittsburgh fan would readily give up this book?)
- One of the prime motivations for getting the book reprinted is to allow more of Bruno's fans to read the book, at a far more reasonable price.

Pro Wrestling Intellectual

I've reviewed the 1990 book, and want to point out a few things: 1) that book was published in 1990! That's ten years before Mick Foley broke the mold of public perception, and at the fading years of the rule of kayfabe.

Now, I know the ongoing perception of Bruno's book was that it was terrible because of kayfabe.

On some terms, I'd agree, but overall, and if you read it carefully, Bruno isn't exactly protecting the business. Sure, he avoids the obvious question and answer, but his opinions and stories on steroids, drug use and certain promoters that we all know aren't exactly kind.

A careful reader can also readily discern that Bruno is much more about keeping the tradition of professional wrestling alive, rather than revealing every trick about the sport. I can certainly respect that, and I would hope that most fans could do so as well.

If you're looking for the awesome story of Bruno Sammartino's life, from his own telling, with a pre "Wrestling is a work!" attitude, this is the book to have.

But keep in mind that the 1990 book was written for another era, and certainly stops short of telling the entirety of Bruno Sammartino's life.

What he has done in the past twenty years has solidified his standing in the industry, and has cemented his embodiment of an often antiquated concept of integrity.

Wrestlers of all levels, talents and standings have sold out for a few bucks.

Many continue to grovel for scraps from the McMahon empire. Several notables have had their images plastered across mainstream TV, due to acts, attitudes and infamy. Others who should, could and may have made a difference in the wrongdoings of the professional wrestling industry have hardly spoken a word.

"Outspoken" isn't just a quaint thing to say about Bruno Sammartino.

Few guys in the history of the sport have been so vociferous in pointing out the flaws, in crying out in the wilderness, in making themselves vulnerable to the catcalls, derisions and guffaws of a mainstream that has never taken professional wrestling seriously.

Most people who come into contact with Bruno do take him seriously.

The amazing aspect of Bruno Sammartino is that he, almost alone among the giants of the sport, is able to be taken seriously, even when the industry itself often deserves little more than a sneer.

Joe Babinsack

What Bruno has done, has said, has experienced and has added to his already superlative legacy has made the 1990 book only part of the overall story.

Title reigns, headlining major arenas, world travels and a reputation supported by many other great names in the business are hard facts. For many years, people have taken Bruno's input into his career as an afterthought. It is easy to attribute his success to promoters (one in particular) or to timing or to ethnicity or to a man with world class strength, athleticism or charisma.

There's a depth to Bruno's character, career and drive that is easy to overlook. Bruno is, from watching him in action, hearing him talk, and now, having spoken with him 'off the record' as well as for research purposes, a very humble man, and a down-to-earth person who will rarely sing his own praises, or admit to his own devices in making his career what it was.

But discernment is an aspect of a good writer, and I've begun to see that there's far more to Bruno's career, in terms of his own guiding hand, than many have ever let on to, than what he's given, and he deserves his just due on that.

That's why I'm doggedly pursuing the chance to help Bruno retell his story, in his own words, for a mainstream audience.

Because as much as the professional wrestling industry needs heroes, we live in a world where the example of Bruno Sammartino can be a lesson for all.

Coincedentally, I was alerted by the ever aware Christopher Cruise about an article in the Pittsburgh Post-Gazette about the need to memorialize Bruno Sammartino in the arena being built to replace the old Civic Arena in Pittsburgh.

Yes, it's Civic Arena, not Civic Center. And I never really took to calling it the Mellon Arena, either. Then again, the new building is being set to be called the Consol Energy Center or some such.

Branding of arenas is something we all have to deal with.

The story is by Dean Fleischman, and I've already contacted him, inquiring as to how I (and likely, the readers of this column) can help persuade the naming of a street, a plaque placement or a statue to be dedicated to Bruno's name and legacy.

Pro Wrestling Intellectual

Rewriting Bruno's Autobiography

Ok, ok. Georgie saw my article on another web site, and wanted to know why I didn't send it her way first.

Well, the answer is that I know Bruno's fans are all over wrestlingfigs.com, and when it comes to the mainstream fans, and certain touted experts, there's a whole lot of preaching that is required.

For those wrestling fans, I have to spell out what Bruno's fans already know… that he's the greatest, that he's the most respected name in the sport, and that his story needs to be told.

So, for all my favorite fans, and my favorite web hostess, pull up a little closer to the screen, and let me explain that I've been talking to Bruno Sammartino over the past several months, and that I'm greatly motivated to land a publishing deal so that I can make sure Bruno's life story -- in his own words -- is presented with his approval, and outside the influence of the powers that be in the industry today.

It was about five months ago that I got a phone call from a very important person. I picked up the phone and heard an unmistakable voice saying "I don't think we've ever met, but you seem to know me very well." We both laughed and exchanged pleasantries. I've exchanged phone calls with the man on almost a weekly basis since then.

The person on the other end was none other than the Living Legend, Bruno Sammartino.

Those of you who have followed my columns certainly know that I've expressed my vast admiration for Mr. Sammartino over the years, and have proclaimed him the greatest of all professional wrestlers. I've outlined that argument; defended his legacy against usually modern era fans who never saw him, nor have bothered to research his career; and have touted his mastery of psychology, his ability to know his fans, and his steadfast integrity.

But that one day when Bruno called me up and expressed his gratitude for my efforts was a very good one. It was only bettered by the day when he said someone was looking to write his book, but he told them he already had someone -- someone who knew his life story better than he did!!!

Over the past several months, I've spoken to Bruno as a fan, as a wrestling journalist, as a friend and as a writer. Because of his experience with his 1990 autobiography -- a book deal that saw him get nothing for his awesome life story -- there has been a genuine reluctance on his part to even bother with updating his inspirational career, legacy and impact on the sport.

We had finally come to an agreement where I would, indeed, help to revise and update his autobiography. That arrangement came with what would appear to be a logical and well-thought caveat: first, I must land a publishing deal, and that deal must include a solid advance.

Needless to say, I've spent much of the past few months trying to land that deal!

But let's put aside that effort for the time being.

Let's talk about Bruno's 1990 book. It's a book that persists in legends and presumptions to this day. The original print run was around 10,000, if that, and it was only released in the Pittsburgh area. Bruno was assured that it would see a national release.

Obviously, it did not.

The point being that so many people that I've talked to over the years, exchanged emails or had serious conversations with, all think that the 1990 autobiography is way too steeped in "kayfabe" and way to protective of the business.

On a certain level, I agree... but only a little bit.

But to say that, in the year 2008, that Bruno, in the year 1990, should have exposed the business is a great leap of logic and a greater affront to his integrity.

Bruno's book may not have been truly groundbreaking, but until Mick Foley crashed upon the best sellers list, no one exactly was making waves in the publishing world with professional wrestling as the subject.

At the time, the steroids scandals hadn't made waves, either, but Bruno was in the midst of his virtually one-man crusade about the evils of drug abuse in the industry.

Had anyone truly heeded his words, the "what if" would be immense.

Would it be possible for Bruno to break "kayfabe" and expose the business in 1990? Not at all. Would he do so today? Well, he certainly could, but then again, what part of the business do true fans want exposed?

I don't know about the true fans of professional wrestling, but the nature of the book publishing world over the past ten years has been all about dirt, scandal and … stupidity.

Pro Wrestling Intellectual

I'm tired of reading about wrestlers who have no respect for the entertainment of their fans, or the nature of the business or the trust and emotions that were invested by the fans over decades of loving professional wrestling.

On thing I got from Bruno was that those guys who do their "shoot" interviews, and spew nothing but disdain for the fans, aren't worth the effort.

We're all in on the con, from fans to promoters to wrestlers, and everyone in between. So many books have revealed so many secrets, so many "magic tricks" and so many illusions -- both realistic and unrealistic -- that one more book on the subject of professional wrestling seems to be one more drop of water over the dam. One more drip in the ocean. One more grain of dust.

Funny, though, how much of the 1990 book that people overlook.

Bruno isn't shy about the business relationship he had with Vince McMahon Sr, nor the blackballing he received for not wanting to cave to the promoters, nor his interactions with Rogers.

Bruno isn't shy about what he saw (or who he saw doing it) in the WWF lockerrooms in the 1980's, or the way he was manipulated into wrestling again -- for the sake of his son's career.

Bruno isn't shy about his disdain for the product.

And while many cry that he is bitter and old school and out of touch, I've talked with him long enough to realize his points and his disbelief and his vast understanding of the motivations, dynamics and pure psychology that drive fans into the seats.

While Bruno may not watch today's action, he certainly follows it. And I've promised to keep mum on some of his vastly entertaining comments and insightful observations and his strong opinions on certain talents (both active and not) that have helped shape my understandings of the business over the past few months.

One Bruno secret I want to share with you -- and believe me, there's a lot of things that I've promised not to talk about, and when it comes to Mr. Sammartino, and his word, I know better than to break it.

But there's a very fun thing I've experienced with Bruno, and that's his uncanny knack for voices.

Joe Babinsack

Whether it's the "Hey Brodder" of Hulk Hogan or the raspy voice of Dick the Bruiser (or even the shrill, sissy voice of Mark Madden, squealing that he doesn't want to fight) there's a level of entertainer in Bruno that a lot of people don't get to hear.

Of course, I don't know if Bruno's going to want to do impersonations at his appearances, so don't tell him that I told you about this. Promise?

Now, I'm not exactly sure about the average fan, or the current fan, or even the old school fan, but I'm sure about one thing -- that Bruno Sammartino knows his fan base, and his fan base loves him to this day.

I've written about his appearances in Pittsburgh and the awe of his presence. I've spoken to him several times after he's done radio interviews or signings or charity appearances. And I look forward to speaking to him soon about his attendance at the big Charlotte, North Carolina event.

He has been looking forward to that event, and meeting his fans.

I've tried to connect him to the fact that all these fans want to know more about him, about his life, about the opinions he has about the industry. I'm sure there are millions, if not hundreds of thousands of fans who watched him or grew up hearing about him or just would love to know what he think's is wrong with the Business.

Call me conceited, but having talked to him for many months, I think I know some of that answer.

One thing I do have a surer understanding of is what REALLY happened during the lead up, and during the match, when Bruno Sammartino took the WWWF belt away from Buddy Rogers, and began an almost eight year run that has to be considered the crown jewel of all professional wrestling reigns.

I'm also gaining valuable insight into that run, and I have a series of questions I'll be asking soon.

I have my own theories and understandings and copious notes and a growing interest in fulfilling what certainly would be a dream assignment.

But there remains that little caveat, and I'm at a point where I do have some leads, and await some decisions, but a little public airing of the project certainly seems to be in order.

So forgive me for being a little self-serving and a little presumptuous and, quite frankly, a little giddy about the prospects of getting this deal off the ground.

Because, as far as I'm concerned, there are no books out there at this moment that could very well capture the essence of what professional wrestling really is, really was, and really could be again, like a book told to the fans by the Living Legend, Bruno Sammartino.

And that's not even considering the impressive life of the man: a man who lived (survived being a better term) through World War II; a man who willed himself to become one of the strongest men on the planet; a man who set his sights on being a professional wrestler, and didn't let politics derail his dream; and a man who, after decades of dominance in the sport, had the integrity to simply walk away from an industry that he saw was going down the wrong path.

Maybe that's not inspirational, interesting or scandal-mongering enough for some publishers, but I'm certain that there's a one out there who will think differently.

If you've got a good suggestion, I'm all ears!

And that's the gist of it. I have a few interested parties looking at a proposal, but I'm definitely looking for an answer -- from them, or from the list of twenty more publishers that I've gathered.

Currently, I'm a little busy with a few projects, and my "real" job is taking me to West Virginia for some training, so I haven't had the opportunity to speak with Bruno for a few days. I look forward to doing that and hearing about his Charlotte convention/appearance, and to see how the fans treated him there.

I'm sure we all know how they did!

SYNOPSIS OF BRUNO! THE AUTOBIOGRAPHY OF BRUNO SAMMARTINO

Sections

I) Italy: Bruno's early life, experiences in Italy and attempting to join his Father in America. Primarily, it is the story of his Mother (Emilia) and how she kept the family alive during the Nazi occupation, and how she nursed Bruno back to health afterward.

II) America: Bruno's family is reunited with Alphonso, his Father. Bruno learns that the United States is not paved in gold, and the air is worse than the old country as he settles in Pittsburgh. He begins the transformation from weakling to fanatical trainer/athlete.

III) Breaking In: The transformation is complete, as Bruno competes in bodybuilding and weightlifting competitions. He is discovered on the Bob Prince Show by Rudy Miller, and along the way, he fights a monkey, learns the ropes from big names, gets caught up in pro wrestling politics, gets blackballed, and basically quits the industry. As well, His life is transformed, as Carol delivers David, and medical bills mount.

IV) Making a Name: Chapter Canada: Bruno finally finds the opportunity he craved. He self-promotes, gets the chance to headline, and pops the crowds in Toronto and makes his name across Canada. His exploits hit the press, radio and the attention of Vince McMahon Sr, who struggles to bring Bruno back to New York City.

Chapter: Buddy Rogers: This chapter covers one of professional wrestling's greatest controversies, and most famous matches, and reveals a secret made 45 years ago. The myths surrounding the match are laid bare, and the story is told in complete fashion for the first time ever.

V) First Title Reign: Bruno holds the title for eight years, and it is a masterpiece of booking, captivating the audience and overcoming obstacles along the way. This reign will likely never be equaled, and the psychology surrounding Bruno's popularity seems to be lost on current promoters. Along the way, Bruno gets press as being among the highest paid athletes of the 1960's, and hobnobs with celebrities in various entertainment fields.

VI) Taking a Break: We discover that the world of professional wrestling was destroying bodies long before Mick Foley was walking, and that the circumstances, ring composition and toll on the body was immense. The chapter culminates in one of the most awesome displays of professional wrestling history, as Ivan Koloff stuns the crowd at Madison Square Garden by pinning the Champion.

VII) Second Title Reign: Politics are explored in depth, as Bruno is lured out of retirement. It is a series of famous matches, ongoing displays of professional wrestling greatness, and the story surrounding Bruno's near disastrous neck injury, and how he returned to the ring in a risky proposition to save the WWWF from one more financial disaster.

VIII) Semi-Retirement: We see the workings of the business and the respect that the legend of Bruno Sammartino has across the world, and in the clubs he works on a semi-regular basis. The chapter starts with the ascension of Superstar Billy Graham (and the ushering in of the age of steroids,) and culminates with the final storyline, that cemented Bruno's legend and should have launched the career of his protégé.

IX) Vince McMahon Jr. Years: Building upon the previous chapter, Bruno is lured back to the WWF by new owner Vince McMahon Jr, and after a few year away, the industry is almost irrevocably changed. But the McMahon manipulations and promises don't change, and Bruno finds himself headlining when stars cannot perform, being called to work for the sake of his son, and observing the roots of a catastrophe in the making.

X) David: The tumultuous story of Bruno and his oldest son, David, is told, exploring the rift and the political manipulations that made it happen. We also look into the UWF and what went on in that promotion.

XI) Steroids: Bruno began his crusade against the evils of steroids long before deaths became prominent. In this chapter, we explore his understandings and efforts of the issue of steroids, and his understanding of the professional wrestling lifestyle as it was, and as it had become with the nationalizing of the WWF and destruction of the regional system.

XII) The "Bitter Years": We pick up with the story of the 1990 Autobiography, and the TV appearances and outcast status of Bruno, as he toils to get the word out about what could happen with steroid abuse. Was Bruno miscast as being bitter, or was he playing the role of a Jeremiah? Time, context and perspective has proved that Bruno had a prescient understanding of what was to come.

XIII) Modern Sensibilities: The industry changed when Vince McMahon Jr destroyed kayfabe, all for the sake of a few percent of taxes in New Jersey. Since then, the world of professional wrestling went through cycles of downtime and a skyrocketing of popularity, and an irrevocable change in the relationship between fans and wrestlers. Where does Bruno Sammartino stand in the eyes of modern fans?

XIV) Life After Wrestling: What has Bruno been doing over the past fifteen years or so? We look at his participation in the Autograph shows, in the Ring of Honor promotion as a guest and legend, and in how and why he has turned his back on the current (and not-so-current) product. We also look at what Bruno has been doing, from his documentary to his love of the Opera, and finally getting a chance to be with Carol and enjoying his grandchildren.

XIV) Looking Back: Bruno Sammartino had a glorious homecoming to his native Italy, and has now seen his legendary status honored by fans in the internet age. We look at some of the myths and misconceptions, and put perspective on his career, and his accomplishments.

XV) Looking Forward: What wrestling was, can be again. There are glimmers of hope and a wealth of reference that can be taken from Bruno's approach to the sport. We look at ring psychology, the interaction with the fans, and most importantly, the illusion and the acceptance of the fans of what they see in the ring. Despite tell-alls, the dirty business of axes to grind, and the ugly truths and heartbreaking deaths of the past decade or more, professional wrestling fans still have an understanding of the sport that transcends the current product, and which Bruno still can connect with.

XVI) Responses: Much has been published by pretenders, by challengers to Bruno's status as a Living Legend, and by petty, jealous and third rate wrestling minds. In this chapter, we explore some of the painfully ignorant statements and fallacious commentary of names like Ric Flair, Bret Hart and Hulk Hogan, and provide Bruno's heartfelt responses.

XVII) Greatness: In many ways, and in a logical presentation, the claim of Bruno Sammartino as the greatest of all professional wrestlers is explored, not by the legend himself, but by his greatest supporters.

XVIII) Fans: A book on Bruno Sammartino cannot be complete without the comments from his many fans, and many peers who have always looked up to him. I will gather comments from wrestlers, fans and other names to support what Bruno has meant to many generations of fans, and to his hometown and adopted hometown, and anywhere he has went.

XX) Training: One of the enduring aspects of Bruno Sammartino's life is a passion, bordering upon fanaticism, for training and keeping physically fit. Despite serious back conditions, a broken neck, and years of pounding from other wrestlers, a full and hectic schedule, and from the ring itself, Bruno has persisted to this day in extensive training. This chapter is to serve as an inspiration for readers to be active and keep in shape.

Interspersed throughout the Book:

For perspective, we will present snippets of context, articles and photos, to explain how Bruno Sammartino fits in the cultures of several generations.

We will provide "Family Portraits" to show what was going on with his home life (or what amounted to his life away from being a world-traveling champion.) His wife Carol, his parents, his twins (Danny and Darryl) and his grandchildren will all be covered.

Pro Wrestling Intellectual

We will also provide Ten Great Wrestling Moments, showing the happenings of some of Bruno's great matches. These include his lifting of Haystacks Calhoun, his cage match with Billy Graham, his hour plus face versus face match with Pedro Morales, his posing with Hulk Hogan, his getting his neck broken by Stan Hansen, his Shea Stadium match with Larry Zbyszko, and others.

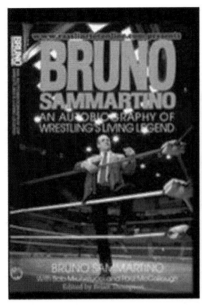

Bruno and Carol (Teyssier) Sammartino

NOW

THEN

**SEPTEMBER 12, 1959
CELEBRATING 50 YEARS OF MARRIAGE
WITH A CRUISE TO THE FRENCH AND ITALIAN RIVIERA**

Joe Babinsack

ADVENTURES IN LARRYLAND!
BY LARRY ZBYSZKO
ECW Press

This is a good read.

Larry Zbyszko writes in an easy to read and compelling manner. With his history in the industry, he is an important figure: linked to Bruno Sammartino and the pre-national WWF era, his appearances on Georgia Championship Wrestling and other regional promotions, his run as the last AWA World Heavyweight Champion (Gagne's classic promotion) and his runs in WCW (notably as ½ of the Enforcers with Arn Anderson) and his vastly interesting run as color commentator and final pop as the man who saved Nitro from the New World Order.

Or is that Odor?

The great thing about Larry's career is that he's been everywhere, and done almost everything in the business. Tag Team champion with Tony Garea. World Heavyweight Champion for Verne Gagne's fading national promotion. Western States Heritage Champion (hah!) and some memorable matches and some world traveling and some great insight into what wrestling was, and what it has become.

The one disappointing thing is the gaps in the story.

While the link to Bruno Sammartino is made clear, there's a span of time between 1973 and 1980 that really gets rushed over. There are some great scenes with Bill Watts, regional wrestling politics and the influence of Bruno in helping his career, but we don't get much of the WWWF tenure, and the tag championships and the interactions as Bruno's protégé. We get a goofy story about Haystacks Calhoun, and not much else.

Larry doesn't provide many dates, and that sort of hides the gaps. But his insight is incredible and his stories are compelling. The biggest story, of course, is the exhibition match with Bruno Sammartino and his clocking the master over the head with a chair after being "humiliated" and unable to compete fairly with Bruno.

That angle was white hot.

What Larry provides is the run up and the psychology in creating it and making it work, which he attributes to Mr. Sammartino. He also plays back on the psychology during his recreation and great match setup with Lord Steven Regal in the fading days of WCW's Saturday night show.

There are great points and great insights to be made, if you want to understand them, throughout this book. It doesn't take a reading of Glenn Gilberti's take on what's going on in TNA to understand what needs to change in the business. Reading Adventure's in Larryland! will set you straight.

What part of giving the fans what they want is so difficult to promoters these days? What part of slow and steady build ups, setting the stage and manipulating emotions is so difficult to comprehend? What part of Larry's history, and his near greatness in virtually every promotion he found himself in, is so hard to capture?

Talent isn't just what someone can do in the ring in terms of technical excellence, but then again, Larry could do that. He acted as an enforcer, then twenty years later, captured the essence of his character and entertaining ability in his role as an Enforcer with Arn Anderson. I can recall that time and that tag team. In a period when muscle-heads and complacency ruled the WCW roost, these two veterans gelled and made wrestling fun to watch.

And there's Larry, playing up his ability to generate heat by doing pretty much nothing.

Although Arn Anderson did have an issue when he did it during a sandstorm. There's a time and place for everything, I suppose. But most often Larry Zbyszko knew when to do it, and how to do it, and most importantly why to do it.

There's always a what if with careers. With Larry, you can play what if in both directions of "if he wrestled in a different decade." Imagine Larry and his look and his connections ten years earlier, starting out in the 1960's. He could have easily transitioned into the belt picture after Bruno. Imagine Larry ten years later, starting in the 1980's, and he would have been huge with his talent and his promo work during the explosion of the 1990's.

But Larry's career was top notch and undeniable.

Even past his active career, when he followed his mentor's footsteps into commentating, he was able to seize the moment and understand what the fans wanted during the whole NWO era. Fans were begging for someone to stand up for WCW. Larry was one of the last guys you'd imagine turning face, but like all great heels, he made a smooth transition.

(Larry nearly blew out Easy E's knee in training?!? Way to go, Larry! Forgive me, I jest! ;-)

Anyway, Larry almost had to sense the underlying need of the fans to rally around someone against the NWO, and he knew how to play it. So much that the powers that be (ok, not quite that name yet) played into his hands and allowed him to triumph. His ability to pop the crowd that was already big for Hogan, Hall, Nash and company trumped almost anything that group could do at the time. And they all knew it.

The most hilarious exhibit of Larry's ability to work the crowd, to deliver what the fans want, and to make them happy with what they get is this book. In particular, there's a chapter called "Love" with a three sentence length.

I guess that explains some of the gaps.

While part of me is always yearning for more about professional wrestling psychology, here's a book that satisfies some of my cravings. Larry learned from one of the all time masters, and pays homage to Bruno Sammartino throughout. His book is an excellent portrayal of some of the inner workings of pro wrestling politics, from old school cigar chomping types to suits who allowed WCW to destroy itself.

In many ways, Adventures in Larryland! is an appetizer, for someone awaiting the main course. But I mean that as no insult. Larry's book is 190 pages or so, and is a quick, good read. It makes you understand the depth of the business, despite some gaps and some areas where more details and explanations could have been presented.

But ultimately, as a history of Larry Zbyszko's life and his impact on the professional wrestling industry, and his awesome insights into the strange and not so strange workings of the business, it's well worth the read. And not an effort at all to understand or enjoy.

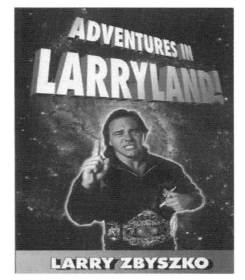

Studio Wrestling

Professional wrestling and television have a long history together, mostly starting in the 1950's. In many markets, professional wrestling, and its own form of broadcasted and controlled violence, was the highest rated of all TV shows.

In Portland, Oregon and in Memphis, Tennessee, let alone Atlanta, Chicago and New York City, professional wrestling shows – fighting for the benefit of the fans –dominated the TV landscape.

Pittsburgh, which up until the late 1960's was a Top Ten TV market, was no exception. And Pittsburgh, with its legacy of champions and hard work, it put its distinctive slant on the concept of such fight shows: a small studio where the live broadcast took place, bringing fans at home intimately into the action; colorful characters -- both in-ring and out; and a particular formula for success that combined the independence and cross-roads mentality of this region.

There are so many directions to go with what Studio Wrestling was, and remains, that a full write-up would require a book. But any brief history of professional wrestling in Pittsburgh is dominated on what happened at the Fineview studios of what was then WIIC TV, on every Saturday night, on every day of the 1960's, plus a few years before and after.

What was Studio Wrestling?

It was the fans.

Two hundred seats were available on a weekly basis, and those fans who sent in Self-Addressed Stamped Envelopes for free tickets were rewarded with seeing the action up close and personal.

Strangely enough, one remembrance of the fans was the latter period use of cardboard cutouts, providing one more quirky reality to the show.

But the biggest of all fans, in truly heroic Pittsburgh fashion, was an elderly lady named Anna Buckalew, but Pittsburghers all over the world remember her fondly as …. Ringside Rosie. Maybe the stories of the hatpins and physically assaulting the heels – the bad guys

– were a little overblown, but Rosie truly was a staple of the show, who sat in the first row every Saturday, and never missed a Civic Arena event.

Early on, crowds of wrestling fans would begin to line up at noon for the 6pm live show.

Afterwards, the fans were truly part of the show, being interviewed by Bill Cardille as the show concluded and they exited the studio, giving their immediate reactions to being part of a city's cultural landscape, while weaving themselves into the that same tapestry.

It was Bill Cardille.

He's Chilly Billy to hundreds of thousands, but to Pittsburgh's fight fans, he has almost always been the face of Studio Wrestling. It is also said that he was WIIC Program Manager Shelton Weaver's first choice for the announcer position, but Club 11 Teen Dance Party was too big a gig to turn down in 1959.

So for a few years, wrestling fans and Studio wrestling had Mal Alberts.

But Alberts left WIIC, and sometimes being the first choice is being the best choice. For the rest of Studio Wrestling's life on WIIC (long before it grabbed an "X" and became WPXI,) to watch the show was to be regaled by Cardille, who was "The Voice of Wrestling" in Pittsburgh, the favorite of fans and wrestlers alike, and the glue that kept the insanity together.

From the opening "Welcome to Studio Wrestling" to the closing interviews with the departing ringsiders, Cardille was the ultimate MC, quick with the lines and always on the ball. Whether the wording was "Where anything can happen, usually does, and probably will" or "Where anything is liable to happen, probably will, and usually does" – Chilly Billy brought the catch-phrase to the ring, or beside it, four decades before Dwayne "The Rock" Johnson.

"He added so much to it." said Bruno Sammartino.

It was an awesome roster of colorful characters.

Whether you called them "good guys," "baby-faces" or "Heroes," the fan-favorites in the ring were a bit fewer, and almost invariably side-kicks to the aforementioned Sammartino, the World Champion of the then WWWF, and for many years, the Pittsburgh promoter to boot.

Pro Wrestling Intellectual

Fan-favorites in that era were everything they were supposed to be: straight-shooters, friendly to the fans and almost ultimately successful in the ring… or ultimately vindicated by the return of the Champ himself. Fans knew Tony Marino more in his Battman costume (note the spelling, to avoid the DC Comics people!) but they certainly knew him, Dominic DeNucci and "Jumpin'" Johnny DeFazio – himself destined for Union organizing and politics.

But like professional wrestling through the ages, and fighters to this day, the most colorful – and secretly appreciated – were the bad guys.

And Pittsburgh had plenty of them.

Foremost among them? George "The Animal" Steele.

He'd call Bill Cardille "Daddy-O" and be the antithesis of his WWF days, a smooth talking villain, capable of outwrestling his good-looking opponents, and sounding more like his professorial career than his latter day craziness, when the green tongue and the chewing of turnbuckles took over the best of him.

But Steele showed the wild side when it came to the big matches. Whether DeNucci, Defazio or Sammartino, "The Animal" sought out to destroy, with a reckless abandon remembered by many. His finisher was the flying hammerlock, and he could finish the best with them.

Bruno felt his wrath on many occasions, and they had a feud that lasted decades, through gimmick matches, best of three falls matches, and the not-so-rare DQ win by one or the other of them. It has to be remembered as the greatest feud of the Pittsburgh scene.

Dick "the Bulldog" Brower was a bulging eyes madman who barked and beat up people. Gimmick wrestlers like Eric the Red; Germans like Waldo von Erich, Kurt von Hess, Hans Schmidt; and wildmen like Pampiro Firpo and Killer Brooks, all enjoyed success, bringing a diversity of characters and many a bad guy for fans to want to see beaten.

Seeing guys get beat is always a secret vice of fight fans. Seeing guys who seem unbeatable get beat is a bigger thrill.

Such was the case with Killer Kowalski, a man who inspired fear in the fans, fear that he would annihilate the good guy, and fear of his crazed look and serious demeanor, that maybe he'd come through the TV and do something despicable.

It was a unique show, with a distinctive local flavor.

Who can? Ameri-CAN!!!!

How many times was that commercial done live in the studio? How many fans can remember the pitch and the voice of Pirates legend and all-time baseball great Pie Traynor?

Traynor gained a new measure of recognition long after his playing days, and his stats began fading from memory (as if a batting average of .320, 2416 hits and reputation as the greatest Third Baseman of all time could ever diminish!)

He was the resident old-timer who did the American Heating Commercials, but whose presence tied Studio Wrestling into Pittsburgh's long and storied sports history.

Studio Wrestling opened with the distinctive "El Capitan" by John Philip Sousa.

It had that distinctive bell, and the announcer's favorite phrase "And in this corner, from parts unknown…"

Everything associated with Studio Wrestling became larger than life, and such was the fate of fame of its referees: Paddy Grimes, Izzy Moidel and Andy DePaul.

Moidel was said to have beaten Rocky Marciano in an amateur boxing match. DePaul was a noted boxer, inducted into the Golden Gloves Hall of Fame.

It was a revolving door of talented wrestlers.

Pittsburgh was a stopping point for wrestlers headed in and out of the WWWF. It was a well connected promotion, no matter who was actually running it, and saw the kind of rotation of talent that kept the sport viable for decades.

National stars like Johnny Valentine had long runs in Pittsburgh. Local talents, like Baron Mikel Scicluna, became so great as role-players that they were later seen on nationally broadcast TV. Dominic DeNucci launched his career in Pittsburgh, and became a champion in Australia, and known across the world.

And then there are guys like John L. Sullivan.

Pro Wrestling Intellectual

Sullivan gained greater fame as Johnny Valiant, but his career was made as a strutting heel in Pittsburgh; his talent talked up matches, riled up the crowds, and he had great in-ring action.

The names of the greats were impressive: Giant Baba from Japan, Da Crusher (Lisowski) from Chicago; Cowboy Bill Watts, Haystacks Calhoun; local favorites like Ace Freeman and Johnny Defazio and Chief White Owl; and big guys like Dr. Bill Miller (the veterinarian from Ohio) and Gorilla Monsoon (born in New York, not Manchuria.)

But the point is, Pittsburgh fans had a strong understanding of the fight game, and a stronger appreciation for talent they saw in the ring. Johnny Valentine was a no-nonsense fighter. George Steele was a refined gentleman with a wild side when it came to the big fights. Sullivan and other heels made the fans want to see them get their beatings.

All of it revolved around the fights.

It was professional wrestling as it was meant to be.

Strange how the fight game has turned profitable with MMA, and turned into sports entertainment with the modern version of professional wrestling.

Pro Wrestling was once the place where fights were the staple, and building up fights that the public wanted to see was the vehicle to success. Main events made the big shows at the Civic Arena, but the events were all about the atmosphere, the involvement of the crowds, and appealing to the sensibilities of the fans.

Today?

Let's not start about today. Today's fights are found at MMA events, where matchmaking makes sense, where colorful characters aren't the brainstorming of out-of-work Hollywood scriptwriters, and where paying your ticket means watching what you expect, not being insulted with vulgarities and bad showmanship.

It was Bruno Sammartino.

Bruno wasn't just the greatest wrestler of all time, he was Pittsburgh's perennial champion. He was the man in this city, and the ultimate of all champions of the 1960's and 1970's.

Few could beat Bruno, and the few that did became legends of their own. But Bruno also ran the promotion that stocked Studio Wrestling for a several year span, holding one of the most prestigious belts, defending the belt upwards of twenty eight days a month, and all the while putting together the shows that Pittsburgh fans rarely missed.

The Italian Superman, the Living Legend, the man who held a Championship Belt longer (it's the duration, not the number,) than any other man in the history of the sport.

Few could challenge Bruno. Few ever dared to do so.

Bruno's grasp of professional wrestling is as great as his reputation as an honest man, a man with integrity in a sport with little of it, and his record threatening athleticism – he truly was a power lifter, and recorded feats of strength that impress the hardcore weightlifters of today.

But more than anything, the connection between Bruno Sammartino and the fans lives on, even with the legacy of Studio Wrestling.

It was violence made mainstream.

Studio Wrestling, above it all, was about the matches. Professional wrestling, despite all the guffaws and the whispering of its true nature, was about appealing to the fight fans in all of us.

Today, in an arena with many thousands of fight fans, we are living the atmosphere and the reputation and the expectations of those Studio Wrestling fans from way back in the day.

We want to see some great fights. We want to see championships on the line. We want to come to the big event, to see the big time atmosphere, and to enjoy watching one guy beat another guy, all in the spirit of competition.

Rules in the days of professional wrestling were unwritten and civilized.

Today, despite the media sensationalism, MMA is regulated even closer than the days of Studio Wrestling. For all the brutality certain elements of the media want to imbue upon the modern day fight fan, think about this: have you ever seen a fight end with a wooden (or steel) chair to someone's head?

Pro Wrestling Intellectual

Back in the day, fight fans were professional wrestling fans, and were boxing fans, and wanted to see the action in the ring (today's octagon) and knew the good guy from the bad guy, knew the rules of conduct and the expectations of a fair fight.

Studio Wrestling extolled the virtue of the clean fighter, but fans took glee in the comeuppance of the bad guy. But they also took entertainment in seeing the fights, staged as they were, with an eye towards understanding the presentation, and believing in the nature of the sport.

Pittsburgh's professional wrestling legacy is all about a dominant TV show that, for lack of better words, glorified violence.

It mostly kept it in the ring, and mostly presented a morality play, but it was what it was.

Today's fight fans can keep the tradition by watching professionally trained, professionally sanctioned, and officially regulated fighters do battle in the center of a huge arena, and enjoy the outcomes, just as they have done for decades.

From November 15th, 1959, (newspaper ads featured Mr. Moto, the Great Scott, Killer Kowalski, Argentina Rocca and Hillbilly Calhoun appearing) until August 3rd, 1973, Studio Wrestling was THE show on Pittsburgh TV, launched by a conglomerate of professional wrestling's greatest promoters: Toots Mondt, Vince McMahon Sr, and Fred Kohler.

In 1974, Studio Wrestling was cancelled by Channel 11.

Management wanted to shift the reputation of the station from that channel with the wrestling, into one based on news reporting. It already laid the groundwork of professional wrestling's demise, by moving the times, by renaming the show, and then claiming that the fading rating reflected a lack of interest by the fans.

Afterwards, it was a fading sunset of a show, renamed Super Pro Wrestling and appearing on WPGH Channel 53. Studio Wrestling faded from TV broadcasts, but never from the hearts of Pittsburgh's fight fans.

And to many, the belief is that the hearts of Pittsburgh's fight fans yearn for something to replace that tradition.

Joe Babinsack

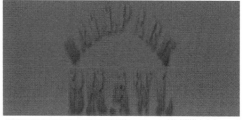

DVDReviews

All Logos TM and/or © their respective companies.

Set It Off
Absolute Intense Wrestling

Different to me is a good thing.

AIW is definitely different. It's pro wrestling, that's for sure, but the overall vision and presentation isn't quite what you might expect.

The primary impact is a camera angle taken over a corner post, not from the traditional side/over the ropes. This presents an interesting perspective for the viewer and distorts some of the size and heights involved. I'm not about to get into a discussion of art theory, not do I want to start considering that this would be Rob Liefeld's dream wrestling promotion, but it is a distinctly interesting twist.

There is also a darkness issue, which I imagine some might find difficult to adjust to. The intros of new wrestlers are hard to follow (although the intro video packages seem quite well put-together.) When the match starts, the lighting improves, but the fans are drowning in darkness. Take that for what you want.

Absolute Intense Wrestling is an Ohio based promotion in operation for two and a half years.

Overall, it's matches are well put together and they make excellent use of top notch indy talent, home grown wrestlers who are capable of mixing it up, and getting back to that vision thing, a definite sense of direction, with interesting factions, a mix of heavy satire, as well as an over-the-top feel to some of the angles.

I also greatly appreciate the attempts at thinking out of the box.

For one thing, the promotion touts its motto as "Philly is Dead!" Which has a hell of a lot of levels of consideration. Some of the workers are Pittsburgh based, some (especially guest wrestlers) of course have the Philly connection. With so many groups running out of Philly, it has the sense of both being contrary and satirical, being that Philly remains arguably the current hotbed of indy wrestling, but then again, if you're tired of everything coming from that city, here's your alternative.

Like I said -- thinking out of the box and with a vision of the big picture.

Joe Babinsack

Music was interesting. I thought they did too many snippets and not enough entrance music fare, but it was hardcore metal and the like, interspersed with gimmick related varieties. Nice touch.

While the "featured" skit may not be entirely new, it was a nice way to change things up and present fodder for an ongoing feud. The action was out of the building and nicely set up. IT was a great change of pace and really cool to see the "he got taken out before the event" to be seen, not just heard.

I will certainly warn the reader that its going to take a few matches to get a solid "feel" for the presentation. The announce team is a bit of a distraction -- an overlay that seems to be live to the crowd. And again, the visuals, with the perspective and the letterbox/movie tone format, as well as the darkness, takes some adjustment.

The lead announcer is quite up to speed with the terms and maneuvers (except for a call of a quebrada as an Asai Moonsault, but who's being picky there when he can call a Koppo kick and a half dozen other Low-Ki specialties in an excellent, fast paced match later on the DVD!) - and the lead has a strong announcing cadence and voice, there is a redundancy with the second voice, being of the "me too" "wow look at that" mentality.

We start the "Set It Off" DVD with an interesting match. "Upgrade" Tyrone Evans is a massive physical specimen. Johnny Gargano is looking like a lightweight. The match, quite frankly, ends up with no relation to my expectation. Not that it wasn't hard fought or reasonably solid, but just like I said, not what I expected. As an opener, it was very good for a variety of reasons. The number two slot is labeled "Thrillbilly Attacks" on the match list.

That's important.

It's a definite homage to ECW's "911" wrestler, and a strange way to reference Philly being dead (although, well, who else has done that bit since ECW?) I just loved the angle, it just was confusing coming into a promotion I've not seen before and seeing some rather horrific work, before looking at the back cover for the line up and not seeing the listing, just this "Thrillbilly Attacks" label.

When I got it, I got it. And I liked it much.

Next up is "The Savage" against "The Masked Fish" This had me worried big time in terms of racial connotations. Then comes out a white guy doing a Louis Farrakhan knock off, and a pasty white Kamala looking fellow. The package and dynamics of the roles, charismatic and bombastic manager and dim witted beast, would be explosive with certain racial composition. Here, its sets the stage for AIW's quirky, satirical direction, and is equally entertaining and though provoking.

The match was merely a backdrop, but that's alright here.

The Absolute Intense style really busted out with the four way tag match. Way too "busy" but a great introduction to some of the factions of the promotion. "Alpha Beta Duke" is a frat boy association lead by a really thick and powerful guy by the name of Duke. They do some beer bong stuff which I thought wasn't exactly appropriate, but hell, we're past the age of Austin.

Another group is the "Cut Throat Crew" which is an 'ahoy ye maties' pirates gimmick (as opposed to a perennial jobber team patterned after Pittsburgh's baseball team.)

[As an aside, the major issue I encountered here was the prop of a sword. Later on, a member of Revelation 13 carried a machete. Now, perhaps I'm being overly picky, but it a wrestling promotion replete with dives and lots of action, I don't think it safe to have guys walking around with pointy objects.]

"The Virgin Slayers" are a high fashion gimmick, with a porno type intro (no sex or nudity, but hell, it was leading up to it.) They are smaller but highly athletic.

The last of the four is the tag champs, "Q&A" who are Luchadores and impressive. The only odd thing was that they came out without their belts, and it's obviously an ongoing issue, which may be tied into the Cut Throat Crew's trunk of booty, but then again, who knows.

The match was lucha libre style. Definitely inspired and fast paced and interesting all at once. The dives were spectacular and even the big guys got involved. There was the obligatory homoerotic stuff which always makes me frown, and it went a bit too physical for my interests, but not long enough to make me scream about it.

Duke is definitely a player, though I must admit that the proportions of the guys are hard to figure with the perspective. Announced weights are somewhat low, but they do a great presentation (ECW style, again) of keeping the combatants on the same par -- something TNA should have understood long before they hired Kevin Nash. But I digress.

Disc One (two disc set -- I must add that the graphics, wrapper and overall presentation, despite the darkness feel, was beyond the level of any other indy level DVD I'm used to. The sound quality was horribly inconsistent, but aside from that, top notch stuff.) ends with the cruiserweight level championship three way match.

Joe Babinsack

The champ is Starless, whom I don't know much about. He's up against talented veteran Super Hentai from the Pittsburgh area, and Dios Salvador.

The match is a bit short, but the finish is really interesting. It sort of came out of nowhere, but in a fashion that was either so worked to be inexplicably interesting, or so coincidental I don't know how it can be replicated on a larger screen (but certainly should be done.)

I'll let your imagination run, but let me know if you watch it and think the same. There area few spots throughout where there's a similar feel - one guy can't get the other up for a suplex or such, but goes back immediately and rolls with it. I really dig it if its intended, because it gives the work a feel of being realistic, not smooth.

Now that I think about it, the featured skit I talked about concerned a match between Jimmy Jacobs and, in reality MDogg20. The Dogg took out Jay Violence before the festivities began, and they aired the "video" of the assault. It's not listed on the rundown. Cool.

The match itself was excellent stuff. MDogg is the heel and seemingly a veteran of the promotion. Jacobs is the guest. Nice heel/face work to boot.

Disc Two has a factional tag team war between the "Sweet Dude Club" and the lead heels, Revelation 13.

The Sweet Dude Club are apparently stripper types, think Lover Boy and others from Mexico. Great looking physiques. "Deviant" is a main player in the promotion, looking like a cross between Batista and John Cena (and I do not joke here.) I don't care for the name, but the guy's got the stuff on the mic and in the ring. The interplay between Deviant and Vincent Nothing as the prime factional involved feud of the promotion is great.

Nothing is the leader of Revelation 13. He's got the chaos symbol on his shoulder and portions of that eight pointed star on his shorts. (I'm a big Michael Moorcock (Elric) fan from way back, with various connections to chaos (as a word and philosophy) so this is way too cool for me.)

The faction has that nifty satirical bent on religion that is both compelling and dangerous and interesting. "Christian Faith" is the Abyss like member of the faction, and Butcher carries a machete and sports camouflage pants. As long as the satire keeps around the line between subversive and overt dissing of people's faiths, I'm cool with it. (I love the band Ministry despite some of it's over the top, likely super-anti-religious strands, but as long as there's a give and take, I don't sneer at rants against organized religion. Don't agree though!)

The war between Vincent Nothing and Deviant is ongoing and with a quick glimpse at other DVDs, continues to grow.

The factions are always desirable in my view of pro wrestling. They allow for more interactions, set up inevitable angles, and allow feuds to grow and develop without overkilling particular match ups. Anyway, this is a solid tag match, with the dives I'm beginning to expect and some really dangerous bumps. More of a power based style, and by the way, it's a tables match. Clearly, with Deviant as a member of one faction, he's the feature attraction. And he very well delivers.

Next up is Low-Ki against AIW's Kano. I'm sure Low-Ki needs no introduction (though I'll be sure to give him a bio sooner than later, even though he's mired in TNA. Kano is obviously the AIW version of the high flying, danger defying role. This match goes longer than 15 minutes, and I didn't know that other than the announcements at the five, ten and fifteen minute marks. It was that solid.

It was another example of the promotion using guests to further its storylines, develop its own talent, and create measuring sticks to judge its work.

In this case, the AIW guys prove they can hang with the best. Too much action to start calling it (and I've got a main event and another major player to discuss) but the announcer was on the money in calling Low-Ki's offense, and Kano got a lot of the match with which to shine. Check this one out.

"East Side Eddie" against "Johnny Beef" was inexplicitly in the next position, but then again, perhaps to spotlight some AIW talent and transition. Solid work.

Raymond Rowe is an up and coming name. He's on my radar from seeing him on IWC's DVD from a few months back. Like I said earlier, size can be deceptive, but I believe he has it. He's physically most readily envisioned by thinking of the WWE's Albert (now New Japan's Giant Bernard) sans facial jewelry. But he don't work like Albert did.

I hate to say it, and you may take exception, but I'm seeing someone who reminds me of Stone Cold Steve Austin in the ring. Not so much technical expertise, but sheer brutality and realism. He's got that sort of mannerism that screams "I'm going to kick your ass" and then he does it. He sells, he knows the game and he's building up an excellent aura around him.

And he's going to be a player.

Rowe comes with the Path of Resistance, sort of imbuing the Taz FTW attitude with a posse of white bandana gang-bangers. While the appearance is impressive, the drawback is the reality that having eight or so guys around the ring does present an ongoing interference situation that doesn't always work well.

Rowe is pitted against "Romeo Vino" in what is obviously a mafia gang war that again has been going on for a while.

I love how Rowe comes out and says "I made a mistake" and they play on that throughout the match.

The finish is just brutal. But the war isn't over.

The Main Event has "Classic" Colt Cabana challenging AIW Absolute Champion Vincent Nothing. Nothing has his posse at the ringside as well, but they worked it rather fine. Cabana helped set up the match in the opening, with a speech. I don't think it was "classic" Cabana work, but he helps to create a strong championship match.

Somewhere in the opening minutes is this weird noise, which the announcers put over as a message to Nothing "from his Lord."

Weird stuff.

But overall, it's a strong match and worth watching. AIW may not be for you, but with nicely timed matches (several over ten minutes) and a distinct atmosphere and vision of the promotion, it has the feel of something quite different but very interesting.

There are a few flaws, and a few over-the-top discussions of previous angles (one where a women wrestler is announced to have lost her baby in an angle -- not appropriate, to me, but hey, I'm not booking it) which sort of need to be ironed out, and that sound quality (blaring intros, soft mic work) that probably have improved over the past year.

I'm definitely into this group and I have more DVDs to review. I had hoped to be watching them live in Pittsburgh last night, but paperwork and other issues got into the way. Sorry for the long review, but take that as another level of my interest and appreciation for an ALTERNATIVE product.

Ballpark Brawl III
Canadian Carnage

I had planned on reviewing a book (Bang Your Head, the Real Story of the Missing Link) but I took a few minutes to look at the Ballpark Brawl and was so impressed that I stopped reading and kept watching. The Ballpark Brawls are a more than annual event in Buffalo, featuring top notch matches, main event talent and huge names from the past.

The third installment features a Hart Foundation Reunion, said to be the first time Brett, Jim Neidhart and Jimmy Hart appeared in the same ring in fifteen years. And for fans who want to see more of Brett, here's a great opportunity. He doesn't speak too much, but he introduces the DVD, presents the Natural Heavyweight Championship Trophy to the tournament winner, and participates in that reunion moment.

Although the moment is far more epic than the duration of the event, it highlights a card that introduces the next generation of the Hart family legacy, with Harry Smith and Nattie Neidhart making their American pro wrestling debuts, and Teddy Hart shining in a pair of high profile matches.

Considering that the last down time of the WWE started to turn around with the last great Hart Family grouping, it isn't a stretch to wonder if the soon-to-debut Harry Smith can be packaged with a few of his cousins for this era's Hart Foundation.

Perhaps Teddy can grow out of his 'work everyone' mentality -- overselling of worked leg injuries (only to somersault back into the ring after he's 'fooled' everyone) – he certainly can make use of his name, talents and potential. Smith certainly has the size and wrestling base to be a major force in the industry. And Jim's crazy girl would certainly be a great addition to the WWE women's roster.

But I don't want to give the impression that this DVD is all about the Hart legacy and future, even though it weaves its way across most of the matches.

The opening match is a nice angle, with Jimmy Hart offering a contract to Jonny Puma. Well, let me step back a moment, because the actual opening is a montage of clips from previous Brawls, with Raven vs Jarrett all over it, plus the Bret Hart introduction.

Insight from Senior Writer Dan Murphy is presented throughout the DVD, mostly in a small inset. Along with the crisp production values, it really sets the product above most independent level productions, and also puts it above most of TNA's offerings -- with the ability to watch particular matches, Murphy's insight and setting up of the matches, slow motion (sponsored by Mighty Taco!) and multiple camera angles.

Joe Babinsack

The participants are introduced with a screen listing statistics and finishing maneuvers, which makes for a great overview for fans not familiar with the wrestlers. And the announcing is far and above anything I would have imagined. Ivan the Impaler and Scotty Bender offer a great blend of observations, appreciation and comedy that put them at a level above the national guys.

Getting back to the opener, the set up was great. Jimmy Hart putting over the local guy, and the viewers being reminded that Hart and Jonny Puma were in a DJ challenge on the last Ballpark Brawl. Then Puma makes an open challenge, and well, if you didn't expect a squash, with one person taking all the bumps and the other guy getting over, then I don't know what you would have expected.

The NEO Spirit Pro Independent Title was up for grabs between "Completely" Cody Steele and "Dangerboy" Derek Wylde. The angle with Jennifer Blake turned into a real life, unadvertised stip in the end. These two pulled out a pretty strong match, and it was packaged nicely with the angle, the commentary and the feel of an important event. I just hope the winner can look past the "Don't trust a blonde in wrestling" comment from the announcers.

This third Brawl was built around the finals of the Natural Heavyweight Championship, and while the matches were great, the seeding was never really shown. Nonetheless, a matchup between Ron Killings and Abyss brought forth some quality action. Killings shows time and time again why he was two time NWA Champion, and his work on the stick is equally impressive. Abyss remains one of the better big guys around, selling and still looking like a monster.

The finish was way too telegraphed by the announce crew (probably the only weak spot of their game) but removing the two biggest names obviously allowed others to shine and undoubtedly prevented any issues with TNA – as well as elevating the quality of the participants in the tourney. I have to give it to the promotion, since paying for names like these without delivering a satisfying end to their match is a risk.

The Tournament continued with an interesting match between Petey Williams and Harry Smith, and the winner would move on to face Teddy Hart. The outcome of this match, considering the theme of the night, is not difficult to figure out, but the performances of Williams and Smith was exceptional.

Among other things (like a legacy and the physical tools,) Harry Smith shows on this DVD is a keen understanding of the sport and a willingness to sell. Already he shows ability beyond his relative inexperience and a presence that allowed him to keep up with Petey Williams.

It was my first look at Nattie Niedhart, and she shares a lot of the same qualifications as Smith. And she was excellent in a brief verbal encounter with Traci Brooks, combining aspects of her bombastic father with a strong sense of delivery. Her work in the ring was equally impressive. The obvious knock is going to be how she compares to the bubble-headed, anorexic 'diva' type the WWE seems hell-bent to push these days, but by no means does Niedhart fail in that measure. Besides, she has thing the WWE women need to play off of: someone that can work a match, deliver believable moves and portray power and charisma equal to the task.

The show-stealing match may very well be the one between Christopher Daniels and the Amazing Red. It is rare that someone can outshine and outpace the "Fallen Angel" but Red certainly is up to the task. When Red delivered a Missile Dropkick, he came down from such a height that it looked like Sen-she's double-foot stomp. Yet he was halfway across the ring! (admittedly, the ring in use was a bit on the smallish size.)

Daniels kicked out of that spectacular move, and Red returned the favor after a true-to-form Best Moonsault Ever. It built to a satisfying conclusion after finishers were traded.

The Hart Foundation Reunion took place before the Harry Smith/Teddy Hart match, and kept Bret out to watch the match at ringside and deliver the trophy to the winner. I know this match was reminiscent of the famed Bret/Davey Boy match from Wembley, because it was brought up by the introductory piece and the announce crew. This was a solid match between two guys groomed to be lasting stars in the business and a great chance to see Smith before he debuts soon on Raw.

Thankfully, the WWE Creative was not involved in this finish, and we had no interference or breaking of the trophy over the head of the winner.

The last match is a Tables, Ladders and Chairs affair between past, present and future hardcore high flyers. With Teddy Hart showing strong influences by Sabu and the excellence reminiscent of his uncle, and his other opponent – AJ Styles, this was a very fascinating match. High flying, fast paced and quite on target throughout, this never felt like a spot-fest. Although I'm somewhat annoyed by the overly comedic aspects of the typical three-way spots, there is an innovative sequence in the early stages of the match that needs to be seen. Later, there is a series of dives that shines a spotlight on the death-defying talents of this intergenerational dream match.

Whether through top notch talent, excellent matches or valuable insight and entertaining angles, there are few DVD's out there that put forth this level of effort and production values and I strongly recommend Ballpark Brawl III for your professional wrestling enjoyment.

Joe Babinsack

Better Than Our Best
Ring of Honor Milestone Series
www.rohwrestling.com

I have two major confusions in the pro wrestling industry today. One is the continued disdain for tag team wrestling by the "major" promotions. The other is the continued obscurity of Ring of Honor among the more "mainstream" fans.

Every continued complaint, observation and disgust with the 800 pound gorilla that dominates this sports entertainment niche is turned around in the ROH promotion. On the contrary, we consistently see in ROH a highly involved, highly vocal and highly appreciative fans, a booking mindset that allows the slow builds, emotional feuds and meaningful stipulations, coupled with either the best talent available on the independent scene, not to mention the best use of various guest talent, the build up of new stars, and the intelligent presentation of modern twists of old school staples. Add to that an underscored manipulation of emotions, an ongoing development of characters and a traditional build up of storylines.

What more can a promotion provide to make it an interesting product?

How about a variety of styles, performed at the utmost of dedication, involving innovative talent and creativity unseen on the bigger stages, not to mention the ability and a willingness to expand the envelope of pro wrestling expectations?

Better Than Our Best isn't just a trite title. It builds upon the standards of excellence and expectations of the Ring of Honor promotion. But this event isn't just more of the same, or even just raising the bar of expectations. I defy anyone to point out a card that has more styles, more events of note and more displays of top notch professional wrestling and storyline than this DVD.

While ROH is often relegated to this obscure, super-hard-core fan base that lives for one hour draws between exceptional talent that is too small for the WWE, that simply cannot be said after watching this DVD. Of the seven matches shown, there isn't one that doesn't merit its placement on the best matches of the year. Five of them are notable for not only showcasing top talent but for featuring distinct styles not readily seen on prime time TV, cable or not.

ROH's purported staple has been its championship matches, and this is one more Bryan Danielson exhibition that proves his ability to channel the champs of ages past. Furthermore, ROH has proven once again its ability, above and beyond all other current organizations, to take a name familiar to the masses, package that talent, and present an off-the-charts main event match.

Here, Lance Storm isn't a mired-in-the-midcard above average talent just going through the motions. He takes that negative energy and his own familiarity to the wrestling fans, and cuts a promo than no one in a decade had enough confidence to produce.

Once again, Danielson takes it up a notch. What else is there to say?

But the essence of this particular DVD is the displays of styles. The ROH championship style is one – technically sound, submissions based and laden with counters, mat wrestling and using a few high spots as well as a build to a satisfying finish.

The six man match is already one whispered in legend and knocking on the door of match of the year. It was one of those rare matches that you simply didn't want to end, and that is the only disappointing aspect of it.

The only way I can describe the style, and the pushing of the envelope of the talent involved, notably the Dragon's Gate wrestlers, who comprised one team (and one person of the Embassy team) was the full use of the three dimensions of the ring.

While criss-crossing runs have been around for decades, it has almost been entirely relegated to warm-ups and some comedy spots in the middle of a throw-away match. The Dragon's Gate crew build upon the notion, attacking from various angles and taking the double team, dual team and triple team action to another level.

Have you seen a triple drop kick? Can you imagine what it takes to innovate such a spot, and can you imagine what it looks like? And its not a simple line up of three guys expanding the old Rock-n-Roll express finisher. It's something else entirely.

Thus the match unfolds at a hectic pace, but not at a pace that outdistances the crowd. Like true pros, the Dragon's Gate crew works the crowd and works the storytelling of the match. Watch this match alone, and complaining about the deficiencies of other promotions will be quickly forgotten.

(I'm still debating the satirical prospects of one of the announcers saying "what a maneuver!" after rattling off the names of a few dozen cutting edge moves before and after. That comment was a Vince McMahon catch-phrase during his announcing era of the 1980's, whenever he saw anything more complex than a punch, kick or maybe a piledriver.)

The true world's tag team champions of the past year, Roderick Strong and Austin Aries, put on an excellent display of traditional tag team wrestling. While the six man match was more Lucha, this match ended up being more "hot tag" centered, but also taken to the year 2006, with innovative holds and the All Japan tag main event style of the 1990's.

The strange part of this match is that the opponents are called "Blood Generation" – the Dragon's Gate team lead by Cima, partnered with Naruki Doi. Even I overlooked this match on the line-up, not readily associating Cima – and his reputation as a great heel and innovative wrestler (now with All Japan.)

Aries and Strong have been the greatest tag team of the year, and this match was their first defense of the ROH titles, which raised the bar to a height only they could match consistently for months.

Once again, words pale in describing the action, and the blood (hardway or not) only heightened the intensity of the match, without being gratuitous. I simply cannot fathom how wrestling promoters could watch a match like this and not feature such a match on a weekly basis. Tag matches get the fans involved, stoke emotions and present ample opportunities of innovation, the drama of double teams as well as the ability to stretch out booking and build variations into the expectations of the fans.

How about a short interlude before the real main event?

I watched enough ROH to know a couple of things. One, Ricky Reyes was pushed to be the next Taz – a submissions master with a bad attitude, who was headed to the top. Two, the wrestler called Delirious was a hilariously crazy promo cutter, with a wild and frenetic style, but who was nothing more than a jobber to the stars.

In a clinic in long term booking, ability to create stars, and excellent use of available talent, the angle unfolded to perfection. Stir in Jimmy Cornette as the credible authority figure, setting up a logical and realistic stipulation, and this stripped down, throw-away character, wearing a mask and channeling the Ultimate Warrior's insane cadence, moves from enjoyable entertainer to credible opponent.

All that and the debut of a rather interesting variant on the cobra-clutch.

Pro Wrestling Intellectual

And then comes the fourth major style, as arguably Delirious embodies the ROH style, but the variant on expectations and excellence of the angle took it to a noteworthy level.

One may say that ROH is all about the technical wrestling, the dedication of its talent and, above all, the sense of respect for the action, the fans and the opponents. So how is it that an absolute bloodbath is what I'm touting as the most important match on the DVD?

Set up by an impromptu interruption of Commissioner Cornette, the oft thought of comedy figure by the name of Colt Cabana, demands a "Chicago Street Fight" and before anyone can think it merely a cute name, the intro video package to the feud sets the stage for violence, mayhem and an atmosphere of war unseen even in the vaunted "Hell in a Cell" attempts to spike PPV buys.

While I can see arguments that much of this match, its set up and the drama would be unacceptable to network censors, one cannot dismiss the efforts nor the presentation. We've got a fork, a bottle of Drano gel, rubbing alcohol and a noose. Add to that a ladder used as a weapon of bodily destruction (rather than a launching point) a gruesome shot of blood pouring from the head of one of the combatants, and an utterly dangerous situation involving a rehash of the Public Enemy's invitations to fans to throw chairs.

Thing is, instead of using that insanity to put a punctuation on the finish, they used it to set the stage for the finish.

What's great about the match is the inability of a fan to know who won, this many months later. I was actually surprised at the outcome, probably because I'm so accustomed to the expected wrestling nonsense, instead of logic, a slow build and the necessities for a clean finish to a long, violent and bloody war. If you think about it, only one man could win, and only one thing could happen after the match, when a noose and more destruction is threatened.

And I'm not about to spoil either of those great moments. It's too cheap, and its not fair to ROH to spill the beans. Pay your ten bucks or so and get this Milestone DVD product. And if you're not an ROH fan after it, I don't know why you call yourself a pro wrestling fan.

Joe Babinsack

Clash against Cancer DVD
Keystone State Wrestling Association (KSWA)

When professional wrestling gets stripped down to its core, when it interacts with its fans, when it takes itself just seriously enough, and when it knows what its role is, and strives to entertain, that's what I call good wrestling.

KSWA is a local Pittsburgh outfit that puts on regular shows, maintains a solid core of regulars, and really knows what its version of professional wrestling is all about.

KSWA is good wrestling.

Having been to a show recently, I was well prepared to see their latest two events on DVD, as I had some understanding of the wrestlers, the crowd and the atmosphere. Despite some minor complaints, the DVD captured that feel of the live shows nicely.

(My biggest gripe was that during the National Anthem, we got a shot of the ring post, and not the flag!)

KSWA typically draws upwards of 200 fans. For the Clash against Cancer, they drew a record 300 fans. This is an operation that knows what its doing. Running the same location, with mostly the same crowd, and a stable roster of wrestlers, it is growing its fan base.

If you like the Full Impact Pro promotion, you'll probably appreciate the minimalistic approach of KSWA. Admittedly, it doesn't have the talent roster of FIP or the name level guests, but this is a group that works hard, knows its role and the matchmaking is well put together.

Of the eight matches on the show, all were of good quality. I never got an impression that anyone was ever lost, and the number of botched moves was impressively small.

Admittedly, the pace of the action was a bit slow at times, and the small ring and rather low ceiling limits the action to some degree. But the action is of the kind that once you understand the KSWA "take" on professional wrestling, it really grows on you.

With a crowd of all ages, and sometimes frighteningly young, the promotion caters to a family type show. There isn't blood, and the level of violence is kept manageable, as is the language.

Strangely enough, there is a group of hard core regulars who gather at the back bar of the place (The Moose is a social club) called the "KSWA Krazies" that are obviously well schooled in ECW lore and audience participation.

Chants and a rather rowdy atmosphere can be expected at the KSWA events. The other great thing about the promotion is the interaction. The action does spill out into the crowd, but the card is interrupted often by giveaways, door prizes and a 50/50 raffle. While that sort of stuff isn't going to fly on a national stage, it reinforces the notion that a promotion needs to cater to its audience and appreciate it, not just expect it to appear.

The ring announcing duties are capably handled by "Trapper Tom," whose voice lends a distinct professionalism and a sense of controlling the flow of the card, much like a Howard Finkel.

The only real complaint about the DVD was a lack of graphics – no matter who the announcer, you're just not going to figure out the names! On the other hand, the 'music video' recap was a lot more polished than I would have expected from a single camera taping.

Anthony Alexander vs Del Douglas. "Double A" is the big guy in KSWA, and holds the Golden Triangle Championship.

Douglas is the "King of Millvale" – which is the community across the river from the home base in Lawrenceville. Douglas won a tourney last year to gain the crown and the accompanying chants of "Burger King!"

This match-up will decide the challenger for KSWA Champion Shaw Blanchard's defense later that night. "AA" has size, but is a bit plodding. That he uses a few of Hogan's holds isn't that much of a surprise (despite his dark hair,) but even so, he does have a larger hold base than Hogan ever shows in the US.

The match is pretty straight forward. Double A gets most of the offense, then Douglas comes back after some heel moves. Shawn Blanchard comes out to distract, but ends up cheering on the match.

Joe Babinsack

Anthony then emulates Stone Cold Steve Austin, setting up the belt versus belt main event level match later in the show.

Trapper Tom keeps the matches flowing, and announces a mean ticket for door prizes.

The Blood Beast is out next for a rather quick squash of Joey Quervo. Da Beast is a stereotypical worshipper of the devil. Quervo would be a bad stereotype of a drunken Luchador if he wasn't announced as being in a "twelve-step program"

Trapper Tom and KSWA owner Bobby O conduct a brief interview segment. The Latin Assassin is brought out, setting up his imminent return, and announces that his last act as commissioner will be as the special enforcer for the "I Quit" match that will be among the three main events at the next event.

(Promoting your next show ahead of time!!!)

Ali Kaida versus Shane Star. Kaida is the co-holder of the KSWA tag titles with Baracus. Star is ½ of the Lost Boys tag team. Old school split the tag into two singles matches concept. Despite a size differential, Star gets in some offense. Kaida, sporting nifty gold AK-47's on his pants, gets the win with a rather quick roll-up.

Biker Al versus Dr. Devastation Lou Martin is next. I don't think Lou Martin is really a doctor. Biker Al is a rather scrawny motorcycle gang lookalike. Al's angle is that he's rallying to be voted as the new commissioner for the Fan Fest event that will be the next KSWA show.

His attempt to rally the crowd is to install his own referee, and use heel tactics to attempt to win the match.

Somehow, I think he's the favored son candidate for the office.

Lou Martin is a solid wrestler who makes his opponents look better. There's got to be a better slot on the card for him. The interplay between Al, his goon referee and Martin is actually quite refreshing. All the fast counts and heel moves work well and tell a story. Even when the ref goes down, he sells pretty good. KSWA seems to do the little things right, which makes everything seem more professional.

Martin gets some heat back after the match, then gets chased out by Mike Malachi, who in turn does his own "heel ref" beatdown.

Pro Wrestling Intellectual

Kris Kash versus Baracus is the other half of the split tag teams matches.

Kash is a clad in black skater boy. Baracus the nutcase military veteran, and part of the international thugs under the management of Gentleman Joe Perri.

After what looks to be a quick squash, Kash pulls out the jumping boots and finishes up with a hurancanrana, a senton and sliced bread#2 for the victory.

Kris Kash seems young enough and athletic enough to really go somewhere.

An intermission is held, where lots of stuff is given away for the Clash Against Cancer theme. I don't believe the proceeds of the DVD sales are slated for any charity, though.

The high flying/technical match is up next.

Justin Sane vs Zero. Justin Sane is the local Pittsburgh legend, well schooled in the craft, who probably has found his niche as an attraction, coming out as the lovable nutcase, sporting a Hannibal Lector mask which he takes off before fighting.

Zero is his complementary opponent, of a similar knowledge and technical level.

The match starts out slow, but builds into some nice dives and other aerial work. Sane did a rather dangerous flip dive off the apron onto Zero. With no mats, he really must trust that guy. There was one minor "what was that" and the attempt to set up a surfboard just didn't click, but otherwise, the match went smooth and professional.

After some exchanges, they go to the finish, and then Justin Sane heads back to the bar for some handshakes and hugs.

The big belt versus belt match is next.

Anthony Alexander vs Shawn Blanchard isn't an old school classic, but Blanchard (seconded by the legendary Frank Durso) has that championship swagger, and Alexander has the size and presence to make it somewhere.

This match is an excellent example of a promotion working a solid style, and building to a main event, within that style, that works well because of the guys knowing what is expected of them, and delivering.

As the previous match was a bit high flying, this one moves into displays of power and old school moves, and being from Pittsburgh, you should quickly realize where all that comes from.

This is also a classic heel/face battle. With two belts up for grabs, but a bigger event being planned for the Fan Fest show, it isn't out of the ordinary how the finish comes about. But with enough fan interaction and familiarity, that the action spills out into the appreciative crowd is neither unimaginative nor unenjoyable.

La Lucha versus Big Mike Malachi The final main event pits "the Mayor of Mexico City" and crowd fave La Lucha (wearing a mask) against the big heel on the roster.

Building upon the previous bout, it turns quickly into a brawl outside the ring, and surprisingly enough moves into the "stands" and gets a lot more involved than I would have expected.

An obvious plant takes a few punches from Malachi, and assists in catching La Lucha off a dive from the bar itself in the back. Chants of "La Lucha!" show that the response from the crowd is beyond appreciative.

Eventually, they get back into the ring and after a series of patented La Lucha moves, leading to a pinfall, it turns a bit ugly with interference by Blanchard (armed with brass knucks!) and the expected car crash of having most of the participants of the Fan Fest's triple Main Event involved.

Lucha ends up with an "injury" which will undoubtedly play into long term booking plans.

KSWA's next event is called "The Aftermath 2007" and is to be held on Saturday, February 24 at the Lawrenceville Moose, at 7:30 (Lawrenceville is a neighborhood in Pittsburgh) 120 51st St, Pittsburgh PA 15201   For more info, call 412-726-1762

By all admission, KSWA is the minor leagues, and without national stars, I'd rate it at the "AA" level. But it's a well run promotion, with a rabid fan base and a passionate and cohesive roster. If you're in Pittsburgh, give it a chance. If you've got $7 to spare for a DVD, they're also available. It's well worth the time and the small time promotions like this deserve your attention.

Pro Wrestling Intellectual

Pro Wrestling Unplugged
JCW vs. PWU: The Showdown

www.prowrestlingunplugged.com

There's a lot of depth to the legacy of Extreme Championship Wrestling. Avoiding the obvious criticisms and commentary of the WWE's version, there remain strong ties back to the glory of ECW, in various promotions, with various real and significant aspects that can be traced back to Paul Heyman's attempt to create a true third national promotion.

And then there are some arteries of lifeblood that go back further.

Of those various smaller and not so smaller entities that dare to claim heritage from the Extreme, none have the lasting and legitimate claim like Pro Wrestling Unplugged. With Tod Gordon at the helm, the resonance doesn't just end with the name at the top, or the use of the old bingo hall (now called the New Alhambra Arena and looking a lot cleaned up,) or even the sense of templates for the promotion, in terms of how guys seem to look, seem to be used, and the overall atmosphere.

Gary Wolf, as one half of the original Pitbulls, still coming out to Thunder kiss '65 (by the now defunct White Zombie,) and Ian Rotten, with a shaved head, a claim to be the King of the Hardcores, and a battle scared body that should turn most aspirants from that title running away in absolute horro, are the sole regulars from that era.

On this show, the rather rotund and even more world weary Raven makes an appearance, in that typical ECW fashion.

What I love about PWU is the depth. There are enough players that the overall JCW (*That's the Insane Clown Posse's pet promotion, as in Juggalo Championsh*t Wrestling, and I'm not going vulgar, but you can figure that out in a heartbeat) war versus PWU doesn't quite make a dent in the entirety of the lineup.

PWU features some great tag team wrestling, and in AMIL (that's All Money is Legal,) and the SAT's (c'mon, do I have to spell them all out,) and the Rottweilers (Joker and Ricky Reyes) the boast three of the best in the indy circuit.

PWU also features some of the biggest guys seen on that same level, and puts on a "Big Man Battle Royal" to prove it.

The promotion features some up and coming talent, some graying veterans and some potential prime time stars in the making, it also has a great women's champion in Mercedes Martinez, and a great heel faction in the form of Ian Rotten and crew.

The comparisons to ECW are both a curse and a blessing. On one hand, ECW has proven itself to be impossible to completely recreate, and its nostalgia is doomed to failure. Too much talent in too many places have raised the bars -- in terms of violence, stunts and other forms of being extreme.

Ian Rotten and gal-pal Amy Lee take to the extreme in vulgarity on this DVD, and I'm not so thrilled with them pushing the envelope.

But one of the more apt criticisms of the package is the filler material. This is a two disc set, and while the quality is great, the length is a bit too much to handle. I love hearing people cut promos and the entrances and all that, but like ECW in its heyday, PWU is far more a live event and far more appreciated live than on tape. One of the problems on this DVD, as I see it, is too much of the drawn out interaction between the crowd and the talent is played out when it's not necessary.

Now, I'll certainly say that the ECW feel involved working in the crowd and riling them up and listening and giving and taking, but when the ICP is heckled and they go off on a tangent to respond, that doesn't necessarily make for compelling home viewing.

Some of the matches just take far too much time for the talent to get to the ring. There's that mentality of filling up a show, but there's also that ego coming into play where far too many of the guys want to have there say, their matches and their angles too.

It also goes to say that having a few squash-like matches, or at least some fast ones, wouldn't be a bad idea.

For example, and I don't want to diss the Azrieal vs. Aramis feud, but sometimes doing a drawn out match where you've already established one of the guys to not be taking his opponent seriously actually detracts from that same notion. I love the nature of this as an opening feud, but it can use a little less interaction and a little more emphasis on the point.

"You're not Eddie!" is a poignant chant at Mr. Azrieal. Not quite fair, but pointed, indeed.

(Let me back up one second. The opening video, obviously to a ICW song, is very, very good. Kinda reminds me of George Shorewood's "Hand Jive" with all the wrestling clips on MTV, when we desperately tried to name the names of guys we'd only heard of through PWI and The Wrestler.)

The JCW/PWU war is a strange one.

Invasion angles are great, but the problem here is that the DVD comes across as a joint production, not a bitter hatred (which does come off by the end of this show.)

The graphics for JCW and PWU are interesting and great, but then again, after you've seen the same bit go over and over on the big screen, it gets old fast.

And the Tod Gordon interview session ends up being everything you'd expect at this point. I'll say one thing, Gordon continues to be great at selling a beat down. But the whole thing at this point of the DVD seems far too contrived.

Next up is the BMBR -- the Big Man Battle Royal.

If my name was formerly Johnny Ace, I'd get these guys on tape and have their names handy.

Sinister X looks like he should be with Gary Wolf, but I can understand why that isn't happening. That being said, he's got the body type that makes you worried about his long term health situation.

The Krash Krew is on display here as well. Kwame is just huge in that same dangerous manner, big and dangerous looking. His partner, Gemini, has more of the Ray Candy feel. Just a big, big guy.

They have some sort of relationship with Damian Slugga, who's billed as seven foot tall, and of course, being big and black, he's got to be running with the same faction.

The big white victim is a 440 pound hulk (as in the original use of the term) of a man called Big Slam, who reminds me of Vader, but a little softer. He came out to the Halloween theme, or if you've watched the late night music ads, "Tubular Bells." (otherwise known as the entrance music for the Samoan Swat Team.)

On display is the blue chipper of PWU, Pete Hunter, whom they tout as a graduate of the XFC Training Academy. By the way, is it just me or does John House sound like Gilbert Gottfried?

Hunter looks a lot like John Cena, only seemingly taller and a bit less cut.

Putting six huge guys in the ring at the same time sounds like a recipe for disaster, but it wasn't.

At first, they all ganged up on Big Slam and put him over the top rope.

After that, it was a long and tedious wait for the next elimination. That was a time management issue. First they set up the sort of turn on Damian Slugga, then they took turns beating down on Slugga, Hunter and X.

It is interesting in a sense that PWU puts the big guys on at the mid-card level, while most indy level promotions don't even push the big guys except for the main event slots.

I won't give away the result of the Battle Royal, but will only say that these guys are looking better than Mark Henry and the Giant Kalil do on most nights.

Next up is a classic heel versus face type tag team event. The O'Doyles are old school villain types, but with a dearth of tag team wrestling, there seems to be little upward movement possible for a mid-card heel tag team anymore, which is a shame.

After the match, the O'Doyles jump into the JCW war, and in a nice touch, they get some surprising results. Out for JCW is Chuck Wagon and Dyson Price. (who comes up with those names, 2 Dope or J?)

One match I greatly anticipated was between AMIL and the Rottweilers.

They had set up a nice three way feud, also involving the SAT's, on the last show, so this one (minus the SAT's, and their championship belts) is for another trophy.

AMIL is a weird but interesting combination, weird because they're doing a gang type gimmick, but one that is all shiny and orange and tripping. They are a little undersized, but do a lot of unique double team moves, but are still a little sloppy in transitions and hitting those double teams.

I do respect their potential, though. With names like Murda and Pusha, its kinda hard to get around considering them as the faces in this feud, but stranger things have happened in this business. Pusha sells the Rottweilers working the knee most of the match. Ironically, its Joker who limps backstage as well, not sure if or where that happened.

On one hand, all that selling made for a great and classic match, on the other hand, expecting any high flying from AMIL against the methodical madness and violence of Reyes and Joker would have taken the action up another notch. It did drag in the middle.

But hey, tag team matches are meant to be that way sometimes.

The feud's not over and there's lots more to anticipate with these guys.

In another match where it could have gone a bit shorter, Pit-bull (the real, the original and the only) Gary Wolf takes on the "Richie Rich" of JCW, Breyer Wellington (with his butler/manservant)

There's a dangerous DDT on the announce table that sets up the win. The cool aspect is one of those rare "that's all it should take" finishing sequences.

Disc 2 has the three main event matches.

Up first is a mixed match between Mercedes Martinez (PWU Women's Champ) and Detox.

Detox's gimmick of dressing up to get the ambush is clever. Pulling off his clothes in a match against a woman isn't….

I rarely care for such intergender matches, thinking them best left for Andy Kaufman, and by most reports, he's still dead.

But this one worked, as did the last one. I'm not so sure about motivation and keeping it going, but the concept of this skinny, untanned white kid being a match up for the Latina superstar in the making seems like a reasonably fair fight.

Martinez can definitely dish it out, and take it as well.

The real measuring stick is that my wife was into the match as it played out. It was some good work and great effort on both parts.

The finish was satisfying and the match played out well.

At the end, however, it went far to the extreme.

Joe Babinsack

I'm cool with Amy Lee as the biker chick friend of Ian Rotten, but when she comes out with other women wrestlers to congratulate Martinez, it had "I see where this is going" written all over it. That wasn't the problem. Amy Lee cutting a vulgar, profanity laced promo during it was, so I had to turn the set off and go through another one of those "you watch this crap why?" looks….

Just an arrogant reminder from the reviewer. Heels should be hated, but heelishness that makes people turn the channel doesn't sell you tickets.

The card then segues nicely into Devon Moore's defense against Ian Rotten.

Rotten's gimmick as King of Hardcores, who choses to wrestle instead, is somewhat reminiscent of Mr. Foley, but since we really don't think that Rotten can wrestle, when he does, it becomes interesting and entertaining. Rotten turned the tables on Moore throughout the match, with some interesting kicks, (including a handstand into a kick) and refraining from punching throughout.

It's a great gimmick and a great change of pace. This match was slow, but welcome to be slow. It was announced at a one hour time limit, but didn't go that far, and didn't lag at all. Moore showed himself championship caliber with the selling and the nature of the match.

The post match tantrum was a bit weird, as Rotten called out the PA Athletic Commissioner from Philadelphia, and claimed that he was on the take. Strange.

By the way, is that strange scab on Rotten's head a Nike Swoosh or what? Maybe he can get some advertising revenue from that!

The real Main Event is a six man match between JCW and PWU.

On one team is the Insane Clown Posse, but Shaggy 2 Dope just had his knee reconstructed (for the third time!??) so he brings in a replacement. Thus we have Violent J, Too Tuff Tony and Dyson Price for the Juggalos.

Unfortunately, we've got three big guys with guts (yes, I could join that crew) who all look pretty much the same except that J has white paint on his face.

On the other side, we've got the Backseat Boyz. (I think I figured them out. Cashmere is the one with the hoody on, Trent is the skinny version of Lover Boy.) We've also got

Pro Wrestling Intellectual

Corporal Robinson, who the Juggalo Family turned on last show -- upset that he'd sooner be PWU Hardcore Champion over being JCW Heavyweight Champion.

"Corp" sports a JCW hockey shirt with the PWU logo on top of the JCW one.

There's another long-winded promo cut here, mostly by 2 Dope, who shows a strange inability to live down the heckling (in a war atmosphere that is rather evenly divided -- even though they cheer loudly for whomever's in the ring at the time.)

The match itself is an ECW inspired brawlfest that immediately goes outside, and stays mostly outside for all the match.

This is the kind of conflict that you can either love or hate. As I mentioned before, its more interesting live (though far more dangerous to avoid thundering herds of frightened fans, as if Tiger Jeet Singh were running around with a scimitar) but on TV you realize how much of the match you missed because the cameras are only focused on two guys at a time.

It really was pretty good. They kept the violence factor up but the high risk stuff toned down. There's a lot less margin for error when Violent J misses that moonsault he just has to do each match. No surprise that the Backseat Boyz kinda shy away from taking that spot. Robinson is the big violent and sometimes bloody guy who loves the hardcore style. The Boys mostly sell.

In the end, the three man triplet team looks to be losing, when the lights go off. It's Raven.

And if you know ECW, you know the drill.

The great thing is that while the show started with a whimper, it does end with some great heat all around, and the challenges and counter-challenges are intense, promising and make me want to watch the next installment of the war.

Great show.

Joe Babinsack

Strong Vs. Evans
Full Impact Pro
www.fullimpactpro.com

FIP is, like any alternative to the mainstream, a product that can be hit or miss, depending upon your appreciation of the effort and intent.

Since the studio wrestling style hasn't seen mainstream television in decades, the throwback mentality can be nostalgia of the best or worst type. Either its appealing because it reminds you of stuff you used to watch back in the day, or it gets a little tedious if you've never lived for that type of show, nor appreciate the "going back to wrestling's roots" mentality that creates these shows.

What I love is the old school heel vs face mentality, with a southern style overlay; a flow that relies upon the interview area, and making challenges -- with sudden appearances; and most importantly, the playing up of the audience with the subtle and not-so-subtle mannerisms that create the sense of who to root for, and who to get riled up at.

It's fun to sit back and enjoy a show that engages the smaller scaled audience in a small scale venue that otherwise features some top level talent, and while sometimes coming across as try-outs for ROH angles and match-ups in the future, the sense that FIP is its own universe, with its own rules and roster and interactions always comes through.

What I also appreciate is Dave Prazak, as both an announcer and as heel manager.

We've all been exposed to the antics of Jerry Lawler, who in turn has been filling the role (with his own twists) on the good old Jesse Ventura heel commentator (who in turn took the work of Don Muraco and Roddy Piper to new levels and a much more mainstream audience.) I'm sure the heel announcer has been around for decades, but with the modern sensibilities, the little things – the humor, the feigned ignorance, the insistence that everything that happens must go through the referee to be "real" – those things come across as new and different, mostly because it hasn't been really done well in a decade. Especially not in the WWE, where the announce teams get too hostile to each other and to the fans instead of pushing the product.

The whole "Mr. Milo Beasley" as a "homeless man in a wheelchair" is something to behold. You just can't do that today anywhere else, and its so over-the-top, so comedic and so -- pro wrestling – that I doubt the creative geniuses in certain locales could even replicate it.

Old school booking rules the day on the Strong vs Evans DVD.

Danielson and Aries are the big heels doing a program with the underdog faces of Fury and Clark. Of course, the heel stable supports each other and pulls out all the dirty tricks (even if you really aren't going to believe that Danielson or Aries would have much of a problem with Fury or Clark.)

But this is FIP, not ROH, and the attempt to give Clark and Fury time with the technical masters at the indy level is certainly what FIP is all about.

It also gives the guys a chance to really work it out with the crowd, as well as work on their promos. I for one will always look forward to the guy, having just wrestled and lost, coming out to complain, gripe or challenge for another match, with sweat pouring across his face and the emotions coming forth and the talent of switching gears from physical assault to verbal engagement is something I appreciate greatly.

And to throw the twists in, you've got the guest wrester in for some spots, and another heel gets in his face for a challenge. In this case, its Jack Evans, who Prazak makes sure to expose as someone who's getting 'unfair' main event shots – he gets challenged in the opening by journeyman heel Angel Armani.

The matchmaking and set up does well. Evans comes across far too much of an indifferent heel, but Armani helps tone him down. Of course, Evans isn't one to tone down his style in the ring. He's a guy who does a split- legged leap over the top rope just to enter the ring!

Armani heels long enough, and innovatively enough, to bring out Roderick "Messiah of the Backbreaker" Strong, still in street clothes, to protest the nonsense.

Therein is the package that FIP presents, and the wonders of the studio setting. It's not just guys appearing in the ring, nor overblown ring entrances, it's a twist by routing the guys from the locker-room to the announcing booth to the ring, that is different and alternative. Sure, after a while, it might all seem the same, but after watching the same old same old for a decade, anything new is interesting.

The angle that also weaves through the show is Colt Cabana and Sal Rinauro demanding a match with Erick Stevens and Steve Madison. Apparently the latter team interfered on

Cabana/Rinauro's "no DQ" shot at the Tag Team Titles. "We will get our revenge" insists Cabana.

And as they come out before each match, repeating the challenge, and finally coming out in chairs to sit with the fans, the heat is brewing and the explosion when the obvious occurs (and if you don't follow the style, maybe you won't guess how they interact, at last) is the kind of emotion that should happen with properly manipulating the crowd.

This show is much a transition one for FIP, as Homicide (the FIP Heavyweight title holder) is not around, and the Heart Break Express is wrestling in a six man tag.

This allows for a build up of contenders.

With Strong and Evans, the main event is for the #1 contender to the FIP title, and the winner getting a shot down the line against Homicide.

In the first set-up for the belts, the Chasyn Rance /Seth Delay portion of the six man match up prove their worth in doing a double pin of the champs. Delay continues to be a bump machine, and there's no competing with the dynamics of the HBX as the heirs to the Midnight Express legacy, with Sean Davis clearly showing the entertainment value of the Playboy Buddy Rose/Adrian Adonis body.

Black Market appears in FIP, having beaten a few teams, and now getting a squash win against the always interesting Masked Fippers (one with a Masked Superstar hood, the other, a three horned grinning skull which I'm not familiar with.) BM comes out looking dashing, like Meng in the WCW era, with black shirt and pants, and white ties. I think they should have stuck to the old Pitbulls Superbomb as the finisher, as the double team neckbreaker that followed seemed anti-climactic, but it was the good old "stomp the jobber" and "complain about the lack of competition" staple of studio wrestling. Slow builds and expectation works a heck of a lot better than jobbing out the new guys on their first appearances.

The show very much is a spotlight on Jack Evans, who has the agility, ability and attitude to go far in the business. Locking him up with Roderick Strong seems to be a try-out for things to come in ROH, but it also helps to move away from the spot fest sort of match that Evans is prone to put on – or at least to help slow down and story tell between high spots of the high flyer.

Who wins? Who loses? Who says what before and after the matches? All that is for you, the fan, to find out after buying this very good DVD offering by Full Impact Pro.

Overload
Ultimate Pro Wrestling
www.upw.com

With the WWE imposing its will upon the national TV audience, and routinely re-educating even the most talented wrestlers into its "house style," I would like to take the opportunity of reviewing this pretty solid Ultimate Pro Wrestling DVD to explain a bit about various professional wrestling styles. While most are familiar with the WWE and its version of wrestling, there are several other variations of the form, from Japan to Mexico to the American Independent scene, which have different appeals to different audiences.

Frankie Kazarian vs Jerry Lynn vs Evan Karagias

This bout was for the UPW Lightweight Championship, held by Frankie "The Future" Kazarian. Kazarian made a splash in TNA, then got signed to the WWE over the summer, only to get lost in the mire of booking insanity that surrounds the smaller guys and quit. In a match with a lot of promise, we get to see a lot of what made the WCW cruiserweight division stand out, and the style which now dominates the smaller federations across this nation.

The style, which can arguably be called American Independent, features lots of fast action, building to big moves, and typically little transition from one big spot to the next. With Jerry Lynn in the mix, the wrestling is solid, if not overly flashy. Kazarian continues to show his talent, and as the main event of the original event, this one showcases some good wrestling – and unlike the WWE style, where only the big names get any amount of time, this match went near the twenty minute mark.

Ken Shamrock vs Predator

Shamrock once had a chance of going to New Japan, but chose to do the then WWF instead. Predator, otherwise known as Sylvester Turkay, was a dominating college wrestler who mixed it up with Kurt Angle, and has done a lot of Japanese work.

New Japan melded the Ultimate Fighting/MMA concept with the traditional pro wrestling over the past decade – to the point where it put far too many of its top notch talent in real fights, which only served to show the mainstream audience that its fighters weren't quite as tough as they wanted to believe. Shamrock attempted this in the WWF, but the results were mixed. The now WWE incorporates a lot of submission work otherwise unknown to the US scene, but shies away from making submission work a 'respectable' talent.

The educated Japanese audience readily accepts moves like the ankle lock, or choke holds (what we would call "sleeper holds") or arm breakers or other 'real world' type maneuvers that would force the opponent to give up – to "tap out."

So UPW worked this style, first by having a drunk Tank Abbott at ringside to heighten the realism of the event. Ok, poor joke. Regardless, the promo cut by Shamrock on Abbott is equally as good as the match. During the match, before it became a train wreck disqualification so neither Shamrock nor Predator would have to lose, it featured Shamrock constantly going for submission wins by using the ankle lock. Turkay constantly powered out.

If you like a more realistic, slow moving, power based style, this is a strong example up until the point where the Bruiser Brody inspired chain gimmick gets used by both wrestlers to make it more of a WWE event.

Konnan, Psicosis & Juventud Guerrera vs Shawn Riddik, Andrew Hellman and Antonio Mestre (The University) No wrestling style is hotter, in the entire world, than lucha libra. Mexican pro wrestling has always had its quirks: no tags necessary in multiple wrestler events; an ingrained polarity between 'good guys' – faces and 'bad guys' – heels; and two out of three falls to determine the winner of most matches.

Beyond that, the luchadores are primarily high flying, fast paced and strangely enough comedic. There is a lot of well orchestrated moves by tag team members, lots of dives out of the ring and an alien concept of faking disqualifications (something Eddie Guererro brought to the WWE.)

Konnan remains a TNA staple, while Psicosis is slowly getting his head set right in the WWE, where well known talents of other styles simply don't know how to wrestle until they know how to wrestle in the WWE. Juvie was a casualty of that mentality, as well as his well known propensity for self-destruction. It was only a matter of time before the WWE released him, and they did with little fanfare but a few weeks ago.

Although a matchup between three of Mexico's most well known talents, and three UPW wrestlers in training proves to have some clashes in style, as well as some seemingly botched moves, it does present a style only seen on Spanish language TV (and here's to hoping that Comcast gives another episode of LLL on its On Demand feature.)

Pro Wrestling Intellectual

Nevermore: the Best of Raven
TNA
www.TNAwrestling.com

For a while, it looked to be the last, and not just the latest chapter in Raven's storied career, but with his reappearance at Lockdown, the next chapter has begun. "Nevermore" chronicles the involvement of Raven during TNA's mostly weekly PPV era, which means that the bulk of his work has not been seen by most fans, and most likely not at all by the new wave on Spike TV

This provides an interesting situation for TNA, as they have a solid backstory of product that has not been seen on the national level, and during that period, they had a heavy involvement of ECW regulars --coupled with a not so compelling involvement of Vince Russo as his S.E.X. faction -- people like Saturn, Sandman and New Jack, as well as Sabu and Shane Douglas as adversaries.

This "Best of" compilation features Raven against a mixture of talent – long time rivals and new blood, as well as the 'first ever' match with Sabu. The DVD is comprised of the Good, the Bad and the Ugly: with Raven, it has one of the most solid professionals of the past decade; his work typically is underrated, and he usually brings out the best in his opponents, no matter what the style involves. Unfortunately, we also see some of TNA's strange amalgamation of top notch talent, Russo influence and, at the time, weekly PPV booking and the main events that often rushed the storylines. And we see some particularly disgusting sights along the way.

The Good

Raven's interplay with rising talent, whether it be AJ Styles or Chris Harris, is always a positive. His style as a more traditional heel allows him to give much more than his contemporaries, and he knows psychology a lot more than others.

As with most appearances by Raven in a promotion (other than the WWE,) there is a purpose and a distinction to his character. When he arrived in TNA, in a moment that is all too hilarious, he attacks Jeff Jarrett and starts proclaiming his "destiny" as the NWA Champion.

(What is amusing is that Jarrett had just defeated Fallen Angel Christopher Daniels in a bloody battle, so already Jarrett one-ups Raven on his own DVD. Then, the locker room clears out to congratulate the retaining NWA Champ. Out of nowhere comes Raven to DDT Jarrett, take his belt, and jump out of the ring. It took a lot of fumbling around and hesitation by a lot of guys to allow that to happen! And then Raven and Vince Russo move through the crowd with the NWA belt, and you realize what era is being portrayed, and probably the sole reason why there had to be a dozen and a half wrestlers inside the ring at that moment, instead of a focus on the debut.)

Raven's matches with his peers also highlight his talent. Even though a lot of the former ECW guys seem a bit bloated, and a step slower, it never seems to be Raven who's stumbling over the fence, or blowing a spot, or unable to perform at the top level.

In fact, after the first Clockwork Orange House of Fun match with Sandman, it is Raven who gets back into the ring and challenges Jarrett to an immediate title match. After about a twenty minute bloodbath, and his face being a crimson mask for most of it, Raven was still able to cut a strong promo, and go at it (albeit briefly) with Jarrett before AJ Styles jumped in.

(A comment on Clockwork Orange: if you haven't seen the movie in a while (or ever) there is a particularly great sequence, before a very vile and loathsome scene, where Malcolm McDowell's gang faces off with another, in what has to be (in 1971) one of the first true hardcore moments in wrestling history. The fight involves boxes, chairs and a pretty mean dropkick. Stanley Kubrick truly is the Father of Hardcore Wrestling!)

Raven's commentary is interesting; his matches are all solid; and his innovation, ability to put over his opponents and work in a variety of stills remain his ultimate strengths. That, and the presentation of several real bloodbaths are the appeal of this DVD.

Now, for the Bad stuff.

Anything that involves Vince Russo's creativity means lots of disconnected storylines, far too many people involved, and far too many plot twists, run-ins and busy scenes.

Once upon a time, a great wrestler could tell a story in a match. I think Raven is more than capable of doing that. Unfortunately, there are too many matches where it turns into a Russo-fest of run-ins to apparently create the impression in the viewer that maybe one guy, or the other, will win.

Well, hell, isn't that what a match is supposed to be about?

Pro Wrestling Intellectual

The Raven/Jarrett NWA Championship match is replete with that sort of nonsense. Several different factions involved, overbooked ebb and flow of matches, and ultimately nonsensical interaction. A handcuffed wrestler, being beaten over the head with a chair? Where have we seen that before? But wait! Innovation on display as the handcuffed guy gets a comeback and a near fall while having both hands tied behind his back. And then, inexplicably, a series of events that simply make no sense at all: first the ref has a key to the handcuffs (the famed "universal key") and then, when the ref is having difficulty releasing the champ, Raven steps in and removes the manacles, just in time to stand up, make a mis-step, and get hit by The Stroke for another JJ win.

And people at the time wondered why the crowd had turned on good ole Double J?

The other Bad thing was the disconnect between matches. Sure, there was a chronologic order to it, and I realize that filling in the backstory would be excessive at times, but the transformation from Raven as nasty heel to Raven as sympathetic combatant – to the point where overhyping Don West slams down his headset and storms off when Vampiro interferes in the hair vs. hair match with Douglas, is just a bit much to comprehend.

And then there's the Ugly.

Does anyone really want to see Kevin Sullivan with painted stripes on his upper torso, instead of a referee's shirt? Does anyone really want to see Shane Douglas puking all over the ring?

But, in the utmost of professionalism, we don't ever see Raven joining in on the gut heaving.

Raven's back in TNA, all's good in the world, and if you want to see Scott Levy's greatest work bridging ECW to modern day TNA, here's a great DVD full of insight and probably the least seen, truly hardcore matches this side of CZW.

Joe Babinsack

Project Mayhem
Hybrid Wrestling
Myspace.com/hybridpro

This is why I love professional wrestling.

It's not just the talent in the ring, but the creativity outside of it. It's not just the ability to make the most out of that talent, but to invest in production values, in getting top name opponents, and in building up the promotion for the future.

It's not just in putting together world class matches, but in making sure the roster is stacked with local names and guest-stars for comparison. It's not just about putting on an obligatory tag team match, a six-person spotfest, and a handful of solid angles.

It's about putting it all together in one package, and that's what Hybrid is all about.

What's more, Hybrid is all about being a bit different. It builds on expectations and it builds on talented wrestlers, but it also fosters an environment of innovations. There's a six-pack challenge that usually has me disinterested, but I saw several moves that had me saying wow, and had me saying "why hasn't anyone thought of that yet?"

The tag match had me groaning at the sight of the opponents of Faith in Nothing, but by the time I thought about it again, it was turning into a classic tag team battle. And the funny thing was, the JWO-- the Juggalos -- were at ringside the entire event, and there wasn't any concern about them ruining the show, or overwhelming the local audience. Now, there were probably some Juggalos in the matches, but I'm not hip to that scene yet.

Another thing I loved was the signage. Not since Sign Guy in ECW have I been so amused by the commentary. Much seemed planted, but if so, it was well done. Humorous commentary, innovative hyping and a great way to get things (and the talent) over.

But let me not overlook the graphics. Top notch stuff, even rivaling ChickFight. This was more creative. The cover art and the design work is exponentially above anything else I've seen, and Outlaw Productions deserves to get inquiries about their work (Myspace.com/OutlawProductions) from these DVDs. There's a promo on YouTube as well. Check that out!

Project Mayhem actually features the great Sabu in the main event, matched up against Ohio's own MDogg20, Matt Cross. Heck, let's start at the main event and work our way backwards, for a change of pace.

I'm not sure who gave Cross fashion advice, but the Fidel Castro look went out of style in the 1950's, and is really only good for mid-card heels. Wow, that's one impressive beard, and MDogg20 has an incredibly ripped physique, but the look has got to go.

Pro Wrestling Intellectual

What I've always loved about Sabu is his inherent wrestling mindset. Even at his peak, he was doing the little things that make his work so much more interesting. One can never tell if it's a sell or a real injury. Of course, over the years Sabu has paid a hefty price for his daredevil stunts.

But here, one can tell that Sabu has the experience and understanding to play off his past, build up expectations and deliver when necessary. If this match is the reason you want to buy Project Mayhem, you won't be disappointed. Because as good as this match gets, the rest of the card holds up to it.

I was really looking forward to seeing Faith in Nothing (Vincent Nothing and Christian Faith) in action. These guys are an awesome team. Not just because they've got a cool gimmick, but because they sell, they know tag team psychology, and they made two geeky looking guys called MegaSexy look like world-beaters.

One sign of an excellent tag team match is getting the crowd behind the face team. When Faith in Nothing do this against what should be an inferior team, and do it without cheerleading, I'm screaming that these guys know what they're doing.

Innovative and old-school at the same time and great stuff.

Jake Crist (of the Irish Airborne) and Johnny Gargano are the third from the top match, and they put on one awesome display of wrestling. I've seen Gargano around, and he's got talent, and of course, Jake Crist can mix it up with the Briscoes, so there's no lack of potential in this match. It's about twenty minutes of solid action, ending with a pretty nifty angle to set up the next DVD.

Billy Taylor and Josh Prohibition have a slightly less intense match, but an interesting one nonetheless. Taylor has a cameo earlier in the card, and while he has a look that doesn't scream for bigger and better things, he has a talent that will take him far.

Prohibition has been around some of my other reviews. He's got something, but doesn't seem to want to break out of some of the comedic efforts.

Chris Cronus is a stud for the promotion. His match with Robert Paulson (Sign: His name is Robert Paulson!) was a squash, but boy did he show some power in it. Military pressing a guy around, showing him to all four the sides of the ring, and delivering a F-5 with airtime were BIG moves.

I didn't quite catch the manager's name, but he's a good "sports agent" type for the heels. Why he has both Gargano and Cronus doesn't make much sense, but I'll never complain too much about a good manager. Before that was a top notch "Junior Heavyweight" caliber match between Starless and "Nasty" Russ Myers. Starless is a facial piercing type of guy with an otherwise Low-Ki type of look. He's not quite as intense as Ki (but who is?) but he makes up for it with high-flying ability.

Myers is a red-headed heel who came out with a SWAT team member, in full riot gear. There's an image there that was awesome (although it screamed "angle alert" if you're schooled in wrestling lore and look out for such things.)

I dug the match.

Wow is all I can say after seeing Jason Bane battle the behemoth "Notorious" Jack Frost. Since we rarely see such bulk in the ring, it's easy to get into the kind of hard hitting match like this (or the Evans/Thrillbilly spectacular in AIW.)

Frost has a sort of combination R-Truth and Rikishi look, but he showed a heck of a lot of talent. He slammed Bane and showed that the big man can sell. Then Bane utterly amazed me with several high impact moves, including a scarily short plancha, but followed it up with a scoop slam that opened my eyes, another power move, and finally an earth-shattering spine buster. Bane is just one big, wide guy, but a talented one at that!

The opener pits Morty Rackem (I believe of the "Cut Throat Crew") against Luis Diamante. Diamante has two stooges with him, and they play out some comedy. It's a solid opener, nothing spectacular, and with the comedy, it adds another level of style to the card, so no complaints here.

The close of Disc One is the Six-Pack Challenge, which is mis-ordered on the back cover listing. While I usually have reservations about six guys going at it, as it causes a spot-fest, and usually the rules are first to the pinfall, I was greatly impressed with the work.

Sure, it was mostly spotfest city, but they pulled out some interesting variations. The participants are Sami Callihan, Logan, Brian Lyndon, Myke Quest, some goof named Cockstrong and the ever-popular high-flyer by the name of Flip.

Ok, the Cockstrong gimmick was funny until they overplayed it, and man, I hope that guy was wearing a cup.

But the match was very good. There's a lot of stuff I've seen before, but that doesn't diminish seeing it again. For example, I've seen New Jack and Vic Grimes do dives from way too high, but this Callahan kid leaps off of a scoreboard with a shooting star press that had me worried.

Nice touches included a dive-fest that included the referee, who then admonished everyone to get back in the ring. Also, they went old school ECW pinfall eliminations, which I always think is better than first fall wins. The key to these matches are the flow, which was strong here, and the innovations in the key spots, which was equally strong. All told, Hybrid Wrestling showed me that it has the stuff, and you should definitely check it out. Fifteen bucks for a two disc set, with this kind of production values and this level of talent is well worth the cost.

Cibernetico & Robin
CHIKARA Pro Wrestling
www.chikarapro.com

It is really satisfying to watch a DVD like Cibernetico & Robin. There isn't just one good thing about the Chikara promotion. There are many: from the infusion of Lucha Libre to the interesting, logical and unique approach to professional wrestling matchmaking, from the incredible talent to the dramatic storylines, from the over-the-top characters and personalities to the subdued and professional nature of the in-ring talent.

A couple of months ago, I saw some really good and some really bad stuff in Chikara's product. Fans responded – not with bitterness or anger or irrationality, but with an appeal to stick with it, that there were anomalies in that event, that the fun of Chikara wasn't in what I saw, it was deeper.

I thank Chikara for sending me another DVD to review, and I'm all but begging for more!

That sort of fan base mentality is in and of itself refreshing. Knee-jerk hatred, obsessive defensiveness and a "they're all out to get us" mentality pervades most promotional fan bases. There are some good things about that, but show me a fan base that appreciates instead of defends, and I'll show you a promotion that is doing the right things and doesn't need the defensiveness.

The one thing that I didn't get about Chikara was all the talks about points. That question was quickly answered by the promotion:

Our "three point" system has to do with qualifying contenders for our tag belts, the Campeonatos de Parejas. Tag teams have to accumulate three points - by winning three CHIKARA-sanctioned tag matches in a row - to get a title shot. If they lose a match, their points go back down to zero, and the climb to contendership must begin again.

Which is an interesting and unique approach, and one that makes matches meaningful, and what's cool is that it provides various avenues to the matches made, and the efforts within the matches. Maybe being at one point isn't that big of a deal, but having two points suddenly is a mountain climbed, that can slip away with a bad loss. The depth it imbues in the "chase" for the title is vastly interesting on several levels.

(Of course, one of the big promotions could steal such a concept, but I can't imagine any of them having the creativity to make it work.) But this point system deal isn't the appeal of the promotion.

The announcing, which I was down upon before, comes through to me today. The rotating crew adds depth and interest to the DVD. Whether peppering their conversations with comic book, video game and music references, or simply by selling the product in a logical and consistent manner, these guys, headed by Leonard Chikarason, are the tops.

And Ultramantis Black has rapidly risen to be my favorite heel. That guy is over-the-top! His voice, his sarcastic drivel, his Neo Solar Temple faction, and that awesome mask: what better package exists in the known universe?

"The 'F' is for Fun"! Leonard F Chikarason plays the role of the booker and the lead announcer. It's a refreshingly different perspective, with the heels constantly badgering and complaining about him, all the while taking advantage of him as a businessman.

Having had the pleasure of watching some old St Louis footage, and hearing Larry Matysik on the mike, there's a resonance there. When the announcer is truly excited and interested in the happenings of the match, and the style and the promotion, it cannot be faked. There is no insincerity here, nor the overhyping or screaming. Its passionate calling of the matches, and even the revolving door of guest color announcers doesn't detract or distract from the stability of a great lead announcer.

But off to the match-by-match reviews:

Cheech & Cloudy vs Olsen Twins

The great thing about top notch independents is that first impressions rarely hold true, and talent always trumps looks, gimmicks and everything else.

When the Olsen Twins came out, I all but groaned. Here's a tall, pale geeky looking guy and a shorter, tanned, bearded "brother" … and then Cheech and Cloudy appear, and despite a growing reputation, the obvious short guy/tall guy tag team wrestling template was my expectation.

That was blown away in no time.

This was an incredible display of tag team wrestling craft. Talent on display, whether athleticism, wrestling skill and, most importantly, in the pacing and development of the match. In what became a theme for the CHIKARA promotion, this was a solid style, a bit subdued, but one fully appreciated by this reviewer.

What I loved was what wasn't on display: the too-fast pacing, the senseless high-spots, the dangerous displays of violence, nor the use of tables and chairs and gimmicks.

This was just pure wrestling and professional wrestling at its best. An excellent combination of working tags, working the staples of tag team wrestling, and building to the high spots.

It's amazing when such simple building of a match engages the crowd and the viewer, and makes the important moves all the more impressive. And to that end, this match outshines a lot of the more lauded tag team action of other promotions. "That's his New Gods and Fourth World training on display!" (I love comic book references!!)

Super Xtremo vs. Kris Chambers

Another strong example of building up the match to a specific high spot.

When Super Xtremo finally unleashed an Asai Moonsault, I was jumping in appreciation. Once again, its not just the move, but the building to the move, and a nicely paced style that made such a risky move vastly more meaningful.

The mixture of top notch indy talent, some from Canada, and the masked Luchador influence on another segment of the roster, creates some dynamics that work well and provide a unique style.

I know there are those in important places that think status quo is the only style that the mainstream will accept. Settling for second best isn't something these guys are comfortable with – and the action and effort proves it. Effort is something that cannot be faked, either, and something that a viewer can get caught up into.

Mike Quackenbush vs. Tim Donst

What impresses me about a great card is the set-up of matches, building up themes and then playing off the themes. What impresses me about any great promotion is its ability to use new and unique talent and mix them into the roster, and let the characteristics develop through the matches, and by bouncing off against established stars.

Tim Donst, by the information provided by the announce team, is a 19 year old with superb wrestling skills. So Chikara, of course, highlights that background and plays it up, and then works the development in a different direction, attempting to create a new star from a rookie with great promise. What's amazing is the simplicity of it all, but who's done it on the big stage?

Regardless, this is being done in Chikara in an excellent manner.

Donst is somewhat nondescript, but the whole wrestling singlet and headgear package makes him stand out. The use of fundamental wrestling moves and skills is awesome, and again, not overdone. Some of the pinning positions are hard to describe. But the depth of the match, and the ongoing efforts to establish Tim Donst go beyond simple analysis. Of course, having Mike Quackenbush involved means its being done right, but again, that's far too easy to say.

The gist of the match is that Quackenbush is mopping up the floor with his young student, but Donst just can't be put away. Moreso, Donst keeps at it, and has several near-falls and several unexpected and imaginative counters, pin-attempts and displays of offensive power.

Joe Babinsack

There's a spinning neck breaker applied by Donst on Mike Q that looked frighteningly fast. And it came from such an odd direction that it heightened the effect. There are ways of making sure the fans know a kid's got talent, heart and great potential. This is the avenue to take. And it's incredibly difficult for me to avoid mentioning Cody Runnels in passing. So I'll leave it at that.

Incoherence vs. Neo Solar Temple

Hallowicked and Delirious as a team. That's huge. Neo Solar Temple cutting a promo? That's huger. If you're down with rambling, nonsensical but utterly entertaining projections of charisma, this whole segment's for you. Ultramantis Black is awesome. That voice! That attitude! That utterly devastating mixture of sarcasm, wit and diabolic anger, and set off by Hydra, who growls like Godzilla gone mad.

And that's the praise before the match begins. What I'm loving about Chikara is that they are taking over-the-top personalities and personages and just running with it. This isn't the myriad of very bad characters that have plagued the sport, from the Ding-Dongs to the Gobbledygooker and every bad early 1990's WWF post cartoon, let's do real characters nonsense.

It isn't even the sort of Mad TV stuff that's so bad it's entertaining to watch.

This is pure entertainment!

With talent to spare in the ring as well…. Delirious is sporting an awesome goatee now, and that just makes the madman even madder and cooler. Heck, I'm doing these guys a disservice by not focusing on the match, but it was by no means something to avoid.

ShaneSaw vs Osirian Portal

Shane Storm and Jigsaw are an established team that are growing apart because of attitude and direction. It's a nice backdrop for the introduction of the Osirian Portal, which on the surface looks like a crazy bad gimmick, but these guys can rock.

Storm has that crazy mask that makes him look goofy and indecisive. Nice how that gets played. Amasis is lauded as the Funky Pharoah. His early moves were scant, but suddenly he burst with some great athleticism. Ophidian acts like a human snake. It's off-putting, but like everything else Chikara talent does, he lives the gimmick and by the end of the match, you realize that, wow! He's got himself over and the whole gimmick as well.

Pro Wrestling Intellectual

It's the kind of passion and talent that is refreshing to watch. And a mix of established and new talent that gets the new talent over.

The Colony vs. Eddie Kingston & Joker & Sabian

Once again, another great display of matchmaking, setting up the story, and potential just oozing from the talent involved.

The Colony is another on-the-surface crazy bad gimmick, but the guys pull it off. What's amazing is seeing the serious heel (oops, rudo) mentality of the Kingston Trio come through in the opening promo of the match, where they are ranting and raving about the booker, their opponents, and … well, let me take that back. Eddie Kingston is awesome in his controlled anger promo. I mean, main event level charisma and look and potential.

The match itself was awesome as was the direction of the storyline: multiple levels to the madness.

That leaves some names unmentioned, like Daizee Haze and Brody Lee. Haze is a great heel for the promotion. Her match had a bit of sloppiness from the debuting opponent, but ended up ok. Lee is a giant among the roster, with that sort of build and placement that makes him meaningful.

Oh yeah, the Cibernetico. It's not the Mexican guy of the same name, but a unique approach to a 16 man match. The rules are clearly explained and greatly framed. Basically each team has a line up that must be followed. Guys can tag out to the next one on the line-up. If not, it's a DQ.

With this promotion, it's a slow paced and interesting series of match-ups, that eventually sees some pinfalls, and then picks up some great speed. The greatness of the roster is featured, notably the Kings of Wrestling (Claudio Castignolli and Chris Hero) on the team captained by the eternal Mitch Ryder – who is an awesome promo.

The opening skit, where the rudos cackle over getting more money out of Chikarason, but Chris Hero "missed the boat" was priceless. As was the match, with a unique display and great interactions. There are few such main events that are well worth the price of the DVD, and for this DVD, the worth was paid three times over by the time the Cibernetico itself took place.

My efforts have been to expose greatly deserving pro wrestling promotions to a more mainstream audience. In Chikara Pro, I've found one of the most deserving around. Not just because of the effort, the passion and the talent, but the realization that this roster, young as it is and plying the true craft of professional wrestling, is the future of the sport.

And it's in great hands.

Joe Babinsack

CONTROVERSIES

Eric Bischoff   *Dr. Mike Lano & ???*   *Ric Flair*

Superstar Billy Graham's Tangled Ropes

In the world of professional wrestling, there are few truly unique individuals. Freaks and muscle-heads are a dime a dozen. Fat guys, gifted amateurs and crazed villains once filled the rosters of a score of promotions. In that world of entertainment, with oft-staged acrobatics, power fantasy story lines and emotional conflict, along with the tragic and terrible physical tolls taken by countless wannabes, numerous journeymen and a handful of true superstars, there is only one man whom the greatest wanted to be.

"Superstar" Billy Graham details his life in the pages of Tangled Ropes ($26, Simon & Schuster,) a portrayal of his raw talent, physically and charismatically, that destroyed a status quo. Graham's persona is so multi-faceted that he has spawned numerous copies of himself, many of whom are so utterly unlike each other that it is hard to believe that they pay homage to the same man.

Jesse Ventura and Hulk Hogan took to bodybuilding, looking to Graham and his impressive physique. What they did in-ring was of little importance, as opposed to how they looked.

Dusty Rhodes and Ric Flair, among other inspirational and attention getting talkers, took their patter from the man as well. Brimming with confidence, eloquence and command, Graham was once a preacher, and picked up the mantle later; but his appeal inspired the pudgy Rhodes and the tanned, arrogant Flair to greater heights.

As WWE owner Vince McMahon relates, the "Superstar" was twenty years ahead of his time. Undoubtedly, the boisterous, iconoclastic anti-hero dubbed "Stone Cold" Steve Austin was a direct descendant from the man who battled Bruno Sammartino for many months, in front of rabid audiences from Pittsburgh to Boston, only to gradually win over those same fans, and become a crowd favorite by the time the next champion rolled into the federation.

Wayne Coleman, after stints as a bodybuilder, preacher and football player, impacted the world of professional wrestling like no other, under the name Billy Graham. In his wake, appearance trumped talent, charisma trumped ability, and exceptional roleplaying trumped the fans interests in seeing the bad guy get his in the end.

Unfortunately, the likes of Eddy Guerrero, Art Barr, Davey Boy Smith, Road Warrior Hawk, as well as dozens of others, well-known or obscure, have paid the ultimate price of a misguided connection between muscle mass and popularity; a dangerous trade off of health for financial gain.

Graham went public with his woes, and does so again in the autobiography: a destroyed ankle, hip replacement, liver transplant and other ailments. His war of words with Vince McMahon over the abuse of steroids at the time when the WWE's owner was in serious legal jeopardy has only recently seen rapprochement.

After years of physical ailments, mental anguish and tragedy, Graham's legacy: the use of steroids to augment body image, on one of the biggest stages, and with the dramatic impact of his personality, created a monster that subsequent promoters, and budding wrestling talent, simply could not ignore, even if they failed to understand that the "Superstar" was a unique, total package: not just the look, not just the charisma, not just the natural inclinations to speech, but also in emoting and performing in front of many thousands of fans.

Steroids and the Death of Eddie Guerrero

Thirty year old professional athletes are not supposed to drop over dead.

So why is it, less than a year after Senate hearings on steroid abuse in professional sports, that such events continue to be a little too commonplace in the world of professional wrestling? Perhaps it is the lifestyle, not just the chemical enhancement of naturally gifted bodies, perhaps the wear and tear of poundings and a rigorous travel schedule, not just the drugs that ensue – to help one sleep, to alleviate the pain, to soothe the inner demons.

Wrestler Eddie Guerrero was found dead in his Minnesota hotel room, which Hennepin County has reported as a result of a massive coronary.

A year ago that the WWE touted an emotional life story of Guerrero on a UPN TV special called Cheating Death, Stealing Life: The Eddie Guerrero Story. The documentary describes the life lead by the 17 year veteran, during which he overdosed more than once, had a near fatal car wreck, was booted from the WWE for some issues and a DUI charge, and then how he got his life together.

But what might be missing is how this man, at five foot eight inches tall and listed at 220 pounds, was able to hang with the 'big boys' in a sport dominated by tall muscle bound men. Anyone who has seen Guerrero in action would immediately realize that he had the body of someone who worked hard at looking the part.

Pro Wrestling Intellectual

Maybe too hard, with too much chemical enhancement.

In 2004, President Bush spoke of the impact of steroids in a State of the Union address. Many in the mainstream press snickered at the notion. Many in the sports reporting business took a deep breath and wondered about the call to action. For those knowledgeable about professional wrestling, and mindful of the growing body count, it was a welcome message. This year, the Senate held hearings on steroid use in major professional sports.

"It seems to me that we ought to seriously consider a law that says all professional sports have a minimum level of performance-enhancing drug testing." John McCain, R-AZ

Unfortunately, the likes of Terry Bolea, James Janos and Wayne Coleman were never called to the microphone. By anyone's definition, these are professional athletes, the best and most well known in their sports over the past three decades. They would have made for interesting copy, to say the least. For in their world, they helped to make body image trump wrestling ability, forged a business sense where physicality became far more important than the talent, and created fan sentiments where newcomers were judged on size, musculature and "the look."

The public hearings on steroid abuse resulted in some changes in baseball's policy, a reinforcement of football's established testing, and nothing for the industry where steroid abuse has littered rosters with scores of dead young men, neon signs of use (if not abuse) and a business culture that thrives on the product of illegal drug use.

In the major sports, steroids are said to enhance performance, but the natural talent and overwhelming ability have to be there to begin with. Muscle bound teenagers are not lining up to be drafted in baseball, basketball, hockey or even football. It takes years of learning, experience and competition to rise to elite status in those sports

Wrestling, however, is a freak show, where having size and a particular body type will take anyone, even a teenager, to the center stage.

Ken Patera, who made noise as an Olympic weightlifter, reducing the challenge for Olympic gold to "who's steroids are better" was a professional wrestling headliner in the 1970's and 1980's. His defense of continued use of steroids was that the "word came down from the promoters, especially McMahon, that you had to be bigger than life. The only way to do that was to take anabolic steroids." Vince McMahon is the owner of what is now the WWE.

But Patera is far from the only professional wrester who publicly talked about steroids. The aforementioned trio, better known to wrestling fans as Hulk Hogan, Jesse Ventura and Superstar Billy Graham, have all had their moments in the spotlight.

Ventura's autobiography, Ain't Got Time to Bleed, is ripe with steroid talk.

"I had been talking about them for years, saying, "Doesn't anybody else out there see what's going on?" Steroids came into wrestling with the advent of the bodybuilder physique popularized by "Superstar" Billy Graham, who suffers grave medical problems to this day from his past use."

More significantly, Ventura admits "I used steroids occasionally myself."

Hulk Hogan had his famous steroid moment on the Arsenio Hall show, where he admitted to using steroids – three times in his life for the purpose of healing a shoulder injury. "I am not a steroid abuser and I do not use steroids" he told the talk show host, and the denial had some credibility – until the infamous George Zahorian trial.

Hogan revealed the reasons for steroids use at the trial: "To heal injuries, to keep on going, the schedule was tough. It gave an edge. For bodybuilding. When I first started it was to get big and gain weight." Healing injuries is the legitimate medical reason for taking this drug, but obviously not the typical purpose, as Hogan admits.

Later, the WWF's ringside doctor would be convicted of illegally distributing steroids, to wrestlers and the WWF's owner. During the trial, the prosecution assailed Hogan's public denial.

"Government: The statements that you made to the press about steroids were truthful?

Hogan: No. "

Superstar Billy Graham was a groundbreaking anti-hero who dethroned local legend Bruno Sammartino, and ushered in an era that has plagued the industry. "Steroids made you both psychologically and emotionally intense. They make you feel you can never be hurt."

Graham paid the price with devastating physical ailments. Ironically, perhaps, the WWF in the late 1980's aired Graham's hip replacement in an effort to promote a return to the ring. A decade plus later, Graham had the other hip replaced, his ankle fused, and survived a serious liver problem.

Pro Wrestling Intellectual

"I became bitter at that point, and after the ankle surgery," Graham said. "I began to tell the world about the dangers of steroids, the pain, suffering I was having because of use and talking about the people who use it."

It was only weeks ago that Graham conducted the services for his friend, Eddy Guererro.

The Zahorian trial could have been a turning point for the industry. Mike Mooneyham, in the book Sex, Lies and Bodyslams, writes of the endemic use of steroids, and how the legal team of Dr. Zahorian positioned the sport and its relationship to steroids. "They're used throughout the WWF. Wrestlers either use them or they don't participate."

Phil Mushnick has been an intense critic of professional wrestling, and Vince McMahon's company in particular. On the issue of steroids, Mushnick gets to the point:

'And why, if, as Bush and McCain claim, steroid use among ball players is a health issue as much as it is an integrity and legal issue, is the health of pro wrestlers, scores of whom have dropped dead over the last 25 years, less important than the health of baseball players?'

The number of dead professional wrestlers continues to grow. Names not well known to fans, like Eddie Guerrero's tag team partner Art Barr or Ed Gantner or Eddie Gilbert, are easily overlooked, as well as dozens of journeyman wrestlers who never reached the big stage. They worked hard, abused chemicals and paid the price for their aspirations.

It is easy to come up with a list of dozens of individuals who perished in their thirties or forties, from mysterious medical ailments or sudden heart attacks. But who can discount the tragic deaths of WWF performers Brian Pillman or British Bulldog Davey Boy Smith? And have the likes of Curt "Mr. Perfect" Hennig, Ray "Big Bossman" Traylor, Rick Rude and Road Warrior Hawk died far too young, with far too little publicity, for no apparent reason?

That many of those in the professional wrestling industry have died, with some connection, speculation or appearance of steroid use is a tragedy that has been far too underreported. And the body count continues to grow, all the while under the radar of much touted regulation and government scrutiny.

Joe Babinsack

WrestleMania XXIV truly was the end of an era.

Like most eras, this one really was over a few years back. In many ways, when Vince bought WCW, and Sting and Ric Flair had that last, symbolic match on a Turner Cable TV Station, that was the end.

That Ric Flair lived on, and had some memorable moments and pretty good matches afterwards, is yet another testament to his enduring reputation and his undeniable legacy as one of pro wrestling's greatest performers.

Today, we live in another era. Actually, Raw on Monday Night, March 31, 2008 is the start of the new, "Modern" era of professional wrestling. While there are many who would argue that the 1980's, and some of the 1990's, comprise the Hulk Hogan era, I'll stay true to my heel fan roots, my visceral appreciation for the leader of the Four Horsemen, and my hardcore schooled, neo-old school, well rounded opinion on Mr. Flair, and stick with calling it the Ric Flair era.

We know when the era was over, March 30, 2008. But when did it begin?

If we went with Hogan, we'd say January 23, 1984. Actually, December 27, 1983 or December 26, 1983 would be more appropriate. The former being Hogan's debut against Bill Dixon; the latter being the end of Bob Backlund's long reign as WWF champ, via disputed loss to the Iron Shiek.

Is it then September 17, 1981, the first of Ric Flair's NWA Championships, not so coincidentally against Dusty Rhodes, in a championship reign that would be like most of the Nature Boy's reigns, short but well-defended?

Would it begin with the last great match of Bruno Sammartino's career, the record setting cage match against Larry Zbyszko at Shea Stadium?

Certainly, it cannot be earlier than that. The 1970's were still the age of NWA domination. The WWF still pledged fealty to the NWA back then. And through the Funks, Brisco and Harley Race, the regions thrived, and television was local, popular and old school.

Then again, could it be December 17th, 1976, when TBS first started broadcasting to four cable stations via Satellite? For what was World Championship Wrestling, in any of its versions, without Ric Flair's presence, and the time that the Superstation made its biggest strides was the building of the foundation of Ric Flair's legacy.

But what was the Flair era?

For one thing, it was the transition period between old school and modern sensibilities.

When Flair debuted, on December 10, 1972, the NWA regions were still mostly in place, and there was a solid arrangement between that overarching organization and its two

Pro Wrestling Intellectual

major spin-offs, the AWA and the WWWF.. Television was a tool for bringing in locals to the local shows, which was almost entirely the profit-making arm of the industry. Closed circuit was on the horizon, and cable TV's deep involvement was beginning to bubble up, but only after the war over Atlanta subsided.

Today, at the end of the Flair era, Closed Circuit is an ancient technology, the Internet is an influential tool of pro wrestling fans (and a major thorn in the side of promoters) and the WWE has gone through major name changes and has swallowed the industry almost whole.

Television now dominates the product, being the most watched aspect, and driving fans world-wide to PPV's. That technology blossomed during Flair's intermittent reigns, and is now the significant profit-making arm of the industry. Merchandising is another significant portion, which likely never aspired to such lofty goals thirty-five years ago.

The Flair era saw the explosion of cable TV. He was on the Flagship of the NWA, and lead the transition from centralized NWA hegemony, lead by a loose association and a revolving presidency, to Carolina based Crockett promotional tool. Flair first won the NWA title when there existed demands on his time and schedule, and transitioned to WCW's control of the belt, and then its diminished reputation, and then Flair himself foreshadowed WCW's demise as he took a contract dispute and the digitized title to the WWF. The enemy.

Things change. And over thirty-five years, things changed immensely. The one thing that remained quite constant was Flair.

Sure, he spent some time as a face, especially in his established home base of the Crockett's Mid Atlantic core territory. In many ways, he pioneered the tweener role, the blending of typical heel and face roles. He was a heel that a significant portion of the fans would get behind. He brought a sense of "coolness" to his championship reigns, basking in his greatness, trumpeting his triumphs and gloating over his conquests.

Storyline or otherwise, in the Ring or in the minds of fans who projected themselves into his massive ego, his legendary status, his awesome ability to talk the talk. And walk the walk.

He was the champ, he is the champ. He was the MAN, and he still is the man.. He touted himself as "the dirtiest player in the game" and because his character is and always seems to have been the perfect blend of villain and anti-hero. Even when he lost the belt, he made sure to win the wars. Even as he established his legacy, he trumped it by "creating" the first real, modern pro wrestling fan movement: The Four Horsemen.

Flair undoubtedly tapped into the teenage sentiments and the growingly violent mindset of the 1980s and beyond. His character was no longer the heel of the past, dastardly but cowardly, inevitably doomed to failure, cheating to win, but always to be caught, and destined to be driven out of town.

The NWA's champion transcended heel and face. While they portrayed characteristics, they played a role of traveling champion, matching up with the local drawing power, helping to draw crowds and profit.

The Northeastern branch of the NWA, Vince McMahon Sr's promotion, relied upon a hero as the champion. Heels were transitory. Larger than life ethnic heroes ruled the world, and were legend because of their stature. (Hogan shed the ethnicity for American patriotism, but played the same role.)

The Midwestern and Western branch was mostly the playground of its owner, Verne Gagne. He was the bland face of wrestling's history, and part of wrestling's ongoing reality: domination by ownership; even if deserved it by technical prowess.

Flair embraced his own concepts, and ran with it straight to wrestling immortality.

He made the heel a natural champion. Even if he never dominated through unbeatable spans, he created the legend akin to the heroes of the sport. Even as he became a hero to a growing heel portion of the fans, his reputation grew, larger than any part of his now recognized greatness: his title reigns, his charisma, his superlative ability in the ring, his drawing power.

Ric Flair became the perennial champion. His momentum went unchecked by losses. He became a hero despite them. His connection with the heel fans was simply awesome. And like any heel throughout history, his persistence, his longevity and his cocky demeanor eventually turns fans to him. For Flair, he already created a base.

Over time, he won over more and more.

Flair picked up more than just the mannerisms of Rogers , the pomp of George, the bumps of Stevens, the whooing of McDaniels, the aura of Valentine. He captured the essence of the heel: the ability to draw heat, the psychological attraction, the glamour and the sheer tenacity.

Beyond that, he captured the break-all-the-rules atmosphere that propelled ECW to niche status. He spoke in catch phrases a decade or more before Stone Cold Steve Austin and The Rock captivated many more millions of mainstream fans.

And he was the perfect counter-point to the bombastic pride of Hulk Hogan.

That underlying competition, between Hogan, whom the hardcores, the newsletter readers and the truest of fans, not the kiddies and the mainstream marks, knew to be a media creation more than a wrestling talent, and Flair, the technically superior antithesis, was the stuff that propelled legends to the status of greatness.

Pro Wrestling Intellectual

Like mid-1990's WWF versus WCW, the rivalry raised the stakes and pumped up an already overwhelming character to new heights.

Flair, even after his stint with the WWF in the early 1990's, even after being chased out, forced to second tier status, virtually retired on several occasions, and even after horrific treatment by Eric Bischoff, Hogan and political powers, could not break his spirit, or his connection to the fans.

That is why this is the Flair era. He won the war.

Flair may have moved from WCW to the WWF, back again, and then to the dominance of the WWE, but he never compromised. He never wore out his welcome with the fans. His selfishness is, in many ways, a problem in addressing his ultimate greatness, but despite some odd presentations, some stupid skits and a period where his red-faced rantings were truly cringe-worthy, the fans never abandoned him.

Sure, he could have been used better. People have been saying that for twenty years, intermittently, incredulously, and never indifferently.

So, today, a few days removed from his retirement match, we look to the future.

What's in store for the future of professional wrestling without THE MAN? And who's going to lead it? Those are questions which will arise in hindsight.

For now, let's hope that there is a man who can capture the spirit of the crowds, the essence of professional wrestling talent and the tenacity to be true to himself, like Flair has done, and will undoubtedly continue to be.

Joe Babinsack can be reached at chaosonejoe@yahoo.com. Today is not the day to rain on anyone's parade. So I'll keep my commentary on Shawn Michaels to myself.

Photo courtesy ECW Press and Larry Matysik.

Joe Babinsack

How Great was Ric Flair?

With Ric Flair's role as an "active" wrestler seemingly reaching a point of real retirement – although with Flair, such talk had plagued his career for much of the past two decades – it seems the time to start talking legacy, and reflecting upon his impact, not just lauding him for his longevity and watching the torch pass to HHH.

There is little question that Ric Flair has achieved much, has been at the top of the popularity charts and has been acclaimed one of the greatest pro wrestlers of all time. I don't wish to diminish any of Mr. Flair's professional accolades, but I do want to point out some peculiarities.

The 1980's were less than arguably Ric Flair's decade.

According to Wrestling Observer awards, and notably "Wrestler of the Year" awards, Flair dominated the industry from 1982 until 1992. His style, technical excellence and reign as NWA Heavyweight Champion all contributed to his well-deserved placement.

In that decade, Flair bested many of the greats of the sport, from Harley Race to Dusty Rhodes, from Ricky Steamboat to Sting, as well as Ronnie Garvin and the tragic figure of Kerry Von Erich, just to achieve a standing as the champion of the (then) largest, and still arguably most prestigious promotion in the history of pro wrestling.

Along the way, Flair beat the – not just "a" -- Who's Who of challengers. Far too many to list, but being the king of the NWA, even in its faded glory, Flair traveled circuits and regions. Just like the Funks, Brisco and Race, like Kiniski and Thesz and the title holders going back to the golden age of the sport, Flair headline against the best and the brightest, often on their home court, and traveled the world to establish the dominance of the NWA, and of course his own talent and reputation.

Yet, there remain some points of contention.

For one, the demise of the NWA came, among other situations, business dealings and economic realities, by the acquisition of James Crockett Promotions of the title, and by having Flair under contract, it gained an otherwise undo control of the legacy of the NWA. Flair was, undeniably in the early 1980's, "THE MAN."

But come the mid 1980's, was he truly still the single greatest wrestler known to modern man, or was he the recipient of a lot of merit, but glowing accolades, the bolstering of the magazine trade, and, in many ways, the epitome and counterweight to the growing popularity of Hulk Hogan? Did the hardcores and passionate fan base of professional wrestling cling to Flair as the savior of the industry, against the new found and often disdained influence of the sleek packaging, "prayers and vitamins" and mainstream acceptance of Hogan?

Flair became the rallying point of not only old school sentiments, but also of the intelligentsia of fans who simply resented the WWF, Vince McMahon, MTV and a cartoonish version of a beloved and established American cultural apparatus.

Flair became the steadfast champion against the encroachment of McMahon's empire, an empire that swallowed up Race and Rhodes , Kerry Von Erich and Ronnie Garvin, the Funks and the other Brisco, and virtually every name player the NWA, aside from Thesz and Sting, and through that domination, and ill conceived opposition strategies, the WWF became the industry.

All that despite the talents, popularity and reputation of Ric Flair.

Am I calling Flair a loser? Hardly. It wasn't Flair that overspent or overbooked or underplanned the ascension of WCW and JCP's acquisitions. It also wasn't Flair that tarnished his own reputation, putting over Garvin, getting sidetracked into feuds, and finding himself, as the 1980's wore on, as a champion with a belt and a reputation, but too few deserving or pushed contenders.

Don't start with me about Steamboat and Funk. I'm talking about the period of 1986 until those great matchups. I can get sidetracked into explaining the history, and again, Flair was more the victim of Crockett's inability to plan and completely hideous buyout and dismantling of the UWF, as well as the booking of Dusty Rhodes.

But still, it wasn't the lack of a title match between Flair and Steve Williams that doomed WCW. It still touted Ric Flair as the perennial champion, and still built a lot of popularity around the Four Horsemen. The legacy of Flair from that era, as well as the domination of the Horsemen, pervaded the 1990's until fans turned to "ECW" as the new alternative.

This leads me to some underlying points.

Flair's reign as "Wrestler of the Year" lasted from the early 1980's, to the early 1990's. Actually, 1992. Is it ironic, or more, that Hulk Hogan's departure from the WWE was in 1992 -- the year Ric Flair finally dethroned Hogan in the "reality" of the WWF, and was rewarded with his last "Wrestler of the Year" accolade. But who dethroned Flair? Who dominated the 1990's? Vader, Sabu; Michaels, Hart, or Austin?

Vader held the promise of a huge guy who could go, and who could himself challenge Hulk Hogan in terms of power, visually and with expectations of much greater things. But Vader's domination of the US scene was far more fleeting than had been expected.

Sabu? I loved Sabu, and apparently so did much of the insider community, but his daredevil brand of wrestling and unique approach lasted only about a year before he was no longer all that unique. Also, his own style of being a daredevil was one that he perfected, but far too many have copied to their own self-destruction.

Shawn Michaels, Bret Hart and Steve Austin all have claims to greatness.

Michaels was, in the mid-1990's, the heir apparent. He had a look, the skill, the showmanship and the expectations to be one of the very best. But Shawn had some unfortunate injuries, and more so, an unfortunate attitude at the prime of his career. Unlike Flair, who would put over anyone that the company asked of him, The Heartbreak Kid played politics, pouted and claimed far too many a coincidental injury to be allowed to rise the level of Flair's greatness.

Even as Michaels establishes his legacy in longevity, he will always have the asterisk, or a frowny face, beside his name, a symbol of the smile he lost when he was asked to do a job.

Bret Hart, in terms of being a pure wrestler, surpassed Mr. Flair in greatness. But the Hitman gimmicked and the personality quite frankly paled to the Nature Boy. Wrestling is an artform, but it also is a popularity contest. Tragedies aside, Hart could outwrestle, but never could outshine Ric Flair in terms of all-around greatness.

Stone Cold rose to a pinnacle of mainstream viability that Flair never achieved, and took the industry to heights of profitability that may never be seen again. In terms of toughness, in terms of connecting with more of the fan base, and in terms of taking pro wrestling to a higher plane of popularity, Stone Cold surpassed Ric Flair mightily.

But, in terms of domination of reigns or years, and simply in terms of being the epitome of a champion, even Steve Austin fell short of Ric Flair's grandeur.

We can re-argue that debate of whether the 1990s, or a decade, century or millennium ends at 9, or at the 0, but I'll say the decade ends at 1999, and deftly avoid commentary on HHH. I mean, if HHH is chasing Flair's greatness, in terms of a mythical number of World Championships, then he must think the world of THE MAN.

But, back to Ric Flair's greatness.

On promos, he was the king. Full of passion, enough comedy to be interesting, enough yelling, screaming and catch-phrases to be the fore-runner of the Rock's success, and Flair could put people in the seats, sell a great feud and put over an opponent in the right way. Of course, come the end of the 1990's, some of it became passé.

The heart attack angles were more an extension of his on-air personality and momentum of his expected promo level than an unfair imposition. Being over-the-top became commonplace for Flair. But still, it is hard to argue against him having been, and continuing to be, one of the greats on the microphone.

As a wrestler, it has been said that Flair could put a broom over. Of course, there would be the Flair Flop, the Flair Flip and the slam off the top rope, a lot of begging off, and an eventual Figure Four and reversal spot. I'm less concerned about Flair figuring out how to put the Figure Four on a broom's handle, and more so about how the broom will throw him off the top rope when he lingers too long ... but still, he can pull off such a match, even at his present age.

Once again, Ric Flair is great. His legacy will always be of one of the great champions, and one of the sport's biggest icons. So, if you want to argue with me about my take on his legacy, go ahead. I'm still a Bruno Sammartino guy – Bruno's impact on attendance, his ability to change up his style, and the still glowing passion he instills in his fans cannot be disputed. I still think Lou Thesz was unquestionably great. I still argue that the Funks surpassed Flair in pure wrestling talent and professionalism and longevity. Misawa and Kobashi and other Japanese stars were equal to the task of comparisons on most levels.

For most of the past two decades, discounting some great years and feuds with Steamboat and Funk, and with Savage, and arguably some of the historic battles with Hogan (None of which drew money!) most promotions were looking to put Mr. Flair out to pasture.

He was readily let go to change from WCW to WWF and back again, with little effort (aside from that big gold belt lawsuit) to keep him from moving. WCW in the ascension of its fortunes, and throughout most of its fall, constantly buried him. At a time when his leadership and presence, let alone wrestling talent, could have been used by the WWE in the post WCW takeover era, he was once again mishandled and strangely positioned.

And now, in the true twilight of his career, even with the eternal arguments about his superiority by wrestling intelligentsia, the adoration of one of his peers and strongest political animals in the business, and the ongoing support and appreciation from a majority of the fans, Ric Flair still cannot get a spotlight on his talents.

That "last hurrah" storyline, one that apparently Stone Cold pitched and sometimes seemingly approved and greenlighted, is a no-brainer, and one that would undoubtedly connect with the larger portion of the fans. It would be set up by expectations of Flair talking and wrestling, based on his otherwise undeniably great legacy and the support of some of his biggest fans on the WWE's creative and support payrolls.Even being in the ring with this great talent, whether it be Kennedy or MVP, or a host of others, could and should elevate their status by the rub. But all is amiss. To me, Ric Flair was great, and Ric Flair has a true legacy on the industry.

Forgive me if I refuse to call him the greatest.

And if you think I slight him, then what do you truly feel about those who are doing more to harm his legacy, and denying him a possible crowning moment of his career?

Joe Babinsack

CHOKEHOLD

By Jim Wilson and Weldon T. Johnson

The impact of Chokehold is multi-faceted, and quite frankly, would have been more monumentally important if published more than two and a half decades ago, when the names involved still had power, and the NWA still existed as a business force.

Nonetheless, Jim Wilson's book, part autobiography, part expose of THE BUSINESS, provides an insight into the operations, and notably the underhanded ones, that prevailed in an industry close-minded and protective-at-all-costs of its peculiar form of monopolization of business.

Since Jim Wilson has, at his disposal, some 3000 pages of Justice Department records from three decades of investigation, plus his own eyewitness accounts of various unethical practices, plus his hearsay accounts from other victims of the wrath of THE BUSINESS, it is hard to dispute the facts.

From Eddie Faieta to Eddie Mansfield, from Antone "Ripper" Leone to Roy Shire, from The Sheik to Angelo Poffo (and sons), from probably every scandal that rocked the wrestling world through the 1990's and from every recorded complaint to the Justice department from the 1950's on up, the facts and stories are documented and disseminated.

One simply cannot argue the facts. Yet it is not without its flaws.

Unfortunately, as has been learned in more than one court proceeding, and notably several involving the peculiar state of affairs of pro wrestling, sometimes the facts just don't matter.

So, when Wilson and Johnson bring up the Vince McMahon steroid distribution trials as one more example of the corruption and the unethical nature of THE BUSINESS, the mirroring of that particular trial becomes more than ironic.

At some point, the piling on becomes a distraction, not a condemnation. At some point, the relative ease to grasp and explain, to seize relevance and line it up with the mounting mountains of malfeasance, all becomes overkill. What's more, by quoting, citing and detailing 'facts' surrounding scandal, tragedy and investigations, it enhances negativity.

While many aspects of the professional wrestling business are indeed, and have always been, based on a sense of working the "mark", on exploitation and on predatory business practices, the legacy of the business also includes a hundred years of profits for promoters and for talent alike.

Quoting people before and after lawsuits only leads to the most negative of snippets. After a while, it gets tiresome. After all, no one forced people to get into the business, and it seems the excesses are often taken out on those who don't get the message that they should leave it. (Not that anything excuses criminality or unethical behavior.)

While Sable's story is certainly appealing and apropos to a condemnation of the lack of humanity of wrestling promotions, and a distinct chapter in the exploitation of talent, it remains tangential to the grand story of Jim Wilson himself.

Vince McMahon and the WWF/E as well, and all the trials and tribulations, the tragedies and the scandals that beset the WWF in the decade before it became the WWE, are on one hand a continuation of historical patterns, but still, the nature of the industry has changed so much that indictments do not neatly line up.

So when we discuss the history of the cable TV wars, it starts off connected very deeply to one James E Barnett, the scourge of James Wilson's wrestling career, and completely relevant.

But once we sidestep into the lamentable tragedy of Owen Hart, and the utter horror sideshow that was the Erich Kulas incident, it starts to lose some perspective. And in terms of the Kulas situation, the facts start lining up more with Wilson's contentions of an INDUSTRY out of control than with my recollections of what happened.

And thus, perspective seems to be the largest flaw of the book.

(Oversimplification is another. Promoters put up huge investments of money and their decisions on who to "push" and how to arrange matches are readily dismissed. Roy Shire is quoted that promoters made millions simply by having a territory. By the end of the 1980's, no territories really existed. What happened to that gravy train? The height of the NWA, as Wilson notes, was over 40 individuals controlling the BUSINESS. How did it diminish so greatly if profits were easy to gain?)

The very root of Jim Wilson's crusade against the pro wrestling industry seems highly entrenched in naïvete as much as it is idealistic; while it is highly commendable, it is all the while being futile because of the nature of the business, the composition of the talent and the interests of all involved.

In other words, the crusade is as convoluted as Wilson's history.

Following his career from highly touted athlete and All-American at Georgia to his years as a pro football player, with the Atlanta Falcons and the Los Angeles Rams, it becomes rather obvious that Jim Wilson lead a life of a professional athlete. Not as extravagant as today's players, but one protected, wealthy and hobnobbing with celebrity nonetheless.

When Wilson gets involved in professional wrestling, he can wonder if the industry is meaning to exploit his celebrity and athleticism. That's quite obvious. What's also obvious is that Wilson had access to the highest levels of the NWA at the time, interacting with former and future world champions, with the major players of booking, promoting and behind-the-scenes deal making; as well as the positioning and matches that would build him to be a star in the sport.

In an off-handed way, Wilson speaks of tagging with Tim Woods and Johnnie Walker, as well as Lou Thesz, as if that was all par for the course!

Thesz, the perennial NWA Champion of the 1950's and 1960's, in tag teams with Jim Wilson? This was an industry built upon reputation and ability, and Jim Wilson, at the writing of the book, still doesn't "get" that he was given extraordinary placement on the cards, and was being given the "rub" of being in the ring with some great names, by which his stock would be enhanced, and if he paid attention, his talent would increase as well.

But Jim Wilson got in a position where he feared getting "rubbed" the wrong way.

Not to make light of the potential for sexual harassment and promoters taking way too much advantage of their "independent contractors" but the whole lead up to the much ballyhooed come-on of James Barnett is replete with red flags and innuendo, points of contention and points where both sides let it go on too long and too far.

I'm not about to recap what the reader needs to read.

What I do say is that there's the age old adage of how to make frog soup, when the frog's going to jump out of the boiling water, and how very appropriate that analogy is to this situation, except that a man isn't a frog, and should be able to see the fire being built and notice that the water is getting rather warm -- far before the boiling point is reached.

That being said, the noble purpose of the book, in terms of unionizing the workers, is laudable.

However, the details are far from being strong, and the persistence of Jim Wilson, mostly in partnership with Thunderbolt Patterson and others, seems readily disrupted by the various aspects of the industry on all fronts. The most frustrating aspect is the insistence of changing the industry while wanting desperately to be involved in the industry!

Wilson's perspective takes more hits along the way, when he decries the treatment, the impositions and the nature of the sport.

* He bemoans the use of the blade, yet notes that Jack Brisco never bladed.

Jack Brisco went on to become NWA World Heavyweight Champion as a baby face who never bled. It was possible, by Jim Wilson's own words, to succeed despite that preference. If it was possible, why didn't it happen for Jim Wilson?

* Wilson bemoans having to "put over" opponents and to lose, saying that people who refused would never work again. Blacklisting happened, and is unethical and illegal, and happened for the worst of reasons. However, there are page after page of stories how people refused to do jobs and go away with it. There's an example early on how no one on a Los Angeles show wanted to put over a smaller Mexican worker. If that's not an ability to say "no" then I'm not sure what it is.

* One of the most perplexing issues, the Battle for Atlanta, is one that twists up logic and loyalty.

Jim Wilson was trained by Ray Gunkel, the NWA lead stockholder of the Georgia region. Gunkel made promises to Wilson, about being groomed for championships and the like.

Ray Gunkel dies, suddenly, of a heart attack.

Jim Wilson throws his loyalty, not to Gunkel's widow, but to the NWA group that threw Ann Gunkel out of the promotion, forcing her to start her own group if she wanted to continue in the wrestling business. Apparently, Wilson believed that the NWA would honor the promises of Ray Gunkel more than the late promoters's widow would.

Now, if that isn't illogical enough, Jim Wilson -- in the heat of an all out war between NWA mainliners and outlaw promotion headed by Gunkel's widow -- constantly mentions his loyalty to Ray, and his expectations of big things. Many, including his friend Jack Brisco, tell him to be patient. Somehow, Jim Wilson isn't patient at all, and complains more and more about payoffs, and then the whole Barnett/Australia incident takes place.

The convolution of loyalty and allegiance seems so incredible to behold! He listened in as the NWA big shots declared their intent to destroy Ann Gunkel's "upstart" promotion, and he didn't seem aware enough to realize that in a war, you've got to choose sides, not play up loyalty to both.

Besides, if unethical treatment was the underpinning of Wilson's complaints about the NWA, why did he side with them when he had first-hand knowledge of their intentions to use every means possible to destroy competition in Atlanta???

At this point, setting aside all the convolutions of that Barnett incident, Wilson trumps his own naivete one step more. He refuses to explain his story to anyone in the NWA!

The situation which never went down, but cost Wilson much pay, four weeks of a lucrative tour, and caused him to be blacklisted (blackmailed seems a bad word to use for all of this, but Wilson uses that word as well) ends up costing him friends and financial ties simply because he becomes so idealistic that he won't spill the truth to people he

Joe Babinsack

claims to have trusted.

And then he rails against lost friendship? And he wonders why no one trusts him, or that no one gives him work? And he bemoans Bill Watts, Jack Brisco and a host of other NWA bookers when he wouldn't spill the beans on why he got blacklisted to begin with?

Wilson's demands on all his lawsuits seem to be centered on getting back into the BUSINESS -- that very same industry he rails against and doesn't trust and finds unethical. It boggles the mind!

That being said, the sordid details and the inner workings of the NWA, circa late 1960's to mid 1980's are fascinating and quite frankly, a must read for anyone who wants to "know" the depths of depravity and destruction of which the industry was engaging.

Jim Wilson's participation in the exposure of the business, on a 20/20 show that put blading on the national spotlight, and his ongoing participations in exposing sexual misconducts and steroid abuse and drug deaths are later aspects of his crusade that are more laudable. His idealism is equally frustrating and puzzling, but Wilson truly shows that his heart is in the right place.

I will take another column to go into the concept of a pro wrestling union, the pluses and the negatives, the details (or lack thereof) and the possibilities. The details in the book just don't go far enough. SAG and the NFLPA are mentioned, and Wilson did try to engage those powerhouses in the early 1980's, but somehow when those important guilds gained true power, no one has been knocking on their doors.

Jim Wilson's book on the industry is important and historical, but I woudn't call it great -- in terms of presentation, logic and perspective, it gets pulled down a bit too much by issues of perspective and an underlying chase of the negative, but the facts are the facts, and the nature of the expose is vastly important and one that should be understood by fans of today's product.

While the WWE is the heir to the cynical and exploitative practices of an industry controlling the professional wrestling business across the entire United States, the rolling on of history and assignment of NWA dirty tactics to Vince McMahon's own business practices is a difficult thing to assume. Pro wrestling today isn't the same animal. It's better on some fronts and worse on others.

The underlying issue of health assurances and insurance remain, however.

From reading, it is both easy to condemn and hard to argue the WWE's connection to that legacy. Piling on the facts to make a statement is never a wise move, either legally or morally, it makes the audience cynical and taints the real issues that need to be addressed. With some focus and a better perspective, Chokehold would be at the level of greatness.

Just like the industry itself, excesses and personal views take something away from credibility.

PART II OF THE CHOKEHOLD REVIEW/COMMENTARY

Jim Wilson's book, Chokehold, remains a significant piece of pro wrestling history, often despite itself. But the one gnawing issue, and the focus of Wilson's decades long campaign against the wrestling industry, is an insistence that pro wrestlers have a union.

Wilson's own details are finally put forth at the last chapter. Much about this "debate" typically ends up in platitudes and generalizations, demands from perspectives that don't seem to line up with the reality of the industry, and buried somewhere within the ranting and raving, a strong kernel of legitimacy.

From my own perspective, which is neither one of a wrestler or that of the promoters, but one of a long time wrestling fan -- without an axe to grind in either direction – there seems to be merit for a collective interest of professional wrestlers in terms of securing health care and other group benefits. Other obvious issues include the potential for a pension, as well as merchandise profits.

On the other hand, other aspects of unionizing seem impossible. Collective bargaining, demands of creative control, insistence upon percentages of the gate, and related issues where it's not so much an issue of "tradition" or "that's the way its got to be" as much as the peculiarities of the industry.

It is an obvious comparison that most major sports are unionized.

While the insistence of pro wrestlers as athletes is not an issue that I would even deign to debate, the bigger picture is much more murkier. Professional sports are comprised of well organized teams, each with different ownership, with national broadcasting AND local broadcasting rights. Each of the major sports leagues have established rules, guidelines and some form of cap on salary expenditures.

While it may be easy to point out that the salary cap, with requisite reporting issues and a sense of a "fair" distribution of profits, would be a strong example of what would be great about a unionized pro wrestling labor force, it isn't exactly that easy to jump to that conclusion.

Those sports, as a conglomeration of competing interests, had inherent tensions that needed to be quelled, and a sense of overall fair competition to establish. (Jokes about baseball are not necessary. I live in Pittsburgh and can joke about that situation with the best of them.)

The point being that unions were in some part a tool of the upper management of those professional sports leagues to coalesce league rules, helping to establish a framework, to impose that framework and to create more interests in maintaining that framework.

In the pro wrestling industry, there is no overarching organization. With the NWA at its peak, there was a comparable situation. But at that time the sports leagues weren't exactly fully unionized as they are currently.

Thus a major strike against attempting to unionize is that 1) there is no overarching super-management interested in pitting athletes against owners for the greater good of the "sport"

The other point from previous items is revenue.

While the WWE is certainly a money making effort, its money comes almost exclusively, and for the most part, directly, from the fans. Professional sports leagues do not rely directly upon live attendance for their continued existence. Sure, it's a part of profits, and one that cannot be dismissed, but salaries are rarely tied to gate, they are tied to ratings and to the fees paid by major television and cable networks to broadcast the games and the overall health of the league.

In wrestling, revenue often gets tied to a single individual, a hot program or an upward cycle. While TV and Cable have provided some revenue, at best they provide a bit of profit to the overall picture, and never a strong stream of cash. TV has traditionally been the vehicle to sell fans on going to the house shows, buying the PPVs and purchasing the merchandise.

Because of that revenue flow situation, the industry is based on promotions developing and maintaining solid interest of the fans.

Wilson argued that promoters were making lots of moneys in the territorial days. He quotes Roy Shire in a deposition claiming that promoters could easily make a "million" or such. But anyone who followed wrestling for the past two decades, on a world-wide basis, knows that wrestling promotion is not a guarantee, and that losing millions has been the rule, not the exception.

Pro Wrestling Intellectual

Part of the problem is that the industry is based on a different set of revenue streams, and part of the problem is that wrestling has not established itself in a way in which it can generate money in an indirect fashion.

That successful pro wrestling promotions must generate money through PPV buys and, to a lesser degree, house shows, means that those promoters are incredibly reliant upon the whims of its customers. And while the WWE has captured a business plan that has been able to reap great profits from its positioning in the PPV universe, it has been proven that changing technology, changing sentiments and ever changing interests of fans has created great risk in the industry.

We all know that WCW blew many tens of millions of dollars in a very short period of time. Those who follow the Japanese wrestling industry know that MMA has crippled the viability, let alone the profitability of wrestling promotions. Back to the US, we can rave and give props to Paul Heyman for running ECW as a cutting edge promotion, but it was never profitable. And Mexico, in a vastly different economic situation, ran from white hot to very cool and back to white hot again in popularity. Whether it can sustain itself is yet to be seen.

And of course, TNA has shown that even five years, some of the biggest possible names and a slot on a ratings proven Cable network isn't a guarantee of profitability.

In other words, how can the wrestlers clamor for a union, for health care or for pensions in an atmosphere where promoters are fighting for survival?

Then again, the WWE isn't.

And the bigger picture of the WWE is that it established itself as a publicly traded corporation. Because of that situation, its books are wide open to stockholders, and for release.

Whether the WWE can continue to treat its wrestlers on a par much below athletes, and also below entertainers is something that may eventually become a public spectacle.

Pro wrestlers are not reality TV stars. They follow, much to the delight of WWE's Creative Deparment, scripts instead of the old school dance or old school cutting of promos. With the insistence of the then WWF that professional wrestling is not sport, but entertainment, they jettisoned one of their strongest defenses against their operating practices, and their insistence on using "independent contractors"

To get back to Wilson, he finally brought up his "Bill of Rights" and does mention his efforts to get the NFLPA and the SAG (and other actor's guilds) involved in the struggle. Jim Wilson's contributions to the argument are the following:

1) Health and Safety Standards

2) Union or Guild

3) Restore State Athletic Commissions

They all seem to boil down to health insurance.

The notion of providing health insurance, or allowing the "independent contractors" to group together for such benefits, seems far from unreasonable. The counter-argument is likely that any move towards that direction would only grow stronger once the boys are organized.

But the interesting aspect is that if the industry, in some way or form, provided health benefits, and matched a contribution of the talent in order to establish such a "benefit" then the other issues of health and safety would likely fall in line.

Then again, if health care gets involved, then testing and physicals and many of the underlying issues that have plagued the industry for the past two decades (in particular) would see the light of day.

Maybe that would be the greatest side effect of them all.

Pro Wrestling Intellectual

Extremely Strange

By J.R. Benson

First, let me say that this is one of the most interesting, informative, detailed, solidly written, but vastly controversial books I've read for the column. Second, let me make a DISCLAIMER: **This is not a book for anyone other than an adult!!!!!!!**

The nature and the descriptions of hardcore and extremely hardcore violence, whether one wants to debate calling it pro wrestling, does stay at mostly an "R" rating level, but it goes beyond that.

While the nature and the descriptions of pornography and sexuality and associated perversions, to call it by the most fitting names, are really of the "R" rating level, and really are at the Howard Stern appropriate age level, there are some definite situations and descriptions that would give me pause in explaining to a minor.

However, the use, abuse, descriptions and details of drug use are by far the most offensive, extreme, problematic and difficult to defend. Beyond that, by the sheer nature of the descriptions and presentation, I would strongly caution against this book being sold or read by children.

You may call me a prude, you may call me every name in the book. But I've discussed the drug situation with JR, and while my review is beyond his control, I have clarified some thoughts and appreciate his input on the subject.

I do realize that I am hyping this book to a large degree because of my disclaimer, and I do realize that the curiosity factor, and the nature of saying "don't" in such a situation are likely to cause more interest than not, but so be it.

Once again, let me state clearly, that this is not a book I would recommend for anyone who is not a mature adult!!!!!

The world of professional wrestling has many styles and formats and levels of intensity.

Debates and arguments about the nature of professional wrestling are welcome, and I'll likely delve into further discussions in forthcoming columns. Suffice to say, my definition of professional wrestling is thus:

Professional Wrestling: an entertainment form, to be performed by trained athletes, with a purpose of displays of violence, in the framework of a "match" and with a mindset of interaction between participants, an avoidance of real violence, and under the auspices of appropriate commissions.

Now, we can certainly argue that, and it leaves a lot of interpretation.

To that definition, the nature of not simply hardcore wrestling, but the genre and style of the more extreme hardcore style, the one from which J.R. Benson has made a name, a reputation and a cult-like following, really does take the notion of professional wrestling and expands the envelope.

The obvious and major issue with most of what I've read about Incredibly Strange Wrestling, Extremely Strange Wrestling, and in many ways, the one time explosion of backyard wrestling types, is the "avoidance of real violence" part. A close second is the nature of training, followed as well by the regulation and the mindsets and the displays.

OK, let me simply say that the nature of the "professional wrestling" aspect of what J.R. Benson has perpetrated on the world pushes everything I've ever held about profession wrestling beyond the acceptable envelope.

And yet, after reading this book by a well informed wrestling historian, by someone who fully understands the nature of pro wrestling as presented in modern history, who clearly understands the shortcomings and failures of most modern interpretations, and who admits throughout this book of the extreme nature of his own form of professional wrestling – after all this – I cannot readily argue against labeling J.R. Benson a professional wrestler.

There are examples of matches, events and situations where he clearly has "crossed the line" but he seems to be the first to admit it.

Furthermore, as he explains in detail, in terms of his training with the APW of Roland Alexander, and ongoing interactions, matches and participation with unquestionably legitimate pro wrestling stars and promotions and fan groups, J.R. Benson is no stranger to the world of professional wrestling, nor has he turned his back on the industry in any way.

It's just that his own sick, twisted version of professional wrestling simply isn't made for the mainstream. Now, on the surface of it, I find much of the presentations of ISW and ESW quite abhorrent. In many ways, my thoughts of J.R. Benson, the person, are highly questionable to say the least, and to say that he's diametrically opposed to my own beliefs and social understandings is to be an understatement!

But, after reading the man's book, and scrutinizing his professional wrestling career, after examining his credentials, after figuring out his "take" on the industry, and after exchanging dozens of emails, I'm vastly impressed by his understanding of professional wrestling, and, after wiping away the figurative bodily liquids and frighteningly obscene creative juices, I must admit to a certain level of admiration.

But a bigger question ensues. J.R. Benson is, by his claims and reputation, and the quotes and explanations of notable industry figures, a great promo guy. He's also very creative,

Pro Wrestling Intellectual

has a strong resume of work (even omitting his own psychotic promotions) and has a background of being trained, of interacting with high level names, and boasts of a strong acquaintance with James Cornette.

(As an aside, the wrestler/valet known in OVW as Synn was involved with J.R. Benson and is now with Cornette. The exploits of Stacey and her sister Brenda are detailed throughout the book, as they ran with Benson and wrestled on a variety of events, and their interactions inside and outside the rings of the APW promotion are quite the story!)

What has bubbled up in my own cynical, pro wrestling inspired mind is that there is a good chance that good ole J.R. has his working shoes on throughout this book.

He just has that natural charm, a devious intellect, and a vast reservoir of wrestling knowledge, and a seemingly strong business peddling his twisted DVDs. The book of course is a marketing scheme in and of itself, and has to be taken in that light.

On the surface, the book is a history of J.R. Benson's involvement with professional wrestling from his youth to the present. Living in the San Francisco area for almost all of that time, with an ill-fated move across the country, and briefly in Tennessee, to test the waters of professional wrestling in the mid-1990's.

What I love is the perspective of a wrestling fan, who turns into a wrestler, who then goes back to being a fan. There aren't all that many books that show the fans point of view, and this does a great job of capturing the addictive nature of the business.

This happens to be one of many for the author.

But the history of the west coast wrestling business is interesting. Benson explains the fans perspective during the tail end of the Roy Shire promotion, and the appearances of the AWA and the WWF in the 1980's. It's quite interesting to read someone's growth as a fan, and how much it mirrored my interests, from Apter mags to newsletters to the Internet.

Dave Meltzer's Wrestling Observer is somewhere in the midst of it all. Although the newsletter coverage and Dave himself become both sought after goals and then foils, in the hopes of getting coverage for Incredibly Strange Wrestling and its evolution into Extremely Strange Wrestling. Having followed the sport and being roughly the same age as J.R., I know of his name, his exploits and his reputation to some degree. I recall the controversies and the discussion (and disgust) over some of his productions.

As Benson stumbled into becoming trained as a pro wrestling talent, he all but takes a leading charge at introducing hardcore wrestling to the area. Once again, that is for good or bad, but he certainly was fearless in his involvement
For 300 pages, the book is interesting, albeit with a sick and twisted coverage of the drug scene, and the overall weirdness and outlandishness of J.R. Benson's warped creativity.

Joe Babinsack

The details on the hardcore carnage are disturbing.

The details on the drug use even more so.

The sexuality of the promotions push the envelope, even beyond the Howard Stern level.

For about 300 pages, I was lulled into a false sense of security. It didn't seem as bad as the reputation that preceded it. The untrained nature of some of Benson's wrestling associates was troubling, but there seemed a sense of restraint, and an understanding that Benson was more into the spectacle and showmanship – albeit a warped and 'evil' mindset – and his interactions with the west coast scene, even volunteering for being put through a table by Sabu, seemed crazy but plausibly acceptable.

The drug use was out of hand, and if real as written, begs the question of sanity and existence.

Along the way, we are introduced to Vic Grimes and the burgeoning hardcore scene in APW, as Roland Alexander seemed to have his mind changed on following the exploits of ECW, and moved from staid and traditional wrestling promoter to hardcore maven. The stories of Alexander, notably the Scott Hall incident, are legendary and yet fairly presented.

As are the details of ISW and ESW. At first I wasn't sure how such a self-admitted drug fiend could remember all this stuff, but as Benson relates, his typical posse of Ron Hed and Peter Hinds, the ring announcer and cameraman respectively, more than likely provided through the video taping an ongoing video diary of his own exploits.

And thus the details are well presented and hard to dispute.

But again, shortly after that 300 page mark, everything went to hell. Obviously by Benson's own words in a nightmarish event, and also for the reader, as the shocking jolt of the detailed depths of Benson's style of hardcore wrestling is exposed far more than the business in general.

It was an event called, appropriately enough, ESW, Exposing the Business.

Now, as usual, I'm not one to give a blow-by-blow description of what the reader can read or watch on video. Of course, this doubles back to my concerns about overly hyping J.R. Benson's maniacal and atheistic and outrageous presentations and promotions. You can get those details elsewhere and on line in a variety of forms, and I'm sure J.R. would love it if you bought his merchandise at his web site.

Suffice to say, the details of what happened at Exposing the Business are sickening.

As I presented my own understanding of professional wrestling, violence is to be staged, not felt. And the physical safety of the wrestlers is paramount; actually, the only thing it comes secondary to is the safety of the fans.

All of that is far more disturbing than the perversions presented in and out of the ring.

Drug use, to the extent that it diminishes capacity for coherent thought, for protecting the safety of others, is about the worst thing I can imagine in the confines of a wrestling event. That Benson and others didn't just condone, and didn't just dabble, but completely abused and allowed it to abuse their actions is unjustifiable on any level.

Taking chair shots has been a controversy that has exploded over this year. Drug use as well. And here's a book, and a particular event, that completely destroys any known sense of restraint in regards to either of those horrific abuses of body.

From a shattered ankle that is far more gruesome than any other situation in wrestling history, to taking full bore, ungimmicked guitar shots, to tossing objects into the crowd, it's a nightmarish scene, and completely destroys any notion that the attempts of ESW were in the realm of professional wrestling.

And again, not because of the incredibly distasteful nature of storylines, gimmicks or acts.

J.R. Benson has established himself as almost a cult like figure in the most outlandish style of professional wrestling that has ever existed. But his book is a strong piece of history, both in the nature and the results of pushing the envelopes of acceptable presentations of the sport.

Benson finishes the book strong, with a great overview of what's wrong with the industry today, where it went wrong, and how it can right itself. Which may, in many ways be hypocritical, considering the levels to which he obliterated standards and acceptance of the sport in and of his own promotional work.

But aside from many complaints of subject matter, and controversies of his own making, "Extremely Strange" is an excellent piece of writing. I do wish J.R. would have avoided some rather pedestrian commentary on politics, and he provides a rather incredible defense of Vince Russo that also raises eyebrows, but once again, Benson's style of self-promotion, his professional wrestling expertise and understanding of history, as well as his unyielding creative juices and insistence on pushing every button imaginable all roll into a big question of how much of J.R. Benson's autobiography is real, and how much is worked.

After all is said and done, that is the core nature of any truly masterful pro wrestling endeavor.

I just remain hopeful that some of the damage explained and exploited is more fictional than factual.

Joe Babinsack

Independent Contractor?

We live in a litigious world, and the reality is that professional wrestling remains a billion dollar industry. The only real question about the lawsuit is -- why did it take so long?

Eric Bischoff speculates that some "down on their luck" wrestlers decided to run with the lawsuit. With Scott Levy part of the mix, that seems furthest from the case. Actually, most guys who would have an axe to grind with the WWE, and/or considered desperate, would probably have already settled for a Legends contract, and the several thousand that comes with selling their names and likenesses (and other fine print stuff, I'm sure.)

The lawsuit filed threatens the WWE's long established business practices of hiring out talent as "Independent Contractors" and presents some interesting questions.

Most are concentrating on dollar amount ramifications.

I'm sure the industry can survive with potentially higher employee or contract costs. The WWE is reported to be awash in money, and capable of withstanding several years of downturns and stale storylines.

The legality of the issue isn't easy to predict, although common sense and logic suggests that the points of reality of being an Independent Contractor don't exactly line up with what the WWE practices.

While my opinion likely differs from the WWE opinion, which differs from what the wrestlers would want, the obvious important opinion is in the courts, as well as the IRS and potentially other governmental agencies.

But an interesting twist, one that I haven't heard yet, is that the bigger picture of this lawsuit, if it is won by the plaintiffs, may result in a big positive -- for both the wrestlers (in terms of opportunities, not just back pay) and also for fans.

The question of unionizing wrestlers as workers has persisted for many decades, and still remains a pipe dream. The "Independent Contractor" status has always divided and conquered the ranks of talent. It just never makes sense for the top dogs to put all their economic positioning on the line for the less profitable guys.

Sure, some have tried -- Bruno Sammartino and Jesse Ventura and others, and have come away with mixed results.

Bruno stuck up for the guys making a few dollars a night, and insisted that they get paid better, even if it came out of his potential payoff.

Ventura tried to organize, but the fabulous Hulk Hogan stabbed him in the back, according to the story.

Pro Wrestling Intellectual

Any sort of mixed result from this trial could result in a strong bargaining position for the wrestlers, especially in the WWE. One thing that has killed any realistic hope for unionizing is that the wrestlers are not employees, but contractors.

If that practice is significantly altered in the WWE, then we may see wrestlers labeled employees, and employees have an easier route to organizing.

But beyond that, the opportunities for the talent would increase if the Independent Contractor relationship is better clarified.

Almost all the points of the 1992 IRS guidelines (look at Eric Bischoff's blog, or my cursory look at them on the www.wrestlingobserver.com site) benefit the WWE and their interpretation and how they've been allowed to operate.

Considering that the WWE currently owns names and likenesses, controls appearances by contracted talent, dictates storylines, insists upon various aspects of a wrestler's livelihood (style of wrestling, character, unwritten physical appearance, etc.) and basically denies the opportunity to work at will, or work with other promotions, one can readily see a defeat that redefines the realities of Independent Contractors (ie wrestlers) would greatly change a lot of dynamics.

Let's set aside monetary compensation, back pay or future contracts. That's not insignificant at all, but that's the aspect everyone focuses upon.

My take is this: opportunity will grow by leaps and bounds for wrestlers if the Independent Contractor status is redefined.

So much so that the WWE would almost have to start hiring talent instead of maintaining that business relationship.

Consider:

1) The WWE may be positioned to where they could not dictate appearances, nor deny wrestlers from making appearances.

Ric Flair quit because he had lucrative signings and was denied doing them.

If wrestlers truly become independent, then they should be able to line up their own appearances. Furthermore, they may be able to turn down WWE appearances, and book their own. They may be able to turn down a match, citing a better opportunity.

After all, they are Independent Contractors, not employees.

2) Furthermore, what's to deny someone wrestling in multiple promotions?

Why not see Bryan Danielson wrestle in ROH, TNA and the WWE in a month? If a guy isn't used, and could get better deals here and there, one could envision that happening under a clarification.

That might just affect the UFC as well…

3) One interesting ramification would be better wrestling for the fans.

Imagine if wrestlers are contracted by their talent, not just their contracts to one promotion. It would break up some of the glass ceilings, and it would allow talented guys who went all out on a smaller promotion to get paid a bit more to wrestle for the bigger ones.

Exclusive Contracts would be a logical next step, where it would cost the WWE much more to tie someone up. That goes back to the financial end, but the realities of wrestlers shopping their wares, and showcasing their talent, and the ability of guys to turn down stupid stuff, and run for better storylines, would all make for better wrestling for everyone.

4) That leads into a more full blown point, being that the promotions would have a bigger incentive in creating compelling storylines, and would be compelled to involve talent in such decisions.

Days of crappy angles and stupidity and abject nonsense may fade away. Wrestlers would be more powerful in turning down scripts that don't make sense, or would harm their careers.

If they could be deemed truly independent, then those independent minds would have to be enticed to work, not just with money, but with better product. Just like movie stars turn down scripts and companies and projects, the mid-range wrestlers could shop around and take up offers that would better position themselves.

5) Opportunity would then be a little more centered on talent and drive and choices, not just getting locked into contracts.

I saw Colt Cabana the other night, and screamed at how badly the WWE introduced him. Of course, he's getting paid (likely) a lot more than he ever did in ROH or on the indy scene, but imagine if he had some say in his character development.

Sure, it's a double-edged sword, because some talent would not have the capability of developing their personality, and almost everyone would insist on not losing – creative control that would make Bret Hart or Hulk Hogan look like idiots in their contracts – but things would play out.

Point is, things may very well change because of fallout from this lawsuit against the WWE, and while the financial considerations may be the greatest part, the freedom of wrestling talent to make more money from their own choices, and the potential for upgrading the current situations and creating better wrestling may just be a side effect that fans could really appreciate!

Pro Wrestling Intellectual

Is it Time for Vincent K. McMahon to Resign?

While it may be difficult to call what the WWE has been through a scandal, there are growing signs and continuing revelations that suggest that the fallout from the horrendous crimes of Chris Benoit is not going away any time soon.

And it may not be long before the pressures from the public, the scrutiny of the media and/or the curiosity of the government gets to be too much for the WWE to bear.

Indictments of doctors across professional sports are turning up the heat on steroids abuse. While we can all hope that such legalities can help to diminish abuse, there remains in place far too many examples, expectations and neon signs that steroids are necessary for the business. While other sports have shown to have their own problems with steroids, and even with the reputed levels of abuse, no other sports has the blatant history, look and numbers that continue to scream "STEROIDS" like professional wrestling.

Having followed various media and political critics over the years, one of the surest signs that a situation is uncontrollable is when the media stops worrying about timelines, and starts airing "new" facts and facets of the story, no matter how many times or how many people already know about them.

The "Wikipedia" story blew up, in a sense, late last week, even though it was known earlier.

Then, the "wrestling hold" aspect got air play.

Next comes the Steroid allegations again.

Then, the Dr. Astin raid, charges and further details.

We've got a few weeks until toxicology reports come back. Until then, the tabloids will have a field day, there will be ongoing reports on the news wires, and bits and pieces are going to surface, from this situation, from similar (but not so similar) deaths and related stories over the past decade plus.

It's not going to be too long before certain trials, certain arrangements and details of certain "Wellness Policies" hit the news, get ridiculed and get thrown into the mix.

Whether the news reporting deals with facts, factoids or rumors, the depth of this story is great, and the ties to a multitude of other situations, tragedies and ongoing realities of the industry (unspoken, real, worked) will provide a rabid and tabloid press with fodder for those weeks to come and thereafter.

And God forbid anyone else dies in the meantime. And when the next wrestling death occurs, this one will be attached to it, whether accidental, overdose, steroid related or any other cause. That, above all, is the current reality of this tragic and horrific situation: the news media has its sensational story to affix to professional wrestling. Stock footage and clichéd commentary are already in the can.

The WWE, for its part, had been out in front of the story with an aggressive defense, and sense of deflection of the culpability to the alleged murderer himself, not the company he worked for. While this stance is advisable, it will only last for so long.

Inevitably, the WWE is going to have to make a serious effort to make things right.

It was my initial intent to provide some avenues for that effort. Unionization of wrestlers seems a viable one. An utterly harsh steroids policy would be automatic – and yet undoubtedly unbelievable to anyone with any understanding of the sport. Reduced schedules, rotating schedules and a strong sense of downtime for all its talent is vitally necessary.

But the underlying issues are of control, of public perception and of vision.

And to all that, the single most powerful obstacle to change is Vincent Kennedy McMahon, and therein lies the greatest problem.

And for that, perhaps it is time for Vince to fall on his sword.

McMahon is by most accounts a self-made billionaire, both in storyline and arguable (at times) in fact. It was his vision that built up the WWF into what is now the WWE; his vision and business plan that conquered a nation full of regional promotions, and then his leading competitor; his vision that helped launch the careers of Hulk Hogan, Steve Austin and The Rock as mainstream recognizable talents. (Arguably, one could add Jesse Ventura, Sgt. Slaughter, Randy Savage and Roddy Piper to that list, plus a myriad of wrestling superstars that have always lingered under the radar of mainstream celebrity status.)

It was Vince McMahon who made WrestleMania, and forged a new revenue stream for his promotion in Pay-Per-View technology. It was Vince McMahon who made tremendous amounts of money for himself, for his talent and for cable stations like USA, Spike and even for NBC and whatever network SmackDown has appeared upon.

But it has been Vince McMahon's vision that shaped the look and the feel of professional wrestling, both for the good and for the bad.

For years, he focused on circus-like characters, making pro wrestling appeal to a younger crowd, cutting down on the blood, the over-the-top violence and the adult nature that infused most other promotions.

On the other hand, he has always had a respect for body building, and has been instrumental in pushing the bigger guys, the ones who were muscular, the ones who were taller, and the ones who ultimately had more of a focus on body image than traditional wrestling talent.

In many ways, Vince has grown with his audience, and has taken advantage of its ongoing familiarity of his product. While his competitor seized that aspect in the mid 1990's, and captured an incredible portion of the market by riding Vince's own, older stars, he was able to refit his personal image of professional wrestling, making it more mature, more risqué, and more appropriate to an audience that was then in its twenties and thirties.

It seems to me that Vince was able to create a fan base, then rode that fan base when he had to. He brought most of them home in the late 1990's, and reaped profit, fortune and popularity. He crushed his competition and proclaimed himself the undisputed king of professional wrestling. And there are still few arguments against it.

However, from the moment he bought WCW for a song and a dance, he's run headfirst into controversy and bad decisions.

The XFL will always dog him. While the body building promotion of the early 1990's was also indicative of his inability to shift his passion, control and vision to another genre, his foray into professional football was full of bravado, intensity and expectations, but little else. Unlike the dot.com financial whirlwinds of the era, Vince (and NBC) gambled on flash and glamour and sizzle and failed.

In 2004, in an interview with Chad Williams of the Hollywood Reporter, Vince is quoted:."Some people when they get up there in age tend to be a little too conservative, not want to take as many chances."

Being conservative in terms of taking chances has not been what Vince is all about. But it can be argued that he's gone in the opposite way. Many, many insightful observers have noted how Vince is constantly changing his mind, and constantly derailing his own vision. It's as if he's going out of his way to be controversial, to be cutting edge, and to be current.

In that same interview, McMahon also says: "You need to surround yourself with quality human beings that are intelligent and have a vision, and we're doing that." The main problem there is that Vince has surrounded himself with the best minds of the wrestling industry, but then has ignored, cast them aside, and made yes-men out of many of them.

James Cornette is no longer associated with the WWE in any way. Paul Heyman is on the outs, still under contract, but with no input into the creative end. The creative staff is often criticized, but has been formed to serve the whims of Vince McMahon above others. And yet, Michael "Hayes" Seitz is still around, and so is Dusty Rhodes. And many creative names behind the scenes remain, providing a solid foundation for the future.

More so, his children are reaching the prime of their careers, and should be handed greater reigns of power, especially with Vince available as consultant.

Now is an optimal time for Vincent Kennedy McMahon to step aside.

While it will be easy to make him a scapegoat, it will also be easy to celebrate the success of his career and to allow the "changing of the guard" to move away from his vision as the guiding force of the company.

While the WWE can and will survive without Vince, the main question is, can Vince survive without the WWE?

In reality, that is a pathetic question at this time.

If the WWE is Vince's legacy, he needs to pay heed to what threatens the longevity of it. And for that, he needs to look in a mirror.

Mostly because Vince is the biggest obstacle to changing the business practices, perceptions and realities of the WWE, and as long as he's around, in charge and with the power of the CEO, no one will believe that change can occur.

Without him micro-managing the WWE, it could be another story.

No one has the drive, the energy and the passion of Vince. No one could be expected – not Shane or Stephanie, both who have families and young children – to work so many hours, to insist upon a single vision, to obliterate and reshape the input of dozens of voices.

That single change would be monumental for the company. And to do so, Vince would help to put all this mess behind him, and especially behind the WWE. While it would not solve the problems alone, it would create an atmosphere of change, and from that change there would be a softening of criticisms, and more likely, a wait and see element that could play out (which otherwise would never be allowed with Vince still calling the shots.)

But without that change, can change ever happen?

Pro Wrestling Intellectual

Pro Wrestling Kid's Style

By Shawn "Crusher" Crossen

NWF Books

It's billed as "The most amazing untold story in professional wrestling history" and it is a quite fascinating read about a young group of kids, lead by Shawn Crossen, who put on their own version of pro wrestling, utilizing local access cable TV programming; put on a few "major" events, and otherwise found themselves persevering through a lot of the typical

problems that have plagued the industry.

On a certain level, it reminds us that those who ignore history are doomed to repeat it, even if that ignorance is innocent.

They were doing pro wrestling their own way a decade before the term "Backyard Wrestling" plagued the industry in the mid 1990's, and while their enthusiasm, business sense and re-creation of professional wrestling smacks of admiration, it also reeks of danger, ignorance and the tenacity of Crossen to promote, produce and perpetuate his own vision.

For that, it certainly is an interesting story.

For those of us that continue to believe our smarts are far superior to our physical talents, and could really run a successful local wrestling promotion, this is an inspiring story.

Shawn Crossen makes some interesting insights into the world of professional wrestling, having basically built his own version from the ring up. But along the way, Crossen crossed the myriad of paths that seem to always dog promoters – including other promoting interests, the bureaucrats, and the evils of ego. Then again, there were a few that he seemed to dodge.

The biggest issue I have with the book is the length – basically 150 pages for $20 – as well as the missing pieces of the puzzle.

I'm not sure if Crossen knows enough of the industry to simply go back to the old adage that wrestling "used to be real" but then emerged as a predetermined situation somewhere along the time line. Since Crossen himself ran much of the NWF operation, it's a bit disingenuous to dodge that question. Not that he out and out refuses to explain it, but he does seemingly refuse to "explain" how the operation worked.

A series of ongoing rehashes of storylines and behind the scenes goings-on is hard to damn, when most professional wrestling books these days are themselves an amalgamation of kayfabe, real life and production storylines. But since this story is twenty years old, being told by the ringleader and, despite having DVDs to hawk, has nothing to gain by avoiding what really happened, the combination of a short book and sparse details is hard to forgive.

The biggest example is the receipts from a few of the big "spectaculars" – the first netted some $800, the second $400, and the third a strong $2000. While the numbers don't seem to add up given the facts presented, the one glaring problem is the question of who made what?

That also makes the inevitable double dealing at a cross-promoted show both easily to understand, yet murky in true motivation. Was the headliner merely taking his own version of a fair share, or was the fair share (otherwise unreported or untold) something along the lines of what should be expected?

The avoidance of pressing charges on stolen gate receipts has me humming a Beatles tune, and it ain't the "Yellow Submarine" song. A promotion with a ticket count, strong promotions and sponsorships knows full well how much money was involved!

But to get back to the story, it is one of interesting audacity and tenacity. Despite numerous "venue" changes and red tape of sorts, changes in the roster and changes in friendships, the promotion lived a surprisingly long five years.

It is inspirational in the sense of having a dream, insisting on the reality of the dream, and producing that dream amongst so many nay-sayers.

However, the issues of responsibility and insurance and other implications seem lost on a teenager as well as the adult writing about his teenage exploits.

Nowhere does this book scream "Don't try this at Home!" and despite the claims that backyard wrestling was far more dangerous, which may certainly be true, the concept of teenagers (and younger!) playing around at a version of professional wrestling seems undeniably irresponsible.

At one point, Crossen describes (albeit briefly) about how they trained each other on taking bumps and the like!

Also, Crossen confuses some issues of injury. He laid out an opponent with a piledriver, which he claims was not properly performed, but calls it his only misfortunate incident, and declares both of the participants quite lucky that it didn't do major damage. Later, though, he writes how a dropkick he threw dislocated another opponent's jaw. He also speaks of breaking his own finger.

Even more, at one point, when the wrestling wasn't "predetermined" he writes of an incident where someone was in a hold and couldn't breathe, and that they submitted because of that situation (instead of the submission hold itself.)

Call me a purveyor of pretzel logic, but if two competitors are doing "shoot" wrestling and someone gets upset because they lost, but not because they gave up to the hold portrayed, that there's a snafu involved. Or that such a situation cries for pre-determined results???

The issue of home owners insurance is addressed when an agent for the parents noticed the location of the ring and the performances. Since then, they had to do a lot of traveling to find different places to do their shows, and often did hit-and-run tapings at the parent's house.

Combining the previous two threads of thought, one must wonder aloud, simply how irresponsible it was to allow that stuff to go on. Injuries occurred, anyone who challenged the operation was castigated as a villain, and the tapings went on with convoluted assurances and seemingly dubious permissions.

The Golden Gloves chapter was quite hesitant in loaning out their ring. The cable TV operatives at a certain level were quite hesitant in allowing it to persist. The school district principal gave some space. Obviously, a lot of people wanted it to disappear.

That it kept thriving seems admirable, but also quite dangerous.

Add to that the insistence on using the word "non-profit" when promoting a show where tickets were sold and a profit – revenue over and above the expenses, was made. It seems like the local TV guy who dogged the show was a bit too "on to" the reality of the situation, even if Crossen and company were or were not innocently ignorant of their position.

As of yet, I have not watched the DVD of one of the shows, so I'm really unsure of what level of interaction this "professional wrestling" entailed. Crossen speaks of Eddie Sharkey, and interacting with the AWA's main agent of the era, which raises some other issues, but also suggests a level of professional display that cannot be readily discounted.

This only adds to the mystique as well as the debate.

But again, the strange and interesting parts of the story are the things which a pro wrestling audience (to which this book probably isn't exactly directed towards) would find quite believable and expected, considering the ego of running a company, the use of talent on the shows, and the ability of the promotion to actually make some real money.

Actually, that makes an otherwise too short book a really informative and interesting story, which could have been much more and much better with the details. As a bigger expose of the operation, Crossen would have a classic story, instead of a strange glimpse at what wrestling rapidly becomes over the course of five years with an experimental group run mostly by kids, as opposed to what wrestling became over the course of a hundred years, in various groups and various efforts.

It's a story of deceptions, delusions and double-dealing, which is what the history of the industry of professional wrestling is all about, all the while presenting a rather entertaining package of not-so-safe predetermined matches and the ongoing efforts to run a business when everyone else wants to see it fail.

Interesting, indeed.

VAMPIRO

There are few individuals in the often strange and freaky world of professional wrestling with the uniqueness and exotic style of the man called Vampiro.

And also few with a career filled with constant political wars.

Despite seemingly losing so many of those fights, the essence of Vampiro's tenacity has been his ability to stay with a profession that has spurned him so often.

Currently the Wrestle Society X Champion, Vampiro is positioned once again to be at the centerpiece of the creation of a new generation of pro wrestling fans, much like he had done in Mexico, and what he attempted to do with WCW and TNA.

"The biggest thing I would like to get across is that I am satisfied that I was right all along," he wrote to Mark Keast of the Toronto Sun.

Vampiro started out in the wrestling business in the mid 1980's, and reportedly was trained by Abdullah the Butcher. His repertoire of holds certainly suggests it, as he started with Consejo Mundial de Lucha Libre (CMLL) in Mexico with little more than basic offensive moves. But even so, his look – tattooed, blue dreadlocks and Kiss influenced painted face – was unique to the point it made him a superstar. As Vampiro Canadiense, the "Canadian Vampire" attracted women fans like few others, but his success and growing popularity created friction with rivals.

Despite his popularity, his lack of speaking fluent Spanish and his wrestling skills were detriments. A rivalry with Konnan, who had been the CMLL superstar of note, arose in part due to a potential role in a soap opera.

Konnan went on to be a mainstream figure in Mexico. Vampiro went into martial arts training to bolster his in-ring skills. He now boasts of several finishing type maneuvers, notably the "Nail In The Coffin" – often called the Michinoku driver II, which is basically a simple slam of the opponent, turned into a sit-down piledriver while holding that slam position on the opponent. He also does that move from the top rope, calling it the "Super Nail In The Coffin" Undoubtedly, he honed those moves while working for Michinoku Pro in Japan, as well as the WAR promotion in that country.

The Tombstone piledriver is also part of his repertoire, which is sold as the most dangerous hold in his long time stomping grounds in Mexico.

But the feud continued, and Vampiro's opinionated personality got him on the wrong side of the political scene, which would follow him for years. He was also at the height of his popularity in Mexico, and lived the life of a rock star, full of excesses and creating a reputation that was easily politicized wherever he appeared.

In the late 1990's, he was signed by WCW, after years of being denied entry into the US mainstream, most likely because of his feud with Konnan. But as with Konnan and Rey Mysterio and Eddie Guerrero, the difference in style, work ethic and look from the more mainstream wrestlers created an underlying popularity with the fans. Popularity among younger rivals created resentment by the main event level talent.

On top of that, the feud with the more politically connected Konnan made things worse. Adding to the volatile situation was Vampiro's connections to the music industry, notably with the Insane Clown Posse. A faction called "The Dead Pool" was formed around the face painted wrestlers, and Raven. As the ICP had their own avenues of speaking to the fans, the temptation for Vampiro to air his differences, complaints and opinions only lead to disaster. That plus the uncontrollable nature of the crazed rap stars. The ICP, while being passionate about wrestling, never needed it for an income source, and started a consistently inconsistent pattern of jumping from one federation to the next, leaving at the first sign of frustration.

At one point, it looked like Vampiro was out of WCW, headed to the WWE to hook up with Vince Russo. As one of Eric Bischoff's projects, Vampiro knew he was on the list of those who were out of luck when the bombastic mastermind was out of power. By some accounts, he was fired, and slated for an ECW PPV, but then the jump of Russo to WCW changed it all in a heartbeat.

Vampiro stuck around WCW, and brought in the Misfits, the iconic punk rock band. It was another short-lived association, which put him in a feud with Steve "Dr. Death" Williams. There was an eventual falling out with The Misfits, a dispute over merchandise money from the sale of T-shirts. Once again, an alliance filled with potential and profit went up in politics.

The similarity in looks eventually had Vampiro working with, and against, Sting.

Of course, even with Sting being the follower in the face paint gimmick, his political clout dominated Vampiro's, no matter who was in charge at WCW. After numerous losses, Vampiro would eventually win against Sting, in a "Human Torch" match, but the obvious use of a body double tainted that victory. One would imagine that the "Millionaire's Club/New Blood" angle feud was a little too real in this situation. "He's not too thrilled about me painting my face white." Said Vampiro around that time.

His next strange alliance came with the Great Muta, against whom he lost a first round US Title Tournament match, and then teamed with to win the WCW Tag Team Championship (but lost them a day later.) Along with the ICP and Muta, the faction was known as the Dark Carnival. It was in successive hardcore matches against the late, spectacular Mike Awesome that Vampiro was struck by concussions, and never wrestled in WCW again.

He became a wrestling vagabond.

While his relationship with Konnan was repaired in the WCW years, his political fights in Mexico made for awkward returns, but also a $20,000 payoff in a hair match against Shocker, as he wrestled again in CMLL, took a tour with All Japan (to reunite with Muta) as well as tours in Puerto Rico, then landed in TNA in 2003 to feud with Raven. He lost a blood match, and was never seen in TNA again. Since then, he jumped to Asistencia Asesoría y Administración (AAA) in Mexico, to reunite with Konnan, and has appeared on the US Indy scene and across the world.

Vampiro has held many "world" championships, as well as the AAA's Rey de Reyes (winning a twelve man elimination.) He has held the NWA World Light Heavyweight Championship in CMLL, the Heavywight Championship for Federación Internacional de Lucha Libre (FILL), the International Wrestling Association Hardcore Championship on three occasions, twice the Juggalo Championshit Wrestling Heavyweight Championship, the Italian Nu-Wrestling Evolution Heavyweight Championship; the Universal Wrestling Association World Heavyweight Championship, its World Tag Team Champion twice, and the World Wrestling Council's Universal Heavyweight Championship.

There is a visually impressive web site of Vampiro's, http://www.angelfire.com/vt/elvampiro2/ but it hasn't been updated in a long time.

His current claim to fame is the WSX Championship, where he enters to the song "You Eclipsed By Me" by Atreyu, on the MTV pro wrestling series that features lots of fast and talented, but smaller wrestlers. At 6'2", Vampiro isn't huge by most industry standards, but looks large on the WSX talent roster. He won one of two contracts in the inaugural WSX event, and then won the Championship against former X/6 Pac Sean Waltman.

Joe Babinsack

With his now worldly experience and vast understanding of the fast paced Lucha Libre style, Vampiro seems to have found a niche in the industry at Wrestle Society X, removed from the dominating industry politics that have plagued his career.

From hockey draft pick to one-time body guard for Milli Vanilli, from Luchador superstar to WCW political victim, from rock and roll lifestyle to vocalist for Droch Fhoula, Vampiro has been many things and has done much to excess, and continues to recast himself as a survivor.

Joe Babinsack can be reached at chaosonejoe@yahoo.com. Opinions are always welcome, but facts are facts!

Vampiro and Hardcore Legend Terry Funk,

Courtesy, Bob Barnett

Pro Wrestling Intellectual

Listen, You Pencil Neck Geeks
Book written by Freddie Blassie with Keith Elliot Greenberg

I don't usually do WWE books, but I was loaned this copy for research, and wanted to extol the virtues of Freddie Blassie to a fan base becoming hopelessly out of touch with the glorious past of the WWWF, of the career of Mr. Blassie and of the concepts of a the manager/wrestler dynamic.

But I was influence by watching "The Notebook" recently, and it is a very touching movie, centered around an elderly man telling the story of his life to a woman suffering from dementia. The woman, his wife, is past the point of knowing her surroundings, but connects enough to the story. The ending is pure Hollywood schlock at its finest, but enough to make a grown man cry.

Every time it is watched.

Now, if you think I'm connecting that story with the story of modern pro wrestling, with Blassie in the role of the storyteller and Vince in the role of the dementia-stricken listener, the person disconnected from the past, unable to see the old glory and love, then I have a few descriptive words for you, namely cynical, astute and presumptive.

Freddie Blassie must be on any short list of top names in the history of the professional wrestling business. He started in the 1930's, and appeared on WWE TV in this millennium. In between, he made his impact felt in Atlanta, in Los Angeles , in Japan and finally found a home in the WWWF, and saw the transition into the WWF and then the WWE.

To settle on that footnote explanation of his career overlooks a wealth of details, psychology and oft-overlooked history of the man and the sport.

To say that Blassie was an awesome heel is to put it mildly. Reports of him causing dozens of heart attack deaths as he tore into Rikidozan in Japan , on TV, seem somewhat exaggerated, but ultimately believable. What he felt about that situation is ultimately revealed in the book, towards the end, when it becomes incredibly touching and self-reflective.

Stranger still is that Freddie Blassie took a wife (Miyako) who came from that culture. Even stranger is that Blassie married and settled down with a woman 28 years younger than himself, and proclaims to have stopped the womanizing and the wild life he once admitted to have lived.

Blassie's role as father to his three children and as husband to his first wife, Nettie, seems of the tragic sort that besets pro wrestling families. As he climbed to be a headliner, his home life became nonexistent – and he became estranged to two of his three children -- seemingly unto death. That seems a trade-off all too familiar, but Blassie was an extreme man. While his flings with fame and infamy took him to heights of popularity and mainstream celebrity status, his other extreme was to almost completely abandon any sense of family. It is a melancholy taint to his life story.

But what a ride it was while it lasted, and it certainly lasted many decades. He hobnobbed with Elvis, with Regis Philbin (before Regis was a singular name star, and in many ways, and Regis even admits it, Freddie was brought along to help him get bigger,) with Andy Kaufman and finally with the WWF, and with three generations of the McMahon family.

Above it all, Freddie Blassie was a fixture in the emotional landscape of professional wrestling, notably in Japan and in California. He honed his ability to stoke up the crowd in Atlanta, and elevated his talents to new heights in California and in his terror sprees in Japan. He worked the crowds in the old WWWF, working against Bruno Sammartino, and he gradually, eventually and almost predictably became a face in his long running hotbed of Los Angeles and the WWA.

Heels are so much fun to hate, and eventually, so much fun to love.

But Blassie's enduring legacy thrived through his participation as one of the big three managers in the WWWF, and into the era of the WWF. Blassie was usually the foreign menace manager: his charges, from Nikolai Volkoff to the Iron Sheik, usually guys with imposing looks no promo skills. There were exceptions, as Blassie mouthpieced for Hogan, for Ventura and for a few others (like Dick Murdock) who really didn't need his presence. But they all benefitted from the rub, from the psychology and from the wisdom he showed.

A few paid him back, like Volkoff in an attempt to reconcile Freddie with his daughter. Or like George Steele did when he slipped the man a big bill, in appreciation of the efforts undertaken in the ring, to shine the spotlight on the talent that demanded it, not on the manager, whose role it should be to make the show more entertaining.

There's a lot to learn about pro wrestling from Freddie Blassie's story.

Pro Wrestling Intellectual

Emotion is a main part of it. In Blassie's day, the conflicts were far more visceral. Far more understandable to the fans. Sure, there were dangerous aspects, and every time Blassie got spit upon, stabbed at or had objects thrown at him, those were the results of preying on people's emotions. Freddie could rile up the fans' emotions with his voice, simple moves and biting.

Again, biting and fan violence is a far cry from a respectable entertainment genre. But the aspects of building drama, creating involvements and making pro wrestling work are buried in there. That, to me, is where the connection to a chick-flick movie comes in. Mostly because Vince K. McMahon's words and fingerprints are all over this book, in terms of shoring up his history, in terms of being seen as "cool" because of his association with Blassie and because of his quotes.

The funny thing is that throughout it all, one wonders if Vince is really paying attention.

The manager role, the one he honored Freddie for holding and exhibiting so well, has been dead longer than the late, lamented Freddie Blassie. And it doesn't seem to be returning any time soon.

Is that the way to honor your beloved friend from way back?

Joe Babinsack

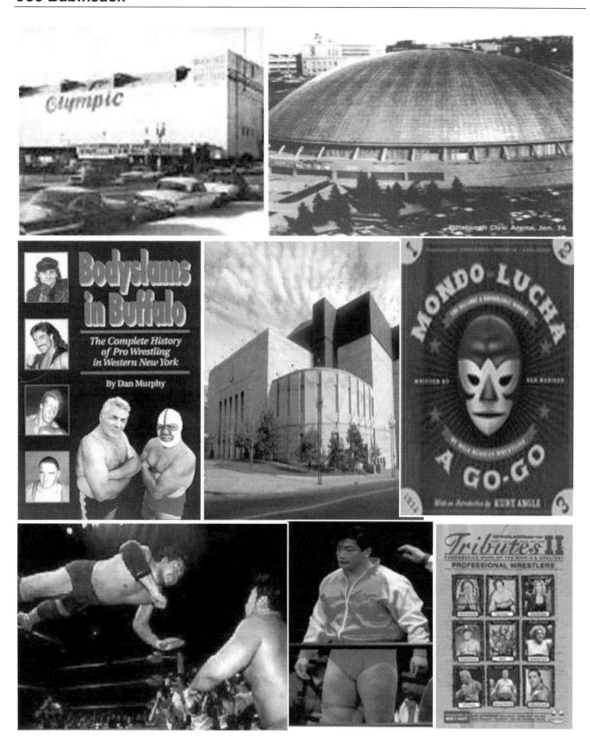

HISTORY

Pro Wrestling Intellectual

BODYSLAMS IN BUFFALO
Book Written By Dan Murphy
Western New York Wares, Inc.

As the vestiges of the significant regional promotions fades away, Buffalo is lucky to have Dan Murphy around to chronicle its strong legacy in the world of professional wrestling. With a worldwide legend in Dick "the Destroyer" Beyer and a long time local legend in Ilio Dipaolo, as well as a strong showing of top notch performers (Adrian Adonis, Mark Mero, Lex Lugar, Mark Lewin) and some significant events, including several top notch PPV's emanating from the city, Buffalo has certainly made its mark on wrestling history.

Dan Murphy is a veteran writer of the Pro Wrestling Illustrated family. While I would have to say that the book is heavily influenced by that magazine's style of prose, I don't consider that an insult. Much of my early wrestling lore was shaped by PWI, and from much of my correspondence with fans these days, the reminiscing always seems to include the mags, as well as the Top Ten listings that were such an important feature of PWI and a great introduction to other feds.

(Which of course leads me to question Mr Murphy as to why he didn't include a Buffalo Top Ten!)

Furthermore, the PWI influence dominates this publication in the avoidance of hard facts and the ongoing creation of a worked history. In the form of hit-and-run facts, figures and an overview of pro wrestling in the Buffalo area, its certainly fine and in many ways an appreciative slant. For a mainstream audience, this book fills in a lot of details, makes the connections back to Buffalo and gives a solid history of Buffalo's two great legends, Ilio Dipaolo and The Destroyer.

What it lacks is that hard-hitting, this-is-real-life, focus on the hidden negatives agenda of most current wrestling books. And, quite frankly, I didn't miss it all that much.

The books details several "Nights to Remember" in Buffalo history, including when the Honky Tonk Man defeated Ricky "The Dragon" Steamboat to start his reign as the greatest Intercontinental Champion of all time. It highlights the first NWA/WCW venture into Buffalo in 1989, as well as the tribute show to both DiPaolo and The Aud, (Wrestling Legends of the Aud) which was co-promoted with WCW.

Buffalo was a home city in the National Wrestling Federation (NWF) and Murphy does an excellent job explaining the foundation and start-up of what became mostly a regional promotion, but seemed to be poised at one point to become a national power. The NWF certainly had top notch main eventers, with Johnny Powers, Johnny Valentine, Waldo Von Erich and others holding the top strap in the US, and then its transition to a Japanese belt, which was held by Antonio Inoki, Stan Hansen and Tiger Jeet Singh, until Inoki dumped the belt, in favor of the IWGP, right before the first tournament for that grand championship.

With Ernie Ladd, Abdullah the Butcher and Ox Baker on the heel side of the roster, the NWF had some heated feuds and Murphy takes the time to sketch bios of the top talent. Equal time is given to Buffalo born and raised wrestling talent, which features a slew of underappreciated and underperforming names that most wrestling fans have heard of, even though many are not well known as coming from the Buffalo area. Adrian Adonis was a talented journeyman who had his time in the spotlight of the WWF before his untimely death, and was probably the basis for Jesse Ventura's getting to the WWF in the first place. (The East-West connection tag team stuck around a bit before Adonis went girly and girthy, while Ventura hit the announcing sidelines and bigger and better fame.)

Lugar…well, anyone who knows anything about the Total Package knows that he had the wrestling world at his feet, but never really lived up to his potential, even when he won a belt.

Mark Lewin was another talented journeyman from Buffalo, who revitalized his career during that memorable Kevin Sullivan "satanic" gimmick in Florida and then called himself the Purple Haze.

Mark Mero's star was certainly eclipsed by his wife, Sable. Some of the depths and inner workings of their WWE tenure seem to be underplayed, but his early career is highlighted.

Johnny Swinger certainly is set up as having a great potential, but he seemed to have been sidetracked by the WCW demise, and his timing with the ECW revival could not have been worse.

As the book was printed in 2002, there is some rough realities that were yet to happen with the likes of Lugar, Mark Mero and Johnny Swinger, but in terms of providing a lot of information in a digestible package, Bodyslams in Buffalo is a great nostalgic ride for people of the Western New York area, as well as wrestling fans curious about both a solid roster of Buffalo bred talent and a lot of the history of the NWF.

Pro Wrestling Intellectual

I think the book was a bit short (107 pages, not including the publisher's catalogs) but then again for $10, who's complaining? My main interest would have been to see what a NWF card was all about, beyond just bio's of the roster and belt histories of the one-time World title.

Before I forget, let me plug another of Dan Murphy's projects, which is the semi-regular Ballpark Brawl:

The Seventh installment of the Buffalo area major independent show takes place on Aug 27, at Dunn Tire Park at 2:00 in the afternoon. Field Level tickets are priced at $25 and General Admission tix are $14 each.

The show features Sgt Slaughter, plus a small tourney to set up a three way for the ROH and the "Natural" titles, defended by Bryan Danielson.

On the card: Samoa Joe, Low Ki, Steve Corino, Monty Brown, Christopher Daniels, Milano Collection AT, Chris Hero, Backseat "Men", Sterling James Keenan, April Hunter and Talia Madison. The Brawl touts 13 matches and 50 wrestlers, and they don't skimp on bringing in the big names and putting forth the top matches.

I've reviewed the Canadian Carnage DVD, and have another one waiting in the wings, and the Ballpark Brawls feature the top indy level talent, lots of nostalgia acts and really, really good performances. If you're one of the growing legions of fading pro wrestling fans, and in the Buffalo area, this is a show you simply cannot miss. If you have to, make sure you visit www.ballparkbrawl.com for the DVD release and the previous five shows.

Joe Babinsack

THE RASSLER FROM RENFREW
LARRY KASABOSKI AND THE NORTHLAND WRESTLING ENTERPRISES
BY GARY HOWARD

"Old School" wrestling is something easy to talk about, but harder to put in details. Gary Howard's book is a great source for getting a feel for what professional wrestling used to be back in the day, and how it was promoted, and how it was starkly different from today's product.

Furthermore, it shows how the mentality at the time – listening to the fans, respecting them and making sure they kept coming back – are timeless fundamentals of wrestling.

I could cite chapter and verse about all this, but hey, that's not a review, that's a book report. And book reports don't sell copies of the book. I really want you, the reader, to check this one out because it is an interesting and informative look, not just at an Old School promotion (the Northland Wrestling Enterprises) but also at what an impact professional wrestling had on a regional culture, and most importantly, on the life of the promoter, Larry Kasaboski.

My fascination is on the promotional end. I love reading and getting the details on the how's, the why's and the wherefores as to how wrestling was promoted and provided to the masses. With NWE and Kasaboski, you learn that Larry and his brother Alex toured and learned the craft across North America. They teamed up with local community groups like the Lions Club or the Rotary Club, having give-aways at the matches, doing countless hours of promotional work, and always moving around, setting up matches and adjusting the wrestling to show new faces and styles – that's the kind of underlying promotional interests that should be done by today's promoters.

And I recommend this book to those of you with those interests.

When Alex died young, due to injuries sustained in the ring, Larry was already well on his way to becoming a successful regional promoter – in the Ottawa Valley of Northern Ontario. His connections were strong thoughout the industry, as he appeared for many promoters, but especially strong with Montreal's promotions, as his audiences had a lot of French Canadians.

It's amazing to learn that most of the cards had very few matches. Often, it was three, with a main event and some preliminaries. Early on, boxing and other challenges set up the night's events. Of course, the typical sideshow attractions brought the crowds in as well, from wrestling bears and wrestling alligators, to the always popular midgets.

Those few matches eventually gave way to a more modern version of cards, but then again, when that happened, the appeal of wrestling diminished. Coincidence or reality?

Pro Wrestling Intellectual

That's something for debate. Of course, the up-close-and-personal nature of small clubs with hundreds in attendance cannot be readily restored, and the nature of heel versus face dynamics are being lost for the ages, but there's always that sense of nostalgia and sense that some of it can be brought back.

Different usually sells in wrestling circles….not that people with Hollywood mindsets every play to that, and different to some these days means to turn one's back on history. But Old School is my favority, and Old School as Kasaboski was, the women matches didn't appear until late in the promotions life.

While lots of names in the promotion were regional, like Dan "One Man Gang" Evans (hmmm…where does that moniker reappear?) and Wild Bill Zim and the Lorties (Bob and Paul) and NWE's perennial champ, Bill Curry; there are lots of colorful names that should be recognized – like Gorgeous George Grant, like Frankie Hart, like Dinty and Herb Parks, and especially the Garvins (from Terry to Ronnie to Jimmy.)

Guys like Maurice (call him Mad Dog) Vachon – who won the first NWE belt while sporting a nifty head of hair – and Roy Shire had some memorable runs in the Canadian outback, and Andre the Giant appeared in battle royals and handicapped matches (much to the chagrin of a local reporter.)

The book is fun, passionate and easy to read (although some Canadian slant on the language does seem awkward to those of use more familiar to the bastardized, Americanized version of the English language.) The details are the work of excellent journalism, and the nostalgia and remembering are well worth the read.

While there are times I would have loved to get a bit more on the details, The Rassler from Renfrew is a book that provides plenty of historic, cultural and picture references to the promotion and the impact of professional wrestling on the small lumber and farming towns of North Ontario. The promotion persisted from the 1930's - 1960's as an important part of the lifestyle.

At the end of the 1960's, the excitement for wrestling seems to diminish in the promotion. I'm a little against the grain of Mr. Howard's take that the entire industry suffered during that time (only to be revived by Hogan!) but obviously the local interests are far more important than the greater industry. Then again, the reality is that TV's dominance and acceptance really did shift the focus away from local touring groups to the bigger promotions that put their product on for free. By the end of the book, the nostalgia takes over, and some of the big picture gets regionalized, but that's ok. This is a book all about the local flavor and the importance of professional wrestling as a cultural institution.

What was wrestling like back in the day? If you have that sort of question on your mind, this is the book for you. Well prepared, well written and well worth the $20, I'd strongly suggest this for wrestling fans of all ages.

Joe Babinsack

Lucha Libre

Professional wrestling comes in many forms and styles, from the kind with six sided rings, to the kind with outlandish characters and very little wrestling content on the weekly TV show.

Well, not all wrestling is like Total Nonstop Action, but Mexico has its own interesting versions of the sport, in the form of the oldest professional wrestling promotion in the world, CMLL (Consejo Mundial de Lucha Libre) and one of the most fascinating sports entertainment organizations, AAA (Asistencia Asesoria y Administracion.)

Lucha Libre is, to most mainstream Americans, a completely alien concept, but with the prominence of Univision in this nation, you may find yourself watching the "caidas" and hearing Arturo Rivera any time now.

When you do, you'll find a high speed style, full of action, dives and bouncing off the ropes, plus a tremendous variety of moves, leaps and jumps off the tops of the ropes. Lucha Libre is light years ahead of the WWE in terms of submission holds. It has a vast array of pinfall techniques.

Another aspect of the sport is a strong sense of reality, often despite the colorful masks, garish costumes and seemingly more 'choreographed' displays. In Mexico, the mats are traditionally harder, and because of that, many common moves in the US version, including slams, dives and piledrivers, are considered much more devastating.

Because of that built up danger, most forms of the piledriver are illegal, and one form (what the Undertaker calls the Tombstone) can put someone out of action for months.

Wrestling, of course, is a worked reality. It consists of traditions, expectations, an oral tradition of rules, and a complete dependence upon the fans to carry on the interactions, attend shows and buy merchandise.

The rules in Lucha Libre include two out of three falls for most matches.

Thus the dynamics of a match, and the storytelling, is enhanced by trading falls, or showing dominance when one wrestler can win without losing a fall. Lucha Libre often overuses DQ's, especially a number of variants of the 'low blow' and surprisingly many matches end in such an unsatisfying finish.

One of the reasons for this is an additional layer of professional wrestling, one that has been diminished greatly in its American form. That involves the referee. In the US, the referee is at best a prop, and hasn't been all that much of a purpose as a character, save for Earl and Brian Hebner, or heel referee Danny Davis from back in the circus era of the WWF. (yes, the pre-attitude initials of the now WWE.)

In Mexico, heel referees (like Tirantes) are part of the show. Actually, Lucha Libre consists of Technicos (the good guys) and Rudos (the bad guys) and how they play or don't play by the rules is paramount to their perception. What is interesting, is that the fans also choose sides, and cheer own their favorites. While heel fans exist in the United States and elsewhere, it just isn't quite as acceptable to be so boisterous and partisan in public about it.

The Internet is another story!

CMLL has Mistico, considered one of the "pound for pound" greatest wrestlers in the world, who uses the Tornillo armbar as his finisher, and has been a great drawing card over the past two years. CMLL has Los Perros del Mal ("the Bad Dogs") headed by second generation wrestler Perro Aguayo.

Both these wrestlers are smaller, highly technical talents, much in the vein of Rey Misterio Jr. CMLL also features L.A. Park, Dos Caras, Jr, Los Villanos, the Casas brothers (Heavy Metal, Negro Casas,) Shocker (who appeared in TNA for a spell, Blue Panther and a host of solid Luchadores.

If you like wrestling more old school, more technical, more involved in the ring, then CMLL is your style. If you want more outlandish characters, a more Americanized mindset and a more elaborate – out of the ring emphasis – then AAA would be more entertaining.

AAA has Cibernetico, the Dark Sect, Mesias and the Hell Brothers (Charly Manson, Chessman) and a lot of crazy characters from the mind of the late Antonio Pena. Now, nephew Dorian Roldan runs the show, sometimes assisted by Konnan. Yes, that's the Konnan who appeared in WCW, had a run in ECW, and was the unforgettable character of Max Moon in the WWF many years ago.

If you want to see other somewhat familiar faces, AAA has had a "Foreign Legion" faction that has included cast-offs like Sean Waltman. (CMLL has use Mark Jindrak, otherwise known in Mexico as Marco Corleone, as a regular.)

Of course, the most important staple of Lucha Libre is the mask.

In Mexico, masked wrestlers are a tradition of great importance. A wrestler must keep his identity a secret, and protect his face from discovery. Much of the storylines, both ongoing and internally in a match, revolve around the mask: Rudos tear up masks and try to reveal the Technico's face; when a feud gets heated enough, challenges are made for a loser gets unmasked match; and after some time, a wrestler who wins many masks becomes a legend.

Like El Santo.

Lucha Libre had a brief explosion of mainstream exposure last year, with an otherwise foolish comedy starring Jack Black. While some thought it might have made a difference on the American scene, that never materialized.

In part, because in this country, the WWE is considered the dominant promotion, and all others merely pretenders. Today, the WWE has secured a show on Televisa, and threatens the long standing traditions of Lucha Libre in its home country.

Sadly, over the past two and a half decades, Vince McMahon has made a living by moving into other territories, stealing up top notch talents, and out-doing promotions at their own game.

Has the WWE met its match with a version of professional wrestling that it will never comprehend?

That's the big story brewing in the industry today.

Pro Wrestling Intellectual

Hardcore History:
The Extremely Unauthorized Story of ECW

By Scott E. Williams

The best analysis of the saga of Extreme Championship Wrestling is the result of Scott E William's latest book, Hardcore History, "the Extremely Unauthorized Story of ECW ($24.95) by Sports Publishing, LLC.

As the second recent publication on the subject, Hardcore History provides the depth and perspective of an "unauthorized" accounting of what happened, who did it, and what motivated most of the main players in the now legendary story of ECW and its impact on the professional wrestling industry. Williams, who daylights as a court reporter, shines in his presentation and examination of the subject: he asks the right questions of the right people, and provides motivations and depth to the story.

While John Lister's Turning the Tables painted an excellent picture of what ECW looked like in literary form, and retold many of the stories from a superficial perspective, Hardcore History is a strong analysis of the operation, far from being superficial, and undoubtedly touches more truths than the WWE would ever dare.

For the more hardcore fans, Williams provides the insight of well suited observers, from tape trade Bob Barnett to photographer George Tahinos to Hat Guy John Bailey; to lists of names either seldom mentioned or easily overlooked - despite their immense contributions: like the producers of the innovative TV shows, who created magic out of a basement studio set-up; to the PPV consultants and must-hires who offer telling commentary on ECW's last gasp attempt to survive; to various talents with assorted feelings on Paul Heyman and his creation and its lasting effects.

This book is well researched and well presented. The mini-chapter approach allows for a hit and run examination of the details, without getting bogged down with the often complex storylines that permeated both on-air and behind the scenes storylines. It is not so much history as it is analysis, and the resounding voice of Terry Funk, the solid introduction of Shane Douglas, an the voices of a wide range of talent not otherwise locked up by the WWE or perhaps silent by other motivations, proves the lifeblood of ECW on many facets.

The impact of ECW's style, its innovations and its treatment of the fans are all detailed. Also explored are the dirty little secrets and the controversies that made ECW legendary:

Joe Babinsack

Raven holds little back in terms of his abuses; New Jack's situation in Revere with Mass Transit is dealt with; the unfolding of the strange relationship with TNN, where it seems most likely that ECW was testing the waters for the big acquisition of the WWE. Well explained are the controversies surrounding the dueling revival shows of last year.

Probably best explored was the corporate interactions between the big two, WCW and WWE, and the little group out of Philadelphia, and how all three played each other, and the who's, what's and how much's that went down in the various jumps between federations. It is hard to imagine the WWE presenting any depth on these matters, let alone dispassionate perspective.

The potential chasm of being unable to directly cross-examine Heyman, Dreamer or Tazz, and the various other voices unheard throughout the book, is well avoided, but remains a point of contention.

Instead of quoting the braintrust, we hear from people like Stately Wayne Manor and ring announcer Bob Artese to explore the early days; Steve Corino, the only guy to diss both reunion shows, for the end times; a variety of voices that fill in the pieces in the middle: we hear from friends of Tod Gordon, on the backstory of the Dennis Corraluzzo and NWA conflict; on how Heyman was out of his element when it came to PPV operations; and from the talent, like Axl Rotten, on how Heyman managed his true element, the creative aspects and the backstage handling of issues.

But this sidestepping of what should be a gaping hole in the story is the most intriguing element of the story. Scott E. Williams, throughout this book, makes sure to dot all the i's and cross all the t's. He uses mouthpieces, from Hat Guy to Axl Rotten to Steve Corino, to verify and explain the situations throughout ECW history.

Are Heyman's fingerprints all over this book? That isn't an easy call. But for a few pages, the evidence, in a book filled with tremendous insights and excellent cross-examinations of various ECW figures and insiders, the tell-tale signs of the mad genius' involvement are arguably evident: so much of the perspective comes across as neutral to positive on all fronts, which is strange considering the passions that have surrounded this, the most volatile of promotions, considering the bad debt accumulated by so much of the talent, considering the factions within the group and how many people left.

There are some rather interesting situations explored in Hardcore History, many of them coming from a rather voiceless perspective that seems to strongly indict the silent partner in the presentation. One such incident is the telephone call from Sabu to Paul Heyman, revealing the "proof" that Tod Gordon was conspiring to take several of the big names from ECW to form an invasion angle for WCW.

Leading to this particular phone call, we read "Heyman received a couple of other calls from wrestlers who seemed eager to flip on Gordon, which gave him all the proof he needed." Prior to that, we learn that Sabu "evidently smelled a rat." And afterwards, the conference call is explained, as Heyman called Sabu, telling him 'he didn't want to know' who was listening in on their conversation.

I can certainly believe that Sabu was not quoted because Sabu might want to avoid breaking character. But Sabu's perspective is strangely lacking in the big contractual issues -- ECW's side is not. Which leads to the question: if the conference call exposing Tod Gordon was attended by "Heyman, Dreamer, Taz, and Buh Buh Ray Dudley, among others" then who provided the play by play of this scenario?

Those four listed individuals are not quoted throughout the book. The first three are obviously under WWE contract. Buh Buh Dudley is absent, undoubtedly for many reasons. So if the individual who related this story to Williams is an unnamed wrestler who happened to be in on the scene, why no input when painting this particular scene?

A page later, this message is conveyed, just before a convenient AOL chat allows Heyman to be quoted, "Heyman refused to speak negatively about Gordon even years later." Since this America Online chat was in 1998, the timing seems a bit off -- not "years later" in the least!

But the biggest piece of the puzzle, to me, is how such an extensive book would be written by an author well versed in the history of professional wrestling, without having the input of the brain of the operation. It would be like performing an autopsy without the head, and I don't believe this talented author would have undertaken such a task.

Working with the corpse of ECW, Williams provides a wealth of detail, motivation, evidence and causes of death, analyzing its painful end, and providing strong and interesting perspectives, which explain the damage and detail the demise. Whether or not he had the participation of the likes of Paul Heyman is a point of conjecture that the reader may want to explore while reading this excellent book.

Joe Babinsack

One of the Boys
Book Written by Jack Laskin

"Heroes are made, not born." --Jack Laskin

In an era where modern the pro wrestling industry is filled with cynicism, skepticism and jaded individuals from fans to owners and throughout the talent rosters, it's a great joy to read something a little more inspirational, a lot more funny and, overall, a lot more enjoyable than typical wrestling fare.

Which only proves that self-publishing can be a great avenue to travel.

Jack Laskin had a vastly interesting and seemingly enjoyable career as a professional wrestler. It was a career that lasted some ten years, mostly in the 1950's, and one that he walked away from before it really left him with no options after retirement.

His is a story of someone with solid talent and a great business sense, and someone who was well aware of the industry, its pitfalls and its ability to use people up and throw them away. Two of his friends in the business ended up taking their own lives. Jack Laskin, however, saw through the double-dealing and dishonesty, and understood it. He also understood that life continues after wrestling cannot, and prepared himself well for the transition.

Thus, in many ways, his is a very positive story. And the dynamics of his association with the industry makes for a great book: he didn't make vast riches as a wrestler, not did he find himself a broken man after walking away from the sport. He does not have a reputation to uphold, or an axe to grind, nor even a business to protect.

He has some great stories and great memories from when he was, "One of the Boys."

Jack Laskin traveled the world plying his craft. He wrestled in front of royalty in Belgium (and was banned from wrestling in that country because of doing what he was asked not to,) in a communist stadium (until Tito decided he needed the arena for affairs of state, and Jack was awarded a tournament championship, plus an offer to coach the hockey team,) and in front of a main event first rows crowd of Jews in South African (who saved his skin from a nearly rioting crowd, due in part to the bad choices of his opponent.)

Along the way, he made use of his Canadian citizenship, he had a great time playing the heel, he toured with midgets, animals and the ladies, and he names the names of prominent talent of the 1950's and 1960's. Laskin was well versed in ring psychology, the business end (at least in understanding it) and saw the color lines broken in Texas, saw the behind the scenes realities of the women wrestlers, and counted himself (as a wrestler) among the subcultures of the era, staying in seedy hotels, scrimping for money on various continents, and knowing the score of the scams and the shady business dealings of the promoters.

He had a final blow-up with Roy Shire; he became a Fuller brush salesman; later became a lay Rabbi (visiting Folsom Prison for some time, at the gracious request of the inmates;) and he wrestled under seven names as a professional -- not counting his Gregor Alexadrovich Kalmikof persona used as a touring/guest speaker.

But through it all, Laskin kept a sense of humor, responsibility and honesty which he obviously holds to this day. It's a vastly interesting book, providing glimpses of the life of a professional wrestler on the road, on different continents and an eye towards the details and realities that any true fan of the industry would find utterly fascinating.

While it can be said after reading the book that wrestling with animals tends not to end well (and I'll let the readers find out what that means for themselves,) that insight alone is worth the price of the book. Alligators and bears are the commonly uncommon animal opponents for men to tangle with in the confines of the squared circle, and Laskin provides a locker room view of what goes on with those spectacles.

He even recounts the time when a wrestling bear was considered "one of the boys!" The alligator story is less positive, but provides a great story about the nature of the business, and the ability of a skilled wrestler to tackle adversity.

Along similar lines (but treading carefully for I don't want to insult the little people) the stories of the midgets are quite humorous and enjoyable. Once again, Jack Laskin provides some of the overlooked details of the industry that just don't surface when reading history books and seeing results listed on yellowed pages.

What's fascinating as well is how Jack Laskin transitioned from being a heel wrestler to being involved deeply in religion. While unorthodox in certain ways, he combines the worldly views and strong experiences of his wrestling years into a tolerant and accepting demeanor in his later years.

Strange indeed, on one level, how heels seem to be the guys that turn out to be the religious ones. Of course, the heels are the ones leading the matches, they also are far more in tune with the responses of the audiences, and from that, they seem to have greater understanding of psychology, and also tend to be pressing the envelope through their actions and attitudes in the ring. And, as history supports, the heels tend to turn into faces if they stay in the same area too long. For Jack Laskin, that wasn't quite an issue. He toured constantly, and only thought of settling down, it seems, when he knew his wrestling career was better left behind.

Joe Babinsack

He writes of his friendship with Skull Murphy, whose plans for post wrestling retirement went sadly awry in purchasing a hotel. Laskin writes that he warned about paying for it in cash. But Murphy wanted to own it clean, and when business took a dive, Murphy took his own life.

Jerry Aitken was a lifelong friend in the business as well, and his overdose suicide also seemed to shake Laskin, likely out of the business, but his plans already were underway.

Promoter Roy Shire took over the San Francisco territory as long time local promoter Joe Malcewicz let the once prosperous area dwindle down. But Malcewicz was trusted, paid well and let veterans hang on. Laskin wrote that he knew Shire "just well enough to dislike him." But Shire's locker room harangue of vet Aitken solidified the dislike, and appears to have lead to that wrestler's untimely demise.

Laskin hung on for some decent pays, and kept himself in shape, but was around mostly to put over new and upcoming talent. In what was his final match with Shire, he was matched against The Destroyer. In what sounds strongly like a set up, Laskin (wrestling as Matt Burns to conceal his salesman job,) took a bad bump over the turnbuckle, and with the bolt put on upside down, he got a hardway gash and bled buckets.

Strangely, The Destroyer played out a few chops before going to a finish, allowing some blood to be seen for the TV taping going on.

Jack Laskin's final words to Roy Shire over the phone are likely the stuff that many wrestlers throughout history had yearned to speak.

Jack Laskin has lead a great life. He plied his trade with the best of them, and on at least three continents. He quit the business young, in his early thirties, and took jobs as a salesman, as a professional speaker and tried other businesses, often successfully.

He also turned a love for the rituals of religion, in the Jewish tradition, into a satisfying side job as a lay Rabbi for Temple Or Rishon near his Penryn, California home.

All told, "One of the Boys" is the kind of book about professional wrestling that inspires, informs and interests me to the core about my passionate fandom for the sport. It also is an inspirational book about a man who may not have been born a hero, but has done many, many heroic things in his life, from walking in unprepared to a serious jail and ministering to the inmates, to successfully transitioning from a career known for chewing up and spitting out its workers.

What Laskin conveys, writing humorously and telling great stories along the way, is a strong understanding of the realities created by professional wrestling, without the jaded outlook that seems to be taken for granted today.

For that, I cannot recommend this book enough.

Pain and Passion
Book Written by Heath McCoy

Stampede Wrestling and the Hart Family are all but synonymous.

This much can be learned from the reading of this excellent book by Calgary Herald reporter Heath McCoy. We can readily make the connection to Calgary itself, and that is the most important perspective of the book. The connection from the greater professional wrestling world to the Harts, to Stampede Wrestling and to the fans of the sport in general is strong and important, but sometimes the details fade away.

But once again, it is the story of Harts, professional wrestling and Western Canada that is the most compelling, not the myriad entanglements of the Hart name to professional wrestling's legacy.

This book offers it all up, because the strange and fascinating, dangerous and dysfunctional, awesome and frustrating world that professional wrestling is, is tremendously encapsulated in the writing of Mr. McCoy.

First and foremost, the story surrounds the passionate love affair of many, many decades of Stu and Helen Hart. It is their pain, and their passion, that drives the story. While I walk away from the book wondering how much passion Helen had for pro wrestling, it's hard to deny that once she married Stu, and raised her children, and was ultimately an equal partner in the business, it had to be in her blood as well.

For Stu, both the pain and the passion were extreme.

What his family went through when he grew up to the pain he frighteningly enjoyed inflicting on unsuspecting wrestlers-to-be; from the harsh winters and the cyclical nature of the business, to the utterly tragic demise of his youngest child, his life was both defined by the pain he endured, and by the passion of being part of the business of professional wrestling.

Yet the chapters of the pain persist. Especially after Owen fell victim to the industry, and the court battled plagued a huge and fractious family. But before and after, the Hart clan and their closest associates felt the pain of the business. Brian Pillman, Davey Boy Smith, Matt Annis, and now the almost unmentionable Chris Benoit: all orbited the Harts, were related and were part of the pain.

Before them, the stories played out across some four decades of Stampede Wrestling's existence as one of the most lauded professional wrestling capitals of the world.

Stampede was a forging ground for greatness; and infamous for its methods of breaking in new talent, but also for the ribs and practical jokes, and for the dangerous conditions and long miles traveled on its wrestling circuits.

But Stampede Wrestling was also an institution of Calgary .

Ed Whalen is just one more famous example of a great announcer who made his mark across the sports world, but found himself linked – more fondly, despite the depravity and disdain for the entertainment genre.

Neither pain nor passion seemed to inflict itself on Whalen, but his passing was caught up in the wave of pain that beset the Hart Family: he died but a few weeks after Helen passed on.

But Ed Whalen was the conscious of Stampede Wrestling for many decades, always attempting to diminish the brutality, always there to derail the violence and yet, often times the person responsible for the products existence and ties to local TV programming.

There are few books written specifically about particular regions, and thus the greatness of the book is without much comparison. Larry Matysik's excellent book about St Louis (Wrestling at the Chase) is an easy one to grab. Unlike Matysik, McCoy is less involved in the wrestling aspect, but more interested in the pop culture and rock and roll atmosphere that surrounded the Harts and Stampede Wrestling.

Because of that, the perspective is certainly different.

There's more dirt, and more details on some sordid aspects of the Hart clan. But there's a little less of the global impact that the Harts had on the industry, and a little less perspective on how the Harts fit in with thing. There's a particular place where McCoy speaks of Bret winning the WWF championship off of Ric Flair, where the measure of Flair is pushed, but ultimately, Bret's triumph wasn't over the champion, but over the image and vision of professional wrestling that Vincent K. McMahon imposed on the business.

Thus there are some annoyances about overlooking size, and overlooking the realities that were professional wrestling. It's a double edged-sword, but ultimately a better book because it dwells on Calgary and the region and the cultural impact much more than the wrestling related impact.

But both stories vastly intersect.

So many of the big names and impact players had more than tangential ties to the Calgary promotion: sure, over the past fifteen years, the Harts and their last generations of trainees were of high quality, and dominated many promotions. But over the previous few decades, many dignitaries appeared and learned at the feet of Stu Hart.

Pro Wrestling Intellectual

Superstar Billy Graham, Bad News Allen, Gene Kiniski and many many others.

But the most remarkable talents of all has to be Tom "Dynamite Kid" Billington, and no other story exemplifies pain and passion than his. He tore through professional wrestling like few others before him, and broke ground for dozens of wrestlers who have either emulated him, followed in his footsteps of high flying greatness, or unfortunately, never learned from his excesses.

The Dynamite Kid was nothing but a scrawny kid, full of talent and passion. After he launched his career in Calgary , he dominated the scene in Japan , and took tag team wrestling in the WWF to new heights. He also self-destructed like few other individuals in history, never slowing down, never holding back and never apologizing for his actions.

That part of the story is compelling, tragic and one more lens of what the impact of Stampede Wrestling meant to all of use wrestling fans.

Filled with retrospections, interviews with great names (Allen, Abdullah the Butcher and family of departed souls,) and a great deal of details on the downward spiral of the Harts and the last days of Helen and Stu, this book was published originally by CanWest publishing, and I was fortunate enough to get an advance copy – more of a notebook, and I devoured the book and was thrilled by its insight.

Who knew back then that the latest and most tragic chapter of the Stampede story was yet to be written?

Heath McCoy has updated his first edition, covering the Benoit horror, and updating the book to the careers of Teddy Hart, Natty Neidhart and Harry Smith.

The legacy of the Hart Family endures, and the stories of the brothers and sisters, the children of Stu and Helen, are compelling. All of that is part of this great book, and all the warts as well.

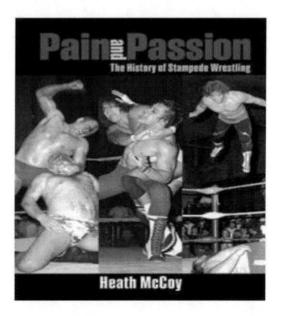

In terms of the big picture of professional wrestling and what it means and what impact it has on a region, a city, a family, an industry: this book cannot be missed.

Joe Babinsack

Mondo Lucha A Go-Go
The Bizarre & Honorable World of Wild Mexican Wrestling
By Dan Madigan

Mondo Lucha a Go-Go is an utterly fascinating look at Lucha Libre, a great homage to its long and unique history, and a must-have for hard core pro wrestling fans of any stripe.

Dan Madigan, a one time writer in the WWE's Creative department, explores the roots of Lucha Libre, tracing back to its origins in Spain, and the factual reality that it came to Mexico because of the Spanish Civil War in the 1930's. In terms of a history of the sport, this book is an invaluable resource, with a strong sense of honor and respect, as well as the cultural importance of professional wrestling (Lucha Libre is the accepted term for the style; it means free fighting.)

The evolution of professional wrestling in Mexico ran in parallel to that in the United States, as well as that in Canada and Europe and Japan. But in Mexico, with the traditions, unique cultural mix, film participation of its biggest stars, and greater mainstream respect, the impact of professional wrestling is far more important and iconic.

That respect and uniqueness has intermingled with other versions of the sport.

An intermingling of Mexico's Lucha Libre and Japan's proresu version created a cultural explosion in that latter country in the early 1980's.

In the 1990's, following the trendsetting of Paul Heyman and an otherwise ignored (but rather successful) PPV called "When Worlds Collide" the intermingling of Mexico's Lucha Libre and the United States versions of professional wrestling were part of another explosion, but the ultimate impact of Lucha Libre seems to have been a sideshow in America.

Madigan does explore that US based sideshow mentality, explaining the disrespect of the use of masks, the use of smaller (but faster and often more talented) wrestlers as only jobbers, and the great hurdles that were overcome before Luchadores reached the mainstream of professional wrestling in the United States.

While some of the more recent Lucha Libre history seems to be glossed over, notably the explosion of popularity of Mexico

Madigan does explore that US based sideshow mentality, explaining the disrespect of the use of masks, the use of smaller (but faster and often more talented) wrestlers as only

Pro Wrestling Intellectual

jobbers, and the great hurdles that were overcome before Luchadores reached the mainstream of professional wrestling in the United States.

While some of the more recent Lucha Libre history seems to be glossed over, notably the explosion of popularity of Mexico's major groups, and some new groups during the 1990's, and especially in the likes of Rey Misterio, Vampiro, Konnan and Mistico, the wealth of information concerning the formative years, and the notable and iconic figures of the 1930's-1960's is overwhelming.

Foremost is an introduction and detailing of the histories of what Madigan calls the "holy trinity of Mexican wrestling" -- El Santo, the Blue Demon and Mil Mascaras.

That triumvirate starred in over a hundred films, which in turn raised the mainstream cultural awareness of Lucha Libre in Mexico to a new level, and eventually exposed the peculiarities and legends of those three men to the rest of the world.

Dan Madigan's love of filmmaking and scriptwriting (he penned the WWE's vehicle for Kane -- "See No Evil") creates a passionate and reverent observation of the film making in Mexico. Often wacky, black and white and low budget, the often hard to categorize Mexican films starring Luchadores remain a vastly interesting genre in and of themselves.

Part fantasy, part horror and mostly a strange kind of action film, the starring of Mexico's top hierarchy of wrestling talent was a cross-promotional effort that worked wonders for both industries. Lucha Libre gained much fame and fortune and heightened exposure. The film industry gained a lot of solid stars as talent, who could do their own stunts, and had a vast number of supporting cast members at hand.

Eventually, the cross promotion started working in the opposite direction, creating roles fit for Luchadores, and then getting talent to fill those roles. The likes of Huracan Ramirez, and to a certain extent, Mil Mascaras, among others, came to prominence by filling the mask and/or shoes of film roles already established by the filmmakers.

But it is the masks that make Lucha Libre vastly interesting.

And the history of the mask is provided in great detail, as well as a strong and complimentary take on the vast honor and importance of this unique aspect of professional wrestling.

Masks are iconic, unique and vastly important to the industry. The use of the masks are heavily regulated by the wrestling commissions, and their existence creates a number of important match stipulations, as well as another layer of intrigue between the good guys (the technicos) and the bad guys (the rudos.)

Strangely enough, many of the earlier Luchadores who wore white masks were actually the bad guys. Medico Asesino, Angel Blanco, Dr. Wagner and others wore white while playing the roles of evil doctor types.

But the pageantry and the honor of wearing masks, and hiding one's identity from the public is a core notion of the tradition. Wrestlers are not supposed to take off the opponent's mask, but the bad guys will do so anyway. A wrestler should and invariably always covers his face instead of immediately retaliating.

It is the strange cultural differences such as the mask, the hair matches and the drama involved that makes Lucha Libre vastly interesting. And Madigan provides great insight into that world.

About the only criticism I have is that Madigan's perspective as a WWE writer provides him a different focus on the spectacle of the match. As a long time fan of multiple styles, my first interest is always the moves. Lucha Libre is a vastly fast paced style of wrestling, replete with dives, unique pinning attempts and a foundation of rules that are peculiar from the American styles.

While Madigan does overview the ways to win a match, and provides a glossary of terminology, there seems to be a disconnect in describing the holds as opposed to my understanding of them. (Meanwhile, his translations of names and nicknames seem vastly on target.)

For example, the senton is describe with a convoluted wording:

"Covering the opponent with the back bump after coming down hard with a splash."

I'd simply call it a splash landed back-first, instead of face-first.

I also thought a tope was a flying head butt, not just a head butt.

Madigan's focus on the films over the wrestling at times is a different perspective, but one which cannot be faulted. The iconic nature of El Santo, Blue Demon and Mil Mascaras are tied into the films, the films into Lucha Libre, and the fame of it all builds upon each other.

While one can argue about giving Mascaras such due, he was Madigan's favorite and the wrestler he grew up on.

El Santo's reputation, as a man, a wrestler and an icon cannot be questioned, and Blue Demon holds up on every level as well, but with Mascaras, there always seems to be a murmuring about him. From the name -- taken from a fan contest, to taking up the mantle of the film star turned Luchador, to the ongoing refusal to do jobs, there always seems to be someone ready to say something about Mil Mascaras.

But again, he was arguably more well known outside of Mexico than the other two....

Another strange focus is the use of Los Angeles based promotions, from FCW and FMLL

Pro Wrestling Intellectual

to Luca Va Voom instead of CMLL and AAA. Madigan details the origins through the Lutteroth family, and gives great history lessons throughout, but somehow the 1980's and especially the 1990's seem to fall by the wayside.

What's more, a lot of the L.A. locals don't get the benefit of being named, so there's a lot of cool photography with generic descriptions and without naming names.

Since I am in the critical phase of the review, I simply must point out two vastly disturbing quotes.

First, Madigan makes note of the "intelligent booking" of Vince Russo....hold on while I count to ten in Spanish ... ok -- Russo can be called many things, and I have done so myself, but calling his work "intelligent" isn't and adjective I'd ever use.

The other statement is made by Ranjan Chhibber in an essay that helps wrap up the book. He notes that, in terms of Tiger Mask's success, "it was the mask that lead to the big money."

Sorry Ranjan, you may be a PhD, but I disagree.

The name and tie to the manga character, the lucha style, the valuable opposition in the name of Dynamite Kid, the marketing connection to kids, and other things may have contributed, but I think the overwhelming talent and innovation of Satoru Sayama made him big bucks, not putting something on his head.

All due respect and honor to the Luchadores performing their craft and living the life!

Another point to note is the hyping of ECW and its impact on getting Luchadores into the US mainstream.

While Paul Heyman's efforts were laudable and important, to suggest that ECW was "successful" is a huge stretch. That WCW stole away ECW talent is hard to argue against, but the timing – suggesting that WCW took all those guys in one fell swoop – is also misleading.

On the other hand, there's the glossing over of the nonsense the Luchadores went through in WCW and the WWE.

There is some mention of the jobber status, but it's painful to have the whole unmasking of Lucha Libre stars by Eric Bischoff ignored. With the WWE, there remained that reluctance to push the Luchadores, and even after Eddie and Rey made it to the championship level, there remain doubts and questions. (By the way, I don't get why Rey Mysterio gets passed over so much!)

But those points are trivial in terms of the overall wealth of information, and despite some repetition in some chapters, the writing is great and easy to understand. Which, considering the ample opportunity to become lost in translation, and the unique lifestyle

Joe Babinsack

and such, is an accomplishment to applaud.

What makes the book, also, is the great photography and the inclusion of movie posters and handbills and the like. Vintage wrestlers are all accounted for, and each of the early stars is given ample space to flesh out their stories.

Again, there is a chapter on some of the family ties, and another round of Lucha stars and their histories. What is lacking in the past decade and a half is more than made up for in the previous several decades, and in the end, that stuff would be far more difficult to dredge up.

We get a strong understanding of one of the first enmascarados -- El Murcielago Enmascarado (the Masked Bat) who had an incredible and legendary reputation, ranging from his taking live bats in a bag to the ring (apparently true!) to taking out someone's eye in the ring (probably not so true!)

The fascination goes on, as someone else laid claim to being El Murcielago II after the first finally lost his mask. That person went on to make his own legend -- as EL SANTO!!!

If you've heard of, but don't know the following, they're in the book in grand details: Angel Blanco, El Solitario, Dr Wagner, Medico Asesino, Huracan Ramirez (innovator of the huracanrana,) Tinieblas, and La Parka.

(Once again, the disjunction between 1960's and up top star Tinieblas, followed by 1990's impact player La Parka is a bit disconcerting.)

Later, we get Los Guererros, Rey Mendoza (and Los Villainos,) Tarzan Lopez, the great Maestro Diablo Vleazco and Rene Guajardo, all in their splendor and legendary status.

And it truly is the splendor and legend of Lucha Libre that comes out in Madigan's book. If you've never delved into tape trading or deciphering the small print and Spanish jargon that surround Lucha Libre, this is your chance to open up a whole new world of professional wrestling.

Mondo Lucha a Go-Go provides the names, the masks and the history, and more than that, gives Lucha Libre all the due respect it deserves, and a then some.

Pro Wrestling Intellectual

Misawa vs. Kobashi

*H*ere's the blow-by-blow of one of the greatest matches of the past decade:

Mitsuhiro Misawa (GHC Global Heavyweight Champion - Pro Wrestling NOAH) vs. Kenta Kobashi; on March 1, 2003.

Arena is darkened, no overhead lights. A brief, but strong chant of "Kobashi" rings out. Silence. Darkness. Screams and names are hollered out. Mostly "Kobashi". Music plays. Ominous, then Star-Wars like, fans clap. A light show explodes in the ring. Flashbulbs go off across the arena. Lights appear at the head of the ramp.

Backstage, Kenta Kobashi, draped in a black robe and blue lined cowl, heads to the ramp. Fog machines obfuscate the entrance, and Kobashi comes down the ramp, into the ring. The cowl covers his eyes, the robe is open. Kobashi has a bit of stubble (he's usually clean shaven)

A "Misawa" chant erupts with his music. Misawa heads quickly down the ramp. Dressed in green and silver leggings, with a green and silver robe. An announcement is made off of a large piece of parchment. The belt is presented, first to Kobashi, the to the ringside official. All lights above the ring are on.

Kobashi, Kenta is announced and streamers fly (purple) Misawa; Mitsuhiro is announced and green and silver streamers fly.

A strong "Kobashi" chant ensues. They circle. Collar and elbow. Misawa back to the ropes. Kobashi wildly swings a discus-punch, which misses. They circle, collar and elbow, then Headlock Kobashi. To the ropes. Misawa knocked down. Up. Exchange of chops and forearms, then Misawa hits a few forearms. Misawa pushed Kobashi back, then Irish Whip to the ropes, which is reversed by Kobashi, and turned in to a side suplex, but Misawa floats over into a body press. Kobashi kicks out at one. Both stand up immediately. Arm drag by Kobashi. Head scissors by Misawa, break. Both up. Crowd appreciative.

They circle. Collar and elbow. Misawa fireman's carry into an armbar. Kobashi to his knees. Misawa with pressure, hammerlock, then Kobashi reverses. Misawa reverses. Kobashi reverses, then Misawa gets an armbar, blocked by Kobashi, until Misawa brings him down to the mat with the arm bar. Both up. Misawa with a twist. Test of strength off

Joe Babinsack

the arm bar with a twist. Kobashi reverses the hold. Misawa flips, punches, and Kobashi hooks a brief half nelson, moving behind, teasing an Exploder suplex. Misawa blocks, escapes, then underhooks with his left arm, into anarm drag take down. Kobashi grabs a leg scissors at the head, but Misawa immediately escapes. Both stand up.

Kobashi rushes into a side headlock, but Misawa powers into a "dangerous" belly to back suplex (Gordy's Back drop driver.) Both down, but Kobashi sells it big, eventually rolling out of the ring. Misawa takes his time getting up. Kobashi crawls on the floor, Misawa stands, then gets to the apron, then climbed the ringpost.

As Kobashi rises, Misawa hits a tope/forearm smash. "Kobashi" chant. Kobashi down, Misawa gets up faster this time. Misawa climbs the apron, then does a running moonsault block on Kobashi (still on the mats/floor.) Misawa gets up, then picks Kobashi up, tossing him into the ring. Misawa hits a missile drop kick. Then goes to the other corner, and hits a frog splash for a solid two count.

Kobashi sells, Misawa puts on a figure four arm bar. Kobashi is face first on the mat. Kobashi sells the arm, and maneuvers to get a foot on the bottom rope. Hold broken. Misawa gets an arm bar with a twist, and pounds the arm twice. Another twist, and Kobashi is on his knees. Misawa applies pressure with a forearm to the triceps. Kobashi forces him to the corner, and gets a Flair-like chop in.

Misawa comes back with the arm bar. Kobashi escapse, and goes to the ropes, coming off, but gets hit with a forearm on the rush. Misawa grabs the armbar once more. Pulls Kobashi to the corner, after pounding the arm. Irish whip is reversed, then Misawa stops his own momentum with a foot to the second turnbuckle.

As he spins around, Kobashi puts on a Sleeper hold. Misawa breaks with an elbow. Misawa hits a drop kick, knocking Kobashi out of the ring. He hits as baseball slide. Misawa goes to the opposite ropes, and backs out of a plancha by grabbing the ropes and landing on the apron. He then misses a forearm/tope. Kobashi sells his own arm, and Misawa is down, perhaps busted hardway on the chin.

Kobashi picks him up and drapes him on the (WCW) barrier, then does a legdrop, and another. Misawa drops to the mats. He is bleeding from the mouth. Kobashi sets up an Exploder, but Misawa blocks. Kobashi hits a big chop, then the Exploder. Misawa on his back, selling. Kobashi in the ring, selling his arm, big. "Misawa" chant big.

Kobashi back out. Pulls Misawa up to the apron, then to the post. Elbows to Misawa's head (three.) Kobashi pulls Misawa in. High vertical suplex, dropped frontward. Strong

Pro Wrestling Intellectual

two count on Misawa. Cranking headlock on Misawa. Misawa makes the ropes. Kobashi chops his collarbone. Foot stomp to the upper back. Chop, forearm traded twice. Spin kick to the gut by Kobashi. Legdrop off the ropes to a bended Misawa. Facelock by Kobashi. Intense resthold. Misawa falls prone, Kobashi gets a two count. Kobashi picks Misawa up, tosses him over the second rope, outside the ring, on the ramp. Kobashi picks him up, and delivers a DDT.

Kobashi paces, then picks up Misawa, and tosses him into the ring. Solid two count on Misawa. Wrestlers are shown watching around the outer wall. Chops by Kobashi on Misawa in the corner, directed at the side of the head. Irish whip, reversed. Misawa rushes for a monkey flip, but Kobashi escapes, then hits an Exploder, then a second Exploder. He puts on a flull nelson with a body scissors. Brief but strong "Misawa" chant. Misawa eventually gets to the ropes.

Kobashi picks him up. Chops to the side of the head, then both sides. Kicks to the back of the head, then big chops. Misawa gets up, Kobashi continues with the chops. One forearm, then another by Misawa. Belly to back/side suplex by Kobashi. Two count. Kobashi picks Misawa up by the arm, teasing another side suplex. Elbows to the neck, then as Kobashi goes for the side suplex again, Misawa hits several forearms to the neck/upper back. German suplex by Misawa. Tiger suplex by Misawa. Kobashi stands up. Discus punch, but follwed by one by Misawa. Both down (crowd shot.)

Still down. Misawa up first. Teases an Exploder?, then they trade chop for forearm. Misawas tries a Tiger suplex, but settles for several forearms to the back. Misawa with a flip legdrop to the back. Picks Kobashi up for a Tiger driver. Two and a half count. Misawa up first. Kobashi up. Tbone suplex? Both down. "Kobashi" chant. Misawa applies a facelock, but Kobashi blocks. Misawa overhooks the arm, and applies a headlock. Misawa breaks, Kobashi on the mat. Tiger Driver for a Two plus count.

Both down. Misawa up.

Body slam attempted by Misawa, but Kobashi blocks it pushes Misawa into the corner, then hits an Exploder. Misawa bounces up to his feet, but Kobashi hits a second Exploder. Misawa climbs the second rope of the corner, but Kobashi connects with a forearm before Misawa can fall back with the elbow. Both down. Kobashi sells the arm. Rushes to get hit by a forearm. A second by Misawa, but Kobashi hits a clothesline. Misawa down for one count. Kobashi up. Tries a vertical suplex. Misawa backs Kobashi to the ropes, then flips over Kobashi to the apron. He then suplexes Kobashi to the ramp. Both down.

Joe Babinsack

Misawa in the ring. Both sell, Kobashi crawls to the ring. Misawa to a knee. Misawa hits the opposite ropes, then hits a tope/forearm on Kobashi on the ramp. Kobashi sells big time. Misawa up. Misawa tries a tiger driver, blocked twice. Misawa hits a Dragon suplex off the ramp to the mats at ringside. The crowd is hushed, and stands to see. A big "Kobashi" chant ensues.

Both are down. Ref hits nine count. Kobashi tries to get in the ring, but falls down. Fifteen count. Misawa on his knees for sixteen. Misawa in at eighteen. Kobashi in at nineteen. Misawa gets a two count on Kobashi.

"Kobashi" chant, with "Misawa" underneath. Kobashi uses the ropes to stand. Misawa hits a shining wizard. Kobashi goes straight down. Two count by Misawa. Kobashi grabs the ropes. Misawa takes a breather, but stands up. Misawa pulls Kobashi up to his knees. Kobashi hits a chop, then falls back to the ropes. Misawa pulls him, but Kobashi with two chops. Discus elbow by Misawa. Picks him up, Emerald Frosion. Two plus count.

Kobashi down. Crowd shot. Misawa tries for another Tiger driver, but Kobashi uses his knees to escape, then back body drop. After draping on the ropes to stay standing, both come across with clotheslines. Both down. Kobsahi up first. Picks up Misawa. Kobashi screams, then picks Misawa up and drops a Brain buster. Both down. Kobashi up first. Picks up Misawa in a torture rack, then drops him on his head (Burning Hammer.) 1-2-3

Both are down, selling the match big time. Huge "Kobashi" chant. This is Kobashi's first pinfall singles victory against Misawa. Both stay down for a good five minutes. Towels and water abound. Kobashi shakes it off, and rises to his feet first. He is handed the GHC championship belt. Misawa gets to his feet. "Misawa" chant ensues. Kobashi comes over to shake hands, then Misawa rolls out of the way, for Kobashi to speak on the mike. I don't know Japanese, but Kobashi is overly emotional.

The crowd responds big time to Kobashi. Suddenly, several big guys his the ring. Predator, Tom Howard and Steve Corino. They tease attack, but all shake hands vigorously with new GHC title holder Kenta Kobashi.

Pro Wrestling Intellectual

History of The Ring of Honor (ROH) Championship

On July 27, 2002 (a few days beyond five years ago,) the Ring of Honor World Title was determined in a four way match between Low Ki, Spanky, Christopher Daniels and Doug Williams.

Low Ki won the match, launching the history of a title belt with far more prestige than all but a handful of belts in the world.

Its matches have ranged from brawls to draws to scientific displays to complete mat warfare. Its style has morphed in much the same way, but it remains a true alternative to the mainstream players. And moreso, as exemplified by two of the best and longest reigns in the industry, those by Samoa Joe and Bryan Danielson, it has proven that a World Title can be meaningful and acceptable to modern fans.

The list of Ring of Honor title holders has nine names on it. Nine names in five years is a testament to the splendid booking and more than capable talent that has held that belt.

In an age where hot shot booking and antsy (if not booked by the pants) decision making and impatience, as well as "even-Steven" booking practices have all but killed the concept of a true World Title. And that's not even delving into the killer concepts of screw-job endings, gimmicked matches and outlandish, can-you-top-this scenarios that ruin reputations and make the pops brought about by a title change a solid representation of the law of diminishing returns.

Think about this, of all the belts in the industry, which one, on any given day (not at a Wrestlemania or other culture-driven, mainstream attending event,) if the title suddenly changed hands, would get the biggest spontaneous reaction?

TNA has driven its belt into the mire, and now presents it as a prop, equal to one fifth the gold in its promotion.

Even the vaunted Pro Wrestling NOAH GHC Heavyweight Belt, the obvious final destination for current ROH Champion Takeshi Morishima, is weighted down by having few challengers capable of working to Mitsuhiro Misawa's vaunted reputation, and worse, almost no one ready, willing or capable of taking the mantle from his weary shoulders.

And the WWE? Well, the Smackdown belt has changed hands a half dozen times by fiat of an injury, and John Cena remains the mystery of charisma, who gets the chicks and kids to scream, but gets the guys to wonder what they're missing.

The old "someone new" pop is one of the worst forms of cheap heat, because it means nothing for the new champion!

What's interesting to me is, having watched half of the ROH Interview with Bruno Sammartino, how putting together a title reign isn't exactly working on automatic pilot.

Sammartino comments upon his successor, Pedro Morales, and offers some striking insight on the nature of maintaining a championship reign. Bruno praises Morales for his athleticism, his talent and his ability to connect with the Puerto Rican fan base.

But Bruno, in his ever bashful way, lets on to the little secret about making the championship work, and putting in the effort. More importantly, Bruno explains that a champion must alter his style -- to the opponent, to the crowd and to the long term viability of his reign.

Bruno's first lengthy reign began with the strongman reputation, and his background fleshed out the expectations, and his exploits put him on the map, notably his impressive feat of lifting "Haystacks" Calhoun up off his feet. By the way, as Bruno put it, Calhoun wanted none of that situation, and tried to sit down on him. But with the leverage and by grabbing the legs of "Haystacks" and using his God-given strength, Bruno would not be denied.

But Bruno didn't live off of that one notorious act.

He built a reputation as a strong man early, then morphed into a wrestler, having reasonable amateur experience by practicing with the Pitt collegiate team while in high school and having the talent to gain a scholarship. Bruno was a natural at being a brawler, and by most accounts, was heavily cheered against the freakish monster types, from Gorilla Monsoon to Killer Kowalski to Bill Watts.

But the key point remains that Bruno wasn't a one-dimensional act.

He could have been, but how long would that play out? Thesz didn't draw well in Madison Square Garden, and Buddy Rogers had played out his act in the region. And when Pedro Morales had his run, as Bruno put it, "He played too much at being Pedro"

In other words, he didn't respond, react or grow as a wrestler, and in many ways, that's the secret to longevity at the top.

That secret, by a look at the ROH Championship list, is one understood by Gabe Sapolsky and more notably by the reputation of those who held the belt, and raised it to a significant level.

Pro Wrestling Intellectual

Low-ki	(2 Months)
Xavier	(6 Months)
Samoa Joe	(18 Months)
Austin Aries	(6 Months)
CM Punk	(2 Months)
James Gibson	(1 Month)
Bryan Danielson	(15 Months)
Homicide	(2 Months)
Takeshi Morishima	(current @ 5 Months)

Low Ki was the inaugural champion, and most of the issues are ancient history, but his obligations in Japan and his ability to play off of TNA and ROH made him a hot property in 2002, and it also proved to be his undoing in some ways.

CM Punk was in a similar, but higher stakes situation. He was rumored and then announced to be headed to the WWE under a Developmental Contract. But the underlying chase for the ROH gold, with several 60 Minute matches, draws and near misses make Punk an underdog who's story demanded a happy ending.

A good booker takes something obvious and works with it. A great one takes uncontrollable demands and makes it work for the good of the promotion. Both Punk and Gibson were obviously headed to (or back to) the WWE, where they would become faces on Television. They (along with Low-ki) were hot independent talent destined for bigger things, and putting the belt on them, even for a short time, did well for a rub.

Xavier by most accounts was the first attempt to make someone great by holding the belt. ROH in its first year was associated with so many great wrestlers, from Christopher Daniels to Punk to the late, great Eddie Guerrero, including Spanky and other noted talents, and up-and-coming stars like Samoa Joe, AJ Styles and Paul London, that it sort of made sense to get someone home grown and let them grow with the belt.

After six months of holding that belt, Xavier mostly disappeared.

But that transitioned into Samoa Joe's reign, which is about as old-school as can be imagined, and in many, many ways follows the tradition of Bruno Sammartino.

Joe was highly though of, and powerful, especially in relation to the regular top of the indy circuit talent. He was also different, and in many ways, being different opens up more doors than looking like everyone else.

But Samoa Joe had both talent and drive, and more importantly, he was booked, and he brought his game to every match, such that he morphed from a monster who destroyed smaller opponents to a powerhouse to a submissions specialist to a guy who could go toe-hold to toe-hold with CM Punk, AJ Styles and the other pure wrestling talents.

If it was a war with Homicide or a brawl with BJ Whitmer, Joe could handle it. If it was wrestling with Bryan Danielson or Rocky Romero, Joe could handle it. If it was German talent in Germany, English talent in England or whatever talent Chris Hero claimed ethnically from Wilmerding, Joe could handle it.

And after Eighteen Months of domination, it was time to change.

Samoa Joe didn't just make the belt, he didn't just build the house that ROH played in, he simply made himself into a rare, living legend. And sometimes, its best to shake things up before it gets stale.

So Joe loses to Austin Aries, but hangs around to eventually challenge a bigger living legend in Kenta Kobashi.

It will be a long time before Joe loses in an ROH ring, and likely he'll never get the opportunity to truly have that return match with Kobashi, but the ROH belt and booking established the big man as being above the crowd, as being the "Babe Ruth" of the promotion.

So when Morishima jobs to Joe before getting the belt, it really isn't much of an issue.

But back to Aries.

Austin Aries was another attempt to create a home grown star, one who hadn't the reputation preceding him. No matter who ousted Joe, the backlash would have been harsh, but Aries had enough talent to make it work, and the inner drive and motivation that caught on with fans.

While Austin Aries wasn't the dominating force, he could wrestle with the best, and his methodical ring style (perhaps better suited for tag teams) was a change up in style. One could argue that Aries was the transition to get the belt off of Joe, but he held his own and held the belt for six months.

Then came the dual transitions and interesting interplays of Punk and Gibson, which created some vastly interesting tension and lots of insider expectations. Would Punk win? Would Gibson win? Would the WWE allow them to have the belt, defend the belt or simply drop the belt to whomever ROH wanted?

That's an interesting change of delivery for the World Title.

And then came Bryan Danielson. Pound for pound, he's simply "the best in the world."

And he's just as old-school as Joe, but with that Southern style, not the Northeastern one.

Danielson built matches from scratch, playing to his opponent and playing up the opponent's ability to win. He was the modern day Funk, the modern day Flair, the modern day touring champion (who may be destined for the NWA belt.)

Pro Wrestling Intellectual

Where Joe had you respecting his dominance and Aries gave you passion and the all-around package, Danielson was a different champion, and he had you expecting the Title to change, no matter who he was matched up against.

That's a combination of talent and booking that doesn't seem to mesh very well anymore.

Homicide was a storyline champion, but one who utterly deserved his spot. Having fought in ROH since day one, Homicide was always there for the promotion, and his style, brawling, garbage and take-no-prisoners, was perfect for a change of pace, and even more so, since he was "put over" during the CZW-ROH war, and became embroiled in a centerpiece feud with Cornette.

Homicide was obviously also a transition, keeping Danielson away from Takeshi Morishima.

Morishima is someone who's destined for greatness, and it remains interesting to see, to watch, to get the glimmers of his transition from potential to superstar.

One day he will carry the mantle of Misawa.

But the current scene is based on this powerful, wild-eyed overgrown kid who towers over ROH's main talent roster, who is mostly brawler with glimpses of absolute talent, and who needs to grow into the championship and into his potential.

Based on the performances of ROH's booking of its champions, the pedigree of those champions, and the talent roster surrounding its budding superstar, I don't worry much about how great it is, just about making sure to keep tabs on it happening.

And with ROH on PPV, that's even easier than ever.

Joe Babinsack

TRIBUTES II
Book Written by Dave Meltzer

Professional wrestling always has, and likely always will be, a strange and unique slice of sports and entertainment. Because of that, it seldom gets the full recognition of the sports world; because of that, it seldom gets the full recognition of the huge entertainment industry.

Despite the passion and crazes spawned by professional wrestling companies over the past twenty-five years, and its seeming dominance on local markets, venues and even with national broadcasting, over the course of arguably 75 years, coverage by the more mainstream avenues of journalism is typically impossible to rely upon.

Yes, there are exceptions, but they tend to be unsettling at best, and fleeting at most.

What's worse, is that the human interest stories involving pro wrestling's top names, and not so top names, are doomed from the start to be ignored and quickly passed over. Even when events merit coverage, we see little, learn little, and at this point, expect little. Honest portrayals, in-depth details and accurate histories aren't just hard to find, they are impossible to find.

The lives of notables like Andre the Giant, Lou Thesz and even Wahoo McDaniel and Freddie Blassie had mainstream appeal and either longevity, ties to major sports or simply American cultural notoriety. And while footnotes and clips surfaced on some of those names, we all know what happens at that point. A few guffaws, a snide look and a modern and utterly dated reference to a company that had only some connection to the name.

And for the likes of so many of professional wrestling's most colorful characters, a passing glance, a quick peek at footage, or even that snide look would be asking too much.

Thankfully for the industry and its illustrious history, we have Dave Meltzer to chronicle the details.

While Dave's first book called Tributes, a compilation of his coverage of pro wrestling's fallen warriors, is hopelessly out of print, his second is readily available in a great deal through this very website. In many ways, it's an advertised special that can be quickly overlooked. And if you have, here's one more chance to look at it:

Pro Wrestling Intellectual

We now have available personally autographed copies of Tributes II, our latest book, as well as a DVD that comes with it talking more about the subjects in the book. The book covers the life stories of Lou Thesz, Wahoo McDaniel, Elizabeth, Fred Blassie, Road Warrior Hawk, Andre the Giant, Curt Hennig, Johnny Valentine, Davey Boy Smith, Terry Gordy, Owen Hart, Stu Hart, Gorilla Monsoon, The Sheik and Tim Woods. To get all of those biographies as back issues of the Observer would be a $60 value today. This is a collection of some of the best Observer articles of the past several years in a hardcover, full-color format that is 239 pages. There is also a foreword by Bret Hart. The book price is $12.95 plus $3.50 for shipping costs in the U.S., $10 for shipping costs to Canada and $12 for shipping costs outside North America. You can order the book the same way you order the newsletter.

Now, if that doesn't sell the book, I'm not sure what I can do to appeal to your fanhood, but I'll give it a try.

If you read the Wrestling Observer, you know it's almost a religious demand upon your time and industry knowledge to read it on a weekly basis. Dave's output is monumental, and his insight is immense. But the most important aspect of his efforts is in covering the histories of those who pass away.

Tributes II is frighteningly full of names that passed on far before they should have: from Owen Hart to Terry Gordy, from Davey Boy Smith to the lovely Miss Elizabeth, from Curt Hennig to Road Warrior Hawk. All these stories are part of our modern pro wrestling lore, and while many of us know the names, Dave Meltzer provides the details that we'd never find in mainstream media coverage.

There are threads of current events in many of these stories, from abuses of chemicals to abuses of the industry. But there are also threads of a passion for the sport and excellence and stories that warn, entertain and warm even the most jaded and unbelieving hearts.

Because at the core of it, most pro wrestling fans are so battered with deception and failed expectations and belittling condescension that sometimes you just want to give up on the industry.

Thankfully, again, we have Dave Meltzer to carry on the spirit of these individuals who, in the end, had given up so much of their lives to mostly entertain us in an often bastardized entertainment field.

But it's not merely the fallen warriors of today that are of interest.

It's the legendary figures like Andre, like Thesz, like Blassie and Stu Hart and The Sheik and Tim "Mr. Wrestling" Woods and the late, lamented and awesomely talented Johnny Valentine that really shine in the writing.

Joe Babinsack

You may have heard of Wahoo McDaniel, and you may have only conceived of him as a battle-scarred vet, but until you've read that his name was cheered by tens of thousands of football fans on the fields of the American Football League, when he played linebacker for the New York Jets, do you really know the man?

Some may hear of the "gorilla position" and know what it means, but did you know the incredible stories of Gorilla Monsoon, a man who was part owner of what is now the WWE, who was vastly integral to the eras of Bruno Sammartino and Hulk Hogan, as well as the growth of pro wrestling in Puerto Rico, and who's tragedies and accomplishments in the industry are analogous to his crazy name, behind which hid a man of great education and sports achievement -- someone who was a three sport star and earned multiple degrees?

Andre the Giant's immense size and more amazing wrestling legend are even more awesome after reading the well researched, fully quoted and painstakingly written history of the Eighth Wonder of the World.

Was Lou Thesz the greatest champion of all time? His longevity is something a more modern fan may have never seen, let alone understood, being that his prime was in the 1950's and 1960's, even though his impact has stood the test of time, and his influence in Japan and across the world is vastly more appreciated in cultures were journalism treats professional wrestling as a combination sports and entertainment, not a bastard child of each.

And the refrain goes on and on.

But the underlying picture is one painted by the industries foremost journalist, and someone lauded by the likes of legendary sports writer Frank Deford. Dave Meltzer continues to be at the forefront of making this industry respected, if not for its honesty and integrity, which is an almost impossible task, then for the efforts of any legitimate reporter, which is to bare the bones of the misdeeds, comment upon the history in accurate terms, and provide the details for those who do not have access to the truth of the matter.

Bret Hart provides the forward to Tributes II, and considering the book covers the lives and details -- warts and all -- of his brother, his father and his brother-in-law, it would be easy to understand if that coverage was soft, but the forward alone explains Hart's appreciation, concluding with the congratulatory message of admiration for Dave and his efforts, for "doing his utmost to find the truth, for all our sakes, to preserve the legacy of what we broke our bodies and spilled our blood for, for the love of wrestling."

It is the love of professional wrestling that abounds in the 239 pages of this compilation, and the output of professional wrestling's foremost journalist. What more can I add?

Pro Wrestling Intellectual

PHILOSOPHY

Joe Babinsack

THIS IS A SHOOT.

I **don't** watch pro wrestling on television anymore.

Which is why, if anyone has wondered, I do book and DVD reviews and avoid the current scene....

It's going on a year since I religiously watched wrestling on a weekly basis. Before that, it was a few sporadic viewings in the late eighties, when I was in college, but kept up with the internet (rec.sports.pro-wrestling, and its forerunner, rec.sports.misc, where wrestling shared the bill with soccer.) At that time, however, Crockett's NWA was doing regular stops in Pittsburgh, so I made up for missing the weekly 6:05 Saturday show by seeing those guys live.

I was that 'go-to' person in college whom the casual fans and even the more hard-core guys came to for serious information. I have kept up that information and standing, even though I'm not terribly social and my family seems equally less interested in pro wrestling. Sure, we all were watching, attending and reading over the past few years. But the spark just isn't there anymore.

At some point, the raucous talk about the big angles and the mysteries and the feuds turned into moaning and complaining about how stupid it all got. At some point, the talk of hope and watching good wrestling and seeing some newcomer – and believing someone will come around as the new Rock, the new Steve Austin, the new Bruno Sammartino, the new Ric Flair, the new Terry Funk, the new … well, the next big thing, the next superstar, the next wrestler who makes wrestling seem cool in the mainstream again.

That talk faded and no one seems to care about the male soap opera much. No one emails about what's going on, no one jumps on the phone and asks what that was all about and who is that guy, and where did so and so go? So here I am, still reading religiously about wrestling, and realizing that its been a year since I've watched a show from start to finish, let alone watched two weeks in a row, let alone stayed up past midnight to write up a recap of RAW or SMACKDOWN, or to catch the PPV results, or to actually want to make the visit to watch a PPV.

I ordered the ECW One Night Stand -- last year. That blew me away, and I had hope, until I realized that they weren't going to follow up on it. I speculated that maybe it was for the best – that an ECW done today would never be the same, would never feature a counter-product, would never attempt to capture the past glory, and would find it hard to be revolutionary in the WWE.

And here it is, and everyone's complaining about ECW. So many people barking about how it's not EXTREME and how it's using all the wrong people and how the wrestling is boring and the violence is tamed and that Sandman can't even get his F'N Metallica.

Here's the thing everyone's missing. Actually there are two things, but as for ECW, the point of the matter is that ECW was a show. It wasn't about the wrestling, it wasn't about the violence, it wasn't about the talent. It was a mixture of intelligent storylines, current culture and that one thing that has been missing from mainstream professional wrestling for years…. EMOTION.

I got hooked on ECW by watching tapes of the Sandman/Dreamer angle. Sure, there was layers of storylines, intrigue and the oh-so-popular turn. But the reality of ECW at that point wasn't cut-and-paste angles, overbearing announcing or ring entrances. It was a compelling drama that unfolded over time, with wrestlers as characters who developed real personalities, and the packaging of the presentation in a format that made you want to get involved, and made you feel.

In other words, there was a connection that several performers strove to create between fan and fiction, between wrestling performer and television screen. That was a time where I could show a pro wrestling product, cheap production values and all, to casual or non-wrestling fans, and not be embarrassed, and more so, be excited about watching the story unfold.

Which is, in many ways, where I'm frustrated with the current scene. Maybe I'm too "inside" to properly enjoy the entertainment anymore, but then again, the excitement was there when the wrestlers did there thing, and the booking surrounded in-ring talent with strong storylines.

It's been said time and time again about the lack of passion in the interviews, and how Mick Foley and Ric Flair can grab at the script points and make something out of going from points A to B. Far too often, we're being presented with mindless points and stories that over-focus on point A (introduction of conflict) to point B (resolution of said conflict.) It never takes a brain surgeon to figure out the conclusions anymore. The problem is, that with few outcomes possible, guessing what may happen has never been a major mystery.

Watching it unfold properly has been the issue.

It's funny, because WCW's first major stumble was Eric Bischoff thinking that by telling the world that Mic Foley would win the WWE belt, that no one would care to see it. Problem is, everyone did want to see it – because Mic was such a talented and passionate performer and how he would get to that conclusion was compelling to most fans.

I think that most wrestling fans want to be compelled to watch. I know I do. But I'm underwhelmed by the creative aspects of the WWE, and their overwhelming indifference to the details, let alone a complete aversion to present what I want to see when they can certainly do so. The WWE knows they are kings of the mountain, so why bother with the fans?

And while I would love to give TNA more of an effort, they are far too overfocused on being second stringers and far too satisfied with their situation. In other words, they are content. So why bother with the fans?

So, my only response is to look for some other avenue of enjoying professional wrestling, even if it is merely nostalgia and learning new things about old things.

Update:

Well, with a move and cable being cheaper, I've watched the WWE and TNA a bit. But I'm still no longer in that routine – if not ritual – of watching wrestling on a certain night, at a certain time, for the full show.

Even myDVD watching is irregular now.

But my appreciation of good wrestling is still kicking…. It's just that good wrestling is hard to find these days, and seldom on the major cable TV stations.

Pro Wrestling Intellectual

Kowalski's Blueprint of Success

The big ongoing conversation is why the WWE has been losing interest of the fans. The big event recently was the passing of Walter "Killer" Kowalski. Strangely enough, examining the first debate by reflecting upon the life of one of the greatest pro wrestling heels seems appropriate....

As a lifelong wrestling fan, my remembrance of Kowalski in the 1970's was one of watching this perennial contender and rival of Bruno Sammartino, and realizing that he had that certain something that made professional wrestling more than just what the mainstream types see in it.

Kowalski portrayed this mean, vicious and nasty heel, one that made you cringe and fearful for your favorite, and one that instilled believability.

Did I know at the time that Kowalski was one of the masked Executioners? Probably not. But it seems so obvious now that someone must have made the connection, someone like my Dad or Grandfather. "Oh, that's Kowalski. Has to be, considering the way he wrestles." As if putting a mask on a main eventer would hide the passion and the talent, the interview style and the gruff voice, the aggressiveness and the believability!

After reading Dave's bio, and talking about Walter with Bruno, I've learned much more about the man, and have grown in respect for his legend.

I was aware, in the 1990's, of Kowalski's training. So many names came through his school, the obvious and the not so obvious. The Eliminators were built up as one of the great tag teams of the era, and sadly enough, one of the few original ECW names that never got tested in the "Big Two" -- but the story of Perry Saturn is one that has its own twists and turns.

One thing Kowalski's trainees seemed to have was a dedication and a style. Sure, his greatest protégé has spent far too much time criticizing other people's styles, even to the point of criticizing fellow trainees, but Kowalski's legacy seems to be one of having instilled more than just the basics.

Looking back at the life of Killer Kowalski, from my own perspectives, having been informed by the sport's leading journalist, and it's greatest talent, it seems completely obvious to me that Walter's legend and legacy clearly points out where the WWE is going wrong with it's product.

APPEARANCE.

Apparently Paul Boesch worried aloud if the vegetarian outlook of Kowalski would ruin his former "Tarzan" image, and the softer, less muscular physique would ruin his main event marketability.

It didn't seem to matter.

Kowalski pretty much proved that reputation and promo ability and sheer passion superseded any concerns about look. Of course, being six and a half foot tall also meant that he was a 'freak' of sorts for the era, but his ability to work and his dedication all upped his drawing ability.

Of course the underlying theme of this is that ability trumps any concern of appearance.

And the reality is that a Killer Kowalski who looked like "Tarzan" would get himself many shots in the current WWE. But a Killer Kowalski who reached his prime, and softened his muscularity for the sake of endurance, well, he may have been relegated to mid-card status at best.

I could rant about Vince's inability to think outside the box of bodybuilders as the best template for a main eventer, but Kowalski, Gorilla Monsoon and Ray Stevens were all of notable main event status, and all looked significantly different than what we see today.

NONCONFORMITY.

A vegetarian who didn't drink, didn't take drugs and kept to himself is a recipe for disaster in today's industry.

And that's a sad thing.

Which of course is a perversion of immense proportion. Kowalski lived to all but purify his body. We all know what wrestlers over the past several decades have done to destroy their own beings.

While I will have a difficult time laying the blame on anyone in particular, the reality is that the industry needs more Kowalskis and more CM Punks, not less of them.

Peer pressure is one of the most scariest things around, but Kowalski obviously had an immunity to cave in to the current trends, fashions and styles of his wrestling peers, as much as he had a passion to succeed and portray himself in this strange industry.

Strange too, how the big names are the ones that broke out of the pack. Austin, Hogan, The Rock and Goldberg were all names because they didn't conform to the current scene. (One wonders how Kurt Angle's career path would have looked like if he wasn't so hell bent on keeping up with his peers, and instead insisted on his own way.)

BELIEF SYSTEM.

Kowalski's inherent religious belief was certainly an aspect of his life that impacted his individuality. It also was far more important to him than professional wrestling.

The story of his life has him retiring from the game to attempt to become a priest. Obviously, the promoters believed him. He had the intensity of his belief, and a passion for questioning reality that made him a better human being.

Professional wrestling, to me, has always been an aspect of a belief system.

Those of us who are passionate fans don't just follow it, don't just "play around" with it, and don't just turn on and off our fanaticism. That, to me, is the crux of the problem with today's product. The writers and the talent are all painfully removed from kayfabe to the extent that they cannot possible comprehend that professional wrestling is a masterfully crafted work of art.

They focus on the work, and they focus on playing on the worst aspects -- duplicity, twisting perceptions and working the fans.

If, instead of working against the fans, they worked with the fans, the whole perception of the current product would change.

With Kowalski, he obviously knew how to work the emotions and work within the framework of what professional wrestling reality was. Sure, we can snicker that Bruno and Walter would never be seen in public together, and their social interactions were destroyed because of their passion to make professional wrestling "real"

But the thing is, we live with producers and decision makers who just don't carry that passion. They don't allow the belief system to persist and to imbue their creativity with ways of enhancing the enjoyment of the fans.

CREATIVITY.

Nothing speaks to the greatness of Walter "Killer" Kowalski like the praise heaped upon him by Bruno Sammartino, in terms of never seeing him wrestle the same match twice.

Kowalski was obviously a talent of epic proportions.

He was innovative in comparison with his peers, having broken ground on a style that is in full force in today's top independent circuits. He was fast paced, worked a body part, and aggressively improvised his craft.

At the time, there were those who claimed he lacked psychology. But he also held to the higher standards of his own perceptions of the sport. To him, as Dave mentioned, if his opponent could not keep up, then when it was time for the opponent to make a comeback, then his opponent didn't deserve his chance to shine.

There's a level of selfishness that could be claimed, but it seems more intuitive than that. Kowalski created perceptions and made sure that the fans believed that he was as powerful, as dangerous and as vicious as he claimed.

If you wanted to work within that creative reality he crafted, you had better be able to perform.

TRAINING.

Muscle wasn't the basis of Kowalski's look, his appeal or his craft.

Endurance was.

Today, the overemphasis is on muscle, and look where that has gotten guys. Sure, there are other aspects that cause injury, but from the reports and stories, Kowalski wasn't exactly play acting out there, and he wasn't holding back his physicality.

The rings back in the Old School days were hard and were boxing style -- not the springy, trampoline type of today. Just moving around, taking bumps and the basics of a match were painful, debilitating and destructive for someone with a long career.

Kowalski wrestled, to some degree, into his sixties.

Was he just a creative, idiosyncratic genius, or did he truly have a grasp at how to maintain his body for the profession he chose?

Maybe those in the know, and those who care about such things, should take heed to his endurance training. It certainly didn't stop him in the ring, and it didn't impact his main event status, and it allowed him to endure when his peers were retiring.

ROLE.

Walter was a perennial challenger. Sure, he was a regional champion, dominating Eastern Canada, but he also headlined in Australia, in Japan, in the main cities of the US (Houston, St Louis, New York, etc.) but that only enhances his reputation.

But was Kowalski always winning his matches?

He knew his role, and he played it up. Most of the time, he was the heel, who protected himself with his aggressive style, but when the time came, he didn't seem to have much of a problem doing the job.

Wrestling is a binary outcome. One guy loses, the other guy wins. Sometimes, the results are important enough, but if the grand scheme is organized, or if the guy cares enough about his role, and his status, he does the little things that keep him on top.

We live in an era where static rosters are destroying long term booking plans. But "Killer" could come into a main event in a major pro wrestling town, build up a match, and lose it, and still come back a year or so later, and get the same reaction and the same main event status.

He did it in Australia, and put over new stars constantly, but was still the go-to guy.

How was that possible?

MASK.

Setting aside the nuances and importance of the gimmick in Mexico, Kowalski had an understanding of how to use that piece of cloth, undoubtedly from watching Beyer in Japan and others, but he used the mask to his benefit when he was showing signs of age.

Killer Kowalski

Joe Babinsack

Funny how he wore it interchangeably at times.

But he used it as a tool.

Today, and in the past decade, the mask is laughed at, belittled, insulted.

But mystery was part of the plan, and when he was one of the Executioners, the guessing was only a small part, but it was part of the appeal.

How it is that current promoters and writers cannot comprehend the illusion and importance of the mask is beyond me.

Some of the biggest and best shows on TV are medical and detective shows, wrapped around mystery. Some of the biggest runs in wrestling have been wrapped around situations where fans guess at who did it, wait to see someone unmasked, or just respect and appreciate how a worker plies his craft without knowing who the guy is.

It's simple and it's Old School, but sometimes it has been proven to work.

Walter "Killer" Kowalski had all the tools of being a great professional wrestler, as explored above, and he deserves the respect of fans across the industry for his career, his teaching and his insight into this crazy entertainment form that some of us love with a passion, and hate that others are demeaning with indifference.

Kowalski was the ultimate professional, who respected the sport, who portrayed a heel like few others could imagine, and who had a promo style that put people in the seats, not just one that put himself over or one that sounded interesting, but proved ineffectual for the box office.

Studying Kowalski should be a primer for anyone who enjoys professional wrestling, and should be a must for those so-called creative types that are steering the ship of the industry into bland and boring waters.

Pro Wrestling Intellectual

THE LACK OF PASSION IN WRESTLING TODAY

Those who have followed my columns for the past few years already know who I respect, what I watch and who I know. I've been able to talk to some big names in the industry, have read the original newsletter source of this site for closing in on two decades, and have watched wrestling for most of my life. I've seen the WWWF on HBO in the 1970's, and watched in live on many occasions; I saw WCCW, GCW and Polynesian Pacific Pro Wrestling (and others) on cable in the 1980's; I visited the Bingo Hall a halfdozen times in the 1990's, and threatened to be a regular on the infamous rswp newsgroup; and I continue to write for the most prestigious site in the industry, twice a week.

Wrestling has been a quasi-religious part of my life. I have watched programs -- the weekly WWWF and WWF shows, Georgia Championship Wrestling on TBS, likely seven syndicated shows of the WWF in the 1980's, Raw, then Nitro, and taped or local TV showings of ECW. Wrestlers to me have their own hierarchy, much like the saints. And let's not even go to the point of a belief system. With wrestling, if you're a true fan, it's a question of making it real, not debating if it's real. Wrestling fans don't just attend, don't just watch, don't just buy things: they make wrestling a lifestyle, a sports that trumps entertainment, a passion.

I count as my peers a once large, but now dwindling number of internet pundits, wannabe journalists and otherwise participatory and outspoken fans. I've seen the arguments rage. I've seen passion and anger and flame wars. I've seen the stupidest of fans spout the most mindless of sayings. I've seen debates that make any talk about the 2008 Presidential election, by partisan hacks, look like a nice conversation.

Over the past week and a half, I hesitate to say, I've conducted a bit of an experiment. Not that my criticisms of ROH, TNA and the WWE are unfounded, inflated or any less logical, but my other impetus was to dip my toe in the waters of passionate fandom.

The water, my friends, is cold.

If you've been around the industry as long as I have, you can recall the times you've debated, defended and dialogued with fans of the other promotions. You've had arguments with non-believers and the cynical; teachers, so-called-friends and parent figures; those who challenge and those who dismissed. If you were around circa 1998, and you threw a pebble at a WWE Raw fan, or a WCW Nitro Fan, or an Extreme Championship Wrestling fan, you'd get a smackdown in return. Call one of those groups crap, and the flame wars would spread, the internet fatwahs would rain down, and your

Joe Babinsack

name would be cursed in three languages and your effigy pilloried with every real or imagined hold known to man.

In 2008, I just called you out. Yes, you! If you're reading this, you follow the WWE, you follow TNA, or you follow ROH. You have, in fact, read about these groups, watched them, paid some ducats to "enjoy" them and you just sat back and let me unload a buckshot of on your favorites.

And more, you sat there!

Now, I may have been lauded by big names and small, by fellow fans and huge figures in the industry, by real writers, by real journalists and by really great names in this business, but I'm not so unhumble to believe that I nailed, logically, the flaws of the industry's leading promotions to such a degree that no one could throw a few stones at me.

(ok, I'm sure there's a few blogs, a few Bischoffs and a few ROH'ers hiding behind pseudonyms calling me out where I'm not reading.... but they don't count.)

The problem today is no one cares. It's malaise. It's apathy, but it's definitely not the emotionally charged atmosphere that makes fans fans, and marks marks, and passionate and crazy men made into hardcore belligerents. Who made it this way? We've all pointed fingers. And while some would say we have ourselves to blame, I say we have timid and weak authority figures, a lack of profit-driven businessmen, and a whole lot of people who have forgotten what the sport was, and what it should be.

So, while my peers continue to shake their heads and threaten give up the ghost, in terms of watching the WWE and grabbing the final straw, I'm still going to be plugging away at maintaining some sense of what's right with professional wrestling. I've continued to provide reviews and commentary on the independent scene, and the book scene, and other aspects not dominated by the WWE business, or quite frankly, perverted otherwise by perspectives that also see wrestling fans as a commodity, not as an integral part of the operation. As I see it, sometime when the bloom was fading on the last cycle's upturn, Vince decided to make his corporation public, and attempted to neuter the rabidness of the always fickle fan base.

 He destroyed the original ECW, he detached any sense of 'getting behind' this guy or that guy, and he did this half-hearted (well, halfassed) branding.

All of which seems, to me, to be a sort of mainlining of interest, enthusiasm and support.

Pro Wrestling Intellectual

None of which works so well, as the experiments have proven. Instead of depending upon fans as a solid, predictable base, the WWE has to realize that they've detached the passion and the emotion, and now see the dwindling results. Vince didn't want rabid ECW types demeaning his product with chants of ECW!ECW!ECW! and now, no one chants that anymore.

Vince didn't want wild and crazy things to happen on his Cyber Sunday fan selection, so he waters down the choices. (C'mon, Undertaker/Show has three match types that are EXACTLY THE SAME CONCEPT!) Vince doesn't want any one guy to rule his WWE Universe, so the only guy he really touts is his son-in-law, and sycophants suggest the Game is underappreciated. And there's TNA, which claims to want to be a competitor, but remains an imitator, and the only passion its fans really show is to scream that the direction is horrible, and the mind behind it should be fired.

Would Bill Watts, Vince Sr, Jim Crockett, James Barnett, Sam Muchnick or one of dozens of NWA power brokers sit there and insist that their vision is correct, or would they fire the damn booker?

We've gone from an industry audience that steered the course of promotions, but was wildly unpredictable and had highs and lows, to one where the powers that be want it to be steady and predictable, especially at the expense of the most passionate parts of their audience.

Look at what that has wrought! PPV buys -- down. TV ratings -- stagnant. Audience at arena shows -- struggling. Pro wrestling is, by the thoughts of Terry Funk, cyclical. Pro wrestling is, by the words of Bruno Sammartino, never going to be the same. And yet Dave Meltzer continues to note that there is a sentiment and understanding of the core audience that yearns for established staples -- who's the face? who's the heel? We have lived in an era for ten years or so where crap is thrown against the wall, where angles are rushed, where no time is allowed to invest in long term feuds or any sense of mystery, or any backing of a new star.

All the time, the people who know suggest that we can't go old school. Why not? The age of Bruno is gone, but the characteristics that made him a superstar are out there to be used. Why haven't they been tested? Well, Paul Heyman explains that pretty well.

To me, there is tremendous positive out there in the apathy and the malaise. Anecdotally, far too many people respond to the notion that things were once better, but now they are no longer the same. Far too many people come up to the legends and suggest that they once watched wrestling, but do not do so any more. Far too many responses to my pieces suggest that there's an untapped source of lost audience that could be re-ignited with the

Joe Babinsack

right approach. But we're stuck in the mentality that it would take a 100 million to put a new promotion into competitive mode.

So no one tries.

What some businessman should realize (or some established promoter) is that the tools of a successful promotion have been established over the history of the sport, and those tools are fading fast in the WWE, and outright ignored with TNA. While ROH continues to promote excellence in talent, booking and atmosphere, it continues to lack in marketing, in grasping at the lost fan bases, as well as connecting with a growingly disconnected mainstream audience. Business cycles are all about making what is old new again. Old school mentalities are what is fading, and as they fade away, the fan base dwindles.

Call me a fool for hoping that the past can make the present business new again, but I'm the kind of person foolish enough to watch wrestling and enjoy it despite what it is -- and because of what it is. The invisible thread of what makes fans, fans, as Larry Matysik has noted, and I have learned from other sources, is that fans want to believe what they see is real.

They invest time, energy and money into that, and the result is passion.

Take away the passion, and the time, the energy and the money are removed as well. I've said it for a long time, in many media, but the bottom line is that the most rabid professional wrestling fans are not only integral to the concept of the genre, but they are the ones that infect their friends, family and coworkers with their passion. Take away that passion, as the industry has done, and it's no secret why we are where we are today.

Pro Wrestling Intellectual

THE WAR ON THE FANS

I've been debating the subject of this week's column, bouncing between the Harley Race book (very good) and the Ballpark Brawl IV (not so very good) and the trailing off of the Vince vs ECW war, which many seem to debunk, but I'm not one of them.

As far as I'm concerned, the VKM – Voodoo Kin Mafia – skits by TNA have missed the boat grandly. Do I digress? Actually, no… The rants by Misters BG and Kip James, or whatever we're supposed to call them last night touched upon the war, and while some have already touched upon the inherent hypocrisy of TNA's calling the WWE's product out of touch with the fans, they do bring up the notion of the war on the fans.

And nowhere has that war been felt as in the revived ECW.

I speculated on the destruction of ECW as a brand name in response to the first One Night Only PPV event. At the time, I figured A) Vince couldn't ignore the response of the hardcore audience and B) Vince couldn't tolerate that such a response was being given to something he owned, but never created.

It is obvious that ECW = Paul Heyman in the mindset of the WWE. Well, that may be a perspective worth noting, but I've never held that belief. If you were a fan of ECW, on the surface, you saw very little of Paul Heyman as a character for many years. And mirroring Vince himself, Heyman became a character at that point where he needed someone on the screen who wasn't ever going anywhere, and arguably, someone who wasn't going to get paid to be that foundation. Heyman had always been the behind the scenes genius (but business wreck) and that was very much known to the internet savvy.

But once again, the internet crowd was a subset of the ECW crowd. Sure the Internet spread the word, but late night wrestling fans in New York, Florida, Buffalo, Chicago and my home base of Pittsburgh discovered ECW and didn't exactly need the internet to visit local shows.

Don't get me wrong, the work of people like Tom Misnik and Dave Scherer and the Philly Internet conventions helped to make a hardcore internet fan base that kept the ECW name alive for a half decade past its real death, and I don't dispute the internet's participation in trading tapes, hyping the product and making comparisons, but ECW was the alternative voice to mainstream wrestling fans in the mid to late 1990's and I'm certain that the

"ECW" chants that sporadically appeared at events (both WCW and WWF/E) were more a reaction to moribund products.

Because it became hip to certain fans to do the chant AND because of the internet savvy, hardcore fan base AND because of the reaction to crappy wrestling – before and after the explosion of pro wrestling popularity and the benefits of real competition – those chants persisted and existed.

Which leads me back to the war.

What I'm saying is that Vince declared war on ECW, revived the name as a brand, and then dismantled its legacy, cut the legs out of its promise, and all but decapitated Heyman. It is my belief that disrupting the ratings potential of someone taking the ECW talent base and going to Spike, or going through TNA or using a new or smaller federation was a core interest in the revival of ECW. I also believe that diminishing Paul Heyman's viability as a wrestling genius and savior was also in the works.

So what is the basis of the argument that ECW was doomed to fail?

I don't accept that putting Test and other WWE rejects on the roster was part of that. Heyman, by most accounts, wanted Test. Heyman has always done well with the rejects, and his security force, his heels and his minimalistic storylines to start out were all arguably working well. Look back to the first One Night Stand. Even with the imposition of Raw and Smackdown forces, once Heyman was allowed to assert creative control, there weren't overbooked and overblown scenarios.

ECW got its revenge on Bischoff, and Taz(z) got an ultimate appearance. The show excelled because of hard work and effort of the wrestlers, even those who never really excelled at the technical parts of the industry. There was no real heel and face contingent within the ECW roster, but they played their roles. And the only disappointment was the Rey Mysterio/Psicosis match which looked far too much like the WWE product than the crowd wanted to see.

Imagine that, ECW fans crapping on its own talent … that doesn't exactly support the notion that Heyman controls his fans like they're mind-numbed robots.

But to get back to the major point, ECW was warred upon by Vince and the WWE sycophants in many ways.

Pro Wrestling Intellectual

It seems to me that one overlooked aspect of the revived ECW roster was the inclusion of Big Show and Kurt Angle. Angle was already proven unstable, with a real fear of his health and career and his SummerSlam snub showed that he had no stroke and there was no confidence in him. Big Show was already winding down his career, with his body ravaged by a physical sport and his overly large frame.

We've already seen the speculations on how ECW destroyed Paul Wight's career, to the point where he very well may not do the Hogan/Giant 20 year rehash angle. As Wrestlemania approaches, how much more will that story grow?

What would have happened if Angle completely self-destructed or worse, while on the ECW roster? That he jumped to TNA only suggests that the competition would be even farther removed from the WWE brands that matter.

The pettiness and/or oversight of removing Sandman's music has been well documented. But beyond the obvious, a roster with significant, legendary ECW talent and a mixture of WWE retreads and potential stars, would have left Paul Heyman with a veritable wealth of storylines and potential, from which he could have worked his magic. And thankfully, he would have no budgetary or business input!

But the old ECW contingent was cut down at every opportunity, and immediately deprived of the one anti-establishment thing that ECW thrived upon. No rules.

Not that ECW never had rules, but the subtleties of having No DQ's, of fighting through the crowds and of going to finishes had no respect from the WWE, and no future in the revival. Vince, as always, doesn't seem to want to be tied down by regulations, but at the same time, his inability to differentiate the ECW brand, let alone give it some classic flavor, let alone at least have Heyman's fingerprints in terms of consistency, seems more than a coincidence.

Add to that the insistence on intermixing the WWE and the ECW crowd, on playing with dates, on not shooting the tapings at friendly arenas and on providing crappy main events (for ECW fans, not for WWE fans) all seems so idiotic as to be on purpose.

Besides, why is it that a Big Show/Batista main event that gets crapped on by the fans means that ECW isn't viable. But when the fans crap on a lame stunt on Raw show, that the presentation wasn't the problem, the fans were.

The fans... that's the problem!

But its not really all the fans, since most of them pay their $ and enjoy the show. Those dastardly hardcore fans are the problem, they criticize too much, they don't appreciate the creative effort, and they don't worship the spew brought forth by the spawn of VKM himself!

Since the WWE dominates the mainstream internet wrestling world with its own site, and has now dismantled ECW's legacy and ties to its core base, what's left?

See, that's where the war, waged long and hard, hasn't been won, and continues to bubble.

When St Louis fans start chanting "TNA!" at the latest laughable WWE skit, there's a distinct undercurrent of dissent in the wrestling world. That it happened at one of pro wrestling's most traditional and historic capitals is no fluke. That it may spread, that other's may take up the cause, is something to look forward to.

Because ECW wasn't about fans of one promotion, who slavishly responded to a certain hardcore product, and that's all there is… ECW history disproves that fact. ECW merely captured a realistic dissenting percentage of an audience who outgrew the product that was forced upon them. The dynamics of WCW and WWF, and the paltry variations in styles on the mainstream stage readily fell prey to Heyman's manipulations and presentations, but Heyman never created the dissent, he rode it for a half-decade, and the association between three letters and that rebellious fan base grew together.

But now that ECW is all but dead, that doesn't mean that the revolution is over, it just means that it's looking for a new name.

Too bad TNA, and the VKM angle, seem to be far too self-serving, to oblivious to this swift undercurrent, and too insistent on aping the boring, 800 lb gorilla, rather than setting their own course and capturing a growing percentage of the fan base.

Because, as the shirt once read, "Join the Revolution" isn't just an impotent call, but one that can and should be heard. If not TNA, if not ROH, perhaps it will be some concoction of another mad genius in a pro wrestling backwater city, where fans can go and see the stuff that respects their investment and breaks the molds of a boring sense of creativity….

Professional Wrestling: Sport and Spectacle

Book Written by Sharon Mazer
University Press of Mississippi
www.upress.state.ms.us

A professional wrestling intellectual, on the superficial level, is of the utmost examples of an oxymoron around.

Of course, that assumes a mainstream individual who's far too tied up in the concept of "real vs fake" to enjoy the entertainment, athleticism and product that is professional wrestling. It also assumes someone who could care less about the artistic merit, the psychological background and/or the philosophical niceties of being a professional wrestling fan.

Of those definitions, Sharon Mazer is not a representative of a professional wrestling intellectual.

While her book does show some rather off-putting ignorance about the industry and its fans, the emphasis of the book is of utter respect for the talent. There is a definite movement from interested scholar to enlightened aficionado, from someone cheering along with the maddening crowd to someone capable of defending a wrestling school from a snarky smart mark wannabe met on the internet.

Mazer moves from a fan with knowledge of the WWF and the explosion of mainstream appeal, through seemingly extensive research, as well as participation on the vaunted RSPW (rec.sports.pro.wrestling) newsgroup, and attendance as an observer at the famed Johnny Rodz's Unpredicatable School of Professional wrestling.

Mazer knows lucha libre from pro resu, and can spout out the alphabet soup of promotions (although lumping GLOW with the likes of ECW shows a subtle lack of nuance that appears throughout the book.)

Unfortunately, Mazer also heavily relies upon interviews of various names from various aspects of the industry, and a few anonymous ones, RSPW, and uses the WWF as sort of a measuring stick for the industry, in that sort of Captain Lou Albano oversimplification perspective from the 1980's that always grates on my nerves. She is also the product of ivory tower intellectuals, and while her version of Marxism isn't completely over the top, the groupism of homosexuality and feminism definitely intrude on her perspectives.

However, there is amazing insight into the industry, and even more impressive insight into pro wrestling's mutant freak fanbase (of which I, and you, whoever and wherever you are reading this belong, and don't argue it.)

Joe Babinsack

There are, to me, four distinct commentaries on this book, two bad, two great, which I will present in lethal lottery random order.

Foremost is a tremendous and though provoking positive. The insight into professional wrestling fandom is utterly on target and vastly interesting and well worth the effort to track this down, understand what she's saying, and continue to do that same thing.

I quote from page 154, but there are snippets throughout the book as well:

"What astonished me then, what amazes me still is the enthusiasm with which fans actively claim their knowledge and authority, their rightness and righteousness as participants in the professional wrestling event, even as they rail against this wrestler or that promoter. They don't simply cheer or jeer, celebrate or lament as their favorites win or lose. They narrate the event, anticipate a turn or a finish, evaluate the performance as a performance. The tell each other, and anyone who will listen, the background of each wrestler: his current story line, his wrestling history, and the details of his "real" life, his name, his marital status, his original occupation, his wrestling patrilineage, and so on."

The fascinating thing is that it goes further. Mazer observes that the wrestling fan is not just part of the con, but an active part of it. We watch wrestling, knowing that we are being "fooled" and so desperately want the product to fool us that we get angry when it doesn't allow us to be "fooled."

I rapidly switch back to the current "Vince McMahon is blowed up" storyline fiasco and heated debate – there's a sense in all this that we know what we want, what we can accept and what we can, ourselves, explain to each other, and to our family, friends and acquaintances – and this scenario that just played out assaults us on various levels. Not because of this, that or the other thing, but because we all love this sport passionately, and the essence of fandom is perpetuating the "Big Lie" of sorts (my words) which is the "reality" we share in watching professional wrestling.

Wrestling fans, unlike their cousins in most of sports, don't just follow the stats, the wins and losses or their favorites, they must actively participate in the "con" that is the sports entertainment and craft of professional wrestling that is equally performance art and athleticism, male soap opera and pseudo sports/pseudo theatre.

The difference, thus, between a casual wrestling fan and the true wrestling fan is not just the obvious line of demarcation (wanting to question it being "fake" and KNOWING that such a question is entirely meaningless) but the nature of participation.

To me, after reading this book, if you can watch professional wrestling and be detached, then you aren't a fan. If you can watch professional wrestling and criticize it – because of the style, the work rate, the emotion, the 'believability' or one of a dozen technical terms

Pro Wrestling Intellectual

or one of a multitude of your own expressions about the sport, then you are a fan.

There is no true middle ground, as Mazer herself points out in the conclusion – you just can't refuse to admit you're a big fan, and you can't admit to being a quasi-fan.

That being said, the most difficult part of the book is the quasi-homosexual intellectual angle.

When Mazer gets into the existentialist "touch without touching, touched without being touched" perspective of the pro wrestling interaction, there's a pointy headed intellectual talking which most of us fans just aren't going to go with.

When she talks of "sexual tension" and an underlying homoerotic portion of the craft, I know she's lost the vast majority of the fans. She talks of Ricky Starr and Gorgeous George as being flamboyantly gay characters, as if that archetype was predominant in the industry. She could have added Adrian Street and Adrian Adonis, plus other names and some snarky name dropping by myself, but that's not seemingly the point.

Her point is that men grabbing other men and sometimes putting themselves in compromising or inadvertent (or not) sexual positions is proof positive of a homosexual intent, but then she gives Rick Rood coming out to "the Stripper" and his gimmick as another example.

Rick Rood?

I mean, facial resemblances to Freddie Mercury aside, what is there about Rick Rood that ever screamed "I'm gay?" Here's a guy who wanted off the juice to reproduce, and didn't he leave the WWF for that reason?

There seems to be a disconnect between generating heat and imposing intellectual theory over reality in this situation.

Another disconnect lies in the bits and pieces approach to the factual basis of the book.

When journalists start using the "(sic)" tag on quotes, there is an underlying disdain for the person being quoted. Any self-respecting writer can clean up a quote, avoid grammar problems, ignore dialect and simply cut out the offending words.

So when quotes consistently get printed full, with the joyous "(sic)" affixed to the error, there's a definite view by me that the subjects being quoted are not being respected. Furthermore, the NWA mega event of the early to mid 1980's is Starrcade, not Starcade, so there are two or three misappropriated "(sic)"'s in a slew of quotes by fans.

Here and there are little signs of such disconnects. Nothing major, but enough to make one pause and reflect upon it.

Joe Babinsack

That, and the character Vito.... Hmmmm. Is it, can it be, that same Vito that Vince Russo considers the greatest professional wrestler of all time, and who sported a lovely dress the past few years in the WWE to keep his job?

Fascinating.

Some other fascinating stories involve a women training to be a wrestler, but it serves mostly as a vehicle to talk about feminism and the industry. While Mazer provides some very interesting commentary (those of you who do more than "hoot and holler" at the girls in the ring need to read some of this!) the feminist arguments seem more based in theory than in reality.

And then there's the training school

Johnny Rodz is one of my all-time favorite heels and a legendary figure in the WWF. His gym and pro wrestling school is obviously of importance, and the names that come to mind (and that are listed on a card shown in the book) include Vito, Tommy Dreamer and that guy that used to be Devon from that team that used to be the Dudleyz.

But Rodz isn't the only trainer in the country, and his approach isn't likely the same as every other trainer.

That being said, the training insight is very interesting and informative.

Just presenting the observations of rote learning of holds is enough to give me a great feel for what would go on at a pro wrestling school.

Now, it wouldn't be fair to expose all that in a review of a book, but there are two strong chapters about what is going on at the school, not so much an overview or an itinerary, but a definite and real observation of what the guys are doing, what their mindset is, and how it "feels" and how the training goes on.

All told, it is an interesting view of the world of professional wrestling, not from an insider, not from a worker, and not from someone who has an axe to grind about it all. Sharon Mazer is, despite her intellectual credentials, a fan, and her perspectives and perceptions as a writer on the sport are well worth the read.

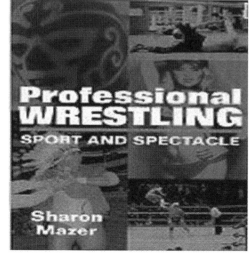

Formulas for Success

One of my favorite TV shows is "Criminal Minds" and it's a great example of an entertainment formula that works.

Some may consider it a spoiler, but if you know the show, you know what I'm talking about, and if you don't, you'll learn pretty quickly how it works if you watch. Plus, I'm sure most crime type shows follow a similar routine.

It's just that some shows get too gruesome, or are just too far-fetched to begin with, just like some pro wrestling is too hardcore, or just too crazy, to be believed. (Believability is another column.)

But when you watch Criminal Minds, the story unfolds in a typical fashion. The evil of the criminal is shown, and the rest of the hour is a chase to stop the murderer from striking again. In that effort, we're shown the potential victim, and the mystery being uncovered, and the criminal working his modus operandi.

Sort of a three way dance, if you will.

The reason the show resonates with me is that the good guys typically triumph, the victim is saved, and the team reveals some deep insights into the mindset and psychology of the criminal who is thwarted. Besides, the drama and problem solving, plus the acting and the stories themselves, are all top quality stuff.

But if you want to boil it down to a formula, you can readily do so.

It's the getting there that makes it entertainment. It's the satisfaction of seeing positive results that make me want to watch again. It's the triumph of good over evil that makes it more emotional, more dramatic and more enjoyable.

The other aspect of the formula is that it can be tweaked. Last season, the finale revolved around a story that did not play out in a typical fashion. This time, the bad guy seemed to have won, and the team was put in jeopardy. Tweaking a formula makes the formula stronger, changes things up and makes the ongoing viewing more enjoyable.

I know I'm speaking an alien tongue to the creative departments of professional wrestling promotions, but then again, maybe someone will learn something, and maybe my viewing of professional wrestling will be enhanced.

Joe Babinsack

Formulas are not just in TV. Writers use formulas. Stephen King and Anne Rice have staples, and I'm sure – if you're an avid reader – that you can recognize that one of your favorites uses the same characters, the same situations or the same genre. Some of those aren't formulas, but when Stephen King ends almost every story in a 'let's go back to the beginning' twist, and when Anne Rice frames her stories in a similar fashion – an interview – those are strong formulas.

I don't see Stephen King wanting for book buyers, nor Anne Rice.

And while both have changed things up over the years, and both have not always kept the same fans, they made their careers on what can be argued a simplistic entertainment template.

Now, I wasn't exactly around when Bruno Sammartino make his mark on the sport, but I've read, watched and listened to the man. I'm well aware that no one in the history of the sport had made the mark – an eight year title run where everyone in the world wanted to book him, wanted him to have their title, wanted to bring him in as often as possible.

Was Bruno's success merely a formula? If not, then his greatness was innate.

If so, then why can't current promotions take a page out of that equation, and try something different? The WWE is, as Paul Heyman has noted, a creative endeavor focused on the perceptions of one man. Obviously, that man has decided that anything but the morass that is the current WWE Universe is not worth the effort.

As a long time follower of that promotion, in its various incarnations over the past three plus decades, I'm well aware that Vince McMahon has a huge disdain for rules. He seemingly has had a disdain for formulaic booking as well, but then again, at the height of his creative and profitable success – in the mid and late 1990's, Vince was formulaic.

In the 1980's, Hulk Hogan took up the mantle that Bruno Sammartino lofted to high levels: Building up bad guys, working programs and prolonging the fight until a culmination was the staple of the Hogan era. That the Hulkster was unable to maintain arena attendance was a sign that despite his mainstream appeal, he was unable to make the real connection to the fans.

Thus there remains a shortcoming to the formula approach, because a formula is the sum of the parts: format, scenarios, talent, build-up and packaging.

Pro Wrestling Intellectual

Formulas quickly become familiar. For the first part of this decade, we all expected every RAW to begin with a 20 minute promo, and end with a pretty solid main event – one that was built up over the course of the evening, and one that lead to further combinations, storylines and drama.

At some point, and obviously after talent with promo ability stopped being produced, that formula drifted away. (Funny thing is, and this is a digression, but as fabulous promo guys are no longer featured, and as managerial roles -- with guys dependent solely upon bump-taking and speaking – are all but antiquities, where are the next generation of talent going to learn the craft? How many guys learned to speak from Blassie, from Heenan, from a variety of Southern style managers?)

But I digress. The point is that, the professional wrestling domination of the WWE has drifted aimlessly since it has long forgotten the dynamics of the Bret Hart/Vince McMahon Montreal event, and desperately needs a reorientation, a big bang event or simply a genuine re-set. But on a different parallel, the WWE (or anyone for that matter) needs to create a new formula or format, and one that reinvents the game.

Any long term fan can come up with a dozen ways that hearken back to the Old School, or a mostly forgotten region, or just a way in which it used to be done.

Maybe the formula can't work, but then again, if it isn't tried, how can it work? More than anything, the hyper pacing and the focus on quantity over quality wore out its welcome.

In a day where competition is a necessity, one day some company may rediscover the tried and true formulas of success. And it might just make watching pro wrestling enjoyable again.

Joe Babinsack

STEEL CHAIR TO THE HEAD:
THE PLEASURE AND PAIN OF PROFESSIONAL WRESTLING
Edited By Nicholas Sammond
Duke University Press   www.dukeupress.edu

I've been fascinated by the "intellectual" perspective on professional wrestling for some time. As someone with a degree in English writing, and having experienced that culture relatively recently, I know there's a lot of perplexing attitudes and amazing insight that these people can provide.

And, I don't use "amazing" as a positive description.

Over my time doing serious reviews on professional wrestling books, one "intellectual" that I found vastly interesting is Sharon Mazer. She has shown, in her own book (Pro Wrestling: Sport and Spectacle) to know the industry, the language and the performance based understanding.

She's done her homework by attending the Jonny Rodz training school, and she's well versed in rec.sports.pro.wrestling (rspw) newsgroup lore. In this book, she once again shows that she has insight and 'gets it.'

I can't say the same for a lot of the other contributors.

The book is touted as a strong analysis of the popular culture impact of professional wrestling. Many of the writers have a strong background in typical English writing, and notably the concept of deconstruction. What is amazing (and note the use of the term) is that these people have a goal of re-inventing writing and communications, to a Marxist end, especially in regards to established mores and traditions, things that the average person considers a given.

(I'll not continue to bore you, or get terribly political. Suffice to say, Marxism has killed over 100,000,000 people over the past century. Ignoring that fact is hard for me to do. Mindless subservience to that ideology is criminal.)

Thing is, these ivory tower intellectuals will target any and every subject imaginable. And then they come to professional wrestling, and … well, we all know pro wrestling fans are mindless idiots, easily lead and all that crap.

So they should have an easy time with it? No?   Bah!

The first major mistake is using someone by the name of Roland Barthes as the subject matter expert. Mr. Barthes is a French Deconstructionist from the Jean-Paul Sartre era. To Barthes, pro wrestling is easily deconstructed. Everything is simple and for the simple minded. His essay from 1957, which was reprinted in his book published in 1972, is

Pro Wrestling Intellectual

considered a touchstone for all writing upon professional wrestling in the glorious (note the sarcasm) intellectual circles of academe.

Problem is, Roland Barthes is writing about an offshoot of professional wrestling in a nation (France) that has a relatively minor role in the worldwide impact of the sport. Sure, I don't want to diss Andre's Posse. Andre is always listed as coming from Grenoble, France. I cannot dismiss Andre's impact upon professional wrestling. He was the Eighth Wonder of the World, after all. And then there's Rene Goulet, with the Michael Jackson glove and the French Foreign Legion gimmick that was cool way back before Lucha Libre reinvented it.

And then…. Well. I'm sure there's more.

If French pro wrestling was so great, why did Andre head out to Quebec to start making money in the sport? Did French wrestling take a nose-dive in the 1960's? Or was it anything to begin with?

Barthes may well merit his own deconstructive dismemberment in another column. I just don't want to waste this review on his nonsense. So, we have a collection of essays by English writing specialists, who love their jargon, love to quote Barthes, and love to attempt to boil down professional wrestling to its core.

Which they can't.

Once again, Sharon Mazer is awesome. She ends her essay with a scene in the "boardroom" or decision making meeting at her New Zealand (Tony Garea!) University home. She mentions how she looks around, wonders about the dynamics, the showmanship of the posturing and whether it's "real" or a "shoot" or how she's "expected to perform?"

And, most of all, how she can put herself "over."

Mazer "gets it" when it comes to professional wrestling. She greatly understands the performance art aspect, the interactions with the crowd, and the essence of the effort put into it. More so, she appreciates the illusions and the "con" of it all. With Mazer, the question of fake isn't one of blaming the promotion, but of appreciating the audience and their involvement in it.

To me, that's the big picture complexity of professional wrestling that the eggheads don't want, or simply cannot, understand. Professional wrestling is a grand scheme of an entertainment genre that engages the fans to a degree that simply is not possible in other sports, theatrics or artforms.

Mazer gets it. Henry Jenkins III doesn't.

Joe Babinsack

And Henry Jenkins IV, simply doesn't have the capacity to know he's so far off the mark that it's laughable. Some of the initial essays, with Nicholas Sammond and the aforementioned Henry Jenkins the third, are simply deconstructionist tripe. They praise Barthes for his blueprint, and then attempt to fill in a modern version of that Frenchman's pathetic insight into an entertainment genre he simply glossed over.

Pro wrestling cannot be deconstructed so readily. This book proves it far more than any social analysis and liberal criticism can. Pro wrestling evolves and changes and does lots of things. When I read about how the 1980's WWF product was all about political satire, I laugh. I've watched Vince McMahon (Sr and Jr) pro wrestling all my life. Sure, there's stuff you can read into anything, but political satire?

In the 1980's?

Hogan was a lot of things, and I can see the satirical slant if I really, really want to, but Hogan was a pale imitation of a greater champion, and Hogan couldn't maintain his drawing power in the same city. The WWF became a national phenomenon by masterful strokes of business acumen, some very risky promotional tactics, and mostly an aging and toothless array of regional competition that couldn't understand the value of cable TV.

But to say that the WWF rode its political satire into box office success?
Please.

The knee-jerk liberal mindset is rife throughout this book. Sure, we can complain about the Beverly Brothers (otherwise known as Mike Enos and Wayne Bloom, who were a pretty good tag team before and after that crazy gimmick.) But homophobia isn't rampant when you keep referencing one tag team that is actually quite obscure.

The other reference, the Billy and Chuck marriage, was 1) pure political satire and 2) a really great angle when it played out. Funny how it's a target of disgust by HJ IV. That moment when Bischoff unmasked was one of my all-time greats. Simply because I saw no way the WWE was getting out of it, and they found a way to do so.

Point is, the inconsistencies of this book are maddening.

But to get back to the gay thing. I've got three names for anyone who complains about the treatment of that alternative lifestyle by the professional wrestling industry: Jim Barnett, Pat Patterson and Adrian Street. I will readily admit that gay-bashing and homophobic leading of the audience is something that happens in the pro wrestling environment.

But there are lots of more important criticisms that can surround the sport. Life and death issues, not just name-calling.

And for all the complaints, I don't see any mention of pro wrestling (notably Sputnik Monroe) and the integration issues in the south. Funny how we get the old "my

Pro Wrestling Intellectual

grandmother was a real racist" but never the wow, Junk Yard Dog really drew big as a black champion figure in Bill Watts' territory, which included parts of the deep south.

But the inconsistencies are laid bare throughout. There's some really good stuff on Lucha Libre, and a cool story about Super Barrio, but no enough world flavor in terms of politicians. What, no one heard of Atsushi Onita, Hiroshi Hase and the Great Sasuke? Those pro wrestlers are in the Japanese government. Sasuke in a freaking mask!

But some flaws in facts really stand out.

There's commentary on Jesse Ventura, and a mindless comment about why Jesse had not stood up to Vince McMahon and tried to form a union.

Seriously?

I guess the Hulk Hogan backstab never took place. That's one of the most egregious lacks of effort in the book. But not the only one. Henry Jenkins IV is touted as the boy wonder, the pro wrestling historian. But his facts are flawed, his insight poor and his addressing of the sport one that just never adds up.

Henry Jenkins III seems to think that Sharon Mazer's insight on interaction is all about holding signs in the audience. What a joke. His son comes through like a 1980's mainstream toy boy. Sure, pro wrestling was marketed to kids in the 1980's, but it wasn't about the merchandise for most of us fans. So when facts are flawed, and the understanding of the sport is just off the wall wrong, what can I say? One can't fawningly write about the impact of ECW one page, and three pages later complain about the violence of the WWE. ECW was exponentially more violent than the WWE ever dared.

And Vince pulled back on that violence to a degree where he deserves credit for it. The WWE could have headed down the road of ultra violence, but they stopped before it destroyed them. (Not that there aren't other criticisms!) But, to the point. There's one page where we're told that Glen Jacobs slapped a TV reporter on camera in the early 1980's. I guess fact checking at the university level is taboo. David "Dr. D" Shultz slapped John Stossel. Not Glen Jacobs!

Glen Jacobs was Isaac Yankems in a forgettable feud with Bret Hart. He was also the fake Diesel. He was also Unabomb in SMW. You know, a name taken from the extremist environmentalist wacko who killed in the name of Al Gore's "Earth in the Balance" book.

Not to get political again.

On the same page, Jenkins (the IV, not the III) touts a brawl between the late Andy Kaufman and Jerry Lawler on David Letterman's show. Weren't no brawl, 'twas a coffee throw. Watched it 'live' on TV and marked out. It also didn't start the feud in Tennessee. It continued it.

Joe Babinsack

On the next page, Jenkins the fourth (no elitism there) explains about "dirt sheets" and his pure ignorance of the fan participation and impact of the newsletters in the industry. He says that the Ross Report was created to take away the steam of people revealing results. Buddy, let me tell you something. I say in my best Jimmy Snuka voice….That ain't the way it works.

Guys like Dave Meltzer don't reveal storylines, they analyze the industry, provide insider knowledge and raise the enjoyment of the vast entertainment genre. They go over storylines, make sense of them and engage their readers to appreciate the efforts.

Newsletters are information sources. Not spoilers.

I could go on and on about the inaccuracies and inconsistencies. Is it a bad book? Somewhat. Flawed to a large degree, and proving, most of all, that professional wrestling is far too deep a subject for Marxist deconstructionism.

Which is hilarious as hell, if you get down to it, because for all the knocks against professional wrestling fans, if pointy-headed intellectual elites can't grasp the concepts, then how can the punch line staple of jokes, that toothless row of front row wrestling fans, be able to understand, appreciate and continue to enjoy it?

There are some interesting articles on masks in Mexico, but some pointless exercises in linking "homological" and masochistic themes to the professional wrestling world.

It's a mixed metaphor of social deconstruction: hopelessly flawed, ideologically driven and ultimately pointless. Except for that thing about killing over a hundred million people who disagree with the concepts.

Which is the most scary aspect of this drivel.

Pro Wrestling Intellectual

What happened to the jobbers?

Once upon a time, they were the staple of any promotion. Those guys who would put on a show for the newcomers, the established stars and those in the first stages of a renewed push. Most of all, they were the unheralded talents that enhanced the reputations of the more deserving – even if those other wrestlers didn't have what it took to begin with.

They were the faces of expectations.

Many of them remained unknown, but their personalities shown through in their work, in their opponents, and in the manner of which they were used. There were guys like Frankie Williams who bore the punishment of the biggest and baddest heels, and there were guys like Johnny Rodz who propelled faces past the mid-card level.

But inevitably, something clicked and they became more than just the job guy. There was that time when Frankie Williams was a guest on Piper's Pit, and through the abuse, that sense of pride just bubbled up. Of course, Piper then waylaid him before he could get much of anything from the sympathy and positioning, but then again, that was expected.

Rodz was always a favorite of mine, sending me to the path of being a heel fan. The "modus operandi" of Rodz was identifiable: he'd give the face on the rise a solid match, and would often get the better of things for a while.

But then, he'd always climb the turnbuckles, and attempt a big elbow or something.

"No!" I'd scream. "Don't do it!" But the inevitability of it all sunk in. Rodz was just playing his role. Being a heel was to be predictable in many ways, even if your nickname was "Unpredictable!"

Even that one time, when Rodz was matched up with Andre the Giant, there was an inkling of belief that "The Unpredicatable" one might just get the Giant in some real trouble. And for an icon like Andre, that really meant something. But at the apex of Rodz' getting the better of the big man, it happened … Johnny Rodz started climbing, and it was all over before the predictable thing happened….

Coming from the Northeast, I have my own set of favorite jobbers, but Pittsburgh seemed to be blessed by having professional wrestling outlets from across the country. I got to see the Mulkeys in their glory, as they made monsters out of the Road Warriors, and stumbled into wrestling lore and history by defeating a seeded team in the Jim Crocked Memorial Cup Tag Team tournament.

Who were the Gladiators and which West Coast promotion did they come from?

Does it really matter?

Joe Babinsack

The Mulkeys became a cult favorite and they continue to get tremendous accolades. How did two skinny white boys get to gain so much attention? All they ever did was lose. But they lost spectacularly. And they were part of the industry and the expectations were almost always met. It's one thing to put powerhouses in the ring. Its another thing to put talented bump takers in that ring and have the exceptionally talented wrester make the other ones look like they are worth a million dollars.

And that's one of the missing elements of the modern era.

Where are the enhancement talents?

When Jake "the Milkman" Milliken ended up captaining a team of AWA wrestlers in that Captain's Cup challenge, or whatever it was called, he wasn't just one of a few remaining and marketable names in the AWA, he was a long time loser and a jobber who had some affection with the audience. Sure, Larry Zbyszko was the star, but Larry was married into the waning Gagne empire. And Jake was the preeminent jobber to the stars.

But who can forget, without laughing uncontrollably, the high pitched screaming of Jake Milliken as he was pummeled unmercifully, in a vain attempt to win a Turkey on a Pole match?

That's the kind of character development, comedy and direction that doesn't appear overnight, and cannot be captured by the Hollywood gazing, script writing wannabes that dominate the current scene and fill in the gaps of decisions made by wrestling immortals.

And then there's Mikey Whipwreck.

Sure, his very name is a joke and a rip on a local promoter, but in ECW – the original one, not the perversion that persists today – Heyman and company played up the jobber role to the hilt. In most occasions, the jobbers were clearly defined. Don E Allen, Paul "The Giant" Lauria and others were very much undersized, and very much played the traditional roles of bumping to the big stars and making them look great.

But Mikey took it to another level. And provides another glimpse at how, within the framework of traditional wrestling staples, great creativity is possible and crowd attention and affections can be enhanced.

Whipwreck took beatings like few others. And then some, and even more.

Even in an ECW where disqualifications were a rarity and rules had their own set of expectations, one traditional sense of DQ was rolled out, and that sense was when an opponent went overboard after a victory, that victory could be rescinded.

Pro Wrestling Intellectual

Couple that with an improbable win, and an untraditional personality display, and voila, here's a new character that "got over" with the crowd in spite of the legends who surrounded him.

Of course, that concept is so outdated, and the jobber role so diminished, that such a character would have almost no chance of surviving today.

Ask Cody Runnels about that situation. But before a Cody Runnels can get over from the jobber tradition, the jobber tradition must be renewed.

Even Barry Horowitz gained a modicum of popularity and push when he upset the late, great Chris Candido in a then WWF match. Horowitz was someone who moved to WCW way before the NOW stuff, and actually showed some promise before politics killed him back down beneath jobber status.

But one of the main perpetrators of assaulting jobbers is someone we all know and love, and someone who deserves a bit of grief for his role in relegating jobberhood, in its historical tradition, into oblivion.

That man is THE ROCK!

Sure, calling people jobronies is fun and was meaningful at the time, but ever since, the jobber role has disappeared. Sure, Heat has some jobbers and jobbers are used sporadically in most promotions, but once the Cable TV wars exploded, there wasn't time for such niceties. And Duane Johnson put the nails in its coffin.

This is unfortunate, because that era ended over a half decade ago.

Jobbers are not of the current millennia. And that has to change. There are many talented individuals out there who deserve a great job, and the exposure, and the opportunity to get over by plying their craft on a national stage. People like Nick Dinsmore and Rob Conway and others deserved to have ongoing jobs – pun intended – in the WWE. Al Snow's Job Squad was a well intention effort to restore the dignity of the jobber status, and could have snowballed into something interesting.

Well, then again, it was Al Snow….But the thought counts, and unfortunately, no one cared.

And now, the only way to get new talent over is to kill dead the promise of talent already languishing in the mid-card. Carlito, anyone?

It's about time for the WWE to return the viewer to an expectation. That expectation is to see new talent develop by putting them into the ring with established veterans who can teach, and at the same time make promising, budding stars look like superstars before their time, and gain that status, instead of squandering their potentials.

But that's just one fan's opinion.

Super Championship

In a PPV environment where the UFC is now able to schedule out big time battles with ever increasing name recognition, the WWE needs to counter with its even bigger mainstream names, and do so without compromising its future and near future stars.

The best way to accomplish this is to create a "Super Championship" that is above the brand titles, and incorporates its mainstream names and the big time current players, allowing new stars a goal to reach for and a measuring stick for several groups of talent. Above all, it also raises the politics and match ups of monthly PPVs to a new level. By placing HHH, the Undertaker and Shawn Michaels, as well as other legends and one off competitors, into a separate mix, it would alleviate the burying of upcoming talent.

At this time, the WWE is at a point where it really has two classes of talent. One group is moving on in years, and while they can work hard, they are better off working part time due to injury risk. Most have contractual stipulations limiting house show appearances.

The second group is one that needs seasoning above all. Some are already draws; some need the interactions, the experience and the payment of dues to move up.
Add to the mix the one-timers and the potential appearances by other legends.

I am distinctly avoiding the notion of a Title Unification, since that talk leads to idiocy.

This direction would keep the three brands at an even keel, and allow those championship holders to really work at being a champion, working house shows, meeting challengers of all levels of competition, and perhaps keeping them from getting their careers cut short. The immediate casualties would be the US belt and the Intercontinental belt, which are both afterthoughts at the moment, regardless.

Of course, discipline and consistency would have to be bolstered in Creativity, which isn't necessarily an easy accomplishment.

The fundamentals of the WWE Super Championship are easy:

One: the title is fought on ever PPV

Two: the title is never fought on a house show

Three: the title is rarely, if ever, fought on a TV broadcast

Obviously, the build up of the Super Fights are done on the TV shows. These can be rotated, making all the stations happy and allowing buildups for PPV events to have another layer of intrigue. The obvious problem is the domination of the Super Competitors, but with four two hour shows, even a small sense of separation would go a long way. That, plus having regular brand title holders as the centerpiece of each show would give each network enough of a reason to force the WWE into not forgetting the main purpose of each of those TV shows.

With HHH out of the mix, Raw and SmackDown! are more equivalent than ever. Keeping said individual out of the weekly mix of one TV show, but giving him a bigger bone to play with, would be a great thing. The other aspect is that it plays to Vince's strength, which is his ability to book ongoing big matches which keep a championship strong. He did it tremendously with Hogan, and then again during the heat of the war with WCW.

Like with the dismantling of the Brock Lesnar unification, any sort of combination of brand titles would be doomed to politics, and any attempt to put all the brands together would create a domination of the top talent, which would hasten any sense of destruction of the next generation.

By raising a Super Belt above the brands, it would presumably raise the politics to a new level, but exclude a lot of vulnerable talent from being victims to HHH, Shawn Michaels, The Undertaker as distinctly part timers who should always be at the main PPV level. I'd throw Batista into that mix, since he has the look and reputation, as well as a injury history and age that suggests that his career is better served avoiding house shows.

Another group to add is Ric Flair, Hulk Hogan, Mick Foley and JBL. These are wrestlers who can compete at that level, and who shouldn't/wouldn't/couldn't be expected to be on house show tours. A third grouping would be (potentially) Big Show, Great Khali, Kane and Chris Benoit—wrestlers who have the reputation and/or size to compete with the aforementioned groups, enhancing matches but obviously not in it for the long haul.

The guys the brands are built around would obviously be the likes of John Cena, Mr Kennedy and Bobby Lashley. Throw in Edge and Orton as major heels, maybe even splitting them up to other brands, and there's the basis for the stars of today, who will eventually compete for the Super Championship in years to come.

I'm sure there are other names to add. Rey Mysterio, William Regal, Fit Finley, Carlito, Jeff Hardy, etc. Also, the guys not at the forefront of the Super Championship are still around to compete for the brand titles, and even with Batista, there can be a transitional period to move him into that higher mix.

So how does this come about?

Joe Babinsack

A massive tournament, which admittedly the WWE has always failed to do well, would be a great undertaking. King of the Ring, to me, has always been misused. It should emulate the NCAA basketball tourney, which it doesn't. It could be a world-wide tournament with ease, and a vehicle to elevate new talent and provide good matches.

*Imagine a European qualifying match with Regal and Finley.

*Imagine a Canadian qualification, with Edge and Benoit or the debut of Harry Smith.

*A Mexican qualification match with Rey Mysterio and the debut of Mistico or Shocker would produce an introduction of note.

*The Japanese contingent would ultimately be a downer, but Johnny Ace's ties and the always rumored New Japan dealings could provide a number of potential candidates.

*Legend qualification matches could match up Flair vs. Hogan, or Foley vs. JBL.

Drama can be added by asking title holders to give up their belts to join the tournament. But then again, another set of mini-tournaments would only cloud the issues. Instead, I'd suggest giving the belt holders an automatic entry, if not a bye into the first set of PPV matches. That would allow for intrigue in terms of positioning to gain one of the belts. By adding a stip to the overall concept, each brand title should have a once per year option of challenging for the Super Title.

With Royal Rumble as another automatic shot, as well as the King of the Ring getting a shot, there would be plenty of opportunities to feed the Super Fight with new challengers – without having to do skits and angles every time, and it would allow time for some natural feuding between automatic shots. That feuding could then spin off of a fight for the Super Title, making for more depth in doing monthly PPVs.

Set over two months of TV time and two PPV events, tell me that a high profile tournament wouldn't draw huge! No matter who the last two competitors end up being, they would have a buildup of two months for a conclusion and an ongoing, mainstream, water cooler talk set of circumstances to keep it in the eyes of old and current fans. Not to mention that it would make a PPV impact in the summer months where the WWE often drifts along until SummerSlam.

Perhaps the WWE would need to summon the spirit of Giant Baba to get a proper tournament bracketing together, and the nightmares of politics, injury and unCreativity would undoubtedly ruin a good thing, but its something to consider for a wide variety of reasons, making money not the least of them.

Pro Wrestling Intellectual

WHAT MAKES A GREAT PROMOTION?

The aspects of a great promotion change with time, and of course are subjective, but here a few things that every great wrestling product must have:

1) Believability
2) Dynamics
3) Talent
4) Matchmaking
5) Simplicity

Now, if you've caught on that I'm an "Old School" type of guy, you're right: today's mainstream professional wrestling is way too fast in developing storylines, featuring too many foolish angles, overplaying a stagnant talent roster, and is as believable as hitting a human with an eight pound sledge hammer and seeing no physical ramification.

I know the general consensus is that the WWE is the best, simply because it draws the most money. While it's hard to argue against a billionaire, it is easy to criticize, and the numbers have been on a downhill curve for the past several years.

The scary part of the equation is that for the first time in the professional wrestling industry's history, there has been no real competition for the most part of the past decade. Fifty years ago, there was somewhere around three dozen major territories spanning the United States, plus thriving promotions in Japan, Mexico, Canada and elsewhere.

Twenty-five years ago, shortly after Vincent James McMahon passed away, and before Vincent Kennedy McMahon's national expansion (and destruction of the territories) there were still closer to two dozen profitable promotions in the nation.

Which meant that every major city had the attention of a local promotion, plus likely TV and or cable coverage that showed other areas, like Superstation TBS and Georgia (soon to be World) Championship Wrestling.

At the time, there were also national magazines – The Wrestler, Pro Wrestling Illustrated, and several others, that chronicled the sport, and allowed fans everywhere to follow Dusty Rhodes, Andre the Giant, Hulk Hogan or Nick Bockwinkle.

Joe Babinsack

Those publications, and the TV coverage, meant that fans grew up knowing that the sport was more than the local promotion, and that wrestling stars, different names and interesting legends existed elsewhere.

Fifteen years ago, professional wrestling was in a low cycle. It was the post-steroids trial era, and Vince wasn't relying upon Hogan or the Ultimate Warrior. It was the post Bill Watts era in WCW, and bureaucrats and office politics were still hampering growth, and Eric Bischoff hadn't quite yet gotten the green light from Ted Turner to start spending money.

But, at the time, the legends and the name values, the memories of local territories and the persistence of long-time fans, all meant that a revival was possible. Fifteen years ago, despite things looking bleak, the tidal wave of mainstream popularity was ready to explode.

Much of the reason? Because the history, the legends and the name value of the stars in the industry remained viable. Whether the sport was followed in magazines, internet newsgroups, word-of-mouth or the fading vestiges of the regions, or the then moribund offerings of the WWF and WCW (and, to some perverse degree, in the claims of Larry Zbyszko as the American Wrestling Association Champion – a claim founded mostly on being the son-in-law of the promoter….my have things changed over the years!)

The scary thing today is that the product produced by the WWE is moribund, but the products elsewhere are mostly worse, unheralded or otherwise unknown to even the locals.

Professional wrestling fans today don't have the history. They don't have anything but a short list of potential comeback types, legends or main eventers. And worse, they don't have the traditions that bridged the chasm of 1980's bubble to the 1990's bubble.

Let's name the guys who aren't currently part of the WWE domination, who could reasonably be brought in to a new promotion…

Rob Van Dam

Bill Goldberg

Ric Flair

Hulk Hogan

Pro Wrestling Intellectual

Randy Savage

Also, an assortment of cronies of the aforementioned Hogan, family members of Flair, and a number of foreign (is that TBS policy still in effect?) talent that fewer and fewer hardcores even bother to follow in 2008.

That's a far cry from 1998, when expiring contracts, still viable main event level names and an assortment of potential stars could fill up the rosters of three different promotions.

The problem is, of the aforementioned nigh half dozen names, only Rob Van Dam is capable of doing a regular schedule, and he has family issues and a reportedly decided indifference to returning to the game. One could argue about Goldberg, but Flair is decidedly retired, Savage looks too much like Santa Claus, and Hogan? Hogan just bombed out on the Country Music TV network, not even a year after he presumably helped draw some noticeable numbers for American Gladiators.

You know, the NBC show featuring overly muscled gals and guys beating up on overly athletic 'normal' people.

And let's not talk about how professionals become 'overly muscled' in this day and age!

But, after a column filled mostly with doom and gloom, let's spin on a dime and get to the positive aspects.

If you've never heard of SHIMMER, a promotion featuring absolutely fabulous and talented women athletes, you've not seen the future of the sport.

If you've never heard of Ring of Honor, which has the potential to break out, perhaps on Mark Cuban's HDNet cable station, then you've not seen how far removed from the current product the passionate ROH guys can be.

If you've never heard of smaller promotions like Full Impact Pro, Pro Wrestling Riot, Absolute Intense Wrestling, Hybrid Wrestling, or one of dozens of extremely localized companies, then there's hope for us all.

It will be the breakthrough of a relatively unknown professional wrestling promotion that changes the landscape laid bare by Vincent K. McMahon, Jeff Jarrett and a slew of other foolish and short-sighted men.

Because, to me, the potential of professional wrestling is too great to ignore.

Joe Babinsack

The 1990's had an explosion because Cable TV is dominated by the ad revenue of chasing young and adult men, and because professional wrestling is cheap, and because the entertainment value of staged violence, creative drama aimed at men, and the emotional resonance of the ongoing battle between good and evil will always be profitable.

Today, we live in a world where Mixed Martial Arts is dominating the scene.

But MMA is not cheap, and the drama is greatly reduced because of physical limitations of fighting, let alone the reality that dramatic fights are few and far in between when talented fighters become overly trained and parity takes hold.

That's the story that made professional wrestling what it became: no one wants to see long and boring fights – they want to see dramatic action, violent threats and emotional investments in promotions, talent and storylines.

Wrestling has rebounded time and time again, and the business cycles are there for historians and fans to examine. But the best solution for the industry is a return to the roots: a simpler product, a more laid-back offering and most importantly, a fan base that appreciates true professional wrestling, and starts to scour the countryside for those gems of talent and matches.

I'll be doing my best, through this column, to provide the necessary insight into relatively local promotions like Hybrid and AIW, as well as the potential greatness of ROH, and especially the inherent greatness of SHIMMER.

Women's Professional Wrestling

One of the Greatest Professional Wrestlers, Manami Toyota.

Photo courtesy of Ed Russino www.wrestlingphotos.net

Joe Babinsack

Joe Babinsack Looks at Women's Pro Wrestling

Maybe women's pro wrestling is under your radar, but I enjoy following the sport.

Once upon a time, women's matches were mostly sideshow, performed seemingly for the wrong reasons, and while standouts in the history of the sport exist (and not just the late, great Moolah's mostly mythological championship run -- I'm talking Judy Grable and Mildred Burke!) it's hard to go back and look for great runs of great matches, or otherwise strong feuds featuring great matches.

That is, setting aside the awesome talents and matches in Japan in the 1980's, and especially the 1990's, and notably with the All Japan Women's Pro Wrestling promotion.

Let's face it, the 1990's versions of the WWE were for one reason, and it wasn't wrestling. And while Lita and Trish could go, they were never allowed to go as much as the talented wrestlers across the indy stages today.

Could they keep up? Likely, but that's a moot point.

The great thing is, that we've reached a point in pro wrestling history where the rosters of women wrestlers are stocked with talent, with dozens of competitors at the main event level, who work in a growing number of professional wrestling promotions, three of which (SHIMMER, ChickFight and WSU (Women Superstars Uncensored) put forth great cards on a regular basis.

To me, the women wrestlers tout a much more purer form of professional wrestling: they interact and react to the fans much better, they don't get caught up in stupid booking (well, I'm talking the above mentioned promotions!) and they aren't constrained by styles or body shapes.

Is women's wrestling perfect? Maybe not. And maybe it's not your "cup of tea" -- but if you're complaining about women's wrestling being all about GLOW (by the way, check out Big Vision's GLOW compilation for some nostalgia!) then you aren't paying very close attention. And if you watch women wrestling, without paying close attention, what's wrong with you?

Just to lay out the argument, let's look at three points: styles of wrestling, and appreciation of the craft, and depth of talent.

1) The top names of the genre are top notch wrestlers, who can match hold-for-hold with male counterpoints, in terms of technical skills, high flying ability and, in many ways, in terms of hard hitting action.

While there aren't exactly reputations for bloodletting, there are names, like Kong and Lee and Danger, and hardcore potential in names like Melissa and MsChif and Jazz, and heck, even the TNA ladies are getting their heads shaved and showing some color.

Pro Wrestling Intellectual

With women's wrestling, we have a growing portion of the industry accepting and admiring the efforts of the women, and these ladies are training hard and learning the craft and displaying creativity that cannot be dismissed.

Even by you chauvinists out there.

On TNA, we've seen that Awesome Kong has attracted solid attention. Of course, they couldn't wait to cut her down, but anyone who's seen Kong in action knows that it's impossible to stop her.

If you want to see punishing action, you can watch Kong vs. Amy Lee in WSU. You can watch Cheerleader Melissa vs. anyone, and especially vs. MsChif. You can see Jazz and Angel Orisini and a number of girls you don't want to see in a dark alley -- that's for sure.

If you want to see technical mastery, look no further than SHIMMER champ Sara Del Rey (recently dethroned by MsChif.) Look to the ChickFight promotion, and it's awesome tournaments, where gals are fighting for several matches before winning the thing. Look at the tag team excellence of Lacey and Rain, and know that they put justice to the "Wrecking Crew" moniker. And how about the "Definition of Technician" Cindy Rogers?

High flying? How about Daizee Haze? How about Nikki Roxx and Sarah Stock and a number of fearless women of wrestling?

How about the fact that we can note several horrible injuries, including one to Mickie Knuckles, and one in 2006 that seems to have derailed the career of Rebecca Knox?

These ladies didn't hurt themselves rolling around in mud, or bopping each other with pillows. They did it when pushing the envelope of their craft.

That's a level passion that deserves respect, not ogling.

2) Once again, it's the purity of the professional wrestling that is displayed by the women that gets my attention. Watch the women in action, and you'll see them interact. You'll see them play face and heel. You'll see them rally the crowd, play to previous matches, and work a match like few of their male counterparts bother.

You want an awesome heel? Watch Amber O'Neal in action. The bonus match on SHIMMER Volume 13 is a gem, showing her and Cheerleader Melissa in a match that would go over well on TV. Besides which, O'Neal isn't just a Barbie doll, she plants her opponent's with the Barbie Cutter, and she doesn't let up on the crowd, or the competitor.

Overbooked nightmares are the stuff of the Vinces these days, but it's amazing what can happen when you cut out all the camouflage and all the distractions. All those distractions are merely a symptom of the disconnect between promoters and fans.

Wrestlers, once upon a time, were a conduit between what the fans wanted, and what the promoters intended to deliver. Today, most wrestlers are robotic, pathetic actors, incapable of controlling the flow of a match. But when I watch the gals in action, I rarely complain about botched moves, or boring sequences or outright bad booking.

That's because the effort is both mental and physical, and in both avenues; I'll take a MsChif match over any other wrestler. I'll take a chance on watching Amy Lee vs. Awesome Kong over watching MMA on a Saturday night. I'll settle down and enjoy Lacey and Rain pull out all the stops in a tag team match.

And there's all that, without even talking about seeing some great looking bodies in athletic garb. Sure, I don't find Lacey Von Erich's fretting about a wardrobe malfunction appealing, but it's cool to see her introduce the Iron Claw to the current generation of great wrestlers.

3) Let's name some of the top women wrestling talents, in no particular order:

Sara Del Rey	Mercedes Martinez	Daizee Haze	Cheerleader Melissa
MsChif	Nikki Roxx	Allison Danger	Amy Lee
Amazing/Awesome Kong		Lacey	Rain
Gail Kim	Jazz	Amber O'Neal	Sarah Stock

Add in another tier:

Cindy Rogers	Portia Perez	Angel Orsini
Mickie Knuckles	Annie Social	Portuguese Princess Ariel
Josie	Serena Deeb	Lexie Fife
Malia Hosaka	LuFisto	Daffney
Eden Black	Becky Bayless	and others… (my apologies for oversights!)

Point is, that ain't including several TNA names, anyone called a "DIVA" nor the Ohio Valley Wrestling gals, nor the Mexican or Japanese contingents, and my apologies, it does not include every wrestler on every roster.

It does represent a very strong roster that currently appear on several solid promotions, and have been seen on TNA.

Women's wrestling isn't confined to one strange promotion, or even one region. It's represented on the West Coast with ChickFight, on the East Coast with WSU, and in Chicago (and other places in the ROH family of promotions) with SHIMMER.

And women's wrestling is steadily making inroads on the major indy level. It's no longer a joke, no longer a sport practiced by one or two troupes, and no longer something just to look at.

Check Out: SHIMMERWrestling.com, www.WSUwrestling.com or www.chickfight.tv

Pro Wrestling Intellectual

Cheerleader Melissa Vs. MsChif

There have been faster matches, more scientific oriented matches, more brutal matches, definitely more bloody matches, and likely, in some minds, more matches worthy of the title "match of the year."

But I present today a detailed run-down of a match that is great because of its subtlety.

It's easy to be jaded with the industry, to be overly impressed with non-stop high spots, to be awed by speed, acrobatics and death-defying dives. It's easy to raise expectations of greatness and at the same time saddle the adjective with time limits, appearances of blood, and over-the-top intensity. But all of that is simply more of the same.

To me, the essence of greatness in pro wrestling is the craft.

It's the manipulation of emotion, the long term build-up, the ability to show talent, to show passion, to show an ability to create a match. Sure, it's always about fighting someone else, but fights get boring, no matter how real or how staged, if they merely go through the motions.

The best of the high flyers, the most infamous of the daredevils, the most renown of the scientific types, and even the best brawlers – if they are disengaged from pro wrestling reality, if they fail to follow the fans as well as lead them, if they insist on rote over improvisation, if they just try to make things faster, harder or more impressive, then they lose the craft.

Believability, passion and telling a story -- those are now considered "old school" by way too many. Way too many wrestlers and way too many promoters, that is. Show me a wrestling fan who gets turned off by any of those three in abundance, and I'll show you someone who isn't, at their heart, a wrestling fan.

And if you wish to take that inference to higher levels, go right ahead….

And so, on to the recap of the match:

To start, we have the ring announcer standing on the red mat of the ring, looking quite old school. There are chandeliers from the ceilings, and it makes me think of

Before the match, the feud is recapped.

To start, we have the ring announcer standing on the red mat of the ring, looking quite old school. There are chandeliers from the ceilings, and it makes me think of "Wrestling at the Chase" and how utterly appropriate a setting for this match, even if it is "Last Woman Standing" rules!!!

Out comes Cheerleader Melissa after being announced.

This match is near Chicago, not the West Coast, so there is a smattering of boos from the crowd. The auditorium is the typically atypical Shimmer venue: not quite the larger size of Ring of Honor, this auditorium allowing for a smaller crowd, but not quite the bare bones, high school gymnasium feel of Full Impact Pro.

MsChif comes out, screaming like a banshee.

The match starts as MsChif slides in under the bottom rope. There's no time for niceties or formalities with these two. Almost immediately, Cheerleader rolls MsChif out to the floor, and slaps her, then begins an Irish Whip. MsChif reverses the Irish Whip, sending Cheerleader Melissa crashing into the far guardrail.

(It is mentioned by the esteemed David Prazak that the only blood spilled in Shimmer has been in a match between these two, as MsChif bled in the falls count anywhere match.)

After a brief scuffle, MsChif begins an Irish Whip to the opposite side. Cheerleader Melissa reverse it, and MsChif crashes into the guardrail. A scuffle ensues, but MsChif is back on the attack.

Both fall over the guardrail, but the crowd has already made room for them, and they proceed deep into the once arranged (but now disarrayed) chairs.

Cheerleader Melissa is up first, throwing forearms and taking control. She bends MsChif over a chair, the first display of MsChif's insane flexibility.

Cheerleader Melissa then grabs a headlock, and drags MsChif nearer to ringside and the rails. She slams MsChif and steps back, awaiting the count.

MsChif is up at the count of eight.

MsChif attacks Cheerleader Melissa with knees to her gut, and then forearms to her back, and then throws her over the guardrail.

Both make their way into the ring.

Cheerleader Melissa immediately sets up the Kudo driver, which is otherwise called the

Pro Wrestling Intellectual

Cop-Killa (Homicide's reverse piledriver move.) But MsChif counters, climbs over the back of Cheerleader Melissa, and nails the Code Green -- her weird version of a piledriver, that resembles the Canadian Destroyer in being a flip plus the piledriver.

Cheerleader Melissa sells it big.

MsChif waits as the referee counts.

Cheerleader Melissa is up at the nine count.

They lock up, and Cheerleader Melissa quickly hit's a Samoan Drop, then a slam, to regain momentum. She's still selling the piledriver. She attempts to put MsChif in a clover leaf (a reminder of their last match) but MsChif rolls through it.

Cheerleader Melissa stays on the assault, though, and puts MsChif in a rather tall Boston Crab. Just as Allison Danger and Dave Prazak note the almost straight positioning of MsChif in the hold, Cheerleader Melissa sits straight down, in an awesome display of MsChif's flexibility.

Both are selling the impact. Cheerleader Melissa, perhaps because of the jolt so soon after the piledriver. MsChif because she was nearly broken in half.

(Allison Dangerism: MsChif has no spine. Choke on that one, wrestling fans!)

Both end up down in opposite corners.

The ref counts, but Cheerleader Melissa is up quickly, and she throws MsChif out on the floor, and waits another count. When the ref hits six, and MsChif rises, she jumps down. They both trade blows, then forearm smashes.

Cheerleader Melissa drags MsChif back in, gets the upper hand, and knocks Cheerleader Melissa down, clubbing the cheerleader's back. MsChif then hits a quick baseball slide, pushing Cheerleader Melissa under the guard rail.

On the other side, as MsChif followed, they trade even more forearms.

"This is the most violent feud we've seen so far in Shimmer!" -- Dave "The Truth" Prazak

MsChif gains the upper hand again, and manages to trap Cheerleader Melissa's arms with a solid chair turned upside-down. MsChif then sits on that chair, tying up the cheerleader's arms in a submission move.

MsChif relents, and the referee counts, until interrupted at seven.

Cheerleader Melissa regains momentum with punches, forearms and then stomps the then prone MsChif, until grabbing another solid chair, and basically tying up MsChif in a camel clutch. Cheerleader Melissa is sitting on the chair, pulling back MsChif's arms and neck.

She pushes MsChif down, and sits while the referee counts, but herself interrupts the count at eight.

She tosses MsChif into the guardrail, then bends her in half over the railing.

MsChif manages a strike, and escapes over to the ringside area, then enters the ring. Cheerleader Melissa tosses a folding chair into the ring, and follows.

Cheerleader Melissa immediately sets up for the Kudo Driver, obviously in hopes of planting MsChif on that chair.

MsChif blocks and sweeps her leg over Melissa's arm, and drops a Desecrator -- a DDT variant. She then drives Cheerleader Melissa face first into the bottom turnbuckle. While Melissa is face down on the padding, MsChif delivers a double foot stomp to her back, and then again.

MsChif heads for the opposite corner, screams and it's a PANIC ATTACK!

(Prazak notes how MsChif trained with ROH's Delirious, picking up the running knee strike to a downed opponent in the opposite corner. (Think face buster without the nonsense.)

MsChif slumps over a bit, and hangs by her elbows on the top ropes.

Cheerleader Melissa slowly and desperately scrambles up, using the ropes to assist her. As she is obviously able to beat the ten count, MsChif attacks, knocking Cheerleader Melissa to the floor.

MsChif follows, but Cheerleader Melissa catches her with forearms, then chops. MsChif makes a comeback with punches, but Cheerleader Melissa tosses her back into the ring.

Cheerleader Melissa attempts a belly-to-back suplex (shades of the late, great Karl Gotch) but the move is blocked, and the two fight their way up the corner's turnbuckles. Cheerleader Melissa maintains control, and basically hits a Tower of London!!!

Pro Wrestling Intellectual

(She delivers a neck breaker, with MsChif being pulled off the top turnbuckle.)

Both are selling strong.

The cheerleader makes it up at the count of eight. MsChif pops up to beat the ten count!

One more Kudo Drive attempt, but MsChif rolls out of it.

She takes advantage of the positioning of the chair and Melissa, and nails the Desecrator -- the leg assisted DDT, on that chair. Even so, MsChif barely makes it up at the count of nine.

Cheerleader Melissa does not.

Both are selling the match huge, and Melissa has a blank expression, as if she's drained of all emotion, energy and capability. MsChif slowly but steadily makes it to the curtains.

Cheerleader Melissa slowly makes it out of the ring, with Prazak and Danger selling it all, noting that she is, after all able to walk out on her own two feet.

The crowd chants "Mel-iss-a"

What more can be said? Let's look at a few things.

For one, note that there are no PIN ATTEMPTS in this whole match. This is an intense, heated rivalry. They don't care about wrestling, rules or formalities. It's all about beating your opponent into a pulp.

There was no fall-back of rope breaks, either. That kind of intensity doesn't come across when you're working a real match. This wasn't a match, it was the last battle of a war, and it felt like it.

The other subtle, great and notable effort was the set up of the Kudo Driver as a finisher. Note how several times Melissa attempts the move. Note how she never plants it. That fact builds the hold up strong for future reference. It is also immensely enjoyable to tease that powerful hold, rather than trade off finishers left and right!

A third note is how Melissa sells.

Once she took the first Desecrator, she's in trouble. From then on, it's mostly a matter of time, although she does her best to win the match. MsChif is on the offense, and Melissa is breaking down. Even Cheerleader Melissa's own offensive actions are jarring her into trouble.

The coup de grace is the Desecrator on the chair, but it was set up a long time before that. And note how it was the chair thrown in by Melissa that did her in. She was, in many ways, the heel, and she paid for it.

Once again, we can argue about match of the year, but for my money, I'd rather see such a match like this, with two talented craftswomen, two wrestlers destined for greatness, and a slow pace despite itself.

This wasn't about the holds, it was about the hatred; it wasn't about a style, it was about the set-up; it wasn't about the finish, it was about the feud. Shimmer, Volume Six is the DVD I caught this beauty on, available at shimmerwrestling.com or at the hotline at (630) 585-3958.

Pro Wrestling Intellectual

SHIMMER WOMEN'S ATHLETES, DVD, VOLUME SIX
WWW.SHIMMERWRESTLING.COM

I'm more convinced than ever that SHIMMER is the best pro wrestling promotion.

Whether its storylines, talent or in-ring action, this promotion continues to put together great DVDs. It never embarrasses the viewer; and it combines an old school mentality, modern day pacing (at times,) different styles, a real sense of tag team action, and a full repertoire of move, as well as top notch talent from most of the world.

And the best part is that SHIMMER has just filmed editions 15 and 16 of its series, which means fans can still jump in on the promotion and get caught up to speed on the talent and storylines and simply enjoy it.

There's no rushed production here.

What I absolutely enjoy is the use of the talent in the storylines. This volume, number Six, still has no hint about a World Title, or a World Tag Team Title, but that doesn't impact the depth and importance of the line up one bit. Eventually a Title holder will be crowned, and by that time, a full roster of contenders, each with a history, feuds and a personality, will be available to make the matches even deeper.

For example, on this DVD, there is a culmination of an ongoing feud between Cheerleader Melissa and MsChif, which I feel is a Match of the Year candidate. It's a hard hitting match, tells a great story, and delivers on multiple levels. I reviewed this one previously, so I'll not gush about it too much, but it's certainly as must see a match as any this year.

There's a unique match with the "Pure Rules" that helped put Nigel McGuinness in the spotlight. I'm often a critic of Allison Danger, and once again, her attire is something to just wonder about, but it's a great match. And it's also part of an ongoing story between Danger and the rise of Rebecca Knox. (Note: Rebecca Knox had a dangerous head injury late last year, and updates of her condition aren't readily available. I will strive to get more info, because Knox has shown herself to be a great and upcoming talent.)

Then there's a tag match featuring top SHIMMER talent: their best tag team (the Minnesota Home Wrecking Crew!) and two of their top flight stars in Sara Del Rey and Mercedes Martinez. The interplay to get to this match is just solid bookmaking.

And there's a great bout relegated to the middle of the card, between Nikita and Daizee Haze, that brings in and elevates a new member to the roster. I believe Nikita is WWE bound, and Haze simply is one of the best workers around, bringing out the best in every opponent she's been matched with, and she's displayed a level of talent that can't be touched on mainstream TV. And I won't qualify that with only talking about the women.

Of the other matches, it's development, debuts and details.

The development of personalities and talent, as well as a lot of effort in the matches, are hallmarks of the promotion. Debuts of new talent (Amazing Kong and Nikki Roxx's string of impressive first matches) is the lifeblood of any promotion, and SHIMMER consistently brings in people 'the right way.'

And the details are what makes a difference. From the announce crew – the great David Prazak and the sometimes annoying Allison Danger, to the subtleties and focus, that all plays a great part of the presentation. As the DVD's pile up, the use of footage – enhancing the continuity and the consistency – has increased as well.

I just don't have a bad word to say about SHIMMER. except a long and somewhat tedious monologue by Allison Danger. She rants about Rebecca Knox and all the cheating, says that she's studied with Nigel McGuinness, and sets up the Pure Rules match. It would have been a bit better a little shorter.

Amber O' Neal vs. Serena Deeb

Amber usually wears orange and racing checks, but comes out in patent leather. I'm not one for blondes, but hey, patent leather is another issue. I like the sense of heel and face, as Serena Deeb plays the rather wholesome face well, and O'Neal has great potential. As an opener, it's strong. There's enough of what you want to see, and enough talent and a strong enough match to know these gals are really good at what they do.

Lexie Fyfe, Malia Hosaka, & Amazing Kong vs. Ariel, Josie, & Cindy Rogers

Fyfe and Hosaka are "The Experience" and the veteran heels, teamed up with the monstrous Kong, who gets the monster push. It's an interesting way to provide a squash without it being a typical squash. We pretty much know that "The Experience" are capable of handling their part, and they basically allow Kong to deliver her power moves and look very impressive.

SHIMMER has that athletic sense, so putting Kong in with multiple people would seem so wrong (although I may eat my words on that.) But here, she gets to powerhouse three faces. Cindy Rogers is the more technically sound face, Josie is debuting, and Ariel rounds out the diversity you won't see on TV.

Pro Wrestling Intellectual

Lorelei Lee vs. Nikki Roxx

Roxx seems like she's moving quickly up the ladder, and this is the sort of strong match where she's going to be gaining experience as much as displaying her assets. Lee has what amounts to a gimmick in SHIMMER, with the denim look and the "lasso" gestures. Unlike the previous two bouts, this is a face versus face match up, and has that Japanese feel of two professionals doing what they do best…wrestling.

Nikita vs. Daizee Haze

Haze is the total package – not in the sense of overwhelming hype, but in terms of ring presence, a nice look and a great interaction with the crowd. She know's her stuff, and sets up everything very well. Those who know her mostly from ROH know she's strong at taking bumps and she can get the crowd involved – as a heel or as a face.

But "The Haze" can wrestle with anyone on the card.

Nikita's no slouch, but with a bigger build and a strong look that will get her to the big stage. She definitely has the tools

Rebecca Knox vs. Allison Danger (Pure Wrestling Rules)

First, we have a(nother) recap of the Knox situations to set up the Pure Rules. The more interesting twist is Daffney on the mike, debuting in a sense, and setting up her future involvement with the promotion.

The Pure Rules, with the three rope breaks, count out rules and such, make for an interesting match. Unfortunately, it also sort of drags out a bit – each wrestler has three rope breaks before the ropes aren't going to break up a submission or stop a pinfall.

The problem with pulling this sort of match out of mothballs is that it's going to go the distance to make use of the uniqueness of the rules. It wasn't bad by any means, just … well, Allison Danger just rubs me the wrong way a lot. But the interplay of heelish Knox and easily ired Danger (who gets beat at her own rules!) is a joy to watch.

Anyway, Rebecca Knox has a great heel personality and displays it beautifully, and the development of her character and talent is well under way and on display in this match. I wish her well on her recovery, not for the business, but for her health.

Lacey & Rain vs. Sara Del Rey & Mercedes Martinez (Tag Team Challenge Match)

The odd-couple team always has its charm, and it gets played to the hilt in this match.

The strange thing is that the MHWC is teaming up for the first time in SHIMMER. The backstory, though, is explained and well done by Prazak and Danger. (Ok, Danger's announce team position, coming back from the previous match, gets a bit old, but it is interesting.) The story, in short, is that Rain and Lacey feuded several years ago, before they teamed up. The long story is better told by Prazak. Listen to him!

This is a solid tag team match, featuring some of SHIMMER's top echelon talent. Lacey is a little more over-the-top than The Haze, and not quite the impact wrestler, but on the same level in terms of all-around talent. The double-teaming of the heel team is exceptional, worthy of the name and of the built up reputation.

Mercedes Martinez, the Latina Sensation, is a heavy hitter, and Del Rey is the protégé of Bryan Danielson, so they can more than handle their own, and the displays of pure wrestling talent, power and building up of the match is impressive.

Sure, the odd-couple team has a rather predictable finish, but its part of an ongoing storyline, and more so, there's not a swerve in the playbook here.

Cheerleader Melissa vs. MsChif (Last Woman Standing Match)

This is simply off-the-charts awesome.

The brutality of the wrestlers involved, the excellent build up of the match (last standing rules) and the emphasis on one wrestler setting up a finisher, and the other knocking her down along the way, until the victory is won, is just great.

What I loved was that there were no cheap pinfall attempts. This was sheer "I'm going to kill you" and an utterly fabulous display of professional wrestling that I'll put up against any other match, anywhere this year.

Bonus matches are excellent. Lufisto vs Josie is just pure power. Lufisto is a sparkplug of effort and entertaining to watch. And any bonus that sees Allison Danger beat twice makes my day. Sorry, Allison.

But I can't overlook Nattie Niedhart. She's going to make it big pretty soon. Standing toe-to-toe with the most talented wrestlers of SHIMMER has proven her worth, as if being a third generation in the Hart lineage didn't already give her the genes and skills already. I think her look, her copying of her father's mannerisms, and her grandfather's innate skills will help her dominate the WWE scene for many, many years to come.

CHICKFIGHT V

Aside from solid wrestling, two ways to get my attention are superior graphics and a well booked tournament, and having it be women's wrestling certainly adds its own appeal.

Chickfight is a San Francisco based operation run by Jason Deadrich, and has recently run events in the UK. It features some of the top women wrestlers in the country, and the world for that matter, but the glory of the promotion is a regular tournament that pits eight top women's wrestlers in a grueling competition.

In the latest DVD installment, Chickfight V, wrestlers from Neo Ladies Pro Wrestling (Japan) join the fray, including Yoshiko Tamura, Tanny Mouse and Sumie Sakai. Tamura is holder of both the NEO Singles title and the NWA Pacific Title; Mouse is a solid veteran; and Sakai is a baby-face looking hardcore dynamo.

Filling out the tournament seeds are ECW great Jazz, the ubiquitous Allison Danger, West Coast standout Cheerleader Melissa, Chickfight IV winner MsChif and one time TNA star Simply Luscious.

The first thing that stands out is the awesome DVD production values. It simply cannot compare to any other promotion on any level. Augmenting that is background and statistical information often lost in other products. We get a stylized ring entrance for each wrestler, with hometown, vital statistics and training background.

The graphics nicely set up the matches, and the announce team of Jason Deadrich and Shane Stoli are exactly what is necessary: intelligent, low key and insightful, providing no distractions and lots of interesting commentary. Unlike so many products, it is impossible to watch Chickfight without coming out of it knowing the names of the participants and a wealth of background material.

The tournament is set up nicely by the graphics, as well as the solid booking.

Since few tournaments in the US hold up to high standards (or low ones, at that!) Chickfight comes across as unique and worthwhile. I'm always a sucker for a great tournament: it forces finishes, it provides a great "measuring stick" and it demands rematches down the road.

Joe Babinsack

From the basis of watching only one tournament, I can see that the promotion excels at the presentation.

Eight fighters is a solid seeding for the tournament, with four first round matches, two semi finals and the championship match.

It was beyond simply interesting how the announce team set up the "unique" styles of several of the first round matches. The Japanese women had some quirks, and a wide range of reputations. It seems as though the announcing was acknowledging the disparities in talent when talking about someone "unique" style. That was apparent with Tanny Mouse, and most notably with Simply Luscious.

The Mouse took on Cheerleader Melissa, the latter having participated in all the first five Chickfight tournaments, but having won none of them. That was a not so subtle hype job. All things considered, this was close to a squash as the promotion is going to put on, as Cheerleader Melissa got to display her talents, aggression and interesting finishing hold -- the Curb Stomp -- where she lifts the prone gal up by both arms, and stomps the back of her head.

There's not a lot of margin of error on that one.

The next match featuring that "unique" style highlights the wrestling talent of ECW/WWE's Jazz. Actually, don't take that sarcastically, although most anyone in the ring with Simply Luscious, on that night, would be taken at the world class level just to get a good match going. The announcers had a field day with Luscious, and there must be more to the story. (At one point Luscious looks for a breather, but Jazz drags her back in the ring for more.)

[Another perspective comes from the bonus tag team match, pitting Luscious and Allison Danger against the Japanes duo of Sakai and Mouse. It wasn't that great of a match, but it put Simply Luscious in a spotlight as being far more annoying than Allison Danger, and for that, I simply remain amazed.]

Pro Wrestling Intellectual

Jazz pulled out the victory with the STF, which is both a rarity for her to use a submission hold, and a rarity anymore for Masahiro Chono's masterpiece of a submission to actually score a win instead of just looking nifty.

Yoshiko Tamura is touted as one of the best women's wrestlers in the world, and she gets to shine with Allison Danger.

[Danger, I learned from this DVD, is originally from Canada, which explains her strange Can/Am/Japan T-shirt image and saying. I always thought she was simply from the less hospitable side of Pennsylvania. I'd love to further reference the "evil Canadian theory that goes back to the Rougeaus, but it doesn't seem appropriate at this time.]

Reputations are lived up to in this match.

Tamura works a stiff, aggressive and technically sound style. She has a particularly devastating knee attack, where she rushes the corner and strikes her opponent's head multiple time with her knee. (sort of like Delirious's clothesline assault.) Everything Tamura does builds to the match, sets up psychology and comes across utterly believable, dangerous and hard hitting.

Danger, as always to me, has that certain something where she manages to do something inexplicable not bad, not crazy, but instills just that sort of "huh" type reaction in me. Sometimes its leading the crowd in clapping when she'd be better off circling her opponent, sometimes its overselling instead of interacting, other times its just a cloying display of personality.

But Danger does tend to live up to the talent of her opponent, and it's a match that builds the reputation of the Chickfight tournament.

Which can also be said of the final first round tourney match.

Sumie Sakai is the perennial underdog, due to size and appearance, but as the announcers hype, she's a hardcore style wrestler. That's pretty much what you might expect of MsChif, but here she shows another facet of her talent. She plays up the overconfidence of being the defending Chickfight Tournament winner (from iteration 4.0) and sells much of the match, selling the point that Sakai came here to prove herself, and took advantage of someone expecting to sail through to the Semis.

Eventually, and likely at the point where Sakai does her traditional kiss of the opponent, Mschif does wake up and show her stuff. Well, she shows that she can batter her opponent and make her tap out in weird contortionist positioning. Here, Mschif grabs one arm in a hammerlock and the other in a crossface position and ties Sakai up in a pretzel.

What I love about the Tournament format is that is presents an opportunity for pacing, for match-ups and for speculation. Chickfight takes advantage of those opportunities to the fullest: while the first set of matches are merely interesting and worthwhile, they strongly set up the second round, having already established certain storylines, match-ups and expectations.

The semi final round is thus set up for big things, and it doesn't fail to produce.

These aren't just matches, they are wars.

Like I said, the opening matches set up the second round, and the second round sets the final match up as even bigger. The pairings are Jazz against MsChif, and Melissa against Yoshiko; the former being a battle of the powerhouse against the last tournament champion, the latter pairing up the most decorated of the contestants against the most rounded wrestler

(who happens to have been in all the tournaments to this point, without winning it.)

Jazz vs. MsChif is a well anticipated matchup. Jazz is all about power, but in the first match she showed she can hang with the faster paced, submission oriented current style of wrestling. The announcers tout her ECW background, and all that plays well against MsChif, who by reputation, move set and attitude has taken those expectations of an ECW wrestler and hyped them up beyond belief.

It comes across as an epic battle, the powerful force against the bendable but unbeatable body. This is the kind of give-and-take that makes a great match, and the believability factor is in full effect. It's also the kind of match you'd expect in a high profile tournament, where everyone's giving it all.

The other semifinal is the hometown favorite, Cheerleader Melissa, against the top of the Japanese food chain in Yoshiko Tamura.

This is another classic, far more technical but no less brutal than the other semi. The big picture is the story, the story of Cheerleader Melissa overcoming odds to make her way to

Pro Wrestling Intellectual

the finals and the tournament championship. The cover alone paints the picture, with Melissa stretched out, reaching for the victory.

But the long term and tournament booking are also flawless and compelling. It's wonderful when the matchmaking and the individual efforts line up "correctly" and make the whole more than just a sum of the parts. Each match builds up the tournament, and each round sets up the next.

Melissa overcomes the "best wrestler" in the field, then is pitted against the most powerful and the "biggest name."

The bonus match, just to digress a moment, is the "consolation" match, between Tamura and MsChif, and a great bonus it is. Ten minutes of solid and hard hitting action. In a sense, MsChif has a lot to prove in this match. She works it a little less stiff, a little slower and a lot more technical than I've seen of her.

She also pulls out the standing moonsault, and highlights her uncanny flexibility in a series of near-falls, crazy submission attempts and a great ability to take punishment.

It was an "old school" feel from the opening announcements, and even in what appears to be a huge hangar with few fans, the atmosphere can barely contain the passion.

Of the seven tournament matches and the consolation, the final four are without doubt some of the best wrestling around.

The final match is the culmination and cannot be looked at without watching the entirety of the tournament. Not that I'm dissing it, but its what you would expect after seeing some hard-fought matches leading up to this championship match. It's a little slower, a little more methodical than the semis, but here's two women who are pounding the heck out of each other, and are telling a match with the utmost of respect for the craft of pro wrestling.

My only criticism is that the finish seemed to come too cheaply, but again, after a long day of wrestling, just winning the match is an effort beyond all efforts, and an accomplishment well worthy of respect.

If I were to choose an "MVP" of the tourney, it would be Jazz. It's easy to cast aside the reputation of the WWE and not expect much from a name level talent slogging away at the indy level, but Jazz stepped up and delivered, working a hard pace in three straight matches, carrying someone in the first, and not losing a beat to two of the top gals in the sport today, and two with whom she matched up well with, in terms of style and expectation.

If you can't figure out who won, well, then that's all the more reason to go out and buy the DVD.

Chickfight has a growing reputation and a great roster, as well as the connections to Japan and elsewhere to highlight the best wrestlers in the world. Its booking is top notch, the amount of nonsense is absolutely nil, and the packaging and presentation of the product is something that needs to be emulated by a lot of other indy promotions.By the way, ChickFight also has a toll-free number for info: The 24-hour toll-free number is 1-888-337-5103

THE VERY BEST OF GLOW COLLECTOR'S EDITION 3 DVD SET
BIG VISION ENTERTAINMENT
BVDVD.COM AND GLOWVOD.COM

Call it equal parts nostalgia, appreciation and a healthy perspective on what professional wrestling can be, but I really enjoyed watching "The Very Best of Gorgeous Ladies of Wrestling"

What's interesting to me is that when you explore the facets of wrestling that otherwise may scream "bad" -- the camp, the variety shows, the badly acted skits and sometimes less than technical wrestling, you find out that when the product is really built around that stuff, and not pretending to be otherwise, it has a certain charm.

Then again, when it is badly produced, foolishly written, hard to comprehend and pretends to be dressing up the core of what is - but isn't - but fakes to be - professional wrestling, then you get TNA, or some of the awful crap that the WWE churns out from time to time.

Nope, for me, I'll take GLOW.

Maybe it's just the big hair, nylon clad legs and workout costumes; the laid back sexuality -- and the often campy gimmicks that were nothing but glorified stereotypes of women; the vastly more interesting and thought-out gimmicks; and in reality, some really good looking women who can also wrestle.

Now, don't get me wrong, this isn't Manami Toyota or Cutie Suzuki level. It isn't MsChif, Cheerleader Melissa and Sara Del Rey level either. Nor is it Wendy Richter or the Fabulous Moolah. It's not Penny Banner or Mildred Burke or one of many dozens of truly class acts, truly impressive talents or classic wrestlers that deserve appreciation.

But it isn't half-bad. Actually, it's stunningly competent and overwhelmingly appealing.

And again, I don't just mean the classically out-dated, hairspray laced and overly bleached blonde mops that adorn these gals.

The craziest thing to me is that seeing women roll around and wrestle, with all the angles, suggestive positioning and "look at that" mentality is far sexier than watching silicon bounce al over the place, with scantily clad women, perversions on display and nothing left to the imagination. Sure, call me a prude. I don't care.

Just take a gawking look at some of these ladies in action. I'm sure you remember Hollywood and Babe -- the Farmer's Daughter, or the fabulous Ninotchka…. Or Tiffany Mellon, or Godiva or Cheyenne Cher.

Sure, some of the comedy bits were straight out of Hee-Haw, and well, maybe I'm dating myself beyond belief, but I'm sure there are those out there that remember what preceded your favorite wrestling shows, whether it was that crazy weird Doctor Who show on WOR, or Lawrence Welk, or the Meadows Racing, or of course, Hee-Haw.

Then again, there was that 11:00 hour when GLOW was on, and you just took in all that visual aspect of seeing ladies roll around the ring.

Watching men in tights?

We know how that goes in school when insidious and ignorant types can't appreciate the bloodletting. But talk about GLOW? That's another story.

And it's all here in the Collector's Edition 3 DVD Set, Gorgeous Ladies of Wrestling: Greatest TV Moments, 80's Classics. All of it, from the horrendously bad Zelda's Zingers, with the nerdy chick spouting off nonsense, in a sort of pre-liberal domination mindset during the last days of the Cold War. How about Tiffany Mellon's warped sense of our own hardcore fandom, spouting off celebrity gossip and wrestling "reality" as if she was prescient to both TMZ and the WON.

We've got Godiva's Bare Facts, and a whole lot of cheeky matches … but hey, almost all of that flesh is covered! Who can forget Big Bad Mama, and her weird campaign to be mayor. Or Fiji?? And how about that opening and the intros to the different characters. It's like someone saw the Chicago Bears rap and decided to run with it past its shelf life. Crappy rapping by white chicks? Is that actually legal?

But then you get to see the women in action, and they're doing old school psychology -- albeit on a faster pace. They're doing fireman's carry's and working the leg and working a body part. They're not just finishing every match with a roll up….or a schoolgirl (to call it more cutesy and pretend that the fans just don't care.)

Man, I just can't get away from being a critic, now, can I?

The point is, GLOW featured sound wrestling talent. They weren't going to go broadway (wow… Hollywood writers can't come up with a line like that, can they?) And they weren't going to go hardway, either. What I love about GLOW is that it was a self-contained universe. You could almost imagine THE GREAT MOOLAH appearing on one show, but she wouldn't be MOOLAH, but Slave Girl Moolah, and she'd be campy, talented and awesome in her guest appearance.

Pro Wrestling Intellectual

These days, one problem with wrestling is that Vince has opened up to acknowledge pro wrestling's history, and he stopped filtering it through his own unique perspective. What that has done is stop the WWE from being it's own universe, where you know coming in that you must suspend your disbelief, that you must acknowledge that the promotion is it's own dimension of rules and illogic, and that nothing that happens in the ring really means much -- except that it is the product.

GLOW was able to do the skits, the "back stage" zaniness and the campy reflections on what others thought that professional wrestling was. And it didn't even pay James Hold for any of his great one-liners.

But it remained a self-contained comedy and an overall sense of atmosphere that rarely broke it's own sense of kayfabe. And that's refreshing. Argh, I can't do the requisite "original ECW" segue….I just can't! So let's skip it and go straight to the requisite continuance of complaints about Vince McMahon and the current state of the WWE: wrestling today absorbed the concept of worked reality, and we're paying the price for it.

Wrestling is no more real than House, MD.

Wrestling is supposed to be taken with a grain of salt, and a self-contained reality, and it's own set of rules. Since Vince doesn't comprehend rules, and since he destroyed his products sense of self-containment, the WWE has been adrift. In part because it's no longer about personalities, because HHH has no personality, and of course, he cannot allow talent to outshine him.

With a great TV show, you can get into the reality that it conveys.

You don't watch House for learning about how to be a doctor, you watch it to get into the head of a conniving, super-cynical and super-brilliant bastard who solves every medical mystery he sniffs.

You don't watch wrestling because you want to be a crazed athlete. You watch it for the ongoing drama of it all. You watch it because it rewards you for knowing the history of the characters. You watch it because you identify/appreciate/idolize or even adore one character over another. Oh, yeah. I'm talking about GLOW here.

What did you think I was talking about? Professional wrestling circa 2008?

GLOW may not be the greatest professional wrestling of all time, but it shows a side of the product that once made pro wrestling interesting, enjoyable and most of all entertaining. And sure, almost all of it was about the eye-candy. It sure wasn't about the acting, no matter how bad it got, or the comedy, no matter how bad it got, or the scripting, because that was bad as well. Ah… nostalgia. The place where you can enjoy and experience professional wrestling at it's finest

Joe Babinsack

SHIMMER: Women Athletes DVD Volume 18
SHIMMER: Women Athletes

If you're looking for the best professional wrestling promotion in existence today, you've got to look at SHIMMER.

I know I've said it before, but can you imagine what Lou Thesz would be thinking about the product today, when the only promotion with true Old School values, the best assemblage of a talent roster, and the most respectful and traditional attitude of any modern organization is one that only features women?

Aside from the bevy of beautiful women, what I love about SHIMMER is the slow pacing, the dynamics of the card, the meaningful matchmaking and the psychological basis of the matches themselves.

Gimmicks are at a minimum, and this is a promotion that didn't bother with a World Championship until they started a tournament on DVD #10, and began hinting about a Tag Team Championship with this installment -- #18.

For the first ten Volumes, I would have barely worried about the lack of a Title. The revolving of main eventers, the ongoing feuds and the dedicated buildups of matches, the slow rise up the card, and the slow fall down the card were all well crafted enough.

Add to the mix a solid roster, with veteran talent, enough up-and-coming players, as well as guests and names and an always interesting undercard.

Maybe it's Dave Prazak, or maybe it's Allison Danger, but the nature of the SHIMMER business, from the DVD model to the atmosphere to the genuine feel of the wins and losses, the stellar announcing (even when I don't like Allison behind the mike) and especially the crafting of the wrestling, it's all vastly superior to other promotions, and it's all in the attention to the details.

But SHIMMER is more than just the framework. It's about the talent. It's about allowing the talent to shine, to be creative and to connect with the fans.

Pro Wrestling Intellectual

Match descriptions don't do the promotion justice. How do you capture the multi-dimensional nature of this product? This isn't about nonsense. It isn't about stroking the egos of the owners [WWE], about recreating the format (with no basis in any known, profitable reality, [TNA]) or even about upping the ante of extremism, fast pacing or hard-hitting action (often without a foundation in the historically accurate aspects of the industry [ROH].)

Comparisons are due.

Sure, those mainstream lemmings can complain about a wood paneled auditorium, a chandelier hanging from the rafters or the lack of dazzling displays. Sure, if you're appreciation of wrestling is all about star-power, or pyrotechnics or larger than life bodies and egos, this isn't for you. Sure, we can complain and nitpick and criticize everything, but the bottom line for me, and hopefully for you, is that the love of the sport has to come out somewhere, or we should all just give up.

But enough pontificating. SHIMMER just has the feel of an Old School promotion. And right now, that feel seems to me to be the best potential for the industry. Simplification of storylines, slow builds of feuds, rotation of talent and making each match meaningful, dramatic and worth watching.

What more can we ask for?

How about an assemblage of vastly interesting characters, with enough gimmicks, but not a whole lot of craziness. Sure, Shark Girl is nuts, but Shark Girl is the only masked wrestler in 18 Volumes of excellent SHIMMER DVDs.

On the other hand, I still don't get why Amber O'Neal is jerking the curtain. I've not seen a fresher heel, someone who plays to the crowd, sells and displays all the right moves along the way. And what's better than a blonde in fishnets?

What I liked about Volume 18 is that the card works from top to bottom.

The opening matches feature varying degrees of talents, crafting matches with athleticism, with psychology and with comedy. Newcomers like Nicole Matthews, Jennifer Blake & Danyah, and the rapidly established Jetta are able to shine, to earn their spot. Veterans like Lee, Haze and Fyfe & Hosaka aren't just displaying their talents, they are making the promotion thrive with their ability to make their opponents look good, and to provide measuring sticks for judging that talent.

Sure, there are rough spots. But there are far too many smooth moves, interesting interplays and in the end, you know if one lady beats the other, then next Volume she'll move up a little, or get a better opponent to challenge her, or be positioned to build upon momentum.

One of the most important matches on the card, quite frankly, isn't the big Championship match, or the big Tag Team match that will help spur the chase for the Tag Team Championship, or the awesome semis, with displays of intensity by Kong and Busic, or the sheer talents on display from Stock and Melissa.

To me, one of the most important matches was Mercedes Martinez pitted against Cindy Rogers. Rogers triumphed in her series against Allison Danger, and put together good momentum, moving up the card. Martinez was missing from SHIMMER for some time, and returned to the promotion with this DVD.

From what I know about SHIMMER, this is a match that will play out a few Volumes down the road. The winner progresses to challenge for the Title. The loser? Well, they won't be dropped, but there are ramifications to losing, just as there are for winning.

Which means it is a match well worth watching, not just because of what they will do in the match – these two greatly talented women – but because of what they will do with the loss, or the win, or the nature of the battle.

Mercedes Martinez is one tough, talented lady who can outwrestle, outmuscle or outmove her competitors. Cindy Rogers, in whatever variant of Bret Hart's phrase, has proven to have the mettle to eke out victories.

So while I can laud the Title Change, and extol the virtues of the purity and simplicity and technical nature of MsChif against Sara Del Rey; while I can do the same and more for the altogether embarrassing (for TNA) match that features the beautiful Sarah Stock and the stunning Melissa Anderson, while they do a hard-hitting match that they'd never be able to perform on a stage of fools; while at the same time, I can watch the awesomely Amazing Kong display the instincts and craft that allows a newcomer like Wesna Busic

Pro Wrestling Intellectual

look like a young Ricky Steamboat, a just breaking through Tommy Dreamer, or one of many talents that relied upon veterans to put them over.

(Which, of course, is a skill and a situation not worth trifling with today, in the money promotions....)

But, to get back to the point, I love SHIMMER because I can drill down into the core of the card, and find a gem of a match, and realize that the booking isn't about one wrestler, the atmosphere isn't about playing to the likes of one owner, and the announce crew isn't pretending to be awful or funny or something that they are not.

Which, as far as I'm concerned, is the depth and detail that I can't find in very many other places.

SARA DEL REY

Women's wrestling has been overlooked a lot as of late.

The number of solid matches on the main stage has dwindled, and for the most part, the notion of a match involving women reaching the duration that is expected of their male counterparts is nigh impossible to conceive.

A few minutes of action, and a few revealing shots, and then it's back to the next skit. Not that there aren't women wrestlers of note. If left to their own talents, there are some main stream women wrestler's who can go. It's just that they never get the spotlight.

But on the indy scene, that's a different story. Especially with SHIMMER, which produces some of the best action available, as well as other groups like Chickfight. As the number of solid women wrestlers gets larger, that talent base has been put to use in matches, as well as in managerial and valet roles, notably by Ring of Honor, and in various more regional indy promotions across the country.

Of the ranks of women wrestlers on the indy circuits, one name seems to stand out above the rest, in terms of toughness, technical ability and solid wrestling. The ironic thing is that she's also one without a belt. That person is Sara Del Rey, otherwise known as the American Angel in Mexico, and once known as Nikki in All Pro Wrestling.

Daizee Haze is certainly higher profile, as are Allison Danger and Lacey, but it's Sara Del Rey who has the endorsement of Bryan Danielson, and also his theme song when entering the ring. Haze has held far more gold, and has likely wrestled more men, but it's Del Rey who squashed someone at a recent ROH event.

Lacey remains under-rated as a wrestler, and Danger has been more over-rated, but one thing that Sara Del Rey brings to the ring is a solid sense of power, technical ability and respect. Which makes her one of those rare talents that can put on great matches with a wide variety of other styles, and it's no wonder that she lists her favorite wrestlers as Chris Benoit and William Regal. Well, she lists Bryan Danielson as well, but go figure -- he had a hand in training her, as well as Donovan Morgan. She also lists the Pro Wrestling IRON dojo and the Inoki dojo as critical to her training.

Del Rey is the kind of wrestler who makes opponents look good.

Pro Wrestling Intellectual

She combines a solid base for the more high flying types to work with, and her submission and suplex style works well in Mexico and in Japan. Del Rey notes "any wristlock counter" as her favorite wrestling hold, once again reinforcing the notion that she has the basics down pat, and is well advanced in working the details and the crowd in a more technical manner.

Although she's strongly linked to the aforementioned Bryan Danielson, and his moniker of being the "best wrestler in the world," Sara Del Rey isn't the gimmick type. She is quoted as saying "I want to prove myself through hard work and quality wrestling" and in 2002, she considered her trying out for Arsion as a career highlight.

Speaking of Japan, she has a DVD that is being sold on her myspace site. It's called "Sara Del Rey in Japan DVD" and features several matches with the Japanese pro wrestling goddess Manami Toyota, one with Yumiko Hotta, as well as tag matches (with Mika Nishio) against Toyota & Mima Shimoda, and one with Nishio against Nattie Newhart & Yuka Nakamura. These are touted as some of the most "grueling" matches of her young career.

You can find an order form at:

http://www.myspace.com/saradelrey

And it's $20.00. Another item of interest is the "Death Rey" T-shirt, also $20.

Sara Del Rey is another of the current generation of indy level wrestlers who has traveled the country and the world to gain experience and develop the craft of professional wrestling.

She calls her favorite type of match one that is "old school and technical" in one of her internet profiles, and in watching quite a few of her matches, she certainly sells the style.

Her matches in SHIMMER, both tags and singles, have proved her to be a center piece for that promotion. She has seen impressive action in All Pro Wrestling, CHIKARA and ROH, and for Lucha Libre Femenil in Mexico (where she lost her mask as American Angel to Tsunami on December 16th of 2005,) although she once again competed under a mask as Nic Grimes for MTV's aborted Wrestling Society X promotion (obviously posing as a man to throw off the Mexican pro wrestling governing bodies ;-)

Like her favorites, she wields the German Suplex and the Tiger Suplex and others, but adds an impressive twist to the Tiger Suplex. First she maneuvers her opponent into a butterfly lock, and the will pick the opponent up in the air, contorting and forcing tremendous pressures. The move is called the "Royal Butterfly" and ends up with a suplex and typically a pin.

The only gold I can find listed for Sara Del Rey is the Impact Zone Wrestling's Women's title, which she won February 15th of 2005 from Adrenelyn.

Of note, she fought Mercedes Martinez to a 30 minute time limit draw For Shimmer, and defeated Daizee Haze on a ROH show in East Windsor CT on June 3rd of 2006. There is a brewing feud between Haze and Del Rey, however, working its way through SHIMMER and ROH and elsewhere.

With Allison Danger, they make up the team "Dangerous Angels" and have fought in FIP, ROH and SHIMMER. Del Rey has fought classic battles with Cheerleader Melissa, the aforementioned Manami Toyota and Mercedes Martinez, and spent most of the year 2005 in Japan, competing with All Japan Women and the A to Z promotion.
If you're looking to see Sara Del Rey live in action, here's her schedule, taken from the myspace room:
For DVDs, don't forget her own "Sara Del Rey in Japan DVD" which is available at www.myspace.com/saradelrey as well as her work in SHIMMER, ROH, FIP and All Pro Wrestling.

MsChif

Analogies can be a great way to paint a picture, but often, they are too superficial to be taken in their entirety. If I said MsChif was a combination of the Great Muta and WCW's scream queen Daphne, It would be a start.

Of course, the first of many questions is, why Muta?

On the surface, it's the use of the almost mystical green mist. One of the coolest aspects of MsChif's web site http://www.mschif.net/ is the Victims section with close ups of peopled "misted" by the goth wrestling queen.

Beyond that obvious connection is the sort of primeval stalking stance, looking around for prey, and a quickness, agility and flexibility that more than suggests danger. It's a sort of aggression and tenacity that Muta had before he slowed down a bit and became the Triple Crown winner Keiji Mutoh.

It's not just the mist, its the mystique, the exotic look and the tenacity.

As for Daphne, yeah, MsChif can scream with the best of them. And she's not a guy. And she has long black hair.

MsChif's been around since 2001, starting out in Gateway Championship Wrestling, having been trained by Johnny Greenpeace and Jack Adonis in the Midwest promotion that brought Matt Sydal, Daizee Haze and Delirious to Ring of Honor.

A feud between MsChif and Haze raged across the Midwest, involving promotions like NWA Missouri and IWA-Mid South, culminating in a give and take for the NWA Midwest Women's championship. With Delirious, the alliance was known as Diabolic Khaos, and they often feuded with the combination of Sydal and Haze.

More prominently, MsChif has appeared with TNA, and the Shimmer promotion.

Her vicious feud with Cheerleader Melissa highlights a run of Shimmer DVDs, and the brutality of their conflicts is beyond belief. From an upset victory in SHIMMER 1, through a Falls Count Anywhere and a Last Woman Standing match, I dare say that there isn't a blood feud on the national stage that approaches the carnage of these two combatants. If you think MNM/Hardys is rough, avert your eyes and don't buy DVDs with these matches!

Joe Babinsack

These two – MsChif and Cheerleader Melissa – go at it like Buzz Sawyer and Tommy Rich. Beating, clawing and drawing blood, but then again, I don' t remember any of those epic battles ending with one bashing the other's foot against the back of that other's head.

Ok, that was awkward. Let me try to make it more clear.

There was a match where MsChif was beaten into submission with her own foot hitting the back of her own head. That, you've got to see to believe and understand the flexibility that MsChif endures. As well, these two show what rivalry, hatred and throwing out the rulebook actually means in terms of building a heated rivalry.

Normally, I'm not one for "cutesy" names for holds, but I can't pass up naming MsChif's repertoire: The Desecrator (a DDT variant,) Code Green, Unhallowed Grace (a quebrada,) The Call from the Grave (a cutter variant) and The Gates of Hell II.

And then there's the Green Mist!!!

Raise your hand if you've played around with green Jello to emulate the Great Muta.

Ok, put your hands down.

Nothing caps off a unique look, a smashing costume and a physical presence like the mysterious use of the green yucky stuff. Although it's not appropriate to win matches, let alone championships with that matter, who's going to tell the demoness who enters the ring to Satyricon's "Repined Bastard Nation" to stop? And especially one who's not afraid to mix it up with the men…

MsChif's been around in some 20 promotions, including the always interesting ChickFight Tournaments, of which she one number four in San Francisco. She's held the tag titles, in the Coastal Wrestling Alliance, with Cindy Rogers. For seven months, she held the NWA Midwest Women's championship in 2005. In Gateway Championship Wrestling, she held the GCW Light Heavyweight Championship for an equal amount of time, in 2004.

MsChif was voted as best female wrestler in St. Louis, in the second, third, fourth and sixth years of the current millennium.

Most prestigiously, MsChif holds the NWA World Women's Championship, a title whose lineage can arguably be traced back to the decades long run of the Fabulous Moolah.

Visit her web site for a tremendous amount of merchandise, including DVDs, photos and other cool stuff. She also has her contact information on the site for bookings.

Pro Wrestling Intellectual

WSU: Dawn of a New Day
Women Superstars Uncensored
www.declarationofindependents.net

I had a discussion the past few days with a celebrity wannabe from the west coast, who decided to lecture me about the realities of professional wrestling. As if I needed schooling on that subject.

There are those who look at the sport we love and follow, and can't tell the difference between a suplex and a hammerlock, let alone the stylistic differences that exist in the country of Japan.

These people can't tell a strong style match from a hardcore one, or a gauntlet match from a scramble rules fiasco recently booked (in triplicate) by the WWE.

Ok, well, I can understand not comprehending those rules.

Point is, there's a depth and breadth to professional wrestling, and if all you can point out is stereotypes, storylines that fuel hatred and finalizing the talent of the individuals in the squared circle, then don't waste your time with me.

In the Womens' Professional Wrestling genre, there are some established indy promotions, notably SHIMMER and ChickFight.

I've reviewed quite a few SHIMMER DVDs (and more to come!) and I've had the pleasure of doing some bios on top stars (Sara Del Ray, Cheerleader Melissa and MsChif (with more to come!) and I've also seen my name on the back of the ChickFight Goldrush collection (yes, Dr Keith and company, I've got Big Vision DVDs to review in plenty!)

But recently, I'd been alerted to WSU -- Women Superstars Uncensored.

While the name is a mouthful, the action is vastly comparable to those other women's promotions. ChickFight is comprised of tournaments that do resemble wars. SHIMMER is an old-school booking atmosphere, with movement up and down the card.

WSU? Well, they're more of a modern day promotion, but without all the typical WWE related nonsense. They rely more upon familiar faces, but they have a strong roster, with ladies like Mercedes Martinez, Angel Orsini, Nikki Roxx, Alexa Thatcher as well as more of the East Coast crew.

In terms of WWE names, the then current champ was Tammy Sytch, and Dawn Marie appears on this DVD, plus we get to see Awesome Kong, Lacey Von Erich and of course, this site's favorite prognosticator, Missy Hyatt.

The matches range from top notch bouts that could headline SHIMMER or ChickFight, but also some more comedic interludes.

WSU promises a more family based product -- strange in conjunction with the name, but the wrestling is solid, better than your typical WWE crap, and the storylines are interesting enough.

Sure, there are some stereotyping, but nothing terribly insensitive.

Hate? Well, hate in wrestling is an interesting thing. When done right, and when it builds dynamics such that the crowd thinks two wrestlers are going out there to kill each other, then it pretty much works well.

When hate incites the crowd to violence, well, that's another story.

Dawn of a New Day features the best of what WSU has to offer. It has the connections to bring in top names, it has the foundation to draw in up-and-coming names, and it certainly has the ability to make excellent use of talent.

Watching Mercedes Martinez battle Mickie Knuckles is certainly watching a war. (By the way, best wishes to Mickie and a speedy recovery from her bad injury.) When I say that there's another promotion that shows wars, well, WSU can do the same.

Between this match and the Kong/Lee epic, if you're looking for hard hitting action, you've come to the right place.

If you're trying to keep track of names across promotions, the names stay the same, but sometimes the "alignment" changes. Cindy Rogers is a face in WSU, and Nikki Roxx is a heel. But they're both great talents, and they shine in a tag match.

There's a six-person tag as well, that combines some stereotypical roles. But anything with Annie Social in it is well worth the effort. Roxxi Cotton and Rick Cataldo do an interesting "mall rats" mixed tag, and establish the storyline.

There's something about Alere Little Feather that is crossing the line, but I'm sure it will all work out. But the heart of the tag is the Soul Sisters, who do a great job in the ring.

One feature of this DVD is Lacey Von Erich's debut in WSU. She's with Missy Hyatt, and I'm not quite sure why Missy didn't go out of her way to instruct her charge on the finer points of ring attire.

Not that I'm complaining too much, but looking for a wardrobe malfunction does distract from the match. Angel Orsini plays the perfect role in this match.

Lacey certainly has talent, looks and understanding of the business to go far.

Becky Bayless is the Ring of Honor interviewer, and heel persona in WSU. She of course gets into an angle with Dawn Marie during an interview session. A bit long with Bayless, but satisfying in the end.

But the absolute can't-miss match here is Awesome Kong and Amy Lee.

I know that far too many people dismiss women's wrestling as something to overlook, but show me a match this year with the inherent potential and deliverance of this battle.

I don't think there are that many (OK, Cena/Batista, but they just can't rev up this level of intensity.)

But here we have two powerhouses, one a leather jacked biker chick, and the other, the Amazing and Awesome Kong. It's well presented throughout the DVD, and it only takes a few glances to realize the dynamics.

These gals want to kill each other.

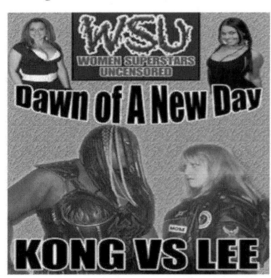

And, they very much show it in the ring. At one point, the action spills out off the apron, and the announcer talks of "two monster trucks going at each other" -- and I can't think of a better description.

These two ladies (hey, I don't want them mad at me) are just crushing each other with the punches and non-stop action.

The end looks a little familiar, but with the TNA Women's champ in the ring, there has to be an acceptance of inevitability.

It's a match I highly recommend, and should be at the top of anyone's list of best matches of the year. Seriously.

If you're into watching women's wrestling, don't overlook WSU. It has the talent, the looks and the booking that puts it in line with the other promotions out there.

Joe Babinsack

CHEERLEADER MELISSA

If I were to list the names of top indy wrestlers whom mainstream fans may not be aware of, but very well should if they call themselves hardcore, one of the first names on that list would be Cheerleader Melissa.

Having recently won ChickFight VII in Norfolk, England, only a few months after securing her first ChickFight tournament in its home base of San Francisco, Cheerleader Melissa has definitely proven her talent and capability around the world. Her training background includes teachers Christopher Daniels, Brian Danielson and Robert Thompson, as well as stints in California's All Pro Wrestling and three months of touring and training with Arsion in Japan.

ChickFight has been her home promotion, and she has been involved in all seven of the promotion's events, which typically features an eight woman tournament, with top flight talent from around the globe. Those DVD's are available through www.chickfight.tv, for a price ranging from $9.95 to $14.95. For fans of tournament style action, no promotion currently does a better job in booking, and the quality of the DVDs is exceptional.

The other major US women's promotion is Shimmer, and in those events over the past year, Cheerleader's feud with MsChif has been one of the ongoing highlights. With brutal action, a stiff style and as a backdrop for the
talent's of both women, it is clearly the greatest feud of the year, and a portrayal of professional wrestling that will not disappoint.

What Cheerleader Melissa brings to the ring is a sense of reality and believability that few other modern talents bother with. Its not just that she does the little things right, she does a lot of things right -- like entering the ring with an all-too-overlooked sense of seriousness, and avoiding the mind-numbing excesses of a high-spot happy, psychology diminished, let's get the crowd behind me mentality that just pervades today's top talent across the
board.

Despite her name, Melissa is not a cartoon character.

As a second generation wrestler – her father wrestled in the early 1980's – she seems to have picked up the inherent talents, and built upon a lifelong knowledge and a natural ability to work, not so much unlike a Bret Hart or a Terry Funk. Maybe name dropping

Pro Wrestling Intellectual

seems over the top, but the Cauliflower Alley Club awarded her the "Future Legend Award" and I'm not going to disagree with the Old School masters of the industry.

Armed with an array of holds and maneuvers picked up across the globe, Melissa has shown her ability to brawl, wrestle and innovate with the best of her peers. She has brawled with the aforementioned MsChif, has outwrestled Yoshiko Tamura and has outmuscled former WWE and ECW talent Jazz.

But at the top of her attributes is simply psychology, as it takes a brilliant wrestling mind, along with the physical talents, to be able to perform great matches with a wide variety of styles.

Of her most used moves, the most powerful is what she calls the "Kudo Driver" which is another name for Homicide's "Cop Killa" and is otherwise described as a reverse Gory Special Piledriver. It's a move that requires some set up, but is clearly a finisher of finishers. She's also known for her "Air Raid Crash" and an "Inverted Texas Cloverleaf" and has also pulled out the Frankensteiner from time to time.

But once again, its not the high spots that make her matches, but the stiff and realistic action, and that style has proven to be gold.

She has also won in Japan and in the UK, having captured the Transatlantic Women's Championship in Chickfight, the Future Legend Title in All Pro Wrestling, and two of the seven Chickfight Tournaments, as well as the Pure Wrestling Association's Elite Women's Championship.

In a brief email exchange, she made mention to note her personal website:
     www.cheerleadermelissa.com

and the ubiquitous myspace: www.myspace.com/cheerleadermelissa

She also notes that "everyone of my matches is available on clickerestle.com"

There's a particularly excellent article by Bill Kociaba regarding her award from the Cauliflower Alley Club which can be found at
     www.caulifloweralleyclub.org/Melissa

If you want to know more about her, that's a great piece, and I would be remiss to even try to distill information from it.

Whether ChickFight, Shimmer or even the rare appearance on WWE Heat, Cheerleader Melissa has proven herself to be one of the top talents in the business and someone that the average wrestling fan needs to see in action.

Pro Wrestling Intellectual

FAVORITE COLUMNS

Joe Babinsack

Fifth Year Festival: NYC
Ring of Honor
ROHwrestling.com

As the opening event in celebration of Ring of Honor's five years of promoting, the kick off of festivities in New York City are an apt one.

The talent roster is indicative of five years of success, and in ROH fashion, it highlights the appreciation and dedication of both the fans and the individuals who have built the foundation a great professional wrestling organization.

This show has a sampling of the talent that made ROH shine, from those, like Homicide, Samoa Joe, Xavier, Christopher Daniels and Allison Danger -- who had been there at the beginning, to the likes of Austin Aries, Roderick Strong, Jimmy Rave and Colt Cabana -- who kept the workrate high over the course of time. It also features the guys who built reputations on their blood and effort, like Nigel McGuinness and BJ Whitmer, Jimmy Jacobs and the Briscoes. But this show is no retrospective, the present stars in the making are already shining, like Takeshi Morishima and Sara Del Rey, as well as Matt Sydal and guests like Shingo. And the future is building as well, with Jack Evans shining brighter, with Brent Albright finding a home, and with guys like Pearce and Delirious, and the gals like Daizee Haze establishing themselves for greatness.

ROH's celebration is to last over six dates and six cities, from NYC to Dayton, from Chicago to Philadelphia, and all the way to Liverpool, England. But it's also the kick-off of the farewell tour for Samoa Joe, so it's an ironic mixture of appreciation and thank-you's concerning the past and the future.

The one unheralded but major part of the ROH promotion is also on display.

While I've never been one to attempt to link the fan response to the greatness of the action in the ring, I do understand the concept. Professional wrestling is all about eliciting emotion and, when done right, appreciation from the crowd. A pro wrestler who cannot make the fans believe in him or herself is not as talented as they need to be. A heel who cannot get the crowd against his actions is not being a heel. A face who cannot generate support is not being a crowd favorite.

To me, in an industry heavily influenced by arena sized crowds and TV saturated attention spans, the ability to truly interact with the paid attendance is rapidly dying on the vine.

Pro Wrestling Intellectual

Despite the criticisms about the work rate, the high spot mentality of some of its spectacular workers, and the influence of a Japanese style of matchmaking (where crowd reactions are hardly an intention of the workers,) in ROH, the strongest aspect of the product is the fans themselves.

With the Fifth Year Festival, there are some notable tweaks and changes to the DVD formatting -- both on the cover and with the on-screen graphics. The match listings outside are more detailed -- no guessing as to the combatants, while the on-screen "chapters" are more like titles than matchups.

Another coat of fresh paint comes with the ring color. It's now red, with "Ring of Honor" in a black circle in the center of the ring, and four ROH logs around that circle. Definitely a Japanese feel, and surprisingly more distinct than changing up the geometry of the ring.

But the fans are still the appeal.

It starts with the ring introductions, and the meaning of all those metal panels that adorn the now standard guard rails that separate fans from the action. No matter what the intro music is, the fans are banging along, bringing the talent to the ring. Next up is either streamers, in the Japanese style, or various forms of applause, chants or, when the timing is right, dueling chants for both participants.

As Samoa Joe states in a solid promo on the newswire feature, ROH is the trendsetter, not the trend follower. Much like ECW, this is a smart, hardcore fan base that not only knows new talent, appreciates effort and applauds work rate, but it constantly out-does itself in creating new chants, and vocalizing its feelings toward the in-ring product, the personalities and the finishes.

This show also has more of the match-to-match flow, also from its ECW origins. That sense of matches ending and segueing into the next one, without concern to ring introductions and emphasizing the conclusion of the previous match with ring music, and announced decision and the like.

Speaking of announcers, the ROH team is exactly what it should be. Knowledgeable about the holds and maneuvers, able to sell the subtleties of the ongoing match (to previous history, talent histories and other matches) and a seeming effort to avoid distracting from the matches or making the matches anything but a professional wrestling competition.

Fifth Year Festival: NYC opens with Pelle Primeau making a daring challenge for anyone in the back to come out. We hear Samoa Joe's music and the fans respond in kind. "Here comes the Champ" and all that. Primeau is, of course, a bit taken aback.

But it's not Joe coming out. It's Takeshi Morishima.

A nice twist to slap Joe in the face and get the fans riled up. But the fans greet the debuting Japanese star of the future like he was a star of the present. "Mor - i - shi - ma!" they chant. The actual match takes about thirty seconds -- enough for the nearly 300 lb monster to destroy Primeau with a "dangerous" style back drop driver.

Morishima definitely has that Terry Gordy look. He's a big boy, with boyish looks and long hair, and a softness to his physique that belies his athleticism. As will be displayed later in the show, he can do things few big guys would even begin to consider.

The nifty set up was Morishima grabbing the mic and calling out Samoa Joe in Japanese. This brings out Pro Wrestling NOAH fellow roster member Nigel McGuinness to calm Takeshi down and tell him its not the proper time to do so.

As the pair head to the back, Adam Pearce and Shane "man-servant" Hagadorn enter the ring.

Hagadorn berates the still destroyed Primeau, brandishing the "Top of the Class" trophy he maintains as the best ROH wrestling school student. Pearce begins to fend off "Repo Man" chants, as the fans call him out for looking like the fourth or fifth iteration (but ultimately the cult favorite image) of Barry Darsow.

Out comes Delirious, the singly most unique ROH wrestler, who proves wholeheartedly that being different can get you over far more than being just another face in the crowd.

Where are the masked men, by the way? In an industry where mystery and speculation never really fails to pique interest, and in an industry where false presumptions and winks-n'-nods are part of legitimate marketing, I can think of a dozen different directions a masked man could pop a crowd, even without being subtle.

Regardless, Delirious had been working a program with Pearce, where he's basically taking on both Pearce and his stooge, and losing out because of that.

In this installment, we get some nifty nods to Ric Flair, and a conclusion based on the use of brass knux versus a loaded mask. Find out the satisfying conclusion by watching the match!

Pro Wrestling Intellectual

In a Shimmer special attraction, the team sometimes known as the Dangerous Angels is set to take on Daizee Haze and newcomer Alexa Thatcher. Actually, Haze and Thatcher make their way out first.

Actually, to digress even further, check out the news wire feature for footage of Daizee Haze getting a huge goose egg in a match that involved her nemesis Lacey, Jimmy Jacobs and Brent Albright, against herself, Colt Cabana and BJ Whitmer. You can really tell how out of sorts she is, and then when they let her get out of the ring on her own feet -- there it is…

Anyway, Thatcher's name isn't her greatest asset, but Haze takes on the early part of the match, doing well against Danger in a cool set of pin attempt exchanges, then Del Rey.

Not that I want to continue my rants against Allison Danger, but what is the deal with that costume? Red white and blue in the front, Canadian Maple Leaf on her asset? Does ROH regularly do Canada and I don't know about it?

After some tag team typical exchanges, Haze tags out and Lacey tags the hell out of her, and they battle to the back.

Just when the announcers start even talking about taking on two people, Del Rey slaps on the Royal Butterfly and suplexes Thatcher into a pin.

That, my apologies, is a spoiler.

An FIP twist on the four way comes into play with the Four Way Fray.

ROH usually does the blah WWE single elimination with tag off stipulations which I can never figure out. (Where's the mentality in ever tagging out if you can lose the match on the apron?)

So they go back ECW style, with tornado (all men at once) rules and elimination stipulations (eliminations until one man remains.)

Davey Richards was injured, and could not compete this weekend, so ROH in a nice gesture, brings back their 2nd ROH champion, Xavier!

So we've got a dark and post-Lacey depression Jimmy Jacobs up against the former ROH champ, as well as Dragon's Gate's powerhouse, Shingo, and Jack Evans (also in the same Dragon's Gate faction with Shingo.)

Joe Babinsack

One thing I'll have to say. Jack Evans is laying the foundation of being the greatest high flyer of all time. His work in ROH is with some of the best wrestlers around, and with Dragon's Gate, he's ahead of the curve in terms of fast pace, high flying styles.

With Jacobs being debilitated by the knee and Xavier seemingly here for a look and a nod, it ends up being a showcase for Jack Evans.

His first spectacular dive is a space flying tiger drop, which misses his target.

After some power exchanges by Xavier and Shingo, and some double-teaming, Evans comes back to make too short of work for Xavier, but once again, does so in vastly interesting fashion.

This time it's not flying by innovation.

First it's a reverse rana, followed up by what I can only describe as a reverse roll-up for the 1-2-3.

Jacobs attempts to hit the Contra Code a few times, and Evans throws a hand-spring elbow in there somewhere, but Jacob's departure is easy to miss.

This lets the two Dragon's Gate alum in together.

It's a cool double-double cross, as the both shake hands and stab at the same time. But the expectations of this match are all set squarely on the shoulders of Jack Evans. If you love the high-flying style and are into the evolution of Evans from loaded with potential to superstar, this is more than just a highlight reel match, and that 640 degree splash is something to behold.

Table matches aren't always great and aren't always something to behold.

Brent Albright's introduction was a little off kilter, with him eyeballing tables, either trying to see if the grain was true, or making a bad impression of a billiards player without the pool cue.

But any match with BJ Whitmer and the slightest hint of violence is worth going out of your way for.

Albright may be discovering a home for himself in ROH. He certainly has the tools and what amounts to a good look in this promotion. On one hand, the tables gimmick is a great stepping stone to being taken seriously.

(On another, do we really need to escalate tables matches up to the point of stacking them by fours around the ring so the fake Undertaker and Tommy Dreamer can go at it like "Night of the Sky-Walkers" without the requisite ankle-breaking inherent in the big bump?)

This is, however, not an escalation but a great and violent match.

Thus the first half of the show ends. Four more main event level matches to come, with barely enough room to cover them all.

Homicide is the ROH Champ, playing on his home turf of NY, and he cuts a solid newswire promo for the match. Jimmy Rave was given a push to get to this place, with the good ol' heel hook as the submission du jour.

This was a solid effort on both sides, but Homicide as champ is only great when he's battling against the odds, and quite frankly, Jimmy Rave needs more than just a push, but a makeover to take him from mid card to upper card in the present of the other main event contestants.

Look, in this event, the dual tag team matches on the top of the card are worlds away better than this, and I think any fan would be hard pressed to expect Rave to come away with a high profile win against any of the other ten individuals on the second half.

The Briscoes are clearly being established as the Tag Team of the Future.

It's not just that they can fly, they can innovate and they can flat out wrestle, but despite the complaints about high spots, these guys can sell and these guys are proving that they have professional wrestling egos of the proper dimensions.

What's nice is that Daniels and Sydal are the champs in an atmosphere where they aren't expected to be the champs, and they play off of that situation nicely. Daniels is utterly ironic in his mannerisms and looks at the ego-inflated Matt Sydal (who touts the Open the Brave Gate title from Dragon's Gate.)

I've spoken of this match recently, notably the follow-up.

There are few places anymore where tag team matches aren't just meaningful, but where the art form is being practiced and taken to new heights. ROH is tag team wrestling and hopefully they'll highlight that notion on the PPV's -- because tag team wrestling is the bridge to the past and is the way to engage fans in ways that most mainstream shows just don't care to do anymore.

In that same vein, we've got Takeshi Morishima and Samoa Joe.

In an emotional promo at the opening newswire, Joe says "I'm Somoa Joe. I Love Professional Wrestling. I'm leaving all of that here at Ring of Honor."

With it being the swan song of Joe's ROH career, the first of the last matches is a great one.

Morishima is obviously the big man who can be the future of NOAH. For now, he's slated to be the present of ROH, and to do so, he must prove himself to Samoa Joe and win over the fans.

He seems to do that in spades.

A big guy who can go toe-to-toe with Samoa Joe and display gifts of athleticism few would even consider from a 300 pounder, is not going to have much of a problem wowing the ROH crowd, which appreciates effort, welcomes highly touted newcomers and is more interested in the match than the finish.

I can see where it's hard for fans to get behind the big guy, but I'll leave that for a bio…

Suffice to say, this isn't Joe/Kobashi, but it doesn't fall far from it, being above and beyond most of the big man matches seen on the big screens these days and well worth the $ and time to watch it.

All said, the Fifth Year Festival starts out with a bang with the NYC installment, and is befitting the top indy level promotion in the United States (which has already spread to the UK and will be on PPV in July.)

ROH is all about the matches, featuring the talent and allowing them to do their craft.

And it more often than not succeeds on all fronts.

Pro Wrestling Intellectual

Last Call: Raven and Sandman
Big Vision Entertainment
www.bvdvd.com

When I opened the mailbag and saw the "Cheers" inspired set, font and packaging on the "Last Call with Raven & Sandman" DVD, I knew it was going to be … interesting. Raven and Sandman both have a sort of weird reputation of being, at the same time, incredibly astute, witty and off-the-charts hilarious, while at other times, showing disinterest, disdain and playing dumb.

One can only wonder how Big Vision, and the unwitting accomplice named Dr. Keith Lipinksi, managed to cajole these two into doing the video in the first place.

For the first few minutes, it gets really uncomfortable. These guys are on the wrong side of the 'let's entertain the marks' coin, and it certainly feels like its 2am on the seedy side of town. Well, we all know that both Raven and Sandman have seen their fair shares of closing seedy bars.

Not that the set is exactly seedy. It's downright pristine, and I doubt if it reeks of stale smoke and spilt beer, like any reputable dive-bar should smell. Maybe the guys are just annoyed at having to work the whole concept. Maybe they're annoyed at how Dr. Keith could possibly pass for a bartender with his geeky, skinny, dorky look.

Man, did I just write that?

But to get back to the story, Big Vision sets the stage with two of professional wrestling's most endearing characters. In 2008, these two can still go, and they can still remember much of their past, despite making unearthly attempts at destroying their own brain cells with chemicals, chair-shots and dealing with Vince Russo's booking and Eric Bischoff's management style.

Again, for the first few minutes, it looks like the pair will just take the money and run, and corner the good Dr (Did Keith Lipinski graduate at the same school as Tom Pritchard?) into wondering how he can possibly make the whole thing happen.

But then Terry Funk shows up, and then we really go to school.

It's kind of a funny situation to be reviewing what, in essence, is a comedy piece with professional wrestling's greatest minds and most endearing characters. I mean, it's fun to recap a great match, tout the merits of great booking and thank the ownership of the current promotion I'm reviewing for not having hired some hardcore-hating nimwit to put the product together, but how does one acknowledge great comedy bits?

Should I just quote the Raven? Should I try to do the phonetics of Sandman, with his weird Utah via Philadelphia accents, and wrestling carny lingo?

Can I do justice to Terry Funk's drawl, or New Jack's flavorful language? (I mean how many times can I work in New Jack screaming "I'M SORRY" to Terry Funk? And should I do a word-for-word transcription of the famous Terry Funk Roast/Retirement speech (let's not even try to figure out what year, and what #, that was) where New Jack really went astray?

Nah. This DVD is all about the stories. The kind of stories that 150 years of professional wrestling experience – and the kind of experience that only the Raven and the Sandman can relate to, and the kind of overlap that Terry Funk can appreciate and New Jack can extol upon.

(If you're not down with that kind of stuff, don't bother. You won't get it.)

The DVD is, without a doubt, crazy fun. It just takes a few minutes to liven things up. That's why Terry Funk is there, and that's why New Jack steals the show at some point. I'm still not sure how the whole Mustafa/New Jack story really went down, but the two are back together, and we should be all grateful for that. New Jack is just out of the world funny.

He's the kind of guy that a promotion that really cared about entertaining would latch on to, and pay big bucks for. There's a fascinating dynamic there, one that I won't even try to explain. Just watch this DVD and watch New Jack tell a story, run with a joke and poke fun while holding a boar's head with a broken tusk. (Raven's the one making the goat-head smoke cigarettes.)

Does it get any weirder?

No, but it gets way funnier. Funk, Sandman and Raven have a dry sense of humor. New Jack is just wild and all over the place, uproariously hilarious, and once prodded, they all get going.

Pro Wrestling Intellectual

This is one of the latest of a series of pro wrestling DVD products by Big Vision, which seems to be doing lots of great things for the industry. There's a laundry list of promotions and themes working with Big Vision, with a wide range of interest for any professional wrestling fan:

Full Impact Pro, SHIMMER, GLOW, Chickfight, PWG (Pro Wrestling Guerrilla), Ultimate Insiders, Before They Were Stars, XPW, IWA, Deathmatches, Hardcore Wrestling, NWA, Lucha Libre, WSX, CHIKARA Pro, Documentaries. One thing I've been preaching for years is that professional wrestling isn't all the WWE: it's the talent, efforts and smaller promotions that keep the craft alive.

You may not consider a comedy bit by Raven and Sandman to be part of the industry, but it's the respect for history, the appeal to the fan in all of us, and the intent of Big Vision in putting this together that should be applauded. And, in looking at this piece, and seeing the professional values in production, and the various other DVDs available, maybe you'll be exposed to quite a few new worlds of professional wrestling that you weren't aware of.

Besides, Terry Funk, New Jack and Mustafa as the supporting cast of a terrifically funny DVD is what I call real entertainment, especially after they trash the place.

Joe Babinsack

The Best of Dragon Gate: Volume 1
Wrestling's Future Revealed
Big Vision Entertainment/ROH
www.bvdvd.com

Can you remember the time, and action, where you realized that professional wrestling was bigger, better and vastly more entertaining than you ever thought it could be?

Maybe someone loaned you the Tupelo Concession Stand Brawl way back when. Maybe you saw some of the big New Year's Eve shows from Japan. Maybe it was watching Manami Toyota and realizing that women can actually wrestle, and can actually wrestle a more technical style than the men. Maybe for you it was Lex Lugar showing up at WCW Nitro, or watching ECW live at the bingo hall, or on TNN (before it became Spike) or just a tape trade throw in when all you wanted was the best of Hogan.

For me, the first time I really got jazzed up about what wrestling was all about was when I flipped the channels one Saturday afternoon after 4 O'clock, in the early 1980's, and caught a sight I couldn't comprehend.

The ring was a bloody mess, with two behemoths that I eventually recognized through their crimson masks. One was Terry Gordy. The other… Killer Khan.

Now, having grown up with the WWWF, I knew all about heels and faces. I also knew enough about blood, having seen Larry Z crack Bruno over the head with a wooden chair.

But this? This was two heels absolutely killing each other on a normal show on the TV screen.

Wrestling has never been the same for me, and I mean that in the best way imaginable. Because that day told me that wrestling wasn't just what I knew it to be: it was larger than I imagined, more intense than I could have considered, and had more depth and creativity, more atmosphere, than I had known.

Watching the Best of Dragon Gate, I had that feeling again, just in watching the first four matches!

And I knew after the first disc that I had more than enough for a column, and would save the second disc for another time.

Pro Wrestling Intellectual

Way back when I watched Gordy (of Freebirds fame) and Khan (of breaking Andre's leg fame) battle it out mercilessly, it was still the era when Bob Backlund was champion, Bruno had retired, and before the mass marketing that both made a man a billionaire and decimated the industry as it was known.

To call Backlund vanilla was an understatement. His aura, physique and talent, all while not exactly unsupportable of a world champion, made comments in the 1990's about vanilla midgets seem completely unfair.

Today, I just watched Dragon Gate put a lie to the Creative Department of the WWE, and especially the pathetic apologies of Mick Foley with TNA's utmost lack of creativity. Hell, pay me for a forty hour work week, and I'll fill in two hours of show with, I dunno, 32 hours to spare?

And none of these so-called creative types are typing away and brainstorming (if I dare insult the term) for the love of the industry. But let me back away from bitterness, because Dragon Gate just enlightened me with the future of the sport.

Was it the entrances? BxB Hulk has a choreographed introduction, with hot chicks, a Luchadore stripper look and a light years ahead mentality that made me pause.

No, I wasn't admiring his physique, but merely gazed in stunned admiration of just how they took the whole concept of a ring introduction and made it more than anything anyone else has done.

Ok, maybe some other Japanese intros for MMA were similar, but who's stopping the WWE from recreating this stuff, except for the complete isolation and inbred idiocy that runs the place?

Then, later on the DVD, we see an awesome Old School intro for the Enter the Dream Gate Championship, with suited announcer, stolid intros, serious demeanors and the kind of boxing inspired mentality that WCW sort of did with Michael Buffer, but always stopped with the stentorian voice.

(Hey, what's wrong with Chris Cruise in that role?)

Afterwards, the Championship shines its glory with the complete selling of the match, the awarding of certificates and this incredibly interesting ceremony revolving around a locked gate in the belt itself, and the removal and replacing of a block (holding the name of the Champion.)

Stunning.

On the same DVD, two completely different frameworks that absolutely blow away anything seen on TV today....

And then there's Gamma, the chief heel of the Dragon Gate promotion.

Awesome in and of himself, the coolest part with Gamma is that they've put all this creativity and storyline into a guy that isn't exactly in the title hunt. Think about that with all the crap going on these days, with top-heavy owners/wrestlers and the insistence that everything else is secondary.

The Gamma/CIMA feud is clearly hot, over-the-top and worth watching in and of itself, but at this point it isn't about a title. It's culminating in a hair-vs-hair match.

But that's not all. It's clearly face/heel but face/heel at a level of intensity, details and atmosphere that belies the very concept when you compare it to American style blandness and Tweener dominated dynamics.

Gamma is an awesome heel, who's mannerisms, heelish acts and attitude all get rolled into a complete package. This isn't about playing to the crowd, it's about being a bad guy par excellence, about being disgusting and over the top, and about being a pure villain.

There's no cool, there's no winking at the camera, nor is there any doubt about the fact that you've got to boo this guy.

And, to top it off, he's surrounded by a gang of remorseless heels, and his own personal referee (with an amazing hairdo) that allows some creative nonchalant counts, blatant assistance and a really interesting three count.

It all sets up intervention by Dragon Gate authorities, but in the Japanese tradition, interference rarely results in a pin.

Gamma is featured in two great matches in the first half of the Best of DVD, the second being a Semifinal of the "King of the Gate" tournament championship.

(By the way, Dragon Gate ties in all the titles in this out of the box, creative and poetic fashion, taking even championship names to a higher level.)

His match with Ryo Saito is just worlds above anything I've seen in tournament matches. And you may note, it's a semifinal match. I won't give the match away, but it ties in Gamma's favorite heel gimmicks: protein powder, kendo stick, constant interference, heel referee and at the end, it's a satisfying finish.

Pro Wrestling Intellectual

Going back to the second match of the disc, we have an Eight man tag match, with BxB Hulk, Jushin Liger!, Jack Evans and Matt Sydal against the heel team of Naruki Doi, Magnitude Kishiwada, Masato Yoshino and Keven Steen.

If you haven't seen the speed and technicality, the talent and the futurism, the approach and the atmosphere of a Dragon Gate match, this is an introduction that will blow you away.

Again, from the introductions to the finish, and at every step in between, Dragon Gate is the FUTURE of this sport.

They leave no details unenhanced, and from the comparable size to the mixture of veteran and young talent, the roster just blows away anything in the US short of ROH.

If you're sitting around disgusted with what you see on PPV, take a chance here (at half the cost) and see what not only YOU are missing, but what the so-called creative types in the WWE and TNA can't even begin to comprehend.

Joe Babinsack

Brody: The Triumph and Tragedy of Wrestling's Rebel
By Larry Matysik and Barbara Goodish

IT is vastly ironic that the biography of one of pro wrestling's most intimidating individuals happens to be one of the most intimate of all wrestling books.

Pure Dynamite was brutal at its core, and Mick Foley's books are honest, but there's something inherently deeper to the story of Frank Goodish – Bruiser Brody to you and me and countless other hardcore types. Brody is certainly on par with the greatest of the books on professional wrestling.

Of course, there are few similar instances in the history of the industry, where a superstar on several continents, at the prime of his career, was senselessly murdered by a heartless, jealous piece of human garbage in Puerto Rico. That event immediately draws the reader in, and the layout of the book is excellent as it immediately addresses it.

The whole tapestry of Brody's life is built on reputation, interacting on various levels and sheer willpower, so there should be little doubt that Brody can greatly influence the reader by the expectations and his presence.

Well, not until after a powerful forward by this site's pre-eminent pro wrestling journalist, Dave Meltzer. It's always easy to praise Dave's work, and hard to avoid such praise, even if there are obvious conflicts of interest in writing for his site, but the reality is that Dave excels at detailing the
lives of fallen warriors. But when Dave is passionate about the subject, like he is for the man who helped open doors for him in Japan, then he has few peers in prose.

At first, that powerful outline and introduction to Frank Goodish's career as Brody (King Kong, Bruiser or whatever moniker you know him best by) seemed to be overbearing, but the book quickly rose to new heights.

Larry Matysik himself is a passionate friend and fan of the man, and has a unique perspective, having "bonded with Brody when he made his 1978 St. Louis debut."

And of course, the co-author is the late superstar's wife, Barbara Goodish. Words cannot describe the tragedy that beset Mrs. Goodish and her son, Geoff. Sympathy is readily with her, but her contributions are no mere words on paper. Between the facts and business perspective of Matysik and the shaping of the complex individual that Frank Goodish portrayed to the world (both industry and "reality" as well as those same distinctions in Japan,) there emerges a wealth of details and facets of this amazing individual's life and his impact onothers, his incredible ability to work, and his fascinating mindset that forged his reputation and legend.

While a review can get lost in platitudes, this book does not.

The story of Frank Goodish/Bruiser Brody shows a complexity of a man who grew into the sport of professional wrestling, and created his own incredibly unique style. The backstory is provided through tons of great quotes, from both the "inner circle" of Brody friends, and from the greater fraternity of professional wrestling superstars, including Terry Funk, Gary Hart, Stan Hansen, Buck Robley, JJ Dillon and a slew of others.

Nearly two decades after his death, and the intensity is still there.

The complexity of Brody is laid out in his ability to pick and choose his friends. His public persona was of his creation – rough, inapproachable and extremely dangerous. But those whom he "let in" saw a different man. The interesting thing is, he was such a gentle giant towards children that it is hard to imagine how he could turn that switch to become a madman, a bloodthirsty and overwhelming opponent in the ring.

Brody built his reputation and did a lot of little things to annoy promoters, to impact his fellow workers and to make himself a vastly talented professional wrestler of his own making. It's interesting to read quotes by Nick Bockwinkle, who readily compares Brody to Ray Stevens and places him at the upper echelon of all time workers, and yet admits he didn't really like working with the man.

Brody was unpredictable. A force of nature. A self-styled madman, and yet at the core, and ultimately what this book is all about, he was a gifted intellect, a businessman with few peers, and a man who was able to traverse the wrestling industry even as it was dramatically changing. Whether his style and impressions were his downfall is not addressed, nor should it be.

But those stories of interaction with kids, from the young fan who walked with him from the arena to the parking lot, to the relatives of business acquaintances to the friends and children of his family, these are all heartwarming and touching and really hits it home what was lost in that dastardly murder.

The overwhelming sense in the book is "What if?" Which to me is a little misguided. Sure, Brody had a potential run with Hogan, and may likely have reaped the whirlwind of money – something he always positioned himself for – in the crazy cable war of the 1990's. Sure, he was on the tail end of his prime (his body breaking down,) but in a sport where reputation and image often persisted a career of a talented worker well into his fifties, he was set for bigger and better things.

And even so, he was looking to that run after wrestling. His BAM – Brody Athletic Management concept – how well could that have been in an age where agents really exploded on the scene in the 1990's, and here's Frank Goodish, vastly intelligent, having learned manipulation in the most cut-throat business of all, and an imposing figure even as a rep for really imposing and large men in whatever sport you could name.

Frank Goodish was set for life.

The sad thing is, the whirlwind of a life he lived left little time for his wife and child. You can read how he cherished his time alone, how he deferred a honeymoon, how even a twenty minute ride to or from the airport was important for wife and son. You can gain the sentiment that "Brody" the wrestler was fading and destined for retirement, while Frank the loving husband and father was gearing up for enjoying time with his family.

All that gone. All that taken away.

I for one don't care about how many millions Bruiser Brody would have made and how he would have changed the face of the industry, and how he could have taught a generation of wrestlers how to work in a different way.

I defy anyone to read this book and not come away with the reality that the tragedy of Frank Goodish's death transcended the wrestling industry and impacted his family far beyond anything that should have befallen that family.

Goodish lived and worked in the industry when it was still consumed by non-stop travel, ongoing threat of injury and pushing oneself to the limits, and all that happened to the detriment of a family life.

And here's Barbara Goodish, her story told for probably the first time to a wide audience, and the
realities of her situation – not only losing her husband, but living in a nation she did not grow up in (she's from New Zealand) and on many instances realizing that she was all but destined to meet Frank Goodish, but only to see it end in tragedy???

That's a story that is hard to imagine, hard to consider being made up by any writer with an ounce of humanity or a shred of sentiment.

While there are books that greatly expose the industry and books that provide deeper insight into the daily grind of the business, I have yet to come across a professional wrestling book that can even touch "Brody" in terms of its portrayal of a man, the story of his life and the essence of his being.

I came out of this book with two thoughts, one of importance and one of a trivial nature: One, Frank Goodish was truly a great man in all respects, and Two, I really need to track down that one hour broadway against Ric Flair and see how great a wrestler Brody was.

Pro Wrestling Intellectual

Uncommon Passion Double DVD Set
OMEGA
www.highspots.com

IF you were a hardcore pro wrestling fan in 1997, maybe – just maybe—you heard of OMEGA -- The Organization of Modern Extreme Grappling Arts.

Maybe you were one of the fortunate locals who was able to watch the unique blend (at that time) of lucha inspired speed and creativity, compelling characters and gimmicks, and sense of an evolution of the art and craft of professional wrestling.

Maybe you were such an intense tape-trader that you found a way to get copies of the shows, which despite its independent level production values, the in-ring action, storylines and, well, passion, more than made it worthwhile.

Maybe, and more likely, you read about the exploits of OMEGA in the Wrestling Observer, or one of the other pretenders in the professional wrestling newsletter universe.

But if you want to try and convince anyone that you knew of the impact of that small promotion, and the depth of its talent base, and the heights to which its home-grown and associated stars would grow to, not even five years later, and the likes of whom are still headlining ten plus years later, well, I simply wouldn't take your word for it.

At the time, WCW was dominant, and WWE was starting to turn things around. ECW was firmly established (albeit already being ravaged by its own successes) and the Japanese scene was moving towards MMA mode, but still vastly interesting.

So despite Steve Corino's DVD claim that OMEGA would have deserved billing as one of the four most important promotions in the United States , and in hindsight, that certainly is a plausible claim; it remains hard to believe that many fans were aware of the operations.

Although within a few years, the industry certainly knew of OMEGA and the promise of its talent. But by that time, its core players were already appearing on much bigger stages, and the evolution of the craft that they heralded was already crashing down upon the suddenly huge but mostly ignorant masses of pro wrestling's fandom.

The Carolinas based promotion featured the Hardy brothers, was promoted in part by Thomas Simpson, and featured an emerging style of high-flying action and a talented, hungry and very young roster. Matt Hardy remains the "man who cannot be killed" and Jeff Hardy has cleaned up his act to the point where he is (finally, one might add) one of the true headliners of the WWE.

Joe Babinsack

What's funny about the Hardy's is that anyone who ask's "are they really brothers?" would likely get a response of "well, I think so, but knowing the industry, I'm not so sure." I mean, who'd have thunk that the Major Brothers really weren't of the same genetic descent? Or the Andersons, for that matter?

That Matt and Jeff had toiled the same back roads and small venues in the Carolinas for several years, sharing to some degree the same talent, and exhibiting the same undeniable passion for professional wrestling, well, that doesn't exclude two guys from saying that they are brothers.

But watching this DVD, and seeing the Will-O-the-Wisp storyline play out … after that, there are no questions to be raised about the Hardy Brothers. But before I run with the vastly fascinating story of the Hardyz, let's look at the roster of talent that emerged in OMEGA's well-worn ring.

Shane Helms, better known as Gregory, better gimmicked as the Hurricane, started out his career with OMEGA. He was part of the Serial Thrillaz, with Mike Maverick. The background on Helms is explored in the DVD, but since Mr. Helms was with the WWE at the time, his voice is only heard in previously recorded situations.

But Shane Helms was one cocky, talented, wrestling machine of a talent. It's hard to describe the almost stupid Thrillas mocking dance that he pulled off, and it's hard to imagine anyone else who could play it like that, but Helms was obnoxious and spectacular at the same time. And in much the same way that the Hurricane gimmick came off with him playing it.

Of course, Helms was first scooped up by WCW, in 3 Count with Evan Karagias and Shannon Moore. As much as the group was taken as a joke, the talent behind it was nothing to ignore.

Shannon Moore is the crazy little kid in the early days of OMEGA. Now, looking like a buffed up punk, it's hard to imagine how many years of top notch interactions he had with this talented roster, and harder still to comprehend that he is as much a veteran as half the WWE roster.

That Moore continues to pop up, and had been moved from WCW to WWE, to ECW and always seems to find himself a home, is a testament to the passion and talent and character of OMEGA. For some, that sense of persistence was simply an outgrowth of the camaraderie, and it was ingrained in their nature. Joey Mathews and Christian York were perennial tag team talents. Eventually, Matthews hit his big opportunity as part of MnM, with Johnny Nitro and Melina. Unfortunately, the perils and temptations of landing the big contract and the exposure to money and the like, seemed to have taken its toll on Matthews.

Pro Wrestling Intellectual

Likewise, with the strange story of Jason Ahrndt. The one time talent known as Joey Abs, Ahrndt was, according to the DVD, taken under the wings of Matt Hardy, and with a similar talent base and the fundamentals and intangibles of the OMEGA crew, but with a WWE style of size and look that would have skyrocketed him to the top.

Unfortunately, the passion exhibited by Ahrndt, as well as some personal judgments and a strange sense of loyalty seemed to have created a self-destruction of epic proportions.

As Joey Abs, linked to Shane McMahon and the Mean Street Posse, Abs had the world of the WWE as his potential. He was linked to Stephanie McMahon as an "ex-lover" and well, we can see where that linkage worked for someone of greater importance.

But the DVD explains some of the behind the scenes situations and choices that Jason Ahrndt was confronted with. With him on no-ones' radar screen since his stint with OVW, one can readily make an assessment of a poorly handled treatment of his potential.

And, as the DVD seems to state without stating, in relation to others, his passion just wasn't there. Christian York, Cham Pain, Otto Schwanz had wildly divergent experiences in the business, but the underlying passion was certainly there.

Christian York made his mark, with Joey Matthews as one of the potentially great tag teams, following in the footsteps of the Hardys, the Serial Thrillaz and others. But York, as the DVD details, gave himself a time frame to make it big, and when he turned twenty eight, he felt that he needed to move on with his life.

Still, the fires are still burning, and he's looking to make another shot.

Cham Pain remains a name of mystery and of potential, and after watching Uncommon Passion, one can see how great a gimmick it was. While the concept of a Las Vegas male stripper turned wrestler seems like a staple, how many have done it so well, with such an entourage, and such a detailed backstory to support it?

Sure, Rick Rude was the "sexiest man alive" and played the role. But in OMEGA, Cham Pain was clearly playing a role that presaged the current trend of reality driven characters, in which the character became more than just the in-ring character, and the gimmick transcended working into something that was much bigger.

Otto Schwanz, despite the provocative German phrase as a name, ends up being on talent that the DVD puts over huge. Schwanz became one of the Dupps, and in that gimmick made a bit of a mark in ECW, and further teased making the big stage in the WWE, but timing certainly didn't help him out. In terms of comedic ability, wrestling talent and all-around ability, he clearly was a step below the potential of Jason Ahrndt, but that's not exactly a put-down.

Joe Babinsack

(The backstory of Schwanz and Cham Pain is interesting in detailing some of what was happening at that time of the industry fallout over WCW being bough by McMahon.)

The most passionate of the bunch, aside from the immensely talented Hardys, was the promoter, Thomas Simpson. Having been involved in pro wrestling promotions before and after OMEGA, Simpson humbly basks in the knowledge that his efforts helped to fashion a stage for so many younger talents, and especially Matt and Jeff, to shine upon and to get their just due.

Many, as can be expected, had the same old attitude about size being more important than talent, about mainstream looks trumping passion, and that, simply, such an effort with undersized guys isn't going to be either profitable or worthwhile to begin with.

The efforts of the Hardy's, and of Mr. Simpson, proved otherwise, and the joy of knowing that his efforts, in part, helped many dreams come true, is a a joy that beams across his face.

While it seems obvious that profits were never a great concern, the facts show that while the Hardy's were headlining, and even beyond that, the crowd sizes were impressive.

The rule that OMEGA followed was to get enough advertising to cover the building costs, and then use the attendance to derive profitability. It's a strategy that should honored, although it's obvious from the DVD that the efforts of Matt Hardy truly paid off in doing the footwork to make it successful.

While not every OMEGA roster member "made it big" most of them had an unquestionable potential and a typically impressive desire. This was more a family than a company, and more a learning experience than a job. These guys ate together, trained together and forced a sort of evolution of the industry, from the bottom up, even at a time when ECW was considered the primary impetus for expanding the role of hardcore, Lucha Libre and Japanese influences in the United States.

But OMEGA's efforts didn't just break the mold and ignore the history of the sport. Watching the matches on the DVD, I was struck by the old-school nature of the first match, and how the crazy spots only highlighted the ending of the match.

In the tag match between Surge (Matt Hardy) and Venom (Ahrndt) against Otto Schwanz and Cham Pain, the match is a classic in its simplicity, its working the body and working holds, and its fundamental working of the crowd. As the end approaches, they kick it up into gear, and display awesome talent, in terms of dives, power moves and creativity.

Matt Hardy in many ways was the star of OMEGA.

While shameless, I have to quote that music blurb of eternal arch-enemy Edge, "You think you know me?" Well, I'm guessing most really don't know the depths of Mattitude, and the underlying passion of his wrestling aspirations, but moreso, the incredible mind he has for finishes, in-ring psychology and pure wrestling talent.

From sewing the costumes to laying out matches, from pounding the pavement to advising and steering the direction of the promotion, Matt Hardy did it all for OMEGA. Without him, the promotion ran on vapors, but even then the momentum and reputation garnered generated enough interest in the fans, and in the roster, that many followed Matt (and Jeff) into try-outs and potential.

Of course, not all of them followed his advice, or rose to the level either Matt or Jeff achieved. Ironic, isn't it, that Jeff has finally seemed to shatter the glass ceiling, and is now using Matt as a set-up to build to a huge championship match. But even more interesting is the first attempt by Jeff to escape the shadows of his older brother's acclaim.

As Will-O-The-Wisp, Jeff wore a crazy mask, and played an Australian demon character, with a shrill voice and effeminate mannerisms. He was the kind of heel that old school fans would despise, because of the stereotyping and heelishness, and modern fans would grow to love to hate, simply because of his incredible showmanship and talent.

The DVD has the match in which Will-O-The-Wisp puts up his mask against Surge's championship match. At the time, Surge was known to be Matt Hardy, but despite various clues and cues, the general audience wasn't aware that Will was Jeff.

The match is hardcore action, in all its glory, punishment and displays of violence. The finish is a bit strange, as Venom ruins the show, but the self-unmaksing by Jeff, and the emotional promo he cuts on his brother Matt, who lies in the Raven position at the corner of the ring, is priceless.

Other featured matches include the two tag team epics between the Hardy Brothers and the Serial Thrillaz. What's interesting is that the Hardy's turn heel between those two matches, and the transition for both teams is utterly seamless.

That, my friends, is true wrestling talent.

Another match shows the 'next generation' of OMEGA, with Helms and Moore up against York and Mathews, while one team was under contract with the WWE, and the other with WCW.

All told, this is one great DVD concerning one oft overlooked portion of modern professional wrestling history. While OMEGA may not have dominated sales, it influenced an entire generation of wrestlers, the big two promotions, and cemented the evolution of the business into a faster, more high spot driven style. Maybe some of that was for the worse, but they were doing it the right

Joe Babinsack

The Death of Walter "Killer" Kowalski

On Aug. 30 at 2:15, one of professional wrestling's greatest talents, arguably one of the industry's greatest heels, and strangely enough, one of it's nicest out-of-ring characters, passed away a few weeks after a massive heart attack.

The man's famous nickname was Killer. He was born Wladek Edward Spulnik.

But most of the world, and especially the world that cares about such trivialities and history of an often maligned form of sport and entertainment, knew him as 'Killer' Kowalski.

To his friends, he was simply known as Walter.

I had the blessing of speaking to one of Walter's all-time favorite opponents. I don't know that directly from the late, great champion, but I know the feeling was mutual because of the words spoken so earnestly by Bruno Sammartino, and the kindness in his voice, and the great awe and respect the Living Legend had for his favorite main event challenger.

"He was my favorite opponent, second to none," Bruno told me, after a long week of interviews where he praised Kowalski. I felt awkward enough on the subject, but Bruno was looking for a particular piece on Walter's life, and I was eager to provide some input.

Dave Meltzer, a long-time, well respected professional wrestling journalist, had interviewed Bruno for an hour and a half about 'Killer' Kowalski. Bruno was surprised to learn that "Kowalski" was as made up a name as his other moniker, as well as the 'Tarzan' name given to him by his early promoters.

I, in turn, found out indirectly that Bruno had kept in contact with Walter's wife, Theresa, for the 22 days since the massive heart attack that had done what no man could do — put the massive heel on his back, never to answer the bell again.

Walter 'Killer' Kowalski was a massive man in his prime, billed at six feet six, and easily 275 pounds. He was most famous for his unfortunate ring accident, that left "Yukon" Eric Holmback without an ear, as the knee drop from Walter crashed a bit off-course.

The result, after the 1952 incident, was one of the biggest money feuds of that decade.

Kowalski also headlined across the country, and the world. He was in main event matches in all the top United States wrestling cities — St. Louis, New York, Houston and others, and most notably in his native Canada — Toronto and Montreal and most undoubtedly, his home of Windsor, Ontario.

He was 81 years old when he died and his legacy in the sport is golden. From his star in 1948, and his rapid ascension to become a National Wrestling Alliance challenger, through his domination of Eastern Canadian promotions, often as American Wrestling Association champion, to his most famous matches with WWWF champion Bruno Sammartino, Kowalski toured the world and the largest organizations, leaving his mark as a headliner and a much feared villain.

He was trusted by the greats, admired for his skill, and favored because of his great look and greater abilities to draw crowds; and thus they found him as an often opponent — Bruno. Lou Thesz. Shohei Baba and others.

Walter trained new generations of stars starting in 1977, when he mostly retired from the business as an active wrestler, and began selling insurance, and also opened up a training school for professional grapplers in Massachusetts, moving from Salem to Boston and then settling in Malden.

The names he trained are legendary as well, none so great as John Paul Levesque, better known to WWE fans as "HHH" and also known as the husband of Vince McMahon's daughter, Stephanie.

He also trained John Studd (whom Walter teamed with as the Masked Executioners, a team of giants sporting blue costumes and masks that held the WWWF Tag Team Titles in the mid-1970's) to the Eliminators (Perry Saturn and John Kronus of original ECW fame) to future stars Ken Doane, Frankie Kazarian and Eddie Edwards, as well as former WWE talents Chris Nowinski and Matt "Prince Albert" Bloom.

There's also another semi-famous name, but her impolite commentary on Walter's training ability precludes her name from being mentioned in a column in his honor.

The style and pace of Kowalski's matches were his greatest legacy.

Bruno recalls him as a "terrific" athlete, with a style that was different. In many ways, it is reminiscent of today's top independent wrestlers. Frenetic. Unique. Strangely psychological — if I may use a wrestling term to describe a match's storytelling by the competitors.

With Walter, the most important thing was that every match was different.

"When you went to see Kowalski wrestling, it was never the same thing." Bruno adds. "He would pick a body part, and if it was the leg, he'd work the leg. He'd hook it. He'd jump up and down. He'd twist. He'd bump with it. But he'd just keep coming after it like a machine. Keep going after it. He was all action, and not predictable."

Walter's finisher, second only to the knee-drop that brought him infamy, was the stomach claw. It was a vicious looking move that allowed him to display his intensity, and to instill fear in opponents and audience alike. Here's a bad guy that towered over others, and made the fans, kids and adults alike, believe that he really and truly would rip the guts out of his prone opponent! He didn't just beat people, he tried to destroy them!

Walter was certainly different.

Stories abound about his outside the ring demeanor. In an industry where ripping off students and introducing newcomers to the sport with unimaginable violence and often a glee in doing so, Walter was reportedly the opposite. He would persuade those wanting to quit to stick with it. He would give breaks and bring people in — to the point where he was taken advantage of, not taking advantage of others.

Quite the opposite of what the audience would have expected from the man.

In an industry known for it's abuses of alcohol (and worse, in the modern era) here was a man who never drank. He also became a vegetarian during his prime, which coupled with his aggressive training, made him unmatched in stamina.

But he was unmatched in his capacity for teaching the art of professional wrestling, to the point where his students were rarely questioned about their skills, and his greatest student now sits as one of the most powerful men in the whole industry.

One can imagine the tenacity, the endurance and the passion of the man, especially considering that he persisted for three weeks after a massive heart attack that left little chance of survival.

Here's to you, Walter, one of pro wrestling's greatest athletes, talents and performers!

Killer Kowalski

Photo Courtesy of Steve Johnson

Pure Dynamite
"The Autobiography of Tom 'Dynamite Kid' Billington"
with Alison Coleman
SW Publishing

"I'll be honest: when I started out wrestling as The Dynamite Kid all those years ago, I had no idea things would end up the way they did. But I'd do it all again. And, in spite of everthing, I wouldn't change a thing. Which I know sounds strange coming from a guy whose wrestling career put him in a wheelchair, but it's true. Wrestling was my life, and I loved it. No regrets. I had a blast."

Thus ends one of the most authentic books by one of the most intense and able wrestlers of all time.

Why start at the end? Well, knowing that Billington – innovator, prankster, hard worker, abuser and overall, one of the greatest wrestlers who ever laced up the boots – paid a grievous price for all his years of professional wrestling heightens the reality of the book.

Billington excelled in an industry built for bigger men and smaller hearts. He thrived on a health defying lifestyle, over the top wrestling style, abuses of coworkers and his body, and ultimately, for his success in the ring in entertaining and raising the bar of expectations of fans across the globe.

That, after it all ended, and at a relatively young age of 40, he could still look back, spill his guts and still love the life he lived says it all. This is an industry where those who survive past 40 have often only just begun a lucrative career. Hulk Hogan and Ric Flair are ready examples of talent who achieved much more than Billington, but were able to prolong their careers, working a softer schedule, and get paid immense sums of money for being in the business and riding their reputations.

Ironically, one might argue that Billington came around a decade too early.

But then again, the list of prematurely deceased wrestling talent really started filling up after he had already hung up the boots. Many of those whom emulated The Dynamite Kid did so in avenues other than in ring talent, yet pushed themselves equally as hard on all fronts. With "better' steroids, harder drugs and a direct competition from peers, instead of blazing a trail of innovation and creating a fast-paced, hard knocking style, it is hard to imagine Billington surviving any longer than the likes of Art Barr, Eddie Gilbert or Brian Pillman.

Those wrestlers who were capable of following the Kid's in-ring work, like Chris Jericho and Chris Benoit, lived relatively tame lives outside the ring. Well, relatively in terms of the often incredulous extremes that Billington conveys in his book, where he can casually describe how one guy gave him steroid pills, another speed, and how he managed to excel at his craft despite his own self-induced impediments; surrounded it seems, by incompetence, infighting and indifference; and always struggling to fit in with his peers, even when he was making them money and setting the stage for greater respect for the business.

This book is written in a smooth flow of words. Somewhat strange because of all the English slang and vocabulary, but nonetheless excellent because it comes across as the Kid's own words, and because of all he's willing to spill, it becomes more and more intriguing as he unveils his history. From learning the craft in the Snake Pit to assisting in creating the ongoing aura of the Dungeon, Billington leaves no opinion unsaid. He slices up the myths of the inherent wrestling talent of the Hart family, and pulls no punches in describing the wrestling scene in England – where he did the bumping and running around so an overblown mainstream celebrity type could get all the glory while decrying the very children he was making money entertaining.

To say Thomas Billington was an angry, antisocial creature would be painting him into a corner. On one hand, this is not an eventual coming of age story – Billington is unapologetic about his often dangerous pranks, and never seems to connect that his in-ring persona – his very own creation, seems to mirror his out of ring lifestyle way too much, and isn't that lifestyle of his own choosing?

Where the depth of character is revealed is in his ability to convey his understanding of the errors he made in his personal life. But then again, he never seems to have forgiven Davey Boy Smith for business related choices, even though he very well understands them. He seems at a loss to reconcile his devastating family decisions. Yet there he is, writing a book and baring his soul.

Once again, the question arises, was Billington too far ahead of the curve, or lucky enough to have lived before the realities of professional wrestling were laid bare. The stories portrayed are honest, biting and brutal. But Pure Dynamite came out early, before the explosion of tell-all books and product-like missives meant to shape public perceptions and set forth the "authoritative" history.

The Dynamite Kid is thus able to dance around predetermined matches and expounding upon booking decisions. His timing allowed him to be himself, and not react to others. His story came before numerous attempts to sell, so looking back, his book seems so much more fresh, so much less reactive, so much more pure.

With all the anger and bitterness that is Thomas Billington, it remains difficult to imagine how he would present himself after the establishment that is the WWE has dominated the literary scene. Not that he would succumb to taming down the opinions or holding back for fear of never working for the WWE (moot and already decided) or hurting the feelings of his peers (a laughable notion, after reading this book.) But would Billington be consumed by giving receipts to mentions read in other books? Would he out-duel Mick Foley for broken body parts (self inflicted or inflicted upon others) or move beyond his typical disdain for less capable peers into a self-delusion of importance along the lines of Hogan?

Such speculation, though, is unfair.

Billington, after reading the book, comes across as the classic little bully. He's not only a master of professional wrestling, but also a master of manipulating situations, and putting bigger guys in their place. He seems to do it not only because he can, but because he finds it funny. And the hilarity of the scenes he stirred makes you regret how hard you laugh.

From stirring up David Shults against Hulk Hogan, to swamping Giant Haystacks in misery on an ill-fated tour of Japan, The Dynamite Kid lived up to his reputation as a prankster and a person not to fool around with. Maybe it is pure ego that he writes about how Hogan drunkenly confronts him one day and sheepishly apologizes for it the next, but Billington's reputation for getting back at people, and creatively manipulating others to do the dirty work, was well known by his WWF tenure.

And if the Kid turned someone on you just because he thought the scene would be funny, did you really want to inspire him to do something for revenge?

The classic story of the Rougeaus is recounted, as are the countless times when Davey Boy Smith brightly side-stepped participation in one of the Kid's schemes. But the other partner of the British Bulldog was a constant target and constant whipping boy of Billington's malicious and devilish streak of humor. So, if one must speculate about literary interactions, the heelish nature of The Dynamite Kid's personality – as an innovator, individualist and creative force, rather than a reactive member of the pack, would undoubtedly bring about some interesting and funny stories.

There are few in the world of professional wrestling who can lay claim to forging an innovative and entertaining style the likes of which Tom "Dynamite Kid" Billington unleashed on the world. Utilizing speed, high risk moves, an internal understanding of how to work a crowd, and relying upon solid workers, he was a daredevil with no peer, and his influence created a place in the industry for lighter guys willing to persevere, give their all and use their skills to outperform the bigger guys.

Paired with Tiger Mask (Satoru Sayama) in Japan, the junior heavyweight division was created and paved the way for acceptance in that wrestling culture, and emulation of his fast paced style brought about a huge underclass of followers across the globe.

Teaming with his cousin as the British Bulldogs, the WWF's tag team wrestling, as well as independents and the Japanese federations, was elevated to a new level.

Tom Billington raised the acceptance of his style and stature in the mainstream audience, allowing those who followed him to rise to places once unheard of. The list of talent that owes a debt of gratitude for the price he paid to change the industry is long and continues to grow.

Whether the industry turned their backs on him, or he to the industry, is equally ironic and shameful but utterly understandable. Whether he played the role of miserable bastard full of malicious pranks and disdain for lesser talented peers, or whether he simply acted out his aggressions in every facet of his life, he appears, through his writing and exploits, as a brutal personality, hard to fathom and harder to predict. Whether he would have been even slightly capable of slowing down enough to enjoy a longer career is impossible to comprehend. For him, it was "life in the fast lane" and nothing else.

Billington was undoubtedly more talented than most others in his profession, and his book shows his ability to innovate, manipulate and engage the reader in entertainment forms other than the dangerous sport and the dangerous lifestyles that he played hard and fast in.

The Dynamite Kid paid for his sins, and paid for paving that path to stardom. Rocked by debilitating injuries, often overlooked so he could pay the bills and feed his habits, Billington's devastated body finally collapsed on him. At the time of his writing he was already wheelchair bound. The rumors of how far his physical deterioration has progressed make his story even more poignant, even more tragic. And well worth the effort to track down.

Pro Wrestling Intellectual

Terry Funk: More Than Just Hardcore
Book Written by Terry Funk with Scott E. Williams
Sports Publishing LLC

*H*ow does one prepare to interview Terry Funk?

Do you anticipate the hardcore legend, who trail-blazed for WCW, FMW and ECW the use of blood, foreign objects, and pile-driving opponents on Tables?

Do you gear up for one of the true masters of the sport? A man who reigned as NWA World Heavyweight Champion in the early 1970's and has been involved in significant angles and promotions across the globe? A maverick and a vagabond, who, whenever he appears on the scene, turns up the heat?

Do you speculate on a man who retired so many times (he's either crazy in love with his family, or with the sport, or most likely both and cannot make up his mind?)

Do you inquire as to the peculiar quote from his father, Dory Funk, Sr, who told him "not everything in the world is a work."?

Or do you heed the description of his publicist at Sports Publishing LLC, promting the book **TERRY FUNK: MORE THAN JUST HARDCORE**, and anticipate a soft-spoken gentleman?

Terry Funk is far removed from the character he portrays at the wrestling arena.

"I'm proud to suspend belief," he says. His words are imbued with a live of the sport, a respect for the fans and a lifelong career where he struggled to find the proper balance between family and business.

Strange enough from a man who was born into the business, the son of one of Texas' greatest promoters and wrestlers, who rose to world champion status in short time. But that success and heritage came at a price: the death of his father at the early age of 54, and the rigors and demands of wearing that NWA title took its toll on his marriage and family.

Having regained his wife, his family and, undoubtedly, some piece of mind, the book is a positive one. And Funk, despite his flaming branding iron character, his ornery countenance and his grizzled veteran status through most of the past decade and a half, has nothing bad to say about anyone.

"Wrestling is not negative about anyone." He says about the tone of the book, which is acclaimed by friends and family, and his biggest critic – his wife Vicki.

Joe Babinsack

Tales of wrestlers past and present, hilarious stories, insights into the industry, its promotion, its art form and even its unsavory practices all come from the perspective of an ever-retiring master, always paying respect to the heritage, always finding something good to say about his peers, even if he's laughing about them, or pointing out their tragic flaws.

And for Terry Funk, his peers are the entirety of the industry.

He ran his father's territory in Amarillo and booked, with his brother Dory, Jr, in Japan. He's worked main events in the WWF against Hulk Hogan, and in the WCW version of the NWA, against Ric Flair – not to mention that run as NWA Champion in the middle of the 1970's. His impact on the Japanese rivalry between long time promoters Shohei Baba and Antonio Inoki was significant, and his efforts and legend helped create the hardcore style that still plays big today. The book has an index with nearly eight pages of wrestling names, from the biggest headliners to the old school roster from Amarillo.

Terry Funk hasn't forgotten his peers. He speaks openly about some form of union. But perhaps not in the traditional sense of a bargaining unit, but more of a player's association where the older wrestlers (stars or jobbers) are taken care of, so they don't end up like Wahoo McDaniels or the tragic situation of Ricky Romero.

Although he hasn't given the concept a deep amount of thought, he is outspoken on who should lead the charge (Vince McMahon.) Funk sees a need to "figure out a way to compensate injuries" and "compensate guys later in life." He speaks of both the headliners and the hard workers who put those headliners over, having "seen so many not watch their money, or have insurance, and have reached [his] stage of life."

At Funk's stage of life, there is no negativity on his mind; he's very satisfied with the life he's lead, and with the life he currently lives. His words of wisdom: "The key is to be satisfied when you don't conquer the world."

He relates in the book about his opportunity to take over the booking for the WWF in the early 1990's, but basically ran away from that offer. He has no interest in that job, its travel and the geography issues. Like the cowboy image he exuded over decades, he's far more comfortable far away from the crowded cities and on his ranch. But as for wrestling, some days he wants to do it, some days he does not.

"I love it very much. I loved the business. I loved living the matches."

So what's he doing now? Working. Killing gophers and hauling weeds, working on the ranch with his wife, Vicki.

"We bust our asses more now than ever."

Pro Wrestling Intellectual

The kids are gone, he says, wistfully, and now, the Double Cross ranch is for sale – he's hoping for a million and a half for the 4000 sq. ft. house, and the tens of acres surrounding it. For a man who retired, one way or another, several times over the past three decades, it is not readily conceivable that this might be the time for his last hurrahs.

"I'm old. I'm tired," he says.

So how should Terry Funk be remembered? He offers his own questions and answered.

"As a wrestling champion? Hell no!"

"As a guy who died in a wrestling ring? I hope not."

What he wants is to be remembered like he remembers so few of his fellows, those few who balanced family and business and excelled at the important part.

"I want to be remembered as a good man."

It's hard to imagine anyone reading TERRY FUNK: MORE THAN JUST HARDCORE and not coming away with the impression that, despite his admitted failures and his hardcore image, that he has worked harder at becoming that man than anything else in his life.

Surrounding Photos Courtesy Of Ed Russino www.wrestlingphotos.net

Joe Babinsack

Pile Driver: The Life of Charles "Midget" Fischer
Book Written by Kenneth R. Boness

There is a lot of talk recently about Dan Henderson being the only dual class champion in the sport of MMA. While true in the modern era, it certainly wasn't the first ever. In the professional wrestling world of the 1930', Charles Fischer held the light heavyweight and middleweight championships, and defended them and held them for quite a few years.

While the world of professional wrestling in the Depression Era was a strange industry, the vestiges of Mixed Martial Arts certainly were on display. Many of the matches, it seems, went to submission, and even included "tapping" of the mat to acknowledge the forfeiting of a fall. Submission holds were the rage, and pinfalls occurred usually after a big bodyslam (or series of such) or other high impact maneuvers.

One of which was Fischer's invention, the Pile Driver.

The industry also displayed the flash and the hype, the entertainment factors and the match fixing, the backstage politics and the triumph of ticket sellers over talent; all those 'niceties' that dominate the world of professional wrestling today.

Where Kenneth R. Boness excels is in presenting his large treasury of research. Blessed with a trove of newspaper clips from Fischer himself, as well as his own efforts, Pile Driver is more than just shaped by journalistic accounts. It is comprised, in a large part, of newspaper articles and promotional efforts of the time. This composition helps to authenticate the story, and while repetitious at times, it does present a perspective on the nature of the industry that simply cannot be conveyed (let alone believed) if simply rendered in prose.

Charles "Midget" Fischer was an anomaly in that strange world that grew from the carnival era and bridged the gap until the true transition period where national television airings irrevocably changed the landscape of the sport. Not only was Fischer's stature as a physical specimen "different" but also his approach to the promotional efforts of the time.

Standing 5'3", but with the poundage of a light heavyweight (he had an uncanny ability to move up and down classes, readily getting under the 160 lb level of the middleweight class, if necessary, but mostly wrestling at the 175 lb limit. Even when giving up twenty pounds or so, he grappled with the heavyweights, and more often that not, was able to best the majority of them.

Fischer was also known as a favorite sparring partner of Ed "Strangler" Lewis, since he had the speed and tenacity, as well as the innate power to hang with the legendary heavyweight.

In many ways, I would compare Fischer to Chris Benoit.

He simply mastered those at his own weight, despite being somewhat short, and was more than capable of moving up and mixing it up with the heavyweights, and no one 'in the know' would take him lightly.

But the other, more impressive, distinction of Charles Fischer was his steadfast insistence on being a fighting champion.

Perhaps he blurred the lines at times, and mostly towards the end of his career, but Fischer set out to win the championships he long held by merit. Syndicates in Chicago, New York and other places controlled the important belts of the era. It took years and countless battles for Fischer to get into the ring with Middleweight champion Johnny Meyers, who was controlled and protected by the Sandow ring in Chicago.

But the "Midget" never faltered, and never gave up.

He sought out the contenders and the claimants to the class championship, and defeated them all. Once he gained the rather "undisputed" title, he never stopped defending it, although his domination at the weight eventually made challengers few and far in between. It was shortly after gaining the middleweight belt that Fischer moved up to the light heavyweight class, and took home the gold in that division.

Over the years, the light heavyweight belt became a feature championship. Heavyweight level championships were well controlled by promoters across the country, each ring protecting and touting its own claimant. The commissions of the era, and the more 'honest' promoters had little chance to compete, let alone control the workings at the heavier class. This is noted especially in Fischer's inability to get a title match. That he could compete at that level is unquestionable. That he may have wrested away such a belt from one of many of the well protected, "paper tigers", only proves the corruption.

With Fischer's skills and determination, the light heavyweight level had its fighting champion. With Max Baumann as his manager (who himself was well connected in the industry) the pair barnstormed through the Midwest: Baumann setting up the matches, and Fischer knocking down the challengers.

But Baumann often clouded the issue. His ties, his showmanship and his at-ring antics became more than just a distraction. They impugned the honesty of Fischer's record, but never corrupted his standing in front of the fans, simply because of Fischer's tenacity, poise and talent. It was years before the Butternut native suffered a pinfall, and the number of outright losses was few.

One interesting aspect of the industry was the depth of the matchmaking process. While the bigger draws were mostly two out of three "falls" events, the opening acts often were of the thirty-minute, one fall variety. Also, the nature of curfews, the imposition of two and a half-hour time limits, and other regulations often meant the difference between winning and losing outright, as well as the controversy involved in draws, in referee's decisions, as well as other strange happenings.

That Baumann and Fischer eventually parted was of little surprise. There was always a cloud of showmanship with Baumann, but he at least continued to set up matches among championship claimants, always with the notion that Fischer would "take care of his end."

Fischer eventually ending up with promoter Al Haft, who controlled Ohio and mixed it up in Chicago and New York, once again the blurring of the lines between integrity and showmanship arises with Fischer. Before that, he became involved in syndicate warfare in New York.

Jack Pfefer found himself on the outs, his clubs and promotional strongholds taken away by a loose association of promoters who wanted to control the New York scene. They used the Heavyweight title as their vehicle.

Using Fischer's notoriety and ability to ward off all challengers, as well as an uncanny insight into the nature and actions of the syndicate, Pfefer re-took a lot of his holdings. By using the press to expose the fixing, the matchmaking and the corrupt determinations of champions, the syndicate was broken up, and its promoters went back to their natural squabbling.

Perhaps that bit of politics sent Fischer to another promoter.

Another fascinating aspect of Fischer's career is his devotion to his home town of Butternut, Wisconsin. Billed often as the "Butternut Midget" or the "Wisconsin Wildcat" he never forgot his roots. From a large, immigrant family, Charles Fischer was the youngest, and he made his hometown his calling card, not his ethnicity.

Pro Wrestling Intellectual

By investing his winnings into purchasing land, and building a home, he put Butternut on the map and created a welcoming hometown to return to once his career wound down. His exploits as a clerk for the school board, his opinions on rebuilding the school, and his participation with the community show a depth of his personality that didn't always come through.

While Boness never deeply delves into the personal side of Fischer (he tells me he had more insight, but word count intervened) the story and Fischer's life strongly suggests that the life of a professional wrestler was simply his life at the time. Which is far more fitting.

Training, traveling and competing left little time for anything else. He was married before his career wound down, but there seems only one "tour" where his wife accompanied him. She quickly disappears from his professional life, but the family life burgeons once Butternut's favorite son retires from the strange world of professional wrestling.

The deepest compliment of his hometown was the renaming of the high school teams.

Now, the Butternut "Midgets" truly are the embodiment of the pride their champion, Charles Fischer. With the gymnasium known as "The Ring" and their athletes are named to reflect the efforts, integrity and championship nature of a diminutive but powerful nickname.

Pile Driver is an excellent book, well researched and well presented. It provides a fascinating perspective on that transitional world of professional wrestling – the time at which the displays of talent were being replaced by displays of entertainment (which evolved into today's displays of another sort of talent.)

If you have any interest at all about the world of professional wrestling in the Depression era, and how some of the rings were run, and great insight into how a champion was made at that time, this is a book that must be in your library.

Ken Boness, being a Butternut resident himself, presents a great picture of one of the unsung champions of the sport. While the invention of the pile driver will have Fischer's imprint on the world of professional wrestling for all time, his attempts to live the life of a professional wrestler as one of dignity and honor is even more laudable.

It is always fun to try to come up with a word to describe the legacy of a man, but often hard to find it. I exchanged words with Mr. Boness on that very subject. "Fischer was, to be sure, a unique individual and it certainly is hard to sum him up with one word."

But Boness came up with a word of note. "Undaunted" was the original title of the book.

Having read the 720 or so pages of descriptions, press and results of his highly successful career, it's certainly a word that holds true.

Ken Boness invites comments on his book. He can be reached at original.piledriver@yahoo.com

Pro Wrestling Intellectual

Cage of Pain II
Full Impact Pro

Have I mentioned that FIP is one of my most favorite promotions?

We open the DVD with a three way. A three way dance in FIP seems a bit out of the ordinary, but it is 2008, and three ways are still a good concept when they feature some good wrestling.

Besides, this is an opener, and openers should be a little different.

I've seen Jake Crist (1/2 of Irish Airborne with his brother, Dave) and he's a solid talent. I've seen Seth Delay, and he is, quite frankly, a human crash test dummy and deserves a strong role as an undercard babyface. Scott Commodity is new to me, but he shows some size and ability to work with these FIP stalwarts, so it turns out to be a solid match.

One thing I love about FIP is the way angles get naturally played out and set up by the set itself. If you miss the good old days of guys interacting with the announcer (ok, there's another announcer in that role of emceeing the event, not Prazak/Leonard, but it's still cool.) There's a part of pro wrestling that is lost when the action is set at big rock'n'roll arenas and with a cookie cutter flow.

Nothing like that here!
We've even got some of the top women talent in the biz, as The Minnesota Home Wrecking Crew, with Lacey and Rain, taking on Bryan Danielson trained Sara Del Rey and the ultimate underdog, Daizee Haze.

Like most FIP matches, this is an ongoing storyline. Not intricate, not overly booked, but featuring a sense of pacing that makes each installment worth watching. Yes, if you think I get nostalgic watching FIP, you're absolutely right. And its about nostalgia, not checking out the chicks, although the patter between Prazak and Leonard is priceless during this match.

The Heart Punch is such a cool finisher.

Next up is Jay "1/2 of the best men's tag team" Briscoe up against veteran CHIKARA talent Gran Akuma. It's a hard hitting match between two guys with great reputations, and a nice change of pace. Cool how the good old match between two guys who like to punish each other doesn't have to end stupidly.

Joe Babinsack

Erick Stevens has been getting an interesting push in ROH over the past six months. There's some arguments against him, and that is always the case with established names and newcomers challenging for a spot. Unfortunately, too many of my peers in fandom are too quick to criticize something different and play too nice with the status quo.

Until this match, I saw Stevens as a big guy type who didn't really really show a lot of fire. Well, this match turned my impression of Erick Stevens around, and I'm sure it will for you as well.

Necro Butcher, of course, is someone you don't see fitting in with FIP, but strangely enough, he's different and brings to play an ability to work through the crowd and make a "Falls Count Anywhere" match true to its intention.

The good thing is, we don't see the over the top craziness of Mr. Butcher. We do see that he has an impressive ring (or is that, out of ring) psychology. And between Stevens and Necro, they put on a really, really interesting match.

What's really cool is how the match plays off of the reputations. Call Necro Butcher anything you want, but the bottom line is that he's a tough wrestler who puts his body on the line in his style of the craft. Pitted against Stevens, you sort of expect a bloodbath and a garbage/weapons match.

But it isn't.

It's more, dare I say, reminiscent of Bruno Sammartino plowing through an opponent worthy of the challenge to the title holder. Here, Stevens isn't quite as over to the masses, but his relentlessness, power and overall ability shines and he comes out of the match a lot better than he came into it.

I know belts are pathetic props these days, but when FIP puts on a display like this, it makes you cheer. It makes you want more. And isn't that what it's all supposed to be about?

Dragon Gate makes its appearance in FIP, and well, that's always a good thing. Actually, usually a great thing… On one side we've got Jack Evans, BxB Hulk and Yamato. On the other, three masked maniacs, by the names of Delirious, Hallowicked and Jigsaw.

It starts out with some comedy, some dancing and other shenanigans, but turns into a quite refreshing change of pace match, even if it did go almost twenty minutes. But, as anyone who watches the Lucha inspired antics of CHIKARA or Dragon's Gate knows, these matches can never drag.

Roderick Strong defends his FIP World Heavyweight Title against the infamous Larry Sweeney. If you've not seen Sweeney, or heard him speak, you're missing out on an awesome talent. Roderick Strong is better known for being part of Generation Next and the No Remorse Corps (or corpse, at this point) but he's another talent you should appreciate.

Sweeney does the Larry Z stall trick like few others – as in, he has enough heat and enough understanding to pull it off. But between the two, it's another solid match. There's a great theme running through this (and most FIP DVDs) and that's the use of different styles and different feels for the matches.

Watching the same cookie cutter match type is not a problem here.

And then we come to what is just a brilliant display of pro wrestling sensibilities. The Cage of Pain is a throwback to the War Games. Sure, there's no JJ Dillon flipping a coin, but the enclosed fencing and the four men to a team and the carnage is just all there.

FIP rarely does the blood and the nonsense, but when they do, it's still in that understated and "FIP atmosphere"

In this match, with light tubes galore and all sorts of "plunder" there's a fine line to be held, and these guys do it well. Of course, any match with a Tiki torch used as a weapon is breaking new ground, and it should be appreciated.

But the best of the match is the build up. It's been a year since the first Cage of Pain, and that was between the Heartbreak Express and the Black Market. Those two teams feuded to a culmination, their own sort of "Last Battle of Georgia" and it played out well. HBX turned face afterwards, and they've teamed up with the Black Market to take on the annoying young upstart heels, the YRR.

What's fun is that the YRR are obviously out of their element, and it never gets played much differently. The veterans are bigger, meaner and more capable of inflicting violence. The heels are set up for the massacre of sorts. It all plays out nicely.

Until the lights go out.

At that point, it's a moment that we all yearn for more often in the sport, and despite the best efforts of Hollywood writer types and the supposed history and brilliance of many who call themselves Creative, it rarely reaches such a crescendo.

I'll not ruin the moment, but bask in the brilliance of it all, and trace it back and see just how well it all plays out, makes sense, and makes you want to come back for more

Joe Babinsack

Photos Courtesy of Full Impact Pro

Pro Wrestling Intellectual

Is Konnan a Professional Wrestling Intellectual?

MISCELLANEOUS

Do you subscribe to the Wrestling Observer?

dave@wrestlingobserver.com or you can order by faxing that information to 408-244-3402. You can also subscribe via paypal at www.paypal.com and using the dave@wrestlingobserver.com address or subscribe via check, cash or money order, as well as credit card, by mail, by sending to Wrestling Observer Newsletter, P.O. Box 1228, Campbell, CA 95009-1228.

http://www.f4wonline.com/ Do you keep up with the best wrestling site online?

Joe Babinsack

Tuff Stuff/Professional Wrestling Field Guide
Krause Publishing

In my vigilant quest to review every book out there on our favorite subject of professional wrestling, I stumbled upon this little gem of a book by Krause Publishing. KP is more well known for books and magazines on collectibles, from comic books and collectible card games to antiques and weapons. (Which, by the way, if your employer has filters, makes it darn hard to view their website.)

While "Field Guide" isn't exactly appropriate for this book, the notation of "Legend and Lore" at the bottom of this small package of a book is far more representative. Covering over 450 different wrestlers from various eras, in a book a little over 500 pages long, the Tuff Stuff Profressional Wrestling guide is an interesting look at nostalgia.

Tuff Stuff is the Krause Publishing department concerned with Sports. The book itself is a compilation from KP's The Encyclopedia of Professional Wrestling, which suggests (in the back page ad) that it covers 500 wrestlers in more detail. (Note to self, why haven't I reviewed that book yet…) Both the Field Guide and the Encyclopedia were penned by Kristian Pope and Ray Whebbe, Jr.

Since the book is in no way "official" but a compilation of photos and facts about the wrestlers, there are a variety of types of photographs, from still shots and takes that obviously were given with permission, as well as action shots taken by ringside photographers and some interesting "street clothes" pictures of some of the bigger stars.

Credit for photo contributions are Dr. Mike Lano and The Wrestling Revue Archives (www.wrestlingrevue.com).

One of the craziest to behold is a black and white shot of Farmer Burns hanging from a noose – showing his incredible neck strength.

I'm sure it would be a fun exercise to simply skim through and figure out who they missed, but it's not easy. The people I found overlooked were Charles "Midget" Fischer (for more on him, see Rick Boness' excellent book "Piledriver") and Sky Low Low – heck what's up with dissing the little guys?

But the Japanese, the Mexicans, the Puerto Ricans are in there. So are the women. There are old school wrestlers and hard core wrestlers. Lots of pre-WWE photos (a cool look at Dave Batista as Leviathan) and lots of what-they-looked like and what-they-look-like now sorta shots. (There is a bit of an inconsistency, but that's understandable when you consider the efforts taken to get 500 or so photographs spanning many decades!)

Several names were honored with multiple shots. These are the ones that often contain images from various eras. Terry Funk as NWA Champion in the 1970's and as Hard Core

Pro Wrestling Intellectual

Legend in the 1990's are an interesting juxtaposition. Dory Funk in the 1960's and in his sixties (perhaps) really isn't all that much different...

I'm really not kidding about that!

While nostalgia is a great selling point, the book is full of interesting facts.

It notes, for example, in the entry for Mike Mazurki, that he was a character actor and got roles in various TV shows, including Charlie's Angels and Bonanza, and got other wrestlers some shots as well. He also co-founded the Cauliflower Alley club, and for that should be greatly honored.

If you want a couple more fun things to do, look for the various championship belts and the people in the background.

If you can name them by sight, you're hard-core! If you can name the jobber or the person getting beat upon by the hair or physique, you're hard-core!

Speaking of jobbers, where the heck is Jake "the Milkman" Milliman? Where's Frankie Williams? Where's Georgia's own Mike Jackson? How about my favorite jobber level heel, Johnny Rodz?

Dammit, it's those guys that make the stars.

I'm really not kidding about that, either!!

While there are some oversights and some omissions, where else are you going to see Vince Sr's face, or Jerry Jarrett as a wrestler? How about Paul Boesch, Sam Muchnick or Sam Menaker? Now all you hard-cores can start putting names to faces, and faces to names. The whole McMahon family is in there, as if you didn't know what they looked like at this point in wrestling's history....

What I love is the nostalgia and the connections you get from seeing the stars of the past decades. You can simply flip through the book and pick up some face from WCCW or ICCW or one of Jerry Lawler's rogue's gallery of forgotten challengers (or the ones that later became famous despite of him.) For nostalgia alone, this is greatly recommended.

On the other hand, it could have had a lot more consistency. Interspersing real names and former aliases, but not always giving the real names or missing a few aliases along the way, sometimes gets a little annoying.

But overall it's a great book to buy for a lapsed fan or just to look at some cool pictures. I hope to track down the Encyclopedia from where it all comes from at some point. But this is a good start.

Joe Babinsack

BodySlam!(Want to be a Professional Wrestler?)
UPW/The Learning Channel

I had already watched the DVD yesterday, and was in the midst of researching the main players, when I learned that BodySlam!
Played on TLC recently. Which should come as no surprise, since it was a rather strong documentary touted by UPW as a feature on that cable station.

I also learned that featured female wrestler Drzan McBee passed away on March 20, 2003, due to complications following a surgery. A tragic loss of an individual who by most accounts had a lot going for her to get into wrestling, but also had a lot of reasons – primarily family and faith -- to not get involved in the industry. RIP.

Details of her story were not readily found, but without speculating, it can only add to the depth of this documentary: the lives of pro wrestlers are often short, harsh and with unpleasant endings.

The perspective of the BodySlam! DVD was interesting and one that any wannabe wrestler needs.

UPW has been around since 1998, is owned by Rick Bassman, and has enjoyed a solid connection to the WWE in terms of being a training affiliate, having quite a number of contracts offered to its talent, and is well situated in Los Angeles as a gathering point for physically impressive, well experienced and a slew of wrestling hopefuls of various talents and expectations.

As a documentary, it maintains an unrehearsed, sloppily put together, yet ultimately insightful and vastly interesting look. This isn't a program geared to explaining all the nuts and bolts of professional wrestling, nor the inner workings of the training and the depth of intensity in workouts and learning the craft. Actually, it comes across as intermingling of profiles, snippets of stories and glimpses of the hardships associated with the industry and its lifestyle.

Because it doesn't preach, and lets the reality of the inner workings come through, it is a strongly recommended DVD. With my mostly "old-school" appreciations of wrestling, I did cringe a lot at the use of terminology – especially when we're introduced to 'writers'

Pro Wrestling Intellectual

'choreographers' and a scene with Juventud Guerrera and Mikey Henderson going over their finish – which was called a 'rehearsal.' Even though they spend the next few minutes with everyone emphatically explaining that wrestling isn't fake, the lack of explanation of that scene resonates.

Of course, it's hard to believe that a match can be laid out perfectly in a dressing room, but the impression is hard to deny. The featured players, with various levels of experience, are the strong point of the DVD. We have Jon Heidenreich, Christopher Daniels, Mikey Henderson and the late Drzan McBee.

Heidenreich's story has been well detailed in the pages of the Observer, and this DVD offers some telling glimpses into his background as a pro football player (with the Saints and with the CFL) and questions of his control of his emotions; as well as a segment where he questions his choice of getting into the sport where he calls pro wrestling a "nightmare on your body." At the time, he had a day where he had a minor car accident in the morning, and broke his hand on the ring apron.

Of course, when Bruce Pritchard appeared to scout talent, it didn't take too long for him to inquire as to Heidenreich, despite the compliments, introductions and praise of more talented and experience wrestlers like Daniels or Henderson. Big Jon billed himself at six feet seven and 300 lbs, and despite his almost robotic promo delivery, he simply had the size and look (carving off 30 pounds of "offensive lineman" body to be chiseled and pro wrestling suitable.)

The comparisons between NFL and pro wrestling are informative. Heidenreich explains how football is very simple in its movements, but wrestling involves 150 different directions. The wearing of an XFL shirt is really funny at this point, all things considered.

Nathan Jones was Heidenreich's training partner at the time, and it isn't funny at all to see how these two immense bodies were better off battering each other and flubbing up moves instead of destroying the smaller guys. At one point Big Jon is practicing leg drops, and questions whether he might hurt Jones. Tom Howard, their trainer, says "look at how big his head is" but it's merely moments later that an errant foot digs a cut in the bridge of Nathan Jones' nose and they're looking for a 'tissue' for the small amount of blood.

Upon viewing, Mikey Henderson's story was the most touching. Here's a kid (20 years old) who wanted to be in the sport since he was 3 years old. He's well aware of his problem – praying to God for some height, and knowing that despite his talent and experience, he's a long shot for the big show because he's only 5'8"

Henderson brings the cameras as he picks up his young son, and wonders if they could tag team in fifteen years. But he complains of not having enough time to be with him, and one wonders how worse it would be if he worked the WWE full time.

(This observation becomes even more poignant with Drzan McBee.)

Mikey gets a lot of wrestling time with Rob Van Dam on the DVD, who was coming back after breaking his ankle in the waning days of ECW. I found their wrestling very slow-motion, which is surprising considering Van Dam and the reputation of Henderson. It's cool to see some cameos by Samoa Joe and a nice angle that turned Henderson on Rick Bassman, and got Christopher Daniels out of the scene when he signed with WCW.

Daniels is portrayed as the most experienced of the bunch, and is touted as the number one unsigned talent in the nation at the time. It could be arguable, but Daniels had already established himself on the indy level, and had nowhere to go but up. Unfortunately, he almost saddled himself with the 'evil priest' gimmick, which he explains, but seems oblivious to how that sort of controversy would play in the mainstream.

Daniels, still with hair on his head, performs through a devastating looking accident in the ring on a Monday Nitro show. He lands after springboarding off the top rope, almost directly on top of his head. He shows Rick Bassman the tape and explains how he didn't have much use of his arm. Surprisingly, WCW signed him immediately after the match. Ironically, look where that got him….

Drzan McBee's story seems so destined to failure, and tragically went in a worse direction. Her husband came across as way too naïve to the sport, and when they bring their child to watch the training, it's hard to comprehend.

A quaint bit with their pastor is shown in the bonus features, where he speculates that Jesus – while perhaps not approving of the violence -- would be in the crowd to attend to the people. That was an interesting twist on things. McBee was shown as wanting to stay true to her faith and her personal morals, but that is beyond impossible in this industry. By the end of her main segment, she turns heel and the point is that she'll have to explain that to her daughter – that there is the character and the real mom.

At the bonus chapters, there are promos cut by the featured players, as well as John Cena. You can see the potential in him shining through in his words, though physically, he didn't quite come across as different, but watching Heidenreich and Nathan Jones for a half hour does that to you.

The lives of those featured are impacted immensely by the commitment necessary to earn a living in the business. And this presentation, even if it comes across as 'between the lines' in many situations, is a loud message to anyone who wants to be a wrestler.

Nathan Jones has a fascinating accent/tone of voice, and the sheer mass that makes me understand why McMahon had him as a special project. But he couldn't seem to remember his words.

Heidenreich moves to LA from New Orleans, leaving his parents, his girlfriend (for good, it seems) and a nice lifestyle, to a life of working out, training, and working as a bouncer to make ends meet.

Henderson travels 90 miles to train, and seemingly never has a shot, but he still works at it.

Daniels finally got a break, and nearly blew it from an accident. A truly telling exchange is when he talks to Henderson, and Mikey sees it as a positive – that at 20 years old, he has another ten years to make it, just like Daniels. Daniels gives him a look that betrays his joy of getting that WCW contract and likely the path it took to get that far.

And McBee, well, she had the guts to train harder, to commit herself to getting to the big stage. While she had the look and the unique physicality to make an impression; faith and family seemed destined to keep her from a mainstream where posing in Playboy is the pinnacle of success.

It would be hard to call this DVD "must see" but hard to put it more than a notch below that level. If you have interest in seeing some of the inner workings of a show, of the training process and especially of the lifestyle one must commit to in becoming a professional wrestler, this is one of the best programs available.

Joe Babinsack

Out of Texas
Book Written by James Hold

In my dedicated quest to review every book about wrestling ever printed, I came across a rare piece of professional wrestling fictional literature, and secured a review copy from the author, James Hold, who has certainly jumped the gun on the billionaire wrestling promotion in getting pro wrestling fiction in print.

Out of Texas is a strange combination of pro wrestling lore, rock 'n roll songs, Texas tall tales, various spoofs of movies and the like, as well as a healthy dose of comedy. The first half of the book is an assortment of short stories, linked by a few recurring characters, a fictional wrestling promotion, and a high energy plot heavily influenced by a lot of weirdness and radioactive materials.

There are many Texas related in-jokes about Dallas and Oklahoma, which makes it more of a humor-fest to the region, but as a Western Pennsylvanian, I simply replaced "Dallas" with Cleveland, and "Oklahoma" with "West Virginia" and transmogrified the other clever insults into local jargon. That helped frame the sense of light-hearted comedy that dominated through ongoing one-liners and other humor.

Hold has obvious influence from the local wrestling traditions. With names like Erik Von Fritz, Brian "the Brain" Toomer, Terry Funt and a villain called the Super Song Machine, as well as angles like multiple masked men, there is a lot of insider wrestling comedy that would otherwise fall on deaf ears (and eyes) to a more mainstream reader.

The stories are send-ups of the following: horror, Godzilla, X-files, pulp novels (as opposed to Pulp Fiction,) the Avengers (the British TV series, not the comic book,) several stories playing off songs and bands, suspense, El Santo (El 7!) spy thrillers and much, much more!

On the negative side, the main women of Out of Texas are reminiscent of Andrew Vachss perennial heroines. At times, the ongoing Jon Raas as apprentice booker, hooded rookie wrestler and secret life as a transformed cat can be a bit complex, especially as the narrator and other characters chime in with the typical "rim-shot" humor which closes far too many scenes.

But as for weird twists of plots, attempts to engage wrestling, comic book and music fans, as well as being a quite interesting read, James Hold wrote a fabulous book and one destined to be well placed beside the series of WWE fiction stories set to be released.

In that vein, Hold sets the standards.

Pro Wrestling Intellectual

If you expect politically incorrect terminology, ethnic stereotypes, portrayals and word play, it's in there. If you want a sprinkling of sexual innuendo, it's in there. (Ok, maybe not as much male posteriors as Vince would love to see, but quite a bit of body parts named, touched and blushed about.) If you want a series of plots, using the same characters, with fits and jumps between the spaces between the stories, like the episodic nature of WWE programming, it's in there.

If you want a lot of wrestling lore, cute twists on names, scenarios lifted from the 'real' world of pro wrestling and some fighting taken from the studio wrestling screen, it's in Out of Texas.

Of course, that pushes me to an aside, and a major tangent, because any speculation on a WWE book written to specifications of WWE Creative, in the year 2006, is simply going to be lacking in such foundations. Maybe a WWE piece of fiction won't resort to "Wotta Manuever" at every finisher, but any sense of building to a finish? News flash to the WWE: characters in a book ain't like wrestlers on the screen: they won't take flimsy, nonsensical storylines and mask them with displays of athleticism and talent!

So when I review Out of Texas and see a strong weaving of pro wrestling tradition and a healthy passion for the sport displayed on the 212 pages of the book, I know it's an endeavor crafted by a talented writer, with the expectation of entertaining a fan base well versed in the century or more of professional wrestling history.

If I ever get to read a WWE novel, would I read the same? I mean, those who bother to watch the WWE and its ever increasing amount of TV time, and further and further removal from a connection to its fan base, to its history (let alone the history of the sport) and its utter detachment from advertising interest, I shudder to think of what sort of output will hit the pages of wasted trees with the WWE logo imprinted upon them!

But back to Out of Texas.

James Hold has written a quite fascinating set of stories using his knowledge of pro wrestling, coupling it with a lot of local Texas flavor, and liberally mixing in rock, comics and spoofs of other media. I found the book enjoyable, not only because I happen to enjoy all of those entertainment genres (and satire to boot) but because I applaud the effort and initiative of self-publishing and I encourage wrestling fans to give it a read.

Joe Babinsack

Pro Wrestling Illustrated's 100th Issue
Cover Date: December, 1987   Price: $2.95

THE more things change, the more they stay the same ... or so the saying goes. One of my secondary purposes to this column has become nostalgia. And what's more nostalgic than looking back at the industry, and it's number one publication from twenty years ago this month, especially when that particular issue was the 100th of Pro Wrestling Illustrated's esteemed history?

In other words, let's get nostalgic over a special issue recap of that magazine's first eight years or so of existence.

But first, a short look at the world of pro wrestling journalism. Today, there are major avenues of getting information. With web sites being the norm, every promotion of note has their own, free and public communications device, which has radically changed the business of producing monthly magazines.

Now, that information is fast, free and far more reliable than ever.

With the WWF starting up its own magazine with a winter issue of '84/'85, the room for the typical type of magazine story – storyline, interviews and analysis, quickly became crowded. While newsletters existed way before that time, the notoriety of the weekly newsletter, and notably the Wrestling Observer Newsletter, began to rise to the level of a true alternative to the magazines. By the end of the 1980s, when internet newsgroup efforts spun rec.sports.pro.wrestling out of its rec.sports.misc home, there became even more opportunities for crazed wrestling mutants to get lightning fast information on a readily accessible forum. Although with the internet, reliability was always an issue.

But I'm sure, for anyone over the age of thirty or so, the growing interest in professional wrestling almost always started with the magazines. Now, there are so many more avenues of following the sport, but PWI persists, and even has its own web site

www.**pwi-online.com**

The Wrestler was the main competitor, with "Thumbs up, Thumbs down" being one of the favorites, plus the ongoing feature that explored major feuding wrestlers – Head to Head, I believe it was called.

But other than those two features, Pro Wrestling Illustrated (PWI) was the top of the food chain. From Bill Apter's "Ringside" column to "From the Desk of ... Stuart M. Saks" and the solid historical perspective of Craig Peters to the wonderfully heel voice of David Rosenbaum, PWI had it all.

Pro Wrestling Intellectual

Even more so, it definitely covered the world, and the "Enquirer" section always had that last minute news that scooped the competition. PWI also had its major awards, plus a recap of the year's festivities. Retrospectives, analysis and great information, plus features and pieces that fleshed out all the important feuds, what more could you ask for?

How about the PWI "Official Ratings" !!!

There isn't a mention of Top Ten lists that doesn't elicit a response from multiple fans about the Top Ten. And PWI was top of the charts on that one.

In the 100th Issue, there were four major promotions covered, and six more regional ones. The ongoing debate was always who deserved top ranking. While the NWA, AWA and WWF were sure fire locks, there was always debate over others. Again, in this particular issue, the UWF was 'raised' to that level, with Steve Williams the Champion, and Shane Douglas and Shaska Whatley holding the last two spots.

Just for Nostalgia, Hogan was WWF Champ, with The Honky Tonk Man the IC/Number One contender. Curt Hennig ruled the AWA, with Nick Bockwinkle Number One. And Ric Flair was the NWA strap holder, with Lex Luger Number One.

Of course, The Honky Tonk Man, the GREATEST INTERCONTINENTAL CHAMPION EVER, was slotted Number One because of the IC belt. Luger likely by holding the United States belt. I'm not so sure if the AWA maintained a default Number One/Belt slot.

But anyway, Top Tens are the coolest of all things, and every old school leaning fan who grew up on PWI and other mags just pines away for them to return. There were a few attempts by the NWA/WCW organization to roll out one in the early 1990's, I recall, but just like a TV Champion, that seems to be another bygone gimmick that should would and could work today, but by gum, Vince never did such shenanigans, so don't hold your breath for someone to put either on display.

But I digress.

The list of "regional" promotions is vastly nostalgic.

World Championship Wrestling is of course the Georgia/Mid South merged territories of Jim Crockett Promotions, which would soon engulf the UWF and usurp any difference between its operations and the NWA itself. But here, it is listed as a regional. And Lazor-Tron is listed as Number Nine. Do you see why WCW is a regional?

World Class (from Texas) was listed, with Kevin Von Erich poignantly listed as World Class Champion, and no other Von Erich on any list. Kerry must have been doing a tour of Japan or such. Brody is listed Number Seven in WCCW, and The Spoiler Number Nine.

(My apologies to the deceased. That's a whole 'nother can of worms.)

Joe Babinsack

Florida is represented by Mike Rotundo, with Dory Funk JR!!!! as Number One, followed by Kevin Sullivan and Ed "the Bull" Gantner, with Teijho Khan Number Seven. And damned if Lazor-Tron isn't Number Ten. But I ain't recanting my snide remark about WCW at this point.

Mid-Southern, which is Jerry Lawler's promotion, which I know because Jerry Lawler is listed as Number One contender, and it's champion is called the AWA Southern Champion, namely Don "the Outlaw" Bass. Rocky Johnson, of all people, is Number Five on the list!

Continental was the long time Alabama promotion that introduced some great names. "Wildcat" Wendell Cooley, who happened to be my favorite wrestler I never saw wrestle much, was the Continental Champion. "Dirty" Dutch Mantel, who languishes in his own hell called TNA (ok, pure speculation on my part) was the Number One. Mr. Wrestling II lived on in Continental as Number Six in 1987, and the Golden/Fuller family representatives, as well as MR OLYMPIA, rounded out that regional top ten.

Puerto Rico was involved on the lists, and despite my acclaim given to PWI as world wide in nature, the addition of All Japan and New Japan (and SWS, I'm sure) came later in the decade, if not the early 1990's, so PWI in 1987 had the sort of blinders on that helped hardcore fans to scream for coverage by the newsletters and the nascent university based internet newsgroups.

Anyway, Puerto Rico was headlined by Hercules Ayala, and of course with Carlos Colon, the eventual Savio Vega as TNT, (then the killer,) and ominously with Bruiser Brody in the Number Six spot. Anyone remember Jason the Terrible? He's Number Ten.

The PWI retrospective following, which typically was the place for spotlighting an even smaller regional promotion, or analyzing trends and movements, lists the initial PWI Top Tens, with Bobby Backlund as the very vanilla WWF Champion, Harley Race as king of the NWA ring, and, surprisingly Nick Bockwinkle as AWA champion, with an even more surprising name as top contender, Verne Gagne, and if your mind can withstand it, Greg Gagne in the Number Three spot!!!

Most Popular and Most Hated were the best though, but 1987 doesn't have that strange irony of Jerry Lawler on both lists, that will come later. Here, Lawler is Number Ten on the most Popular, with Hogan (undoubtedly reminiscing about this today) as Number One, and Ric Flair (undoubtedly reminiscing about this today) and Number One Most Hated.

What the hell, Dory Funk Jr. is Number Ten Most Hated! Killer Khan lives on in the Hated department from his run against Andre, and Larry (I dare you to spell it without reference) ZBYSZKO is Number Seven!

Pro Wrestling Intellectual

I won't bore with further Most Popular names, because I'm a long time heel fan, and I hate those guys.

Tag Teams, you might ask?

Road Warriors undoubtedly and unquestionably at the top, as Number Two contenders to the NWA Tag Team belts held by The Rock and Roll Express, with the Midnight Express holding the US Tag Team belts, and undoubtedly and undeniably the Number One contenders to those belts, even though they are Number Four on the list.

Ok, that is painfully confusing, and a sign of PWI's crack staff playing it like they see it, not like the promotions want the marks to believe.

Tag Teams (with weight and contendership to promotional belts omitted)

1. The Road Warriors
2. Brett Hart and Jim Neidhart
3. The Rock and Roll Express
4. The Midnight Express
5. Tully Blanchard and Arn Anderson
6. The British Bulldogs
7. Tim Horner and Brad Armstrong   (note to self: seriously?!?)
8. The Sheepherders
9. The Fantastics   (!!!!)
10. Dino Bravo and Greg Valentine

Wow. Not much room for much else. I hope this has been an interesting trip down nostalgia lane for you too.

As much as the publishing/magazine industry has been slammed by the immediacy of the internet, and the control of promotions (ie WWE) over talent and in terms of doing their own mags, the history of Pro Wrestling Illustrated in my own fan appreciation of pro wrestling will always be of importance and fondly remembered.

Not that you should purchase PWI over the Wrestling Observer Newsletter, but don't hesitate to check out what they do today. They continue to have lots of good stuff, and a strong journalistic feel to their coverage of the industry, which undoubtedly affects many people to this day.

Joe Babinsack

A Jaunt into the Gaming Industry…

The gaming world, to many, is a source of addiction that rivals the best of Columbian cartels, Beverly Hills plastic surgeons and Starbucks Coffee.

Each decade, a new product arrives, and pushes its habits on another generation of otherwise innocent children. In the 70's, a couple of nerds stopped playing with their leaden soldiers (the hashish of the 60's) long enough to imagine a fantasy battle, then a small scale fantasy battle, which blossomed into this crazy game called Dungeons and Dragons, which subsequently addicted millions of impressionable minds, and purportedly caused several to kill themselves, or others, with modern day implements.

Ok, had they done so with battle axes and two handed swords, I would have worried.

So along comes the computer age, and with it this simple minded, abstract rendition of a fantasy world that could be played on University networks. Moria. Countless academic lives were lost to this plague, and another generation subdued by the horrors of the gaming world.

A decade ago, it was games on trading cards. Wizards of the Coast produced Magic: The Gathering. Or, as those in the know call it, Crack: The Addiction. The twisted genius that brought together the demented fandom of collectibles and the warped sensibilities of the competition prone was richly rewarded. Millions of others were deprived of large sums of money. Anyone want to buy my collection? It's worth five large.

Now we live in another modern era, in need of another widespread affliction upon the youths of America . So the newest style of gaming is rising to the surface, threatening society like LSD, Pop Rocks or Cocaine had in the drug world. These twisted geniuses have combined the internet with a basic fantasy game, where tens of thousands of gaming geeks with no social lives can fight fake battles over fake gold. The best part is that there is an inherent top ten list, expanded and modernized to keep track of hundreds of thousands of data points and keep crazed gamers coming back on a daily basis, if not hourly, to play a 'real time' game of historic proportions.

Massively Multiplayer Role Playing Games are here, and they are set to grab each and every game fanatic, and run them through an intense addiction that knows no cure. Through several devious innovations, these games capture the imagination, the attention and the continuous need to play.

See, in the past, games were one on one. Sure, multiplayer games came and went, but the better ones challenged solitary users and single game buyers, and taxed their skills and later, their wallets. Even those really good multiplayer games came down to one winner, unless you played Dungeons and Dragons, which became a lifestyle and created a subculture best left under a rock. I know, I've been under that rock for years straight.

But when someone creates a game that cannot be truly won, a game that cannot be truly conquered without the assistance of many other people, through alliances, through teaming up to outsmart the programming, or through gaming the rules, not mastering the game, then that game takes the concept of competition and applies advanced calculus to it. The human mind cannot fathom the inherent ability of a gamer to want to fight with, compete with, and do better than a dozen other gamers. But this game raises the odds and the competition exponentially.

Another major component of gaming is cost. Sure, it's easy to freeload on other gamers. University clubs, a rich buddy, and numerous lonely, antisocial types who have no other friends are all sitting out there, waiting for someone to play with.

But along came the aforementioned Crack: The Addiction, and suddenly all gamers interested needed start up money to get involved. And I'm not talking the $6, then $10 dollars for a starter box, nor even another ten bucks in "booster packs" to gather enough for a half-decent deck. No, I'm talking outlays of one to three hundred dollars to collect the entire set, and probably about as much to make sure that multiple power decks are always at hand. So when it comes to MMRPG's, being a web based product, the cost is virtually nil. Yep, nothing, nada, zip! All one needs is a computer and an internet service provider, and who doesn't have that in the year 2005?

Another aspect of this addiction is availability. Up until now, almost every game needs a warm, live body to sit across the table. Sure, there are play-by-mail varieties of games, but anyone who wants to game with a week or two between turns is truly desperate and unworthy of mention. And the biggest problem with live bodies is that they get boring really quick. Plus, most of them actually need to sleep, go to work, class or do social things, and not every person can consist on a diet of pizza and diet pop.

But a web site is not a live body. It's a program. Which means that, unless it crashes (which does happen, and I just shudder imagining the desperation and/or panic on ten thousand gamers needing a fix at 4:30am , their time, who cannot connect to the game site) the web site is up and running 24/7.

So basically, with a Massively Multiplayer Role Playing Game, there's immense competition, free play, and continuous play. What's more to love?

Cheating.

As I mentioned earlier, gaming the system and out programming the program are aspects well at play in this realm of gaming. And what's more attractive to the average win-at-all-costs gamer than being able to cheat? Creating programs to exploit loopholes combines the competitive addiction of the gamer with the insatiable appetite of the hacker, always searching for a new way to subvert computer technology.

And thus, the ultimate game, removing such trifling details as face to face interactions, the emotions of winning or losing in the company of humans, and the reliance upon skill, game play or outwitting the opponent.

Joe Babinsack

Synopsis: Professional Wrestling's Greatest Moments

Introduction: An explanation of the approach of the book: the purpose is to provide an interesting read for long time pro wrestling fans as well as novice fans. The appeal is nostalgic as well as informative.

In terms of a top twenty five book, I will also outline the rationale for the inclusion of the moments, based on aspects such as Star Creation, Money Making, Historic Nature, Remembrance and Statistics – most likely in a points based fashion. I plan on a fact based as well as an opinion based analysis of each moment, allowing for debate and discussion of the findings.

The focus of the list will be positive and moments of a worked nature. In other words, I choose to ignore the train wrecks and the pure business moves, as well as the accidents and the deaths that populate pro wrestling's history.

"Greatness" to me is a matter of positive impact. There will be instances of mixed impact, but I want to avoid things like the botched WCW invasion angle and the various WWE entertainment based vomit like the Katie Vick angle and incarnations of the Undertaker's supernatural powers. That is the stuff for Wrestlecrap and other similar books, an avenue already written about and well documented by capable authors.

I believe that professional wrestling is in great need of positive reinforcement, and that in the midst of a potential upswing in the business cycle of the industry, focusing on the positive should be of great appeal. Of course, the nature of what is positive and negative is certainly up for conjecture, especially in an entertainment form based on violence, emotional manipulation and a history of shady business practices. Also, the nature of positive impact is tied into how the moment is packaged, as well as the statistical evaluation of the impact. Hulk Hogan becoming a bad guy is not exactly positive – but the creation of the NWO sparked an immensely profitable period of business.

Moments under Consideration: I plan on undertaking this project with this list of 50 historic moments, which will be altered, added to and trimmed down in the process of research, evaluation, analysis and perhaps by conducting a survey of writing and internet peers for suggestions.

Twenty five of the following will be selected, based on a solidified set of criteria. I envision five to ten pages for each entry, in strongly formatted chapters. A main emphasis of mine will be leveling the playing field between PPV, Television and Arena situations, and I intend on gathering strong statistically based comparisons for that purpose.

Pro Wrestling Intellectual

List of Potential Entries:
1.) Montreal and the screw of Bret Hart
2.) Hulk Hogan's Heel turn
3.) Andre the Giant's Heel turn
4.) Steve Austin/Bret Hart "I Quit" match
5.) WWF on MTV (first show)
6.) Rock vs Mankind Superbowl halftime match
7.) Ric Flair/Kerry Von Erich match (Freebirds)
8.) Junkyard Dog blinded by Freebirds
9.) Freddy Blassie debuts in Japan
10) Shane Douglas throws down the NWA belt
11) Terry Funk attacks Ric Flair at Clash of the Champions
12) Funks vs Abdullah the Butcher/Sheik
13) Funks vs Public Enemy
14) Dusty Rhodes turns face
15) Dusty Rhodes as the Midnight Rider
16) Larry Zybysko turns on Bruno Sammartino
17) Ivan Koloff beats Bruno Sammartino
18) Sandman is blind angle
19) Goldberg beats Hogan at Georgia Dome
20) Lex Luger turns on Ricky Steamboat
21) Four Horsemen form
22) Four Horsemen turn on Sting
23) Los Gringos Locos form
24) Hulk Hogan wins IWGP Championship
25) Iron Shiek wins WWF Championship
26) Superstar Billy Graham beats Bruno Sammartino
27) Ray Stevens bombs away angle
28) Freddy Blassie Los Angeles face turn
29) Road Warriors debut
30) Ric Flair/Harley Race Starrcade match
31) Tommy Rich/Buzz Sawyer "Last Battle of Atlanta"
32) Hulk Hogan/Ultimate Warrior Skydome match
33) Jerry Lawler/Andy Kaufmann angle
34) Orndorff turns on Hogan
35) Savage/Elizabeth "wedding"
36) Blade Runners debut
37) Lex Luger debuts on Nitro
38) Rey Mysterio Jr/Psicosis matches on ECW
39) Radicals debut on WWE
40) Sabu/Cactus Jack ECW match
41) Shawn Michaels "collapse" on Raw
42) Rock: This is your Life skit

43) Kobashi beats Misawa for All Japan Triple Crown
44) Misawa beats Tsuruta for All Japan Triple Crown
45) Tiger Mask/Dynamite Kid series
46) Bruno Sammartino beats Buddy Rogers
47) Piper's Pit with Jimmy Snuka
48) Roddy Piper saves Gordon Solie
49) Mankind/Undertaker Hell in a Cell
50) Vader/Takada UWF match

Criteria:
Star Creation: Did the situation elevate someone to headliner status, solidify a headliner into a legend, or move a feud from interesting to memorable?

Money Making: Depending upon the intended, or prevalent, avenue of profit (attendance, PPV, TV Ratings) did the angle succeed?

Historic Nature: Did the situation impact the wrestling industry in terms of style, booking approach or audience perception? Was it merely a cool thing that happened or did it create something over and above profit, star creation or a one time event?

Tangents: Did this event lead to other events? Was it the kick-off of a grand angle or the underlying cause for another memorable moment? Does this moment overshadow other moments before or after it took place?

Remembrance: Is this a fondly remembered moment? Is it remembered in the mainstream? Is it known nationally or regionally?

Statistics: Are there numerical facts to support the overall effect of the moment, other than the profit margin? For example, did the moment set the stage for a long run of profitable business, or is there support that suggests that while the moment didn't have quite the impact, did it spark something larger?

Possible Appendices:
(I would envision a book length of 250-300 pages, and using the following lists as "filler" material with far less commentary.)One: Top Ten Business Decisions – mostly Vince McMahon related so pulled from the main section of the book.Two: Top Ten Fizzles – basically items from the main list that doesn't pan out as being memorable, notable or profitable.Three: Listing of the Top Twenty-Five by criteria. Attendance, Profit, Impact, Nostalgia, Star Creation, etc.Four: Honorable Mentions. Those that are worth mentioning in terms of the Criteria.Five: Pre 1956 Moments

Eight suggestions for TNA...

On their move to a prime time two hour slot, and the battle of their survival:

1) GO OLD SCHOOL.

Pro wrestling has worn the same face for a decade. It's arena wrestling, with fly by night booking and larger than life stars (that have been missing in action for years.) Not that I want to get political, but having the same people in charge for too long makes anything else look inviting.

But the worst thing TNA can do is go crazy. Almost any long time fan of pro wrestling has been raised on some sort of tradition that hasn't been seen, respected or understood in far too long. By presenting a product that is so "Old School" that it is new to the newer fans, and a welcome nostalgia to the older fans, TNA can capture the minds of many of the alienated WWE fans. And the WWE just isn't going to readily follow suit.

Simply by changing things up, making more of a studio and impromptu set, maybe giving Don West the mic and letting him go solo, maybe just by having post match interviews and changing up the concepts of "run-ins" (after the match, not during it!) or several of a litany of other fondly remembered gimmicks and production tricks would do the trick.

And that is to present a different product, to go along with the various talents and styles not readily seen on national TV.

2) GET EMOTIONAL

Seriously, when was the last real wrestling feud you watched? I mean the one where you wanted to kill the bad guy yourself, where you were dragged across the line of fantasy and reality so quickly it made your head spin?

Love and hate are things that fall to the roadside in the fast turn, give and take, overly creative world of the WWE.

The strange thing is that TNA has one of the hottest feuds in-house, and all its doing is burying it. As much as James Cornette vs Vince Russo is a backstage, insider information driven situation, its also the classic Old School/New School battle. And unlike the majority of the contrived General Manager battles seen on the boob tube, there's underlying passion, a stark difference in opinion, and, quite frankly, a long history of animosity, associates and angry outbursts to fuel the thing.

Isn't that what wrestling is all about?

And what a great point to introduce Dixie Carter into the mix. She can't be as unlikable as Stephanie, nor as unfriendly to the camera as Linda, so why not have this role? Simply by saying "Let them fight it out" could create an interesting war for control over well defined aspects of TNA. Cornette's already the commissioner (of sorts) and the insiders know that Russo is calling much of the creative shots. Why not define their roles, and let them battle it out – much in the way Jeff Jarrett has described the next evolution of the sport, which would be letting the curtains open a little, showing more of the behind the scenes actions.

3) BRING THE WORLD TO TNA

Face it, fighting the WWE by going global is a fool's errand. TNA simply doesn't have the infrastructure or the financial backing to make a go at it.

But what TNA does have is an open door to wrestling's great talent. It has the prestige of the NWA belt, the associations with Mexico, some ties to Japan, and more of a friendly relationship with the top independent talents.

One could name dozens of top notch talent, marketable names or notable bodies to bring in. The first thing to do is make that list, and cross out the first dozen and a half names. No use overpaying for talent. Bringing in guys with guts, energy and hunger on the card would be more appealing.

Have a few clips to intro the guy, put together an excellent video package, and bring this talent in for a pre-PPV match and the PPV itself. Have a contract where it's a month long situation, with options if the talent seems to connect. If an agreement can be made before hand, then do a few three month programs.

This shouldn't simply be for the NWA Heavyweight belt, and/or the X Division crown, but also to raise the bar of the wrestling up and down the card, and to spice things up without overplaying the same match-ups.

There really isn't a downside to this. If the WWE wants to scoop up that talent, it's really not TNA's problem. Plus, these are mostly jobber-to-the-stars roles, so it's not like TNA overly pushes someone. Yet again, if worldwide or indy talent sees TNA as a stepping stone, that makes them more attractive. It also makes the promotion one that can build stars (but can it figure that out?)

As well, no great wrestling talent is going to end up shining so brightly in the WWE, so it raises the bar of wrestling quality.

4) GO JOE

I've heard it suggested elsewhere, but I'll throw my 2 cents in with the notion that Samoa Joe should win the match against Kurt Angle.

Kurt has the reputation and the storyline and the ability to lose without tarnishing his drawing power. Bottom line is, no matter how great a show Joe puts on, if he loses to Kurt, he's ho-hum.

But if he wins? Then he beat the great Kurt Angle. Not only that, but TNA shows that it has talent superior to the WWE. (which is my complaint about the use of Christian Cage and Rhino and others – why bring in mid-carders and have them sail to the top. It isn't a good situation.)

Kurt, with his innate drive and believability, would be on a mission to prove himself in TNA. And furthermore, after such an event, what brings about more "water-cooler" talk – Angle's debut and victory, or Angle's debut and unexpected loss. For the millions who wouldn't know Joe from anyone else named Joe, he'd be someone to seek out.

The Goldberg method comes into play, until the Angle rematch, or someone else comes along. The foundation of greatness in a pro wrestler is the ability to make someone else look great, as well, the ability to "make" someone an equal superstar. I know Kurt Angle can do that. And I know TNA needs more recognizable names, not just jobbers to the stars.

5) DO THE OPPOSITE

Long matches. Few skits. Short, intense promos. Tag team wrestling.

If it's on WWE, why be second best at what can only work for the top dogs?

The major thing TNA needs to do is run with the Tag Teams. They have the best accumulation of talent around. Which is certainly damning with faint praise, but the combination of veterans and younger guys, of talented athletes and experienced audience manipulators, all this can differentiate the product and take TNA to the alienated wrestling masses.

6) DO AN ANGLE WITH PUDER

Whether or not this match ever takes place, in a pro wrestling ring or a MMA octagon or cage, is immaterial at the moment. Putting this intriguing storyline on national television, with the various insider and speculative perspectives to it, would make it the most wanted match up in six months.

And then there are two directions.

Even if Dana White doesn't give a damn, it's a MMA main event for one of many organizations. TNA can cash in by contracting out its MMA talent; or it can do its thing, and keep it in house. Does the mainstream care if TNA isn't an MMA product? Could TNA simply play the game, not get sanctioned, call it a farce in a not so obvious way, and see if it has legs?

I'm betting it does. And if TNA hedges the bets, it could set up the match with one of the money-throwing UFC challengers and allow it to be real. Because, in the end, one or both of those guys are going to come back to TNA as marketable wrestlers having drawn a big payday.

7) BE CREATIVE

Why is it that when anyone speaks of a Creative, no one talks about doling out the responsibilities?

Didn't Vinnie Ru make his mark by doing all the undercard while VKM made the final decisions?

Why can't TNA delegate creative decisions to various people, who are in charge of their division – tag teams, X division, women's, etc. And then, keep all of those departments separated and out of reach of prying nonsense.

In the end, self-sufficient and self-reliant divisions, each headed by its own creative mind, would be far more logical and entertaining.

8) STRETCH IT OUT

Above all, TNA needs to take its normally overbooked and far too fast paced one hour shows, and simply stretch them into two hours. Don't add a thing, just make all the matches three times as long. Set up skits before and after. And also allow for promotional videos to run several times during the show.

Do the ECW thing and recap last week's show, and always do a tease for the next week's show, and then TNA has a must see show without changing much of anything.

Pro Wrestling Intellectual

Who'd Win: Austin vs Goldberg

Like many fans, I saw a feature on Bill Goldberg, and thought "maybe he ain't a Stone Cold clone."

Similarities remain: bald-headed ex-champions, replaced by corporate counterparts; backed by their fans because of their antiestablishment status; physically, psychologically and mentally superior to their peers.

With comparisons, the dominance of their federations, and no match immediately possible, fans are left to argue: who'd beat who?

To assume that the better man would win assumes too much; the answer is not that simple. In a match between Stone Cold Steve Austin and Bill Goldberg, the where of the match is important: the control of Vince McMahon or Eric Bischoff undoubtedly decides who beats who.

Yet if we play the dream match, supposing an interpromotional event, it reverts to other comparisons. What tangible characteristics can we compare, to set the winner of the match? The better wrestler? The better draw? Or have it a shoot, and determine the better, real world fighter?

Stone Cold Stunner versus the Jackhammer? After the application of either move, the opponent seldom kicks out. The major difference is the duration before their moves are typically applied. Austin's Stunner occurs after a longer match: he's a brawler who takes a tremendous amount of punishment, has more experience, and uses his wrestling skill to set up the finisher. Goldberg is pure power, his martial art skills rarely show themselves; the Jackhammer suplex/slam ends the match after but a few minutes.

In a short match, the victory goes to Goldberg; the longer the match, the better Austin's chances.

With snarls and facial expressions, Goldberg elicits immense reactions; Austin, through vulgarities and obscene gestures, gains the same. Despite the dubiousness of the Goldberg chants at WCW tapings, there exists a huge following for the man who dethroned Hogan, carved out one of the longest winning streaks in wrestling history, and became a media darling.

Joe Babinsack

Austin corrupted the minds of hundreds of thousands, who wear his T-shirts and chant his slogans, many too vulgar to repeat. But how much hype surrounds Austin despite his character, and by the machinations of the better all-around promoter? If virtue wins, we go with Goldberg. But despite the fame the Goldberg gains with wins, no one should overlook the popularity Austin gathers in defeat: Austin never beat Bret Hart in their feud. Realistically, fights do not last long, and neither should this debate. Since being dropped on his head by Owen Hart, Austin has lacked conditioning, mobility and strength. He remains one of the best in-ring, but never gained a reputation as a shooter.

Goldberg is a true athlete, with gridiron experience, a dedication to gym work, and fight skills.

In a real fight, the victor goes to Goldberg. There's a funny thing about pro-wrestling, though, and the reality is that the best wrestler is the one that makes the opponent look the best. For those who want to trumpet their favorite, they've got to consider that the best wrestler is the one who makes the winner look like the winner.

That's a lot harder than hitting a signature move.

Pro Wrestling Intellectual

WWE Draft Lottery Analysis

Nothing has shown the complete disconnect between the WWE's "sports entertainment" world and the "pseudo sports" world that most long term fans seem to gravitate towards, like the concept of the draft lottery.

In a real sports environment, or one that pretends to be so, the draft is a big thing. It would revolve around various interests attempting to select new faces for their benefit, positioning themselves for future dominance, or shoring up a weakness.

Major League Baseball's draft is far too long term to consider for most fans, and ironically, most comparable to the WWE's own processes for developing its own talent -- picking prospects and mostly hoping that they will rise to the major league -- and sometimes ruining major prospects because of a great need to bring them up before they are properly trained or experienced.

Obviously, this sort of long term planning is boring as hell and would be met with indifference.

The NHL is a strange mix. In Hockey, there are true superstar prospects to be had. Sydney Crosby was the most recent example, but every few years, from Wayne Gretzky to Mario Lemieux to Eric Lindros, there's a "can't miss" number one selection that is destined to take a losing team to a contender in a small number of years.

With some hype and video packaging, such a scenario could work. The major issue is that the WWE has clearly had its difficulties in pushing new talent and allowing them to dominate the sport. Brock Lesnar was the closest situation to this, but how many Brock Lesnar's are in the pipeline, if ever, let alone having one every year that has the potential to fizzle out….

The NBA draft runs in that direction as well, but it certainly has the "draft lottery" in reality. The losing teams get odds on gaining that all-important first pick. Over the past few years, the basketball universe is getting younger in terms of draftable players, and the high profile nature of the NCAA Tournaments (there's a great tangent there!) provides star quality players to be drafted, that have been in the public eye.

In many ways the NBA situation is the closest to what the WWE does, except that the WWE never bothers with logic (except to switch people around in a trade like fashion) and rarely ever builds up never before seen guys or prospective talents in these crazy drafts they hold.

So what gets frustrating is that the WWE just throws up this "draft lottery" and expects some sort of interest, but much in the vein of the "Lethal Lottery" or "Cyber-whatever" or other situations where a promotion promises the premise of chance, then delivers its worked results. Layers and layers of badly thought out attempts to create some sense of random results has never shown to be a respectful approach to pro wrestling fans.

It's bad enough that certain angles and storylines and decisions make no sense except for ongoing politics and family ties....

Let's be honest. Most wrestling fans are willing to suspend their disbelief for the overall concept of professional wrestling. The effort of the wrestlers involved in a match often overcomes the outcome. The soap opera nature and ability of the fans to select and back their favorites, no matter what the promotion believes in them (for example, Ric Flair and Matt Hardy.)

So when the WWE comes along and runs with a greatly interesting sports based concept like the draft, it really seems to fall short from the get-go. Not only has the WWE proven its inability to be consistent, it readily defeats the purpose of the concept, and seems to muddle things even worse.

Picking tag teams as a "selection" while splitting up other tag teams via the draft (as happened to the Dudleys in successive years, seems to be a perfect example of complete indifference to fans and to the concept. No General Manager in his/her right mind should be splitting up a tag team, and on the other hand, what kind of rules allow for a tag team to be selected as a 'pick'?

The McMahon aversion to rules has been long and storied. The XFL became a debacle, in part, because the rules were not tried out in a pre-season form, and when ratings plummeted, there was no conception that tinkering with the rules as a sports league's season is underway is completely unacceptable in so many ways.

The WWE has always been a mish-mash of rules, never with consistency, never the same from one period of time to the next. So there should be no surprise that the draft has devolved from something somewhat interesting to something almost embarrassing in presentation.

When it started out as selections, it was fine. Not great but acceptable. When it went to putting names on bingo balls and "randomly" selecting new names, it became asinine. Unbelievable and, to me, a complete waste of an opportunity.

Pro Wrestling Intellectual

Why not take some time and allow the vaunted Creative Department to script something interesting, compelling and worthwhile to its fans? I guess there really was a lot of time invested trying to come up with gimmicks for all those people that routinely get laid off. Otherwise, what are those writers doing all week?

The NFL draft on ESPN is now a huge event, spanning two days, and has months of intrigue, speculation and analysis. It is much more high profile, and combines a few "can't misses" with a solid array of talent that can be easily slotted -- from guys who will make an immediate impact to "reaches" to raw talent that simply cannot be passed on.

Why the WWE absolutely ignores the fan's interest, speculation, analysis and myriad avenues of mystery, expectations and viewer curiosity has been a constant conundrum. Of course, the "draft lottery" probably sprung up as a last minute concept, but once again, if played out for a few weeks, it could actually generate some interest and boost ratings.

Unlike the NFL, the WWE is comprised of few entities, so all that intrigue is diminished.

In my opinion, it screams for a wider inclusion of interests to make the selections, but then again, the WWE cut mangers out of its history and never seems to want to allow them to return. It's another frustrating tangent worthy of review, but the concept of ignoring the promo talents of dozens of individuals who otherwise cannot perform a modern era wrestling match, all the while destroying the careers of talented wrestlers who otherwise cannot read, emote or improvise their way through a good short speech becomes mind-boggling.

It also becomes crazy that the McMahon family cannot be players as manager types. Shane, Vince and Stephanie assuming those roles, as heel counter-balances to the General Managers would at least provide six interests in making selections. Toss in assistants to the McMahan's as true manager/valet roles and what harm is there?

But I Digress…In my own dream world professional wrestling promotion that is, but is not, the WWE, I would go all out with a draft.

I would have a Mel Kiper look-alike, whose name didn't sound anything like Dave Meltzer, to provide draft analysis in a fifteen minute package on both Raw and SmackDown! for a few weeks. I would feature some new faces and some monster types, and at least inject some names into the minds of fans, so that when names and faces appear, they aren't complete unknowns. I would also do a mock overview of what each brand needs. Obviously, the whole worked-shoot mentality is going to be an issue, but with so many injuries, why not simply roll with it and claim that there is a shortage of talent with the Undertaker and Shawn Michaels down.

An avenue to take would be to completely shake up the GM situation with the brands. Whatever angle is going on with Teddy and the girls could end up with a split of the SmackDown! Selections. ECW needs a General Manager, and I can't for the life of me remember who is running Raw, aside from Coachman.

This could all lead to dueling factions, the likes of which can shake out over the course of several months, and also leading to trades and the like. Nothing creates drama, tension and ongoing soap opera like people out of place with the situation they find themselves in. And the WWE is so muddled in terms of faces and heels that doing a bit of set up to re-align those concepts would be helpful, especially in driving some personality into some of the names.

I would add managers, with a storyline $100,000 fee for a license, which would also grant a pick.

Adding HHH to the mix of wrestlers to be drafted would be a major upgrade and worth the intrigue (despite the lack of questioning as to where he's going to wind up.)

All told, though, that is fantasy. Some things will likely show up, but the prediction here is that the lottery will consist of a lot of question marks and a lot of fan interest and curiosity, which will not translate into TV ratings because it was not pre-advertised. The WWE.com site will likely get a lot of hits and the internet will be abuzz with the why's and wherefores.

In other words, the draft will be successful in generating interest, but wholly off-target in terms of manipulating that interest into ratings, long-term momentum or any sort of over-arching programming. But then again, why should that be surprising?

Pro Wrestling Intellectual

KEN PATERA

Ok, ok. For the past few months, I've promised to write about Ken Patera.

And, it's about time I get to it.

I've watched quite a few matches with "The World's Strongest Man" and have been collecting bits and pieces of data, not just from the typical Wikipedia search and countless hours of watching DVDs, but from watching some shoot interviews, pouring over documents and reading various other print interviews.

My conclusion is thus:

Ken Patera was the perfect heel.

From the early 1970's to the early 1990's, Patera had runs in all the major territories, and notably in the "big three" that were the WW(W)F, the NWA and the AWA. He was managed by the likes of Bobby Heenan, the Grand Wizard of Wrestling and James J. Dillon. He challenged for the big belts, and hand a strong run against Bruno Sammartino in 1976, and was a great challenger for Bob Backlund a little later -- he won the Wrestling Observer Newsletter's Match of the Year in 1980, for a Texas Death Match with Mr. Backlund.

Most impressively, from April until November in 1980, Ken Patera held two very important belts, the WWF Intercontinental and the Missouri Heavyweight Championship – simultaneously.

Sure, that was before the WWF went national and made it pro wrestling's biggest threat, but the importance of those two belts cannot be ignored. The Missouri Heavyweight belt, the top title of the St Louis promotion, was often a precursor to the NWA belt.

The Intercontinental belt has floundered over the years, but it was for a long period of time the biggest belt underneath the WWF's Heavyweight Champion Neither of those belts was a mere prop; and both were important for drawing fans, for being a stepping stone and were only held by top notch competitors.

The boom and bust of the past ten years has not been kind to the legacy of Mr. Patera.

At the peak of his career, in the mid-1980s', he had an unfortunate run-in with the law, and a glass window of a McDonalds, that seemingly derailed any potential he established. When he returned, he was back in the mix of the WWF, but when announcers start suggesting retirement on-air, it's a pretty strong signal that the guy is on his way out.

Despite mixing it up with Andre, Ken Patera ended up with the dying embers of the AWA, and while he challenged the ever lovable Larry Zbyszko, his career faded away as a member of the "Olympians" tag team with Brad Rheingans. There was a cool angle with Johnny Valiant/Mike Enos/ Wayne Bloom that tied into the one time Olympic Weightlifting legend (and don't call it powerlifting!) but ever since, it's been low key.

Of course, with Shoot Interviews and having announced the event that became Wal-Mart's top selling pro wrestling DVD, Ken Patera's name still lingers on in the industry.

Watching some of the shoot stuff, I could really catch on to the wit and perspective of Mr. Patera. His interplay with the interviewer is priceless—coming to an interview ill-prepared is not a good thing. But Ken isn't crushing the poor sap physically, he's swatting the guy around verbally, and it just shows how on the ball, sarcastic and psychologically minded Patera can be.

Obviously, from watching film, he was that way in the ring.

There are various avenues to explore in looking at a great heel. Ken had them all. He was physically imposing, had a great background, sold like a big baby, cheated to win, came up with catch phrases and mannerisms, and worked the match from various areas of psychology. Ken Patera was one of the great heels of his era, if not all time.

Look, you don't get the athletic ability to snatch nearly 400 pounds, clean and press over 500, or clean and jerk that much as well, without having big guns and/or a big frame. Over the years, Ken Patera went from big powerful guy to impressive physique. He admits to steroid use, but considering his commentary and his peak performances in the Pan-American games, Olympics and trials and such, he obviously knew how to use them.

Which is still a questionable situation, but when a knowledgeable guy starts talking about people who never come off a cycle, there's an interesting distinction…

It's worthy of a digression. I certainly don't want to condone steroid use at all, but when debating the issue, the reality is that abuse of steroids seems to be the culprit (mixed with drugs) of a high percentage of the deaths of the past two decades. Rarely, it seems, do we speak of someone just using enhancement drugs, but abusing them.

Again, this is a point that I don't want to blur, but if anyone points to people using enhancement drugs and wants to argue legality, that's one issue. The greater and more important one is that obviously far too many talented but undersized individuals don't know when to stop or what to do with the drugs when they get them.

There's something in this perspective that I wish more informed individuals would take up, because I certainly don't have the insight to run with it any more.

So, back to Patera.

What Ken had was physicality to tower over opponents, and provided an imposing visual – massive arms and shoulders – that any fan could appreciate as powerful. Of course, he had the background – the aforementioned lifting accomplishments, medals and Olympic experience to build upon. You knew from sight and from reputation that this was truly a claimant to "World's Strongest Man" status.

But for his size and physique, what made Ken Patera's work stand out was his ability to sell. He could do it to the point of comedic relief, but more importantly, he could – and would – sell for the likes of Jose Lothario, Pat Patterson or Antonio Inoki. And by doing so, he made the good guy look capable and made the match far more interesting.

The thing is, Ken played the chicken not just when he had to, but when he was supposed to. He'd take the offense, and then when the good guy came around, he was ducking outside of the ropes, running out of the ring or otherwise taking a cheap shot to stop the come-back.

There's only so far a no-sell approach can make $. With Patera, you can just see that he understood the process and the psychology, and he enhanced the matches all the more with the interactions with the crowd "Whoooo!" and "Get up, boy!" and his solid promos and his demeanor.

Patera's most famous line, stolen by someone else (like that other catch-phrase, but another guy) was "Win if you can, lose if you must, but always cheat."

Patera seemed to know that as the bad guy, you only won by cheating. While the fans knew he was capable, it was all the more inciting to them that this big, powerful guy bent the rules and didn't just rely upon his ability.

That part of wrestling craft is almost forgotten these days.

It's one thing to play the heel, it's another thing to make the role work. Ken Patera clearly had the ability to work the crowd, to sell for his opponent and to make the fans want to see him be defeated.

That's the making of a perfect heel.

Picture: www.kenpatera.com

Joe Babinsack

Classic St. Louis Wrestling Volume 2
(Looking at Johnny Valentine)

I watched Classic St. Louis Volume 2 over the weekend (Thanks Larry Matysik!) and the coolest thing was seeing Johnny Valentine in action, against Bill Frazier. It's a solid match, but Valentine's style is so awesome to behold. I love the Old School, stripped down, tough guy stance, and Valentine just exudes it.

One interesting thing is Johnny Valentine's finisher – Joe Garagiola calls it the "brain buster" – but it's not the suplex variant made more famous by Dick Murdock. Instead, it's an elbow smash to the top of the head, usually from a jumping Johnny Valentine. That's the sort of impact, expectations and quite frankly, psychology that has been lost today.

Old School finishers, let alone 1980's ones like pile-drivers and such, end up being transition moves these days. When every high impact move ends up with the other guy popping up for his spot, everything gets so watered down that nothing gets over. It's a cliché anymore, but that phrase is so appropriate to so many aspects of the sport.

If I, let alone some six foot four, 275 pound athlete, bash someone in the head with a strong elbow, it should put the victim down for a three count. (It would also likely break your funny bone, but that's the suspension of disbelief I can live with!)

So I started looking for Johnny Valentine (was going to write Johnny V., but that's another name for another piece!) and found some classics. I'm bummed out that the Antonino Rocca vs Johnny Valentine match got pulled, but hey, licensed products are certainly not supposed to be exploited.

What I found was a match (heavily edited) against George Steele, an awesome clip of the match between Valentine and Lou Thesz, a great match between Valentine and Bearcat Wright, and an awesome angle of a match between Crusher (Lisowski) and, as Joe Garagiola called him, "our guy Johnny Valentine."

There's also a very brief clip of the ending of a tag match between Giant Baba/Antonio Inoki and Valentine/Gene Kiniski. Here are some of the highlights:

The Crusher and Johnny Valentine http://www.youtube.com If you've not seen Johnny Valentine on tape, he's a pretty tall guy, with blond hair and sort of a Hollywood look hairdo. To say he looks and acts like a tough guy is an understatement. He's not overly muscled, but you wouldn't confuse him with someone who's not athletic. Crusher, by the way, looks pretty funny as a younger guy. No cigar, no gut, crew cut and just that strong physique you expect from the era. But that gravelly voice cannot be mistaken.

Pro Wrestling Intellectual

It's an 8 and a half minute clip, starting with sit-down promos with the announcer and the wrestler seemingly at ringside. Crusher is just over the top, calling everyone bums and all that. His promos haven't changed all that much over the years, because, well, there's a great charm in his presentation. "That bum's giving me one finger " screams The Crusher!

Crusher has an open contract across the country. Johnny Valentine gets talked up about being a Hollywood star, and questioned if he has an agent.

From what I know about Valentine, he style is best appreciated over months of work, not just snippets and single matches. But the attitude he has, the drive, the toughness, that comes through here. I love the sequences of an uppercut, followed by an over hand punch. Just non-stop aggressiveness, but paced to look realistic and he just exudes the feel of someone you just don't want to mess with.

The interesting set up here is, with Crusher playing the heel, he acts up and refuses to get into the ring. After a minute or so, the referee disqualifies him. It's a great way to pump up the crowd. "We want Crusher!" The crowd chants. Johnny Valentine plays cheerleader. His mannerisms are incredible: he jumps with clenched fists, stomping and cheerleading. It has a sort of Hulk Hoganesque look and determination. Who knows who stole what from Valentine, but that resemblance is easy to see.

The heat was incredible. It's amazing how the set-ups work on the crowd. Here, the match is announced, but Crusher's doing his thing. He speaks a great game, with the growling voice, but he's playing heel, and doesn't want to lock up. He get's DQ'd, and the crowd goes nuts, thinking they won't see the match.

But they announce a new opponent, and give Bad Boy Joe as a replacement. Johnny Valentine just kills him. Five beals and then the brain buster, a jumping elbow smash to the top/back of the head. Twenty nine seconds of a match, and its 1-2-3, and no one in the crowd seemed to lose a beat or disbelieve that such a thrashing could take place.

It's just crazy good. Ring Announcer: "With a brain buster and a body press….the winner, Johnny Valentine!" TV announcer: What can you do but have the Crusher have his way!

It's crazy how the ringsiders are all but on the apron of the mat. Banging the canvas at times and shaking the ring ropes in displeasure at The Crusher, returning to the ring. In the end, the match doesn't take place, but I can just imagine how badly the crowd wants to see it, and that no one's going to miss the next scheduled show!

Baba/Inoki vs. Valentine/Kiniski Valentine's taking huge chops from the legendary Japanese duo. Just brutal. But you can see him just moving forward, taking the punishment, and while it seems like they just go to the finish, considering who's in the ring, it must have been an absolute war!

Johnny Valentine vs. George Steele Crazy! Johnny Valentine just controls the pace with his style. Lots of editing here, but you know Johnny Valentine isn't going to let George do his usual schtick! I'm not sure if that's Lou Albano or not, but the manager rushes the ring, but can't do nothing to our man Valentine. He gets the pin regardless of the interference.

Johnny Valentine vs. Bearcat Wright This is yet another great angle. Valentine puts Wright over huge. What impressed me was the crazy attempts by Johnny Valentine to get out of a front facelock. Just running to the corner repeatedly, displaying effort and strength and aggressiveness you don't see often enough, and considering the simplicity of it, why not? After that, it turns into a slugfest!

Wright end up outside. Even then, those little things, the attitude, the reputation all builds up. These guys are killing each other. Valentine does his patented chop to the chest, as the opponent is draped backwards over the rope.

In the end, it's a screwjob, but man, does Valentine sell that choke. Even the referee bump in this match is pure Valentine. The ref sells the elbow drop, allowing Bearcat to pull out a rope and choke out Valentine, leading to the pin.

Security is noted and seen around the ring – the heat is powerful.

A second ref comes out to point out the miscarriage of justice. Bearcat Wright just clocks him. Johnny Valentine is still out on the mat. Bearcat stomps him then pulls out the rope again. The refs finally pull him away, and both are needed to help Valentine to the back.

Lou Thesz vs. Johnny Valentine Announced by Gordon Solie.... It's Old School Heaven! Gordon Solie : Enjoys inflicting punishment. The more you give, the more he gives back. This clip shows the finish, which Solie describes as controversial. Maybe not these days, as Valentine basically uses the tights to score a cheap pinfall over an older Thesz (well, he still wrestled ten and twenty and thirty years later...) The set up is a nifty crash – Johnny Valentine's brain buster elbow clashing with the Thesz press, and both go down. Thesz begins to roll JV around by a wrist lock, but JV stops at one point, then grabs the tights and gets the cheap 1-2-3. Awesome but edited.

The most important thing is Gordon Solie's description of our man Valentine:

"Relentless" -- which is an awesome and apt description of the all-time legend.

FINAL WORDS....

If you take anything away from reading this book, I hope it would be one thing: That you can enjoy professional wrestling on multiple levels.

(Well, too, that the WWE isn't synonymous with Professional Wrestling.)

Far too often, I'm confronted with the ignorant masses that, in the immortal words of Gorilla Monsoon, "couldn't tell a wristlock from a wristlock." The retorts are clichéd, but some of them apt: "Movies are fake, do you ask the fans of Star Trek or Star Wars whether they think it's real or not"? let me try doing a few wrestling holds on you and see if they're real! or, there's the hard slap to the ear of an ABC reporter by Dr. D, David Schulz.

Ok, slapping idiots who question you about professional wrestling is not an option.

What's frustrating about professional wrestling is that far too many promoters in the mainstream care little about educating the masses. While Kayfabe has faded away, the mysteries of professional wrestling remain, but no one seems to pay mind to them. Too many older wrestling talents have removed themselves from the illusion, and simply play-act at a different level, one that diminishes the participation of fans, and heaps disdain on the legacy of the sport, and worse, the investment of time, effort and money by those fans.

Which to me, is the biggest crime.

Professional wrestling is all about belief, all about participating in the charade, all about creating an atmosphere where the people who are "in" on the game are the ones having the most enjoyment of it. That aspect is becoming long forgotten, and what's worse, as it fades, the fans have been losing their attention span, their investment and their enjoyment... one after another.

I've talked to many a wrestling legend, and the general consensus remains that it cannot be revived, that the clocks cannot be turned back, and that wrestlers simply cannot learn the psychological aspect of the craft, because there is no connection between fans and wrestlers, and no inherent need with the diminished role of live events to the profit of any given promotion.

Certainly there is that aspect, but when no one tries it the old way, does anyone really know how it would turn out, and can we readily say it will not?

I remain faithful to the industry that I love, that some day soon, the Old School methods will become the newest of business cycles, and that business cycle will boom.

Because it's the faith I have as a fan that drives me to a positive view of the industry.

Joe Babinsack

Photos Courtesy of:

Bob Barnett

Steven Johnson

Ed Russino www.wrestlingphotos.net

Full Impact Pro

Ring of Honor

MsChif

Jason Deadrich/Chickfight

Big Vision

Bruno Sammartino (Thanks for letting me use you on the cover!)

Assorted Bibliography

Pro Wrestling Kid's Style, by Shawn "Crusher" Crossen, NWF Books, www.nwfwrestling.net

EXTREMELY STRANGE, by J.R.Benson, www.jrbenson.com

One of the Boys, by Jack Laskin, www.xlibris.com

Mondo Lucha A go go, Rayo (an imprint of Harper Collins), www.ClubRayoBooks.com

Pain and Passion, by Heath McCoy, ECW Press, ecwpress.com

Bodyslams in Buffalo, by Dan Murphy, Western New York Wares, Inc., www.Buffalobooks.com

Tributes II, by Dave Meltzer, Sports Publishing LLC, w/DVD, www.wrestlingobserver.com

The Rassler from Renfrew, by Gary Howard, General Store Publishing House, www.gsph.com

Adventures in Larryland! by Larry Zbyszko, ECW Press, ecwpress.com

Professional Wrestling: Sport and Spectacle, by Sharon Mazer, University Press of Mississippi, www.upress.state.ms.us

Out of Texas, by James Hold, www.iuniverse.com, www.ebookmail.com

Listen, You Pencil Neck Geeks, Freddie Blassie with Keith Elliot Greenberg, Pocket Books

Made in the USA
Charleston, SC
30 January 2010